From my heart and my hands, I lovingly offer this book to the Goddesses of the Moon;
to my teachers in all realms throughout all time and space;
and to the vortex of Sisterhood of the Moon—past, present, and future.
Long may we thrive.

Praise for *Llewellyn's Complete Book of the Moon*

"Jesamyn's writing holds the same qualities of insight and understanding she brings to all her in-person interactions. She deserves this accolade and every success, as this book is certain to bring insight and greater interconnectedness to readers from around the world."
—NADIYA SHAH, author of *The Universe is Wise and Loving*

"*Llewellyn's Complete Book of the Moon* shines like a full moon, illuminating the path to your inner priestess. You will be expertly guided through lunar cycles, goddess mysteries, and potent rituals, connecting you deeply with celestial rhythms."
—AMY ZERNER AND MONTE FARBER, authors of *The Enchanted Tarot* and *The Intuition Oracle*

"Brimming with moon-phase rituals, lunar spells, and celestial insight, it offers a path lit by silver light and sacred timing. Each chapter moves like the tides, inviting readers to attune their magick, healing, and intuition to the rhythm of the night sky."
—MAT AURYN, author of *Psychic Witch*

"A truly rare resource, beautifully written and rich in useful information, offering wisdom and skills for harnessing the enchantment and power of the Moon. It's also a divination tool to speak with the spirit of the Moon."
—PHYLLIS CUROTT, JD, author of *Witches Wisdom Tarot*, *Spells for Living Well*, *Book of Shadows*, and more

"Blending astrology, hermetic correspondences, crafting, divination, and ritual, Jesamyn Angelica illuminates a path to create an intimate relationship with the lunar essence."
—DEMETRA GEORGE, author of *Mysteries of the Dark Moon*

"*Llewellyn's Complete Book of the Moon* is unique in that it presents the path of becoming and being a Lunar Witch in a way that is encompassing and organic. Jesamyn's writing style is elegant and her warmth and wisdom as a priestess shines in every chapter."
—IVO DOMINGUEZ, JR., lead author of the Witch's Sun Sign Series

"A thorough and delightful exploration of the Moon, and its magick, myth, and lore. Jesamyn Angelica shares her love of the Lunar Goddess' many expressions, drawing from her own magickal practice and the many traditions and cultures that also adore the Queen of the Wise."
—CHRISTOPHER PENCZAK, author of the Temple of Witchcraft series

"Jesamyn Angelica has gifted us a luminous and deeply felt guide to the Moon's wisdom. … She beautifully weaves lunar magic, ritual, and practical insight to help us attune to the rhythms of nature. … Whether you are new to lunar magic or have long felt the Moon's pull, this book is a treasure."
—**DR. STORMIE GRACE**, astrologer and author of *Channeling the Zodiac*

"It's been a long while since I loved a book this much! … [This book] holds a comprehensive exploration of scientific and magical information, from rituals to altars to recipes for magically made tools and items, and so much more. … If you only buy one book about the moon and moon magic, this is the one."
—**DEBRA DEANGELO**, author of *Pagan Curious*

"A beautifully crafted guide filled with wisdom and transformative insights. Each chapter deepens our connection to lunar energies through practical rituals and spiritual reflections. Ideal for beginners and seasoned practitioners alike, this book offers fresh inspiration and essential tools."
—**CLAUDINEY PRIETO**, author of *Wicca: The Goddess Religion*

"The definitive guide to understanding Mother Moon. … This book was nectar for my soul and allowed me to sink into deep connection with the Moon. … This book is truly a manual for life and the rhythms of Lady Luna, and if used in loving homage, I believe it will be life changing."
—**ALLISON STILLMAN**, author of *The Sacred Art of Anointing*

"Moon lovers, magic seekers, and wild thinkers will all savor this treasure trove of a book. With applications for both solitary practitioners and ritual facilitators, *Llewellyn's Complete Book of the Moon* will inspire you, guide you, and nurture you."
—**MOLLY REMER**, creatrix of #30DaysofGoddess and author of *Womanrunes*

"A powerful, enlightening, inspiring, and energizing guide packed with an abundance of fantastical moon knowledge. Well-organized chapters with inspiring meditations, magical explanations, and step-by-step spell crafts make this lunar book a valuable resource for every season of witch."
—**SONJA F. BLANCO**, author of the Witch of Ware Woods trilogy

"As a priestess and teacher of forty years, I must say that this is the best book on the Moon and how to follow the energies of the Moon that I have ever read. It will be a book required for my students."

—**BENDIS (DEANNE QUARRIE)**, founder of the Apple Branch and author of *Ogham Twigs*

"Jesamyn Angelica guides the reader to meaningful connection with the sacred power of the Moon through a series of beautifully designed activities, from meditations to divinations to rituals. Whoever you are, whatever your path may be, this book will prove a valuable resource."

—LAURA PERRY, founder and Temple Mom of Ariadne's Tribe inclusive Minoan spiritual tradition, author of *Labrys & Horns*

"A luminous and magical journey! I found myself savoring every word of this powerful book. It's brimming with soulful insights, sacred rituals, and deep wisdom that will bring you into a more intimate connection with the moon."

—RHODA JORDAN SHAPIRO, author of *Fierce Woman*

LLEWELLYN'S

COMPLETE BOOK OF THE MOON

About the Author

Jesamyn Angelica is High Priestess and founder of Sisterhood of the Moon, an inclusive, matriarchal goddess tradition for all. Lunar Priestess, Green Witch, ritualist, teacher, oracle, artist, and muse, she has followed the Path of the Moon since her dedication to the Goddess as a maiden. Jesamyn brings more than three decades of Witchcraft practice and experience in the Goddess Arts to her uniquely inclusive women's empowerment work.

A lifelong student trained in multiple traditions, she infuses everything she does with joie de vivre, combining wit and humor with practical skills and cultivated expertise in leadership, communication, and magick. Her spiritual ministry is dedicated to guiding people of integrity toward authenticity through belonging, truth-speaking, and self-exploration.

Jesamyn is creatrix and alchemical guide of The Women's Mystery School of Magick & Empowerment, which is open to all women, and Lunaversity, which is open to all. Learn more at JesamynAngelica.com.

LLEWELLYN'S

COMPLETE BOOK OF THE MOON

Lunar Wisdom for Magic, Healing & Inspiration

JESAMYN ANGELICA

LLEWELLYN
WOODBURY, MINNESOTA

First Edition
Second Printing, 2026

Book design by Christine Ha
Cover design by Shannon McKuhen
Interior illustrations
Moon phases, void of course, moon journal, astrological glyphs, lunar nodes, star of magic, seven-chakras system, upper chakras, bindu & bridge pose illustrations by the Llewellyn Art Department
The astrology charts in this book were created using the Kepler Superb Astrology Program, with kind permission from Cosmic Patterns Software, Inc., the manufacturer of the Kepler program (www.astrosoftware.com, kepler@astrosoftware.com).
Moonwheel illustration recreated by the Llewellyn Art Department; original © Shekhinah Mountainwater

Library of Congress Cataloging-in-Publication Data
Names: Angelica, Jesamyn, author
Title: Llewellyn's complete book of the moon : lunar wisdom for magic, healing & inspiration / by Jesamyn Angelica.
Description: First edition. | Woodbury, MN : Llewellyn Publications, a division of Llewellyn Worldwide Ltd, [2025] | Series: Llewellyn's complete book series ; 18 | Includes bibliographical references. | Summary: "The latest addition to Llewellyn's Complete Book series, this guide teaches you how to harness the Moon's transformative energies for spellwork, healing, and personal growth. Featuring detailed ritual instructions and time-tested techniques, this complete book is an essential resource for anyone seeking to embrace the magic and mystery of our celestial companion"-- Provided by publisher.
Identifiers: LCCN 2025031554 (print) | LCCN 2025031555 (ebook) | ISBN 9780738780047 paperback | ISBN 9780738780092 ebook
Subjects: LCSH: Magic | Healing | Inspiration
Classification: LCC BF1611 .A554 2025 (print) | LCC BF1611 (ebook)
LC record available at https://lccn.loc.gov/2025031554
LC ebook record available at https://lccn.loc.gov/2025031555

Llewellyn Publications
A Division of Llewellyn Worldwide Ltd.
2143 Wooddale Drive
Woodbury, MN 55125-2989
www.llewellyn.com

Printed in the United States of America

GPSR Representation:
UPI-2M PLUS d.o.o., Medulićeva 20, 10000 Zagreb, Croatia,
matt.parsons@upi2mbooks.hr

Contents

Practices and Rituals

Chapter 16: Healing

Introduction

The Moon, the Mysterious One; in the tarot, she represents the unseen, the unknown, and the yet-to-be-discovered. She is timeless, and yet she helps to shape our perception of time. Though fluidity defines her very nature, she gifts a fleeting glimpse of eternity to our narrow human gaze.

Since ages unrecorded, humans have had a love affair with the rich, rare beauty of the Moon. Who hasn't gazed up in awe at her sparkling body, marveling at her brilliant light streaming hundreds of thousands of miles through the darkness? Who hasn't been inspired by her mystical transformation, her ability to renew herself month after month, year after year, eon after eon?

What happens when we choose to partner ourselves with the Moon, collaborating with her cycles, exploring her mysteries, seeking her secrets? What happens when we tap into her ever-changing nature, synchronize our lives with her tempo, dance in harmony with her myriad of guises? What happens when we tune into the Moon?

Just as the Moon travels through her phases without pause, so do we upon our own life's journeys. The cosmic circuit of our Lunar Lady—from New to Waxing to Full to Waning to Dark and then back to New again—reflects our own humanity, constantly transforming and shifting, flowing through seasons of awakening, growth, flowering, fruiting, harvest, compost, dissolution, and rest, again and again and again.

Life speeds along quickly—like watercolors running together, days into weeks, weeks into months, months into years. On occasion, we glance up, wondering where the time has gone and what we have done with it.

Am I living up to my highest potential? Am I working toward my greatest good? What will be left undone when I slip from the embrace of the Earth Mother and into the welcoming arms of the Cosmos?

Alarm sometimes sets in when we wonder how much time these soft souls have left within these sweetly fragile human vessels.

What if there were a means to slow things down, to bring more mindfulness and intention to each fleeting moment, to each previously unremarkable inhale and exhale? What if we could savor each achingly ephemeral twinkling instead of allowing them to pass us by, unnoticed?

The Moon can help us to make that which is unconscious conscious. As such, Lunar Witchcraft is an aid toward wholly immersing ourselves in the cosmic rhythm, bringing our hopes, our dreams, and our aspirations into manifestation through everyday collaboration with the celestial tides.

Just as the Moon is reborn each cycle, so are we. The cycles of the Moon impact everyone! It may be more subtle for some, but it is no less real or measurable.

Tuning into the cycles of the Moon can help us to ground ourselves more fully into the cycles of our own individual odysseys and the reciprocity we have with all beings here on Earth. As we learn to appreciate and attend to our own fluctuations and transformations alongside hers, waves of calmness and joy suffuse our everyday lives.

My Celestial Confidante

I have always enjoyed a profound and vitalizing connection with the Moon—exquisite shape-shifter that she is—and I have invoked her presence almost daily throughout every age and circumstance I've experienced.

My mother tells the story that when I was between the ages of one and three, she would find me standing up in my crib, distressed and crying desolately on Full Moon nights, reaching my plump little arms out to Luna's luminous body as if in supplication.

When she or my grandfather would pick me up and carry me about, whether it was indoors or outside, I would continue to reach up to the Moon in the sky, forlorn and weeping.

While I don't have any conscious memory of this, I do know that the Moon has been one of my most constant and cherished companions, her ebb and flow informing my own.

As a woman with a natal Sun in Cancer, the Moon is my sovereign queen. For as long as I can remember, I've looked for her in the sky every day and night. When I spot her, I pause to breathe in her cleansing rays, filling my body, mind, heart, and spirit. This practice swiftly brings me into resonance and regulation, at peaceful home within a container of immense comfort and relief.

She has held my hand and my heart through all of my encounters—painful, pleasurable, and everything in between. She has provided a sense of belonging when I have felt misunderstood and utterly alone in the world, when I've been in the throes of the jaggedness of grief, as well as during moments punctuated by sweeping swells of jubilation. Her enduring presence has unfailingly brought tranquility to my soul, as well as instilling awe and wonder regarding the greater mysteries, which govern All That Is.

The Moon was my first teacher in the art of Witchcraft and my inspiration to the vocation of Priestess.

I followed the Moon to my first herbal teacher in rural Vermont, where we, her apprentices, tracked Luna's cycling and applied it to growing, tending, and harvesting medicinal plants. In a circle of women studying healing herbs and Green Witchcraft, this may have been inevitable!

I followed the Moon again to Manhattan, where I helped to facilitate monthly lunar rituals in Central Park, gathering in every season and all weathers at the Goddess Victory statue on the corner of Fifth Avenue and Central Park South.

I followed the Moon to the Bay Area of California, where I met the woman who would bring my Priestess Path from a state of foggy, hazy dreams and inexperience into the ripeness of capable expression.

And from this place of grounded knowledge, I followed her direction once again and birthed Sisterhood of the Moon, a monthly Full Moon circle for women. As time went on, we changed like Luna herself. No longer bound by the Full Moon, I began offering ritual for all of the lunar phases, depending on the month and the magic that felt correct to share.

Sisterhood of the Moon then grew from a local women-only community into what we are now, a tradition where all are welcome. Without fail since 2010, we have honored Lunar Goddesses from many different cultures the world over.

And here I am, again following the Moon, this time called to share with you her lore and her magic, transmitting some of her mysteries as I understand them to you, my lunar kindred.

What Is a Lunar Witch?

A Lunar Witch, also known as a Moon Witch, dances joyfully with the vibrations of Luna's steady yet ever-shifting cadence, aligning their personal energetic stream with the unique frequencies of each phase and sign, welcoming the Moon's shimmering light as a silver thread of magic woven throughout every aspect of their life.

A Lunar Witch recognizes that the Moon holds vast influence over their life, informing emotions, thoughts, and energy levels, providing opportunities to actualize and transform alongside the monthly rising and falling of her powers.

Within the heart of the Lunar Witch lies an intense desire to center an intimate relationship with the Moon not only in the magical or spiritual practice but in every moment, be it esoteric or routine.

Following the Moon is a way of life, a wellspring, the bond with Luna of primary importance. Here, the cycling of the Moon functions as a secure and sacred container, holding them as they do their work in all spheres: physical, intellectual, emotional, spiritual, and magical. Here, they source the Moon—her guises, energies, and effects—as the very foundation of all they do.

A Lunar Witch appreciates that there is far more to life than the capitalistic grind, that although hard work is necessary, this existence is also meant to be ecstatic, thrilling, and, at times, even psychedelic. The Moon Witch accentuates spirituality, love, and belonging—using lunar phases to recharge, reset, manifest, and inspire, applying these energies to activate and express their highest mission in this one precious lifetime.

Lunar Witchcraft is a path and a practice open to all who are attracted to the magic and mystery inherent in each lunation, who desire to open to the inspiration of the Moon, and who want to re-enchant their connection with life's cosmic tides. Tuning into the Moon can be seamlessly integrated into everyday life and into any existing spiritual practice or tradition.

Exploring Lunar Witchcraft

Our Lunar Lady can help us to create lives in which we fall intensely in love with ourselves and the world; lives that are delicious, satisfying, and sensual; lives that have us bouncing out of bed with excitement and anticipation most mornings.

When we give ourselves permission to yield to Luna's fluidity, to increase our receptivity to her pulse and her heartbeat through timing our activities with her, we become moon-blessed, which in turn opens us further to the gifts of living.

We feel less anxious, releasing the need to attempt to control the uncontrollable—plotting, scheming, and micromanaging. We trust that the Divine has a greater understanding of how to manifest our desires. We call upon lunar energies to power our hearts and our magic, living enchanted, expansive, playful lives filled with prosperity, gladness, and delight.

When we cultivate a devotion to lunar living, evolving alongside the Moon's tides, everything else falls into place with grace and ease, springing forth fluidly with less effort. We amplify our gratitude for—and flow with—the beauty of life itself.

On the Path of Lunar Witchcraft, we center, explore, and embody devotion, hope, self-expression, love, compassion, spaciousness, prosperity, vision, empowerment, and service.

On this path we discover beauty, passion, and purpose. We uncover the Moon-Within, embracing our authentic selves as we learn what is truly important to us: what makes our individual soul sing, our heart flutter, our toes tap. With the Moon as a mirror for our individual truth, guiding us with her divine light, we explore our lunar resonance, unlocking our highest magical potential.

On this often-exhilarating path, we investigate our identification with the Cosmos and discover how this helps us to navigate our distinctive life's voyages. As we align ourselves with the Moon's rhythms, we become adept at the art of transformation.

Together as Lunar Witches and magical kindred, I invite you to join us in allying with the Moon Mother, developing an intimate understanding of how she affects our daily experiences and learning the lessons that only she can teach us.

Together, let us uncover ways to connect more deeply with her—and with ourselves—in all aspects. Let us hone our magical skills through spellcraft, dreamwork, potion-art, divination, and more. Let us create ceremonies and rituals that honor the Moon, celebrate our cycles, and empower us through growth, manifestation, release, and renewal. Let us build a profound accord with her and her silvery light, living Moon-drenched lives filled with personal power-within, an understanding of the rhythms of life, and a jubilant curiosity.

Getting the Most from This Book

My students are familiar with me saying, "Take what works for you and leave the rest." Know, though, that this is said with the expectation that the student has actually attempted the practice, project, ritual, or spell in physical reality before discarding it as not working for them.

There are many reasons we may procrastinate or stop ourselves from trying something new or different. Most often, though, it's because we're afraid of "doing it wrong." Here, you cannot do anything wrong so long as you are doing it.

So, please, toss out that perfectionism and dive in. There is nothing to lose.

As we move forward together, we will delve into many ways of developing rapport with the Moon. When one of these interactive processes calls to you, that's the time to procure any supplies necessary for that particular working and then plunge right in.

It is my hope that you will choose to engage with the information presented in this book for the traditional year and a day. In doing so, you will pass through the entire Wheel of the Year, experiencing for yourself the impact of all of the lunar nuances.

To start, you'll want to have a journal or notebook and pen on hand as well as some form of lunar calendar.

Your Lunar Calendar

As an old-school Witch, I use a printed calendar, specifically the *We'Moon* datebook that is published each autumn for the following year. I like this particular publication because it includes a visual representation of the Moon plus a listing of the astrological transits for each day, as well as a thirteen-month lunar calendar and an ephemeris table for the year. And it also includes articles, art, and poetry, making every week a festive gift!

You may prefer to use an app, a website (check out the "Moon Calendar" page on astro-seek .com), or even a lunar wall calendar or other datebook. Investigate and see what is out there, and then select the option that speaks loudest to you and best fits your everyday life.

Your Moon Journal

Your Moon Journal is something that you will use specifically and only for your Lunar Witchcraft. This is the place where you will record your thoughts, feelings, explorations, ideas, mooncraft, rituals, and more.

Your Moon Journal helps to bring all of your lunar practices, magic, and reflections organized in one place. Coupled with your lunar altar (see chapter 5), this simple tool can help you to center your relationship with the Moon each and every day, increasing the collaborative nature of your association.

Begin by finding or decorating a book that speaks to you, that catalyzes your happiness when you look at it, that motivates you to spend time with yourself and write. Your Moon Journal can be of any size and color, lined or unlined, plain or lavish—the only thing that matters here is that you are inspired when you see it, hold it, and work with it.

Inside your journal, note Luna's ever-shifting phase and sign and any other magic or practice you engage with for that day and your experiences, opinions, thoughts, and feelings about them.

A Note on Gender

At the beginning of each chapter, you'll find a short piece entitled "The Moon Goddess Speaks," which gives voice to Goddesses from various regions. Although the Moon is gendered as male or non-binary in many cultures, my personal practice is primarily Goddess-based. Since this is my particular area of study, for the purpose of this book, I chose to focus solely upon Goddesses who are associated with the Moon.

Hail and Welcome!

From my heart, I welcome you onto the luminous Path of Lunar Witchcraft, Dear One. I am so very glad that you are here with me! It is my intention that this book provide you sacred guideposts along the limitless adventure of expanding your relationship with the Moon. It is also my wish that you follow the thread of the Moon wherever she leads you!

While I have been walking this path since before I can remember and will share with you my own processes, practices, research, rituals, and spellwork, it is important to understand that *you* get to choose how you relate to the Moon. You are always the final and absolute authority regarding your relationship with her, which may be, at times, profoundly intimate, private, and highly personal.

It is my heartfelt desire that as you begin to sync every aspect of your life with the powerful energies of Luna, you will also learn more about yourself: your capacity for expansion, your own power-within, and the singular magic that only you can wield.

The Path of Lunar Witchcraft is an ever-unfolding adventure of discovery and exploration. When we embrace both Moon's light and Moon's dark, we learn to also embrace all parts of ourselves, unlocking the profound power of transformation, flexibility, and growth we all carry within.

Together, let's learn, play, and heal with the Moon, creating greater personal peace, deepening our connection with the flow of existence, and amplifying our sense of cosmic belonging with All That Is.

Queen of the Night, we honor you and your everlasting splendor!

Chapter 1
The Power of the Moon

The Moon Goddess Speaks

Sister, lover, galactic mother—I am all these things and more. I illuminate the hidden energies, shifting secrets so that you can see what you must see as I preside over the velvety night sky, rising when the Sun quietly tucks himself into bed.

I hang before you unveiled, unguarded, bare and open. Gaze upon my radiant and compelling face; my light is filled with love for you—soothing, gentle, joyful. This is divine motherlove: unconditional, peaceful, kind, tender, compassionate, empathic, supportive. In my silvery embrace you are held, and you are safe.

Let your light shine like mine; do not hide yourself away. Shine like me, for you, too, are filled with an enduring beauty, a welcome lighthouse rising up out of the rock-crowned cliff at precisely the right moment.

I am here with you now, and I will always return to you. You are not alone, and you never have been.

I am Selene, the Moon Herself.

Journal Inquiries for This Gateway

How do the lunar phases impact me and my daily life? How can I better attune myself to the Moon's endless cycle? What is one small change I could make today toward this purpose?

Affirmations for This Gateway

I willingly transform alongside the phases of the Moon. It is safe to embrace change. I keep my spiritual connection with the Moon at the center of my practice.

The Moon is the Keeper of Sacred Time, her cycle never-ending; she is full of mystery, her brilliant white light sparking marvel and wonder. Each phase—New, Waxing Crescent, Waxing Half, Waxing Gibbous, Full, Waning Gibbous, Waning Half, Waning Crescent, and New again—a guidepost upon the path of our lives.

Welcome to the beginning of our travels together! Before we begin this mystical voyage of honing and polishing our skills in working with juicy lunar magic, let's take a very brief crash course in how the Moon influences us on both the personal and the transpersonal levels. Let's ignite our Lunaversity journey by getting "science-y" for a minute, with an eye toward creating a shared foundation, a practical, functional awareness of the what, the where, and the how of the Moon.

What Is the Moon and Where Did She Come From?

The Moon is peppered with asteroid-shaped craters, and her powdery dust-covered terrain includes regolith plains, valleys, mountains, pits, tunnels, caves, and even basaltic lava domes and tubes.

While the Moon does not currently have an active molten core like the Earth, research suggests the possibility of viscous, almost-solid magma beneath her surface near her center.

Her core contains mostly nickel and iron, and her surface is, thankfully, not made of cheese. It smells of gunpowder and is primarily composed of iron and minerals, plus additional metals similar to those on many other planets in our solar system: aluminum, gold, magnesium, mercury, silicon, and silver. Trace amounts of water-ice are also found.[1]

Her atmosphere is exceptionally thin—too thin for us to safely breathe—and is comprised of gases such as helium, hydrogen, and neon. There is no weather on the Moon, and as such, the most ancient of records of her story survive upon her surface, stored in regolith and rock, intact throughout an unfathomable progression of time.

According to NASA, the Moon's temperature can reach as high as 250 degrees Fahrenheit and as low as −424 degrees near her poles.[2] Because she lacks a thick atmosphere, there is no insulation, and her temperature can vary widely between lunar day and lunar night (each about fourteen Earth days in length).

Our Earth Mother's only natural satellite—the fifth largest and second densest in the solar system—the Moon was ostensibly created about 4.5 billion years ago, a result of an impact with an interstellar object approximately the size of Mars.[3] Debris from this collision with our young planet collected together into an orbit, forming the Moon as we now know her.

1. "Moon Composition."
2. "Weather on the Moon."
3. "Moon Formation."

Let's stop and really think about this: A cosmic body traveled from outer space and joined with the Earth in such a singular manner that the Moon was formed. This celestial object and the Earth produced the Moon from a unique combination of materials from their two heavenly bodies, like all parents do their children.

The Moon contains the DNA of the Earth and the Cosmos. Like our human bodies, she is made of both Earth matter and star stuff. The Moon is a child of both the Cosmos and the Earth, of both Above and Below, just as we are.

We are all magical siblings of the Moon—she is a Sacred Sister to us, belonging to all of humanity, transcending time, culture, and religion. Of course we are enthralled by her, captivated by her, and mesmerized by her; of course we feel this attachment, this irrefutable fascination and draw to know her in all her myriad aspects.

Without a Moon

In 1999, I was thoroughly disturbed and unsettled by the Discovery Channel's *If We Had No Moon*, narrated by the wonderful Sir Patrick Stewart. Whilst I (intentionally!) never viewed it again, that program stuck with me, keeping me up at night worrying long after I had seen it.

This sixty-minute TV documentary investigates the significant effect the Moon has on the Earth, examining what life would be like here without Lady Luna.

Exploring the premise that the Moon's gravitational pull is absolutely necessary for life on Earth, the show delves into her role in creating oceanic tides, livable habitats, and weather patterns and even talks about how mammalian (therefore human!) life may never have happened without her.

Through interviews with various scientists and many alarming late 1990s-style graphics, the viewer is taught about the Moon's importance to both the stability of the Earth and the stability of life itself.

This documentary acutely, even painfully, awakened me to the crucial role the Moon played—and plays—in shaping life as we know it today.

Since the airing of that show, science has continued to prove that the Moon's powers do have an immense bearing upon all of the creatures of Earth. And it is my firm belief that once more analysis involving humans (instead of other animals) is completed, what were once considered anecdotal or folkloric accounts of the Moon's imprint on the human body and human behavior will become proven science, aligning with what we Lunar Witches already know.

Rhythms and Tides

Even though our Moon Sister orbits an average of 238,855 miles away from us, her rhythms are primarily responsible for the Earth's oceanic tides, which in turn regulate the lives of many of Earth's creatures.

About 71 percent of our Earth Mother's surface is covered by various types of water—salt, fresh, or brackish in the forms of liquid, solid, or gas.[4] The energies of the Earth are intimately bound to—and are catalyzed by—the lunar tides as the Moon moves through her perpetual course of waxing and waning.

It is a scientific fact that all life comes from the sea: About 540 million years ago, humans began to slowly evolve from a microscopic water creature named *Saccorhytus*,[5] and all these millennia later, our bodies continue to be composed of about 60 percent water (this varies by age; we begin life at about 78 percent water, and this level decreases over time as our bodies grow and change).[6]

Since humans were originally ocean-dwelling creatures, it is my theory that we continue to maintain this watery lunar link, ebbing and flowing in tune with the lunar rhythms. The Moon tugs and pulls upon these smaller bodies of water that make us *us* just as she does the brackish rivers, the great seas, and the vast oceans.

Her magnetic pull stirs our own inner tides, mirroring our emotional current, subtlety—and sometimes not so subtlety—directing our creativity, our intuition, our magic, and our oh-so-human hopes, dreams, and longings. We are not simply observers of the Moon; we are her partners in a continuous cosmic dance upon a journey of self-discovery as old as the moment when she and our ancestors first met.

By the Light of the Moon

Not only does the Moon's gravitational pull strongly affect us, her glow does as well. Scientific studies have definitively shown that moonlight had a hand in shaping the existence of every living thing on Earth.[7] From bacteria to lichen, plant to fungi, algae to fish, reptile to mammal, we are all influenced, whether we are conscious of it or not.

One large long-term investigation of a coral reef showed that many of the animals there have lunar reproductive cycles, spawning at either the Full or New Moon phase, some governed by brightness at night and some instead by the darkness.[8]

4. Water Science School, "How Much Water Is There on Earth?"
5. Tarlach, "Our Oldest Ancestor."
6. Water Science School, "The Water in You."
7. Kronfeld-Schor et al., "Chronobiology by Moonlight."
8. Lin et al., "Moonrise Timing Is Key for Synchronized Spawning in Coral *Dipsastraea Speciosa*."

What about you? Are you ruled by brightness at night or by darkness at night? (And yes, this can absolutely vary over the course of your life as your own rhythms do.)

Based upon my own adventures over the past twenty-seven years mentoring people in the art of moon magic and informally collecting my students' stories, I've learned that there are powerful things that happen to people at both Full and New Moon phases and, most interestingly, which of these two phases acts more dominantly varies from person to person.

Some have reported an increase in energy and inspiration at the Full Moon and a sharp decrease during the New Moon phase, and just as many have disclosed the opposite, finding themselves energized and creative during the New Moon phase and lethargic and even depressed during the Full Moon.

Lunar insomnia is a real clinical condition, too.[9] Do you have trouble sleeping when the Moon is full, even in a completely dark room? You are not alone!

The bindu chakra, also named the Moon Center, is a little-known energy point located at the back of the head. It is situated directly across from the ajna, or third eye, and these two chakras are equidistant to the pineal gland, an endocrine gland.

One of the roles of the pineal gland is to regulate our body's cycles through the production of the peptide hormone melatonin, which administers our circuit of sleeping and waking as well as our circadian rhythm, and the production of melatonin is thought to be regulated by lunar changes.[10]

While currently the only complete studies regarding melatonin production in relation to the lunar stages were done on animals, I'm going to go right out on a limb here and say that yes, positively, human melatonin production is affected by the cycling of the Moon.

We will explore the bindu and other chakras more in chapter 13.

The Moon Is a Mirror for Our Authentic Self

Unlike the hot blaze of the Sun, the cool, restorative streams of Luna encourage us to go within, to excavate and examine what is happening inside of us, to listen to the quiet wisdom found there, clearly hearing what our own eternal Soul Selves need us to know.

As living beings, as spirits settled within physical bodies, we increase our affinity with our environment when we recognize both our role within it and its sway upon us, at all times both reflecting and absorbing, both receiving and transmitting.

When we follow the mood of the Moon into our rightful selves, we accept that we are not walking blindly or alone through this life, that we are undeniably and veritably interconnected with all

9. "Moonlight May Affect Sleep Cycles."
10. "Pineal Gland."

things. Here, we can reinforce our own belonging, our understanding that we truly are an integral, essential part of the vast cosmic tapestry that expands throughout both time and space.

Wrapped in our reverence for the Moon, we encounter a reflection of ourselves: our own ebb and flow, our movement through times both bright and shadowed, outward and inward, loud and quiet, projective and contemplative, extrospective and introspective, the fluctuation of our emotions and thoughts as things begin, rise, peak, and fall, over and over and over again.

When we allow ourselves to be guided by our own inner wisdom and the light (and the dark) of the Moon, she reveals to us—without judgment—those truths we have concealed from ourselves, those illusions and old patterns that call for shedding. This is where we can also find our forgotten desires and the parts of ourselves that still require acknowledgment and integration.

Linking with her celestial presence brings the Holy Mystery home, a charge to actualize our fullest potential and to exercise the unique creative and magical gifts of our authentic selves.

When we commit to recognizing how we are thinking, feeling, and acting during each lunar phase throughout her travels through each sign of the zodiac, we can increase our cognizance of our own innermost workings, one of the most crucial skills of the empowered Moon Witch.

This practice of tracking Luna's travels alongside our own aids us in seeing ourselves vividly, deepening our connection to who we truly are.

A Self-Dedication Rite of Attunement to the Path of the Lunar Witch

A self-dedication rite is a formal ritual done to demonstrate to yourself and to the Divine that you are consciously and willingly stepping onto a new path. It helps to align your internal energies with your highest objectives and tells the Divine that you are serious about your undertaking.

This particular self-dedication ritual can mark your devotion to the Path of the Moon Witch in its totality, mark a commitment to this journey for the next year and a day, and/or mark other commitments you are freely assuming on your Moon-centered spiritual path.

In many modern Witchcraft traditions, dedications are often made at Imbolc (on or near February 1), and yet a dedication can be made at any time, with the New Moon (a time for beginnings) and the Full Moon (when the Moon is at the peak of her lunation and holds the maximum amount of energy) being particularly auspicious.

This ritual will unlock a finer understanding of the Moon and your Sacred Self, and it can be quite profound and dynamic—sometimes even world-shaking—shifting you into surprising new approaches to perceiving life.

Know this, though: There is no universal ritual for dedicating to the Path of the Moon Witch because much of the artistry and potency here is manifest in you creating a ceremony that is of the greatest service to *your* unique life, heart, and bond with Luna.

You are about to do something that you were probably not expecting! You are going to craft a self-dedication ritual and do it—regardless of whether or not you have familiarity with ritual. In fact, I prefer that you go forward with this ritual thinking that you don't have enough information to do it, because everything you need is already inside of you.

We will broaden our exploration of lunar ritual and spellwork later in this book. For this rite, though, please do not hesitate. Simply trust yourself, jump right in, and complete this ceremony before moving forward. Do not permit self-doubt to cause you to delay.

Performing this ritual will help you to develop your belief in your innate abilities and power-within as well as intensify your union with those energies that are cosmic and infinite. We are all divine. Divinity resides Within and Without, and therefore, every cell of your blessed body already knows exactly what to do.

Your ritual need not be long or drawn out unless this is what you are resoundingly called to do. Often, in solitary endeavors, rituals that are short, concise, and directly to the point are the most mighty. Be earnest, be authentic, be real—and your self-dedication ritual will go perfectly.

I've shared below an effective, impactful framework that you can adapt and personalize to craft a meaningful rite that will set into motion the process of cultivating your partnership with this path on a primal, magical level in realms both Seen and Unseen. In this ritual, you will claim your birthright as a Moon Witch with the aim of integrating this path into your life and fully inhabiting your lunar truth.

Purposefully, the design of this ritual is left flexible. Please engage with this rite in the ways that are of the deepest service to you and your practice at the time you enact it.

This rite can forever be revisited and revised—done again and again and again over the years—whenever you have want or need of it. This is a lovely ritual to use whenever you yearn to reset your relationship with Luna.

To Gather

- Any items you would like to use to create your ritual altar. If you are so inclined, include images and/or symbols that evoke the energies of the Moon for you, such as candles, cloths, and crystals in white, silver, gray, and/or a shimmering opalescent.
- An unlit candle for your altar as well as something with which to light it during your rite
- Something with which to magically cleanse your ritual space. For some, this involves burning dried herbs specifically for purification (such as cedar, rosemary, or lavender). For others this may mean asperging with consecrated water, tossing sea salt, or engaging with sound (such as a singing bowl, chime, rattle, or drum). All will disperse unwanted energies. If you are new to this work, follow your intuition when choosing a strategy. Do not overthink or self-edit.
- Blessed water, a blended magical oil, or a diluted essential oil in a small vessel. Your tap water, drawn mindfully and blessed with your heartfelt words, is fine.
- A bit of food and a libation for yourself, also called Cakes and Ale (e.g., chocolate, fruit, or nuts and a glass of water, wine, or juice)
- Your Moon Journal and pen to record anything that emerges for you during or immediately following your rite

Optional

Consider whether you would like to begin your work with a sacred bath or shower. If so, arrange for this, too.

To Prepare

Be sure to make the time to read through everything and procure the necessary supplies before beginning. As you read through each step of the rite, note any thoughts or emotions emerging for you, and then go on to determine a place, date, and time appropriate for you, marking it on your calendar as a sacrosanct appointment with the Divine.

The magic actually starts in the planning and collecting stage. As soon as you begin considering your rite, a specific space is wrought for you in the etheric container of the Multiverse that will later help to hold your ritual.

Whether you decide to perform this ceremony in your living room, at a beach, in your backyard, in the woods, or in some other place hallowed to you, be sure to select a location where you will be both safe and uninterrupted for the duration of your rite.

If you live with others, tell them in advance that you will be unavailable during this sacrosanct time. Close doors and put up a sign gently reminding your cohabitants and loved ones that you should not be disturbed. Whether indoors or out, turn off all electronic devices (or, better yet, leave them elsewhere).

Choose that date now—ideally within the waxing phase of the Moon—write it in pen on your calendar, and when that moment arrives, take a deep breath and begin.

The Rite

Step 1: Set a working altar. This can be as simple or as elaborate as you would like and built upon any surface: the floor, a coffee table, a nightstand. For example, when I am working outdoors, I prefer to construct my altar directly on the ground.

Step 2: Cleanse and consecrate your ritual space as sacred with your chosen method. As you cleanse and clear, release any fear that arises and do your best to become a full occupant of your physical body.

Step 3: Ground, center, and open the channel. To do so, connect with your breath, and then use your breath to connect with the Earth and Sky. From your body, send etheric roots down into the Earth Mother and etheric branches up into the Cosmos.

Once you are grounded as the pillar between Earth and Sky, come into contact with your bindu chakra, your third eye chakra, and your heart chakra, opening them up to give and receive Cosmic, Earth, and Divine Love.

Now, slowly and with elevated consciousness, open yourself up to the powers, energies, and spark of our Moon Sister.

From this place of loving connection with All That Is, extend gratitude to the land you are on, its Indigenous Ancestors and energies, and your own Benevolent Ancestors of blood and/or choice. (You can research the ancestors of the land you live upon on the site Native-Land.ca.)

Pause here and enjoy the sensation of belonging and kinship for as long as it feels supportive, powerful, and good.

Step 4: Connect with the ritual intent. In your own unscripted words, voice aloud your purpose in this rite. Speak from your heart, and as you do so, activate the divine being you are. You may also wish to say something like, "Enthusiastically and with joy, I now empower myself to remember and to celebrate my birthright as a Moon Witch."

Step 5: Create an energy well. Using the sound of "Ma," "Om," or another tone that resonates with you, create an etheric well of energy to draw upon for your ritual.

Step 6: Move Between the Worlds. Separate your ritual space out from mundane reality in whatever style is appealing or familiar to you. If it is part of your existent spiritual path, you may decide to cast a magical circle, or perhaps you are called to issue formal invocations to the elements or directions, your Guardians or Guides, a specific Lunar Goddess, or to the Moon herself. If you do not have an established custom, then you might simply turn in a slow clockwise circle as you envision you and your altar moving into a time out of time, into a space out of space between the Above and the Below.

It is always okay to experiment with this to discover what speaks most loudly to your Inner Moon Witch. Sincerity—not perfection—is the goal.

To complete this step you may wish to announce: "I am Between the Worlds."

Step 7: Presence yourself. Spend some time considering the Moon and the relationship you have had with her—or have not had with her—throughout your life. What is your first memory of the Moon? What is your favorite memory of the Moon? How do you feel when you think about the Moon?

Evoke the lunar energies within your body through visualizing and remembering what you find beautiful, potent, and/or most compelling, and then, using your intuition, channel these energies toward healing and renewing yourself—body, mind, heart, and spirit. You may experience a pull to place your loving hands upon different parts of your body to better direct the stream. Follow any intuitive hits you receive.

Fill your heart with the pure energy of the Moon until you can contain no more, and then radiate it outward to the world, beginning first with yourself, then your home, then your street, then your neighborhood, then your county, then your state or province, then your country, then your continent, and then out across the entirety of the Earth Mother.

Step 8: Name yourself. When your body is thoroughly vibrating and resonating with the energies of the Moon, stand in front of your altar—roots buried in the Earth, branches open in the Sky, connected with breath and heart and mind and spirit.

Three times, speak aloud your name and say: "Just as the Moon changes, so do I. I am filled with the magic and the power of Luna. I now name and claim myself as a Moon Witch."

Step 9: Embrace your Moon Witch Self. Light your candle, and with expansive love and compassion and receptivity, welcome your full, embodied, authentic, and actualized Moon Witch Self in whatever manner feels right. This may come in words or in action or both.

Step 10: Amplify your connection to the Moon. Read aloud "A Blessing for Opening to the Path of the Moon Witch" whilst anointing each part of yourself as you name it with your blessed water or magical oil.

A Blessing for Opening to the Path of the Moon Witch

May my crown receive messages sent upon her silvery beams.
May my eyes open to the glow of her beauty, Within and Without.
May my nose smell the essence of white-petaled flowers.
May my lips speak honeyed words of transformation.
May my heart beat in time with the rhythm of her tides.
May my belly be filled with the blessings of her ebb and her flow.
May my sacral chakra radiate with the glow of her pleasure.
May my hands do her work on Earth.
May my feet tread gently upon her pathways.
May my entire being—body, mind, heart, and spirit—be filled with accepting welcome of my ever-changing nature, which mirrors hers—now and always.
Blessed be.

Spend some time in quiet contemplation and meditation upon this blessing and the Path of the Moon Witch. Journal and/or draw your thoughts and feelings and whatever else emerges for you.

Step 11: Dedicate yourself to the Path of the Moon Witch. Sit comfortably in front of your altar again and gaze into the flame of your candle, allowing the fire to fill first your vision and then your being.

Consider a simple pledge or declaration that you are willing to make, here and now, to the Moon and to the Path of the Moon Witch. Succinct and sweet is best; this is a dedication rite, not an initiation rite.

When you are ready, stand and speak aloud your pledge or declaration. Express heartfelt words from the depths of your soul to the Moon.

Step 12: Empower and seal your magic. Use your arms to gather up all of the energies from the center of your circle—from the etheric well you created in step 5—and send these energies out across the world and up to the Moon in thankfulness using a "Ma," "Om," or other tone, perhaps rattling or drumming, too.

Step 13: "It is done, it is done, it is done, done, done!" Vigorously and joyfully chant these words aloud three times. You may wish to shake a rattle or drum or dance to move these energies through your body and your ritual space.

Step 14: Enjoy your food and libation. Bless your sacramental food and libation in the name of the Moon and then eat and drink with reverence.

Step 15: Open the ritual space. Offer your gratitude to the Moon and any other energies or entities you invoked, sending them lovingly on their way.

Step 16: Ground and center yourself. Release any extra energies from your body down into the Earth Mother for her health and her healing. Carefully retract your etheric roots and branches, restoring them steadily and firmly into your physical body.

Step 17: Celebrate yourself. You are now solidly upon the Path of the Moon Witch. Blessed be!

The Aftermath

After your ritual is complete yet before you rejoin the ordinary world, take some time to journal about your encounter.

Mark your calendar to journal about your thoughts and feelings again three days later—and then follow through with it! This permits the ritual opportunity to truly sink in and fully land in all parts of your being, both physical and etheric.

Be soft and kind with yourself throughout this time, just as you would a newborn. You have just walked through a liminal doorway and birthed yourself into a new vortex, a new approach to living in the world.

—

Welcome, Moon Sibling. Welcome home! Our bond with our Lunar Sister is woven of moonlight and magic, of practice and purpose, and of love and fascination. Forever we are magnetized to her enigmatic glory, and forever we are drawn to the secrets she whispers to us from the Great Beyond.

Chapter 2
The Phases of the Moon

The Moon Goddess Speaks

I bring you the medicine of the Moon, and I rule her cycles. Each phase holds an important piece, a unique frequency, and a powerful vibration which you can direct in order to bring healing and beauty to your life on Earth.

I hold the power of the sea and all of the movements of the tides. I send rainstorms and floods and hurricanes, their destruction a cleansing force upon the land, bringing in its wake renewal and rebirth. I mind the flow of justice and the dispensing of change. I am the Weaver of the World itself. In exchange for my gifts of fertility and hope, I require your courage!

Allow yourself to be awed by my magnificence and power. Bless your intentions and your dreams and your life that you may be fertile and prosperous. I am the Cave of Life. When you see a rainbow, you will know I am there.

I am Ix Chel.

Journal Inquiries for This Gateway

What is one thing I can add to my daily life to help deepen my connection with the cycling of the Moon? What phase of the Moon holds my personal medicine? How can I lean into the flow of transformation?

Affirmations for This Gateway

I honor and accept the sacred medicine of the Moon. There is a divine plan for my life. I align my life with the cycling of the Moon.

The Moon circles the Earth Mother about thirteen times every year, while the Earth Mother circles our Sun Star once. We are all in constant motion. The perpetual dance between the Earth, the Moon, and the Sun is what causes Lady Luna to appear different to us each day and night. This whirl creates varying angles, which provide more or less light for the Moon to reflect. Let's take a closer look at the science behind it all.

The Science of the Lunar Cycle

The lunar cycle, also called a lunation or a synodic month, is the length of time it takes for the Moon to move through all of her phases as observed from Earth. The word *synod* derives from the Greek language and in this usage references the meeting of the Moon and the Sun.

Just as we round the length of a solar year to a flat 365 days (when it actually takes 365 days, 5 hours, 48 minutes, and 46 seconds to make an entire orbit around the Sun, hence the need for leap year adjustments to our Gregorian calendar), the length of the lunar cycle is often rounded to an easier-to-manage 29.5 days, or 29 days, 12 hours, 44 minutes, and 2.9 seconds.[11]

In actuality, the length of Luna's cycle varies from about 29.18 to 29.93 days, with an average lunation lasting a bit over 29.53 days.[12] Additionally, there can be a swing of as many as seven hours from year to year.[13] To confuse things even more, her revolution around the Earth takes 27.3 days.

There are additional ways to measure lunar months, too. If you want to go down a bunny hole, check out anomalistic months, draconic months, sidereal months, and tropical months!

Beginning around 3000 BCE, ancient Mesopotamian astrologers used the Moon as a timekeeper. As early as 2500 BCE, they also began recording information about the Moon as deity incarnate.

Next, around 1800 BCE, the observable happenings between the Sun, Moon, and planets were studied and decoded as divine messages, communications from the gods to humanity.

Predictive astrology first enters the picture much later, after the end of fifth century BCE, when Babylonian astronomers used mathematical astronomy to create formulas of predicting the movement of the Moon and the planets and their relationship to events on Earth, as well as to develop the concepts of horoscopy and the zodiac.

According to the ZODIAC project, sponsored by the Institute for the History of Knowledge in the Ancient World at Freie Universität Berlin, the term *astral science* references our ancient

11. "Lunar Sidereal and Synodic Periods."
12. Helmenstine, "Sidereal Month Versus Lunar Month (Synodic)."
13. Espenak, "Length of the Synodic Month."

ancestors' "interconnected astronomical, astrological, mathematical, religious, and social practices."[14] This also includes divination.

In a beautiful dance of synchronous rotation, at the same time Lady Luna is orbiting the Earth Mother, so is the Earth Mother orbiting the Sun, both Earth and Sun orbiting in an elliptical manner, in the shape of an elongated circle. And because of tidal and gravitational locking—meaning the Moon only turns once upon her axis each time she orbits Earth—we invariably see the same side of the Moon.

Why Doesn't the Moon Always Look the Same?

Our beloved Sun and Moon—collectively called the *luminaries*—have been fixed in this beautiful, intricate dance since Luna's birth: Every being who has ever lived has beheld the same face of the Moon.

However, we do see tiny variations in the Moon's face at times due to lunar libration, a wobbling effect that occurs because of her tilt in relation to the Earth as well as her elliptical orbit.

When Luna is traveling closest to Earth, her speed is faster than when she is traveling furthest from us. *Perigee* is the name for the occasions when the Moon is nearest our planet, and *apogee* denotes the furthest point the Moon can ever go from the Earth. Libration enables us to see 59 percent of the face the Moon presents to us instead of the 50 percent we would see should she have an unchanging orbit.[15]

The Moon Is Not Only Visible at Night

Have you noticed the Moon in the daytime sky? She is not only visible to us at night, and this can be important to the magic we implement in partnership with her.

Luna does not have her own source of light; all that we see of her is because of the reflection of the Sun's light. That said, she visits in daytime just as often as she does at night, even though it may be a bit trickier to see her and she needs to be journeying through certain parts of the sky.[16]

From our earthly perspective, Luna rises in the east and sets in the west just as do all other celestial bodies. There is a possibility of seeing the Moon during the day throughout any of her phases, except for the New Moon. Where and when she is visible depends upon our location, the time of year, and where she is in her cycle.

14. "ZODIAC."
15. Walker, "Inconstant Moon."
16. Talbert, "Why Can You See the Moon During the Day?"

The Eight Major Lunar Phases

The Moon is in constant flux as she moves through space and time. She reflects back to us varying amounts of the Sun's light, as well as Earthshine—the phenomena of the light of the Sun reflecting off of the Earth, which is particularly visible on the dark side of the Crescent Moon. In addition, Luna traverses perpetually through the twelve signs of the zodiac. Our Lunar Lady's phases are measured by her placement in the sky relative to that of both the Sun and the Earth.[17]

There are many names for the phases of the Moon, both major and minor, depending upon the tradition and worldview. For example, in Indigenous Hawaiian lore, there are as many as thirty![18]

Her light—which we know is a reflection of the Sun's light whilst we also know that it is so much more—perpetually fluctuating as she dances between the polarities of dark and bright.

She is a constant reminder of change, of construction and destruction, of emergence and dissolution, and of all that happens in between. Each of her phases is unique, filled with its own power, energy, and purpose, affecting each of us on an individual level and on a macro level, and affecting the entire natural world as well—plants, animals, sea, and stone.

At the most fundamental level, the Lunar Witch understands that aside from the pause-like moments on either side of her lunation—the New Moon and Full Moon—the Moon is always doing one of two things—waxing or waning—and that her cycling never slows, stops, or changes speed.

When the Moon is waxing, she is gaining power. When she is waning, she is releasing that power. Her phases can also be likened to and matched with the seasonal holy days we find upon the solar Wheel of the Year, every lunar cycle a microcosm of the larger solar cycle.

17. Aceves, "What Are the Phases of the Moon?"

18. "Hawaiian Moon Phases and Traditional Natural Resource Management."

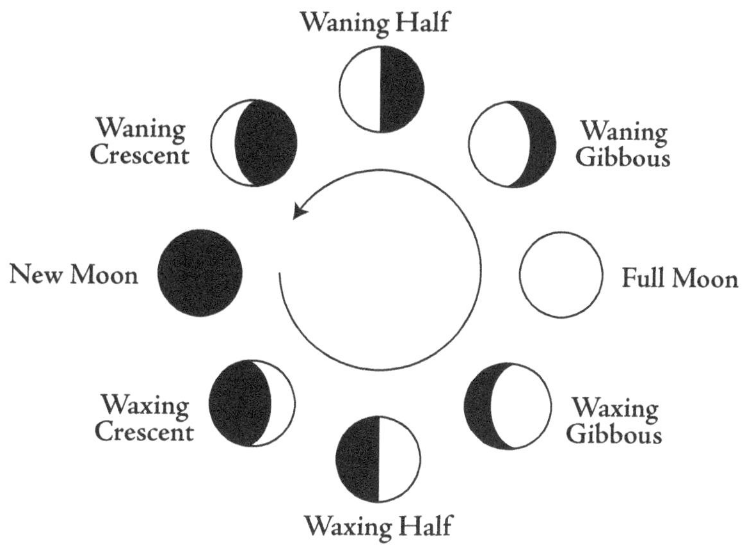

The Phases of the Moon

Daily Practice

Look at an ephemeris or lunar calendar and find out: What phase is the Moon in now? Go outdoors and look—and feel—for her in sky. Sometimes she will appear in the day, other times at night, and there are times when you may not be able to see her at all. The goal of this practice is to develop the ability to consistently *feel* her and to discern what she is doing.

New Moon

When the Moon is new, she is conjunct with the Sun; they are both found at the same degree of the same sign of the zodiac, rising and setting as one. The Moon, the Earth, and the Sun are all aligned with one another at this time. (We will dive into lunar astrology in chapter 3.)

The New Moon takes place directly after the Waning Crescent Moon phase ends. From the New Moon until the moment before the Full Moon, she is waxing (growing larger)—a period of about fourteen days.

The New Moon marks the beginning of the lunar cycle, the sacred spark, a moment of conception. Even though we cannot see her, the exact time of the rebirth of the Moon is the origin point of each new lunation.

Every New Moon features an opportunity for you to start fresh, to consider what you want to invite into your life, and to contemplate the desires you want to manifest. This is an occasion to think big, to expand your sense of what is possible, and to embrace your biggest potential; it is a time for visioning, heartstorming, and discovering where you want to go next. The energies here are unrefined, formless, and ready for you to gather up and channel in ways that will later fuel your greatest plans.

On the solar Wheel of the Year, this phase corresponds to the Winter Solstice.

Where and How to View the New Moon

Because she is one with the Sun's glare, the Moon appears invisible to us on Earth. The only time we can see a New Moon is during a solar eclipse.

Journal Inquiry for the New Moon

What theme or goal will I explore this lunation?

Waxing Crescent Moon

When the Moon is in her Waxing Crescent phase, she is still in near alignment with the Sun and the Earth, and her right side is beginning to illuminate. As the Moon moves in an eastern trajectory around the Earth, the Sun begins to move out ahead, revealing Luna's thin crescent glow, which grows in size every night as her orbit brings her further and further along the ecliptic, the Earth-Sun line.

This phase takes us from 0.1 percent illumination up until 49.9 percent, lasting a bit longer than seven days.

When this Waxing Crescent is first visible in the night sky, usually about three days after the New Moon, she is also called Diana's Bow. This is when we first see the Moon after her rebirth, and it is often a dramatic and awe-inspiring sight as she reveals herself early in the night, not long after the Sun has fully set and the sky is morphing color to dark blue or black.

About one-eighth of the Moon is visible during this time. We see only this small fraction of her illuminated face unless there is Earthshine, when we can see her darkened side, too.

The Waxing Crescent Moon is still young, still new. These are the energies of initiation, of slow growth and setting things in motion. This is the time to create a foundation, a home for your hopes and dreams, a rich and fertile soil in which you can nurture them into fruition.

On the solar Wheel of the Year, this phase corresponds to Imbolc.

Where and How to View the Waxing Crescent Moon

Beginning with this phase, the Moon may be visible high in the sky. For the best view of her inhabiting this phase, look to the western sky soon after sunset when Luna is setting.

Journal Inquiry for the Waxing Crescent Moon

What processes, practices, or habits will I put into place to support my goals and my growth?

Waxing Half Moon

Called the First Quarter Moon by many, this is when the waxing half of the Moon lights up, perched at the central moment between her darkness and her fullness. Fifty percent of the Moon is lit up at this time.

A quarter of the lunation is complete now, halfway between the New and Full phases, carrying half of the light of the Sun. There is a lot of power available within this phase, as the force of the Moon ramps up as she grows and grows in the sky.

You are encouraged to continue to tend to your metaphorical dream garden now, as the energies begin to coalesce and consolidate. Sometimes you can already see your desires slowly taking shape. Or you may choose to make a decision to allow a particular desire to rest because you have realized that now is not the proper time to pursue it.

On the solar Wheel of the Year, this phase corresponds to the Spring Equinox.

Where and How to View the Waxing Half Moon

When the Moon reaches the halfway point of her waxing, she is located approximately the same distance from the Sun as the Earth. Her rising time now is about six hours after sunrise, around noontime depending upon the time of year, and you can see half of her face illuminated in both the day and the night sky before she sets at approximately midnight. Look toward the south around sunset.

Journal Inquiry for the Waxing Half Moon

What course corrections or adjustments will I make now?

Waxing Gibbous Moon

When the Moon has reached her Waxing Gibbous phase, she grows heavy in the sky, her form swelling toward fullness, looking like a round, pregnant belly. *Gibbous* is a word rooted in both ancient and modern Latin, and it can be translated as "humpbacked."

The Moon is more than halfway toward her pinnacle now, her energies growing stronger and quicker as they lead up to the Full Moon. Throughout this time, Luna travels through 50.1 percent illumination and reaches 99.9 percent.

Embrace the power of Luna and connect with it as you lovingly tend to all of the little details of those dreams you have been nurturing. These energies can be compared to the creative, transformative, nesting instincts of a parent-to-be.

On the solar Wheel of the Year, this phase corresponds to Beltane.

Where and How to View the Waxing Gibbous Moon

This Moon is easily visible in the daytime as she rises in the east in the afternoon whilst the Sun is sinking in the west. When the Moon has reached her Waxing Gibbous phase, you can see her as soon as she rises until after midnight. Without fail, she disappears before sunrise.

Journal Inquiry for the Waxing Gibbous Moon

How can I step into full alignment with my goals and my growth?

Full Moon

The Full Moon always occurs in the opposite astrological sign of the Sun. When she is full, she is 100 percent illuminated, solidly holding the light of the Sun.

Here is the peak of the lunar cycle! The Moon has reached her pinnacle, and there is a heightened awareness in the air, the energies strong and intense (and occasionally overwhelming for some). Everything is magnified now, especially our emotions and the emotions of everyone around us. Be aware of this when walking about your day or night!

If she is still waxing, this is the time to quickly set things in motion for rapid results. To determine whether this is the case, check an ephemeris for the exact time of her fullness because it can be deceiving to the eye. Magically speaking, Full Moon energy is commonly said to last three days: the day before the Full Moon, the day of, and the day after.

In my own practice, once the Moon has reached the moment of her fullness and has begun to wane again, I do not consider her energies to be full any longer. Like the movement of an ocean, her powers may still be quite strong, and yet, once they have crested their highest point, they are already beginning to recede.

After this instant, the gentle tides of release start to roll back in. This moment of the Full Moon is a point of celebration, of honoring, of feasting, dancing, and making merry. Feel the height of the energies and pause to honor yourself because you deserve it! The hard work will begin again tomorrow, when it's time to see what needs to be pruned or composted.

On the solar Wheel of the Year, this phase corresponds to the Summer Solstice.

Where and How to View the Full Moon

In the few days leading up to and including the Full Moon, look to the east, where she often rises a bit before sunset. After this, she often sets in the west after sunrise.

Journal Inquiry for the Full Moon

What is culminating in my life?

Waning Gibbous Moon

This phase lasts for about seven days and encompasses the time when Luna transitions from 99.9 percent illumination to 50.1 percent illumination.

During the Waning Gibbous Moon, also named the Disseminating Moon, the light of the Sun fills the left side of the Moon; she has passed the threshold and is already fading toward darkness again. Here is a slow descent toward the end of the lunation, toward the Waning Crescent and Dark Moon. There is a gentle disintegration beginning, where those things that aren't meant to be begin to break down into their smallest parts and reenter the void of potential and possibility.

As this waning feels peaceful and slow, now is a time to consider what you would like to decrease and release once you move deeper into this side of the lunation. Gentle, long-term cleansing, clearing, and healing can be started and are well-supported now.

On the solar Wheel of the Year, this phase corresponds to Lammas.

Where and How to View the Waning Gibbous Moon

The Waning Gibbous Moon generally rises in the east between sunset and midnight and sets sometime after the Sun rises. She is often visible in the morning sky.

Journal Inquiry for the Waning Gibbous Moon

What practice, relationship, object, or action is no longer serving my life and who I want to be?

Waning Half Moon

When the Moon reaches her Waning Half phase, also called the Third Quarter Moon, 50 percent of her sphere is once again illuminated—this time, the left side.

Now we're getting serious again. After the exact moment of the Waning Half Moon, we move forward into her Waning Crescent phase.

Reflect on what has already occurred this lunation, and clear away anything that needs to be moved out of your way. What intentions do you hold for these last two-ish weeks of this particular lunar cycle?

On the solar Wheel of the Year, this phase corresponds to the Fall Equinox.

Where and How to View the Waning Half Moon

This Moon can be seen day and night. She rises in the eastern skies around midnight, setting in the west around noon.

Journal Inquiry for the Waning Half Moon

With what am I now ready to move into a gracious state of conclusion?

Waning Crescent Moon

This phase lasts for a little over seven days, taking us from 49.9 percent illumination all the way to 0.1 percent illumination.

The end of the lunar cycle is coming quickly now, and the light of the Moon is now surrendering to the power of her darkness. It is time to completely let go, to yield to the beauty and power of the shadow, to rest, relax, and renew yourself within her inky blackness.

This Moon, sometimes termed the Old Moon, is a time for cleansing, clearing, purifying, and giving yourself permission to feel the relief of the release. Note the spaciousness you are creating inside yourself and your life—body, mind, heart, and spirit.

On the solar Wheel of the Year, this phase corresponds to Samhain.

Where and How to View the Waning Crescent Moon

This Moon awakens around 3 a.m. and sets around 3 p.m., depending upon the season. Look to the east before sunrise to see her slender sickle hanging in the early morning sky, her illuminated side always pointing toward the direction of the sunrise.

Journal Inquiry for the Waning Crescent Moon

What am I now complete with for all time?

Moon Musings

Once per waking cycle, be it morning, afternoon, or night but best at the same time each day, take up your Moon Journal and note the lunar phase, how you are feeling, and what is happening in your life. Pay close attention to each part of the lunation: listen, chronicle, journal, and experiment. What does your body think and feel like during each lunar phase?

Begin making this part of your everyday practice.

"Bonus" Lunar Phases and Other Happenings

Aside from the phases, there are other lunar happenings and notable positions in the Moon's dance around our Earth Mother. These bonus stages can affect and enhance your magic and work as a Lunar Witch.

Dark Moon

As the Waning Moon phase comes to an end, we reach the nadir of the lunation. This is when the Moon's orbit brings her between the Earth and the Sun, with the dark side facing us, making her virtually invisible to the naked eye. This is the time of the Dark Moon.

The Dark Moon isn't an official lunar phase, and yet for many, it is hugely important for magic. It dials a direct line into our inner wisdom, our unconscious, and the collective unconscious.

There is disagreement around what this phase is composed of, and there are generally two schools of thought about it:

- The Dark Moon is technically the (astronomical) New Moon, the point of total darkness when the Moon is completely hidden from human view.
- The Dark Moon is the final part of the Waning Moon phase, a time when Luna is moving into her brief place of rest and regeneration, when we are held gently and powerfully within her Waning Crescent phase, before she is born again at the New Moon.

Please experiment with these two schools of thought and discover what works best for your unique magic!

On the Path of the Lunar Witch as I walk it, the Dark Moon phase encompasses the final three and a half days before the Moon is again reborn, marking the last segment of the lunar month, occurring just before she begins to wax again. This time, also titled Hekate's Sickle or the Balsamic Moon, is a mirror to the Diana's Bow Moon, each happening in the three-day span that surrounds the New Moon in either direction.

For me, these are the witchiest moments of the lunar cycle, when That Which Is Hidden is revealed, when I allocate time to slow down, go deep within, and listen. This is a profoundly liminal place, that hallowed threshold between dark and light, between gestation and birth, between the invisible and the visible.

There is true healing available at the Dark of the Moon; a loving and compassionate space in which to slow down and savor *what is*, a natural pause in which to take stock of your life, to contemplate that which could use the wisdom of the Dark Goddess and the curative balm of slowness, to acknowledge what you are ready to heal and release, to thin, prune, and compost.

These are the last moments to shed those old skins before it is time to care for the new, to afford space for new thoughtforms to become physical matter, and to begin again.

Look at your lunar calendar and find out when the Moon will next be in her Dark Moon phase. If necessary, mark your everyday calendar so you know when she is next Dark.

Void of Course

The void of course Moon is not a phase but more of a *happening*, a marker of the period between the Moon's final aspect in one astrological sign and when she moves forward into the next one.[19]

Magically speaking, this is considered a poor time for any workings. Luna is said to be ungrounded, untethered to any particular energy, and things begun alongside this interval will have a hard time manifesting, if they do at all.

As Luna changes zodiacal signs every two or three days, she goes void of course at the same rate. The Moon can dwell in void of course from a couple of minutes to several hours or even longer.

This happening is typically indicated on an ephemeris or calendar with the notation "v/c" placed next to a time. You can locate the time the Moon moves out of void of course by the hour and minute listed adjacent to the astrological sign that comes after the sign that the Moon most recently left.

Void of Course Moon in an Ephemeris

19. "Void of Course Moon Dates and Times."

Lunar Void Practice

Using an ephemeris or lunar calendar, begin a practice of charting when the Moon goes void of course. Make particular note of how you feel during these times. Do you notice anything different emotionally, physically, or otherwise?

Supermoons

Remember: Our Lunar sibling moves around the Earth in the shape of an ellipse, which can cause interesting happenings in the sky.

When a New or Full Moon happens at the same time the Moon is closest to Earth, a Supermoon occurs. Supermoons are not rare: There are usually three to four New Supermoons and three to four Full Supermoons every calendar year (although occasionally there can be more; for example, in 2024 there were five New Supermoons).

While you most likely will not notice much of a difference in size, if any, Full Supermoons can appear to be brighter than regular Full Moons because they actually are—and by an average of 15 percent.

The King Tides arrive with these Moons, too, so if you live near a coastal area, you may notice that the water can be appreciably higher or lower than usual, as the gravitational pull is about 4 percent greater than during a regular Full or New Moon.

Micromoons

The opposite of a Supermoon, Micromoons occur when our Earth Mama is farthest from the Moon during any lunation. Like Supermoons, Micromoons generally occur three to four times per calendar year, with some exceptions.

Micromoons are the Full and New Moons that happen when the Moon is at apogee.[20] From our earthy perspective, the Full Micromoon may appear to be smaller and fainter than a regular Full Moon.

20. "Supermoons & Micromoons."

Threshold Moons

Threshold Moons are those New and Full Moons that mark the beginning or ending of a season, those Moons which stand guard over the energetic shifts in the solar Wheel of the Year, where the boundaries and currents are as fluid as the rain pouring through the winter skies.

These Moons include the first and last New and Full Moons of Spring (with Spring Equinox as the beginning point, on or near March 21), of Summer (with Summer Solstice as the beginning point, on or near June 21), of Autumn (with Fall Equinox as the beginning point, on or near September 21), and of Winter (with Winter Solstice as the beginning point, on or near December 21).

Eclipses

Eclipses are powered by the Lunar Nodes—the two points where the orbit of the Moon crosses the ecliptic or the Sun's yearly travels across the sky as seen from Earth. The lunar and solar eclipses each happen when Lady Luna touches either the lower or upper border of this oval-shaped orbit. I will discuss the Lunar Nodes further when addressing the Shadow. (See chapter 4.)

Eclipses can be viewed as the holy union—or sacred separation—of Moon and Sun, a manifestation of their eternal alliance as they glide through the celestial tides.

Total solar eclipses happen about every eighteen months, with partial and annular solar eclipses averaging around two to four times per year (with as few as two and as many as five possible).[21] On the other hand, total lunar eclipses happen only about every two and a half years, with partial or penumbral lunar eclipses occurring about once or twice per year (with as few as zero and as many as five).[22]

Solar eclipses and lunar eclipses are generally paired (i.e., a lunar eclipse will be followed about two weeks later by a solar eclipse), although sometimes there will be a group of three eclipses (solar, then lunar, then solar, or lunar, then solar, then lunar).

Solar eclipses last less than ten fast and fleeting minutes, and lunar eclipses can last almost two hours.

These cosmic happenings carry with them intense, far-reaching energetic signatures, not only because of their astrological impact on the Earth but because even non-magical people are aware and fascinated by them, adding to their mythology and to the collective egregore.

In April 2024, hundreds of thousands of people in the United States alone traveled to view the total solar eclipse. This seemed like the most universally recognized eclipse of my lifetime, and most of the people I'm acquainted with who journeyed to see it have absolutely no interest in astrology and no conscious magical connection to the Moon.

21. "What Are the Three Types of Solar Eclipses?"
22. Dobrijevic, "What Are Lunar Eclipses and How Do They Occur?"

Eclipses can assist us with our own ongoing spiritual metamorphosis, helping us to understand the longer cycles of the Cosmos, cycles much longer than the monthly lunar circuit or the yearly solar circuit. Vibrationally speaking, the currents of an eclipse can be felt for at least a half a year after the event itself, with many of the reverberations playing out for a wealth of years—even decades—afterward.

Referred to as portals or vortexes by some Witches and magicians, I liken them to a magical cauldron inside where far-reaching change is made. Eclipses take the power of the lunar phase and sign in which they occur and then multiply those energies exponentially. As spiritual gateways, these happenings can accelerate our personal growth to lightspeed as well as bring deeply buried issues out into the light of day.

Those who view eclipses as portals generally recognize the point of this cosmic happening as a doorway between the past and the future; introspective moments of reflection, self-care, and growth; and an opportunity to make quick and long-lasting changes.

Eclipse energies can feel raw, jagged, unbalanced, scary, and overwhelming, and many practitioners abstain from magic of any kind during these happenings as it has ample possibility of going awry.

Any eclipse, though, also presents the potential of a suitable time to focus on divination and magic for health and healing as well as workings to increase intuition, psychic powers, and magical skills. They offer the prospect of rapidly leveling up, of bringing greater awareness of the Self and its place in the world.

Just as the Sun, Moon, and Earth move into alignment to create an eclipse, these events can also activate your own alignment—both Within and Without, with yourself and with All That Is—or if you are off-balance, you might decide to make substantial shifts, especially internally.

All eclipses carry the powers of alchemy and promise. Throughout an eclipse, allow yourself to be embraced by the Moon in all of her guises.

A Bit About Lunar Eclipses

Lunar eclipses always happen at the Full Moon phase, when the Sun and the Moon are astrologically opposite one another, and the Moon is eclipsed by the Earth.

Awareness of your emotions, the emotions of others, and the territory of emotions in general is quite heightened during a lunar eclipse. Look to your Inner Self, your inner wisdom, and your inner knowing at this time.

On the outer level, examine your affiliations and your relationships. A lunar eclipse can often contribute depth, perhaps a glimpse or even the full sight of something of which you were previously oblivious.

A Bit About Solar Eclipses

A moment of night in the day, solar eclipses invariably happen during the New Moon phase, when the Sun and Moon rendezvous in the same zodiacal sign. The Sun is eclipsed by the Moon, and the shadows of the Moon cover the Earth like a black blanket.

A solar eclipse is concerned with *personal* cycles and shifts, and there is expansive potential for seemingly spontaneous life initiations and living rebirths to happen as things get rattled around.

The usual order of things is suspended, and we all hold our collective breath, then comes a big exhale, creating spaciousness and a possibility for expansion. Grand questions and epiphanies may also arise, questions such as "How did I get here?" or "Where do I go now?"

You may have an impulse to completely burn down the structure of your life in order to ease feelings of constriction and to begin again at the most fundamental level. Give yourself some grace and self-compassion if this happens, as the enormity of this new beginning can cause everything to appear unstable for a time.

You must always wear protective eyewear to view a solar eclipse!

Blue Moons

A Blue Moon is an additional Full Moon that occurs within a given time period. There are many different schools of thought on how to properly determine a Blue Moon, including calculating (1) by calendar month, (2) by astrological season, and (3) by astrological sign.

In the first method, any time there are two Full Moons in one calendar month, the second occurrence is the Blue Moon. We know that the timing of a lunation and a calendar month are not synchronous; the calendar Blue Moon happens when the first Full Moon occurs near the beginning of a calendar month with enough time for a second Full Moon—the Blue Moon—to occur at or near the conclusion of that same month.

In the second method—which seems to be the most oft-used determination—whenever there is an extra Full Moon during any season, the *third* Full Moon in the sequence is denoted as the Blue Moon. Using the astrological seasons—from Spring Equinox to Summer Solstice, from Summer Solstice to Fall Equinox, from Fall Equinox to Winter Solstice, and from Winter Solstice to Spring Equinox—when there are four Full Moons within one of these vortexes instead of the usual three, the *third* occurrence is the Blue Moon.

The final method, which is my personal favorite because I think it's the most fun, is when two Full Moons occur in the same astrological sign. For example, on June 21, 2024, we experienced a Full Moon in Capricorn. The following Full Moon, this one on July 21, 2024, also fell in the sign of Capricorn, making it an astrological Blue Moon.

Using this also as an example for a seasonal Blue Moon, in the astrological season that began on the Summer Solstice of June 20, 2024, and ended on the Fall Equinox of September 22, 2024, the *third* Full Moon of this four Full Moon series was the Full Moon in Aquarius on August 19. Using this method of calculation, this was the Blue Moon.

Why Is It Called "Blue"?

Our Lunar Lady does not turn blue, so why is it called a "Blue Moon," anyway? We are not exactly sure, but there are a few theories! Try them all on and decide which one makes the most sense to you.

Perhaps the earliest written reference to the general idea of a Blue Moon appears in the 1528 satirical pamphlet *Rede Me and Be Not Wroth*, authored by Friar Jerome Barlow and Friar William Roy. In this tract, these two clergy members criticize Roman clergy members for their expectation that laypeople were to believe their every word, even if they proposed something outlandish or impossible such as "the Moon is blue."[23]

Philip Hiscock, a professor and folklorist, asserts that in the 1600s Cardinal Wolsey, advisor to King Henry VIII, was the first to use this term, writing that his enemies "would have you believe the moon is blue."[24]

In the 1816 poem "Alastor" by Percy Bysshe Shelley, written when the effects of the eruption Mount Tambora were being experienced all over the world, we find these lines of verse: "Blue moon/Low in the west."[25]

Other people pinpoint the genesis of the phrase to the eruption of the volcano Krakatoa in the year 1883. The dust that filled the air as a result of this event caused sunsets to look green and the Moon to look blue around the world for almost two years.[26]

There are at least two other times that the Moon actually appeared to be blue. In 1927 in India, there was an exceptionally long dry season due to the late arrival of the yearly monsoons, and the atmosphere was filled with a dust that appeared to give the Moon a blue sheen. In 1951, the particulate matter resulting from forest fires in Western Canada made the Moon appear blue to those living in the northeast part of North America.[27]

23. "Is The 'Blue' in 'Blue Moon' a Reference to Betrayal?"
24. Wolchover, "If It Isn't Blue, How Come It's Called a 'Blue Moon?'"
25. Shelley, "Alastor."
26. Begum, "The 1883 Krakatau Eruption."
27. Hiscock, "Where Does the Phrase 'Once in a Blue Moon' Come From?"

In 1946, people detected that there was a mistake in the translation of the 1937 *Maine Farmers' Almanac* by James Hugh Pruett, which brought us to the common usage of the term *Blue Moon* to designate the second Full Moon within one calendar month.[28]

No matter how it is calculated and no matter the etymology of the term, there is no doubt that Blue Moons have sparked humanity's imagination! They happen approximately once in each thirty-three-month span, about every two to three years. These are compelling times to make magic (notably potions, which I'll discuss in chapter 10) that will radiate outward for some time, as each Blue Moon is part of a greater Blue Moon cycle.

Black Moons

While this term is far more modern and is sometimes attributed to Dorothy Morrison's book *Everyday Moon Magic,* Black Moons have been an integral part of my Lunar Witchcraft practice since the mid-1990s. They are calculated just as Blue Moons are yet for New Moons as opposed to Full Moons.

Just like determining a Blue Moon, there are three primary ways to calculate a Black Moon: (1) by calendar month, (2) by astrological season, and (3) by astrological sign.[29]

When there are two New Moons in any given calendar month, the second one is called a Black Moon.

When there is an "extra" New Moon within any astrological season (from Equinox to Solstice or Solstice to Equinox), the *third* is the Black Moon.

And when there are two successive New Moons in the same zodiacal sign, the second is the Black Moon.

Black Moons occur in the same pattern as Blue Moons (i.e., we experience one about every thirty-three calendar months).

Moon Stones

For a tactile route to bring all of this Moon phase information home into your body, you can create your own set of moon stones, each one containing and anchoring the energies of a different lunar phase. These stones will help you to integrate the ever-shifting phases of the Moon into your everyday flow.

28. SpaceRef, "A 'Blue Moon' Heralds the Harvest."
29. Whitt, "Black Moon Coming on December 30–31."

Creating Moon Stones

The simplest way to start this project is to buy a package of stones from a craft store. These flat stones are often used for rock painting activities or to create plant displays.

Alternatively, you could instead create your set over time, collecting rocks as you find them in nature. Some beaches are especially known for flat, round stones. As an added benefit, if you collect stones on a beach, you are organically incorporating the tidal energies of the Moon through the stones themselves, which have been formed and bathed by the tides.

Another means to approach this project is to purchase polished crystals that are already cut into the shape of a circle. Choose a stone—or stones—that resonate with the lunar energies. See chapter 7 for ideas.

To Gather

- Round flat stones or polished crystals
- Paint pens. Try the silver ones.

The Process

Step 1: To construct your set of moon stones, simply draw one of the eight major phases of the Moon on each rock. You can also expand your set, using symbols of your own devising to represent the "bonus phases" you'd like to further study.

Step 2: Next, charge and then activate your stones individually, placing each one outdoors underneath the proper corresponding lunar phase so it can draw down and contain the energies of that particular phase of the Moon. This charging and activating protocol is similar to the one used to set a magic mirror with specific lunar and/or astrological vibrations in chapter 15.

Step 3: When completed, store your set of moon stones upon an altar or in another sacred place or in an attractive bag. I prefer black, blue, or purple velvet drawstring bags for mine.

You can use your moon stones to keep track of the changing of her phases by placing the corresponding stone on your altar or in another prominent place alongside each shifting phase. You can also use them as part of a ritual altar, for divination, or even to decide when to perform lunar rites or moonspells. I will address all of these topics in upcoming chapters.

If you create your set from crystals or stones that are shiny, you can use them to behold the glow of the Moon!

Moon stones can also serve as an excellent focal point for your Moon meditation practice and to assist you in tuning into your own deep Lunar Witch wisdom.

Chapter 3
The Zodiac

The Moon Goddess Speaks

I spin the silver wheel of celestial whirling, my hand firm upon the rudder of fate. Not only can I tell you who you are in this lifetime, I can remind you of who you once were, in lives long past. Who are you now? Who were you then? I hold all of these threads in my holy hands, forever weaving them into the unique tapestry that is past, present, and future.

Journey with me through the phases of the Moon as we taste everything that is available upon my buffet of sacred possibilities, all of the flavors—sweet, savory, salty, and sour—that created the singular recipe of you.

With light feet and a joyful heart, join me in this dance through the endless cycling of life. Listen to the cosmic messages that were written in the stars just for you.

I am Arianrhod.

Journal Inquiries for This Gateway

What is my purpose in this lifetime? What is my life's mission? What is one step I can take to place my feet more firmly upon my sacred path?

Affirmations for This Gateway

I surrender to and flow with the infinite cycle of birth, death, and rebirth. I am always in the right place at the right time doing the right thing. I trust the loving hands of fate.

Encoded within you is a galactic treasure map to self-understanding, one which reveals your inherent challenges and strengths and highlights your innate abilities and areas for growth, offering valuable insight into who you are and how you interact with not only life on Earth but with the energies of the Cosmos.

Exploring how your cycling mirrors the passage of the Moon will reveal not only the larger cosmic forces at play and how this macrocosm affects your personal microcosm but how to include upcoming energetic patterns in your plans, too.

If you view the Sun as the main battery of your life, providing your primary source of energy whilst also holding the stored energy that powers you from day to day, the Moon can be seen as a choreographer, distributing these energies and influencing all of the rhythms of your life, from your emotions to your mindset to your biological changes.

While the energy of the Sun is direct, the energy of the Moon is usually far more subtle in nature.

The Moon, like all other celestial bodies, does not compel, coerce, or constrain. Her energies may influence, motivate, and encourage, but you are not bound by them. You continue to have free will to make the sovereign choices that you want to make.

The energies of the astrological signs that the Sun and the Moon journey through combine with each of Luna's phases and your lunar temperament to create different vibrations, which you can then synthesize in both your ordinary and your magical lives.

You are most likely already familiar with your Sun sign, the zodiacal signature that governs your core personality, your greatest motivations, and how you carry yourself through life. Equally important is your birthmoon, the conjunction of the lunar sign and phase under which you were born.

The Moon in Your Natal Chart

Just as with any planet, when the Moon is said to be *in* a sign, this is a shorthand reference to her travels within that sign's constellation. The first step in connecting with your birthmoon is to discover the constellation the Moon was in when you were born. To do this, you will run your natal chart, also called a birth chart, which is a picture of the sky at the moment of your birth, showing you the location of the planets and luminaries in relationship to where you were on Earth at that instant. There are many free apps and websites where you do this; I am partial to astro.com.

Luna shifts signs rapidly, so in order to cast an accurate natal chart—one that includes the correct lunar sign and degree—it is ideal to have your birthplace and exact birth time.

If you do not have your exact birth time—and if you are unable to obtain your birth record from the hospital, from the vital records office of your birth town or state, or from an online search—you can run a chart with just the date and location. On the site I use, a chart with an unknown birth time is automatically calculated for noon. However, if you have a general notion of when you were born (e.g., early morning, late afternoon, evening, and so on) you can instead input that time.

This static chart will show you which zodiacal sign the Moon was traversing on your birthday. Next, look to the degree the Moon was in and, taking into account that Luna moves about 13 degrees a day and that there are 30 degrees per sign, ascertain if she could have moved through or into a neighboring sign during those 24 hours.

You can also determine what constellation the Moon was in when you made your first earthly appearance by creating natal charts for the two days surrounding your birth using your same birth location. If the Moon is in the same sign throughout the two days on either side of your birthday, you can be confident of your Moon sign. And using those two additional natal charts, you can also extrapolate the range of degrees that the Moon traveled through and formulate a reasonable guess as to the degree of your own birthmoon.

If you do not know your birth time and/or place, you might want to hire an astrologer who specializes in natal chart rectifications, a discipline that uses significant life events and themes to discern nebulous birthtimes.

Of course, the planets and luminaries don't stop moving. Your birth chart is purely a snapshot of that particular moment in time when you arrived Earthside. As these heavenly bodies continue their travels throughout your entire life, they simultaneously activate different parts of your chart. These continuous planetary travels are termed transits.

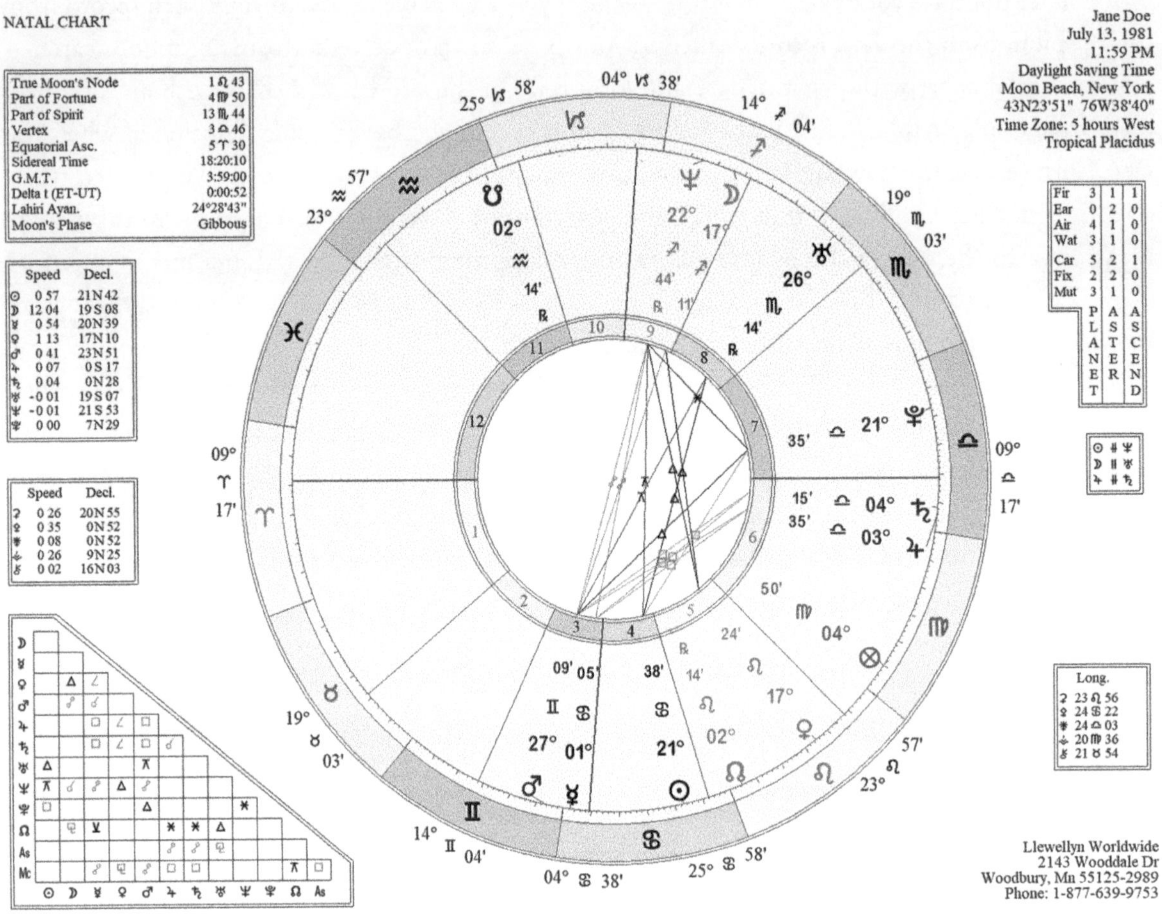

Natal Chart

What Does It Mean?

Your Moon sign is the first component of your birthmoon. This sign of the zodiac represents your innermost Self—your gut, your instinct, your intuition, your reactions, and your desires. This is who you are inside and may not permit many people, if any, to see. Your Moon sign is also at the forefront of your intimate relationships, signaling whom you are attracted to and how and whom you love.

This energy rules your emotional body, defines your emotional development, and is an expression of the unconscious side of your personality. It can also be representative of your Shadow Self or shadow concerns. (We will explore the Shadow in the next chapter.)

Your Moon Sign

Your Moon sign denotes the constellation that Luna was traveling through when you were born. If you haven't already done so, run a birth chart for yourself and find your Moon sign on it. In which sign and degree was the Moon at the moment of your birth?

While looking at your chart, envision yourself in the very center of the wheel with the celestial bodies stretching out around you in all directions. Where is your Moon located? Is she above you, below you, or to one side? Let yourself feel into her location at the moment of your arrival on Earth.

The Astrological "Flavors"

While the Moon describes our emotions and the way we nurture ourselves, each sign of the zodiac through which she travels carries with it its own ambiance, frequency, and vibration—each imbued with its own symbolism, magic, and themes.

Further, each sign of the zodiac is also governed by an element of life (i.e., air, fire, water, or earth), a modality, or way of being (i.e., cardinal, fixed, or mutable), as well as a response that is either projective or receptive.

Additionally, as they are paired together, each Moon phase and sign creates its own novel signature, and each lunar and solar pairing creates an axis, which looks and feels distinctive based upon the qualities of the zodiacal signs and the planets that rule them.

Although there are considerable commonalities, how these vibrations interact with your singular makeup is different from how they interact with mine. As you proceed upon your Lunar Witchery travels, your empirical studies will show you how each sign affects you and your life, how they feel inside of your body, as well as how they impact you and the unique individuals with whom you share your life.

Have you ever noticed that you feel differently during each New or Full Moon? This is natural because each lunar happening has its own essence comprised of layers of spice involving the Sun sign, the lunar phase, and the sign the Moon is in—not to mention all of the other planetary happenings going on up there.

A Full Moon in October bears a significantly different energetic than a Full Moon in June. Likewise, a New Moon in February feels distinctly different than one in August. And so on as we traverse the lunar and solar Wheels of the Year.

If you think of the Moon (and every planet, actually) as an actor upon the celestial stage and the zodiacal signs as the costumes that can be worn, this can help you to visualize the different flavors of the Moon and the unique flavor of your own birthmoon. Not only does the Moon express varying vibrations as she goes through each of her phases, but she also adorns herself with different energies as she travels through the signs.

Just as you may feel better when the Moon navigates certain signs based upon your own unique makeup, nurture, and natal nature, every planet and luminary is said to be happier in certain signs based upon their natural powers. (While the Sun and Moon are not planets, they are historically included as planets for the purposes of astrology and magic.)

A planet or luminary is said to be *at home* or *in domicile* in the sign it rules over and *exalted* in a sign where its energies can reach their highest potential. The Moon rules the sign of Cancer, and so she is at home when traveling through it. She is exalted in Taurus. This is because the fertile, grounded energies of this sign provide a safe and secure foundation for the Moon to express her highly fluid, emotional nature.

Moon Frequencies

Going forward in your daily practice, instead of just noting the lunar phase, how you are feeling, and what is happening in your life, add another component: What astrological sign is the Moon traversing? Do you notice your energies changing alongside the lunar sign?

January 6th, 2025 ☾

◐ ♈

Moon Journal Record

I like to draw something like this at the top of my daily Moon Journal page. I will write the calendar date and year and include the glyph for that day. Then I draw a little circle to symbolize the Moon, filling it in to reflect the phase she is in. Next to that, I will also note the sign, using the glyph that denotes it.

The Moon in Aries

Aries is the enthusiastic, energetic sign of activation, beginnings, and that powerful moment when things accomplish that first movement from flickery vision toward physical form. Aries is that explosive spark, that lightning bolt, that moment when sperm meets egg. This is the power of the passionate pioneer, the adventurous explorer, the one who thrives in challenging, exhilarating situations, who longs to investigate anything that is new, contemporary, or different.

Aries Glyph

Ruled by the element of fire, there is a certain fearlessness that accompanies this sign, the vibrant, vivacious energy of the tarot's Fool, the energy of leaping first and looking later. Aries energy contains thirst for life and all that comes with it, an internal joie de vivre no matter what may be going on externally.

The Aries Moon inspires us to independent action, to dance to our own inner beat, to blaze the trails upon which others can later walk. This fire-starting sign has a sense of contagious enthusiasm and a peerless desire and ability to lead. If support needs to be drummed up for a cause, this is a fitting sign under which to set things into motion.

An Aries Moon is most pleased when working on a challenge, and ideally it is one that helps to create a better world. Their courage and their confidence are rarely lacking, and they often rush in where angels fear to tread. The Aries Moon leads us toward innovative problem-solving using stratagems that maybe no one else has ever before considered.

The flavor of an Aries Moon: peppery spice, perhaps chili crisp.

How to Connect with the Moon in Aries

As Aries is ruled by Mars, one of the best methods to connect with this Moon is through intense physical activity. Fast, quick, precise movements such as rowing, high intensity interval training (HIIT), short uphill sprints, and agility training are some actions to take to align yourself with these energies.

If you aren't called to physically exert yourself, or are unable to do so, try taking swift, spontaneous action based on something you are passionate about in the moment. Don't wait—boldly grab on to your courage and begin!

The Moon in Taurus

Taurus is ruled by the planet Venus and is best personified by the Empress card in tarot. As such, these lunar vibes are luxurious, slow, and deliberate. Taurean energy is grounded, calm, centered, and steady.

Taurus Glyph

There is a great power that coincides with the patient dependability and the fertile energies of the Taurus Moon, one which helps us to grow ourselves and our dreams steadily and strongly. This Moon reminds us to look up and out, to see, acknowledge, and honor all of the beauty that surrounds us at any given moment.

Ruled by the element of earth, the Taurean Moon supports us in tending to our worldly resources and riches and supports us in expanding our value in the form of our self-worth, self-care, and self-love.

This transit is one of beauty and being, a sensual time to slow down and savor every precious moment that is presented to us.

When the Moon is in Taurus, she is in her exaltation. Try to feel this the next time she inhabits this sign.

The flavor of a Taurus Moon: rich, dark chocolate served hot in a fine china cup with a pile of homemade whipped cream and a cherry on top!

How to Connect with the Taurus Moon

A lovely approach to connect with the Moon traversing Taurus is through seeking and creating beauty and through making time for focused self-care.

Look around your home and see if there are any small updates or deliberate touches you can incorporate to create a more luxurious and beautiful space. This need not cost a lot of money! A simple bundle of flowers from the grocery store mindfully arranged in a favorite vase could add just the right touch.

Self-care can be as easy as taking an hour for yourself, simply relaxing and reading a novel or having a good soak in the tub with candlelight, incense, or blessed oils.

The Moon in Gemini

The first air sign in the zodiacal wheel, the playful, curious, and clever Gemini lunar transit invites us along for a fun and fast-paced ride.

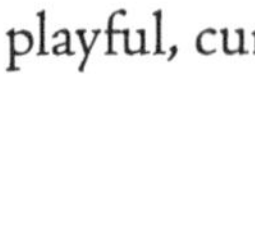

Gemini Glyph

This witty Moon is friendly and social, communicative and connective, a reminder that although we are sovereign beings we are not meant to walk through life alone.

Gemini Moons can help us to cultivate personal gardens of inspiration: new ways of thinking, new ways of being, and healthier ways of expressing ourselves. This transit invites us to set out on a journey of exploration, to hear new messages and learn new wisdom, and to adjust and adapt our view of life and what is possible based on these new insights.

The flavor of a Gemini Moon: air-popped popcorn covered with a sparkling dust of both salt and sugar.

How to Connect with the Gemini Moon

Since it is ruled by Mercury, the planet of communication, you can best experience the Gemini Moon energies whilst in connection with others—to talk through ideas big and small, to share and gain wisdom, to laugh, and to play, play, play!

When the Moon dances through Gemini, you are invited to live out loud and to get out of your own way—to stop telling tired old stories about yourself and your life and to move beyond those boxes that you created for yourself as reactionary and protective devices.

The Moon in Cancer

The Moon is the ruler of the sign of Cancer, and when she travels through this sign, she is at home and our intuition soars. Strongly connected with the element of water and associated with the night, we may become more emotional and nurturing during a Cancerian Moon and discover a forceful desire to stay close to home.

Cancer Glyph

This is the transit for observing traditions, keeping the past alive, and engaging with nostalgia. Pausing to check in to ensure you are speaking the truth—from your gut—instead of saying what you think someone may want to hear is important, too.

The flavor of a Cancer Moon: fresh briny oysters and surprising sushi rolls, like mango coupled with maguro and avocado.

How to Connect with the Moon in Cancer

Cancerian lunar energies can create situations where you are extraordinarily empathic and sensitive to others' thoughts, feelings, and emotions. During this Moon, it's important to notice when you are feeling your own feelings and when you are feeling and expressing the emotions of others. You may be thoroughly surprised by how often the energies you are expressing during a Cancerian Moon are not yours but rather the emotions of your loved ones, those around you, or the complex, aggregated emotions of your community, town, or world in general.

Reviewing your security and your personal boundaries is artfully supported when the Moon is transiting Cancer, and a certain amount of energetic shielding is needed, too. Check the fences of your own realm, inside and out. What needs to be repaired? Where have you let down your guard where you would be better served by holding more prominent boundaries for your own soft and best life? Don't neglect this work—it can revolutionize your entire existence.

Start diving into this during the Moon in Cancer. Take detailed notes about how you are feeling and if how you are feeling genuinely matches your own emotions or experiences throughout this time each lunation.

The Moon in Leo

The golden passion of the Moon traveling through the constellation of Leo helps us to step fully into our self-confidence, to own ourselves as charismatic creatures exuding the vital, glowing energies of life itself.

Leo Glyph

Ruled by the Sun, the luminary that guides our days on Earth, and the element of fire, a Leo lunar transit brings brightness and cheer to our days and a clarion song to pay attention!

The Leo Moon invites us to step into the spotlight, to take center stage, and to shine. When we learn to dance with the lunar flames of Leo, we level up. And as we joyfully play with these energies of self-awareness and self-love, we learn to easily conduct the fiery, expressive, and robust energies of the lion toward our loftiest desires.

The flavor of a Leo Moon: hot honey drizzled on cheesy New York pizza.

How to Connect with the Leo Moon

When the Moon is in Leo, it is an excellent time to do something you have been putting off because you have felt too afraid to make the leap. Go for big goals in this transit: Trust that the scorching power of the venerable lion will carry you through the fires of your greatest fears.

You can take heart from the Lion, allowing your own sacred flame within, your heart-fire, to be a beacon for your magic and your creativity, to express the fullness of your true Self. There is a consistency to this flame, one that can sustain you through anything you may experience.

The Moon in Virgo

Detail oriented and summoned to service, the Virgoan lunar energies assist us in creating systems, in organizing ourselves and others, and in solving problems large and small. As Luna travels through this constellation, our powers of observation and analysis increase, helping us to gather and process all pertinent information before any big decision-making.

♍

Virgo Glyph

When we need to invoke the energies of precision this is the transit to wait for. The Virgo Moon brings a solution-focused energy, one that can assist us in creating the structures needed to secure our roots down into the Earth so that our minds can expand broadly and fly through the stars.

Ruled by the element of earth, this lunar transit can help us ground into the calmness and order necessary to pave the way for personal understanding and growth.

The flavor of a Virgo Moon: a glass of perfectly aged Napa Valley cabernet sauvignon.

How to Connect with the Virgo Moon

The Virgo Moon helps with focus and completing all of the little details of life that you've been putting off, dotting *i*'s and crossing *t*'s. Mercury governs this sign, making it a marvelous transit in which to organize all of the information you've accumulated into accessible concepts and applicable plans.

Meditation, journaling, and yoga are good practices to move you away from overthinking and return you to your physical body, as are earthy activities such as taking long hikes and caring for plants, getting your hands into some grounding dirt.

The Moon in Libra

Often communicative and diplomatic, sometimes whimsical and charming, too, when the Moon traverses this sign the overarching energies are eminently concerned with harmony, balance, and equality.

Libra Glyph

Ruled by the element of air, Luna in Libra is openhearted, accepting, and frequently quite social. When the Moon spends time here, we are often drawn to working toward justice and equity for all—to seeking the point of balance both Within and Without. Beauty is a necessary component, too, found in inspired, expansive thinking as well as cordial, hospitable settings.

The flavor of a Libra Moon: a light, tender scone with fresh garden strawberries and Somerset clotted cream.

How to Connect with the Libra Moon

Ruled by the planet Venus, there is a certain grace, elegance, and self-containment that arrives with a lunar Libra transit. As such, this is another excellent time to create beauty in the spaces where you spend the most time and then invite other congenial people to join you there for a salon, soirée, or cocktail party.

Working with goals and dreams is also supported, especially through brainstorming a list of pros and cons for those things you still need to make decisions around as well as seeking out the wisdom of those you trust, those who hold your highest good in their hearts.

The Moon in Scorpio

Guided by the element of water, the energies of the Scorpio Moon are recognized as intense, passionate, and evolving. This transit can feel elusive, even mystical or otherworldly.

Scorpio Glyph

There is an element of cosmic mystery here, of the undertow, and of the depths. Emotions can be consuming and extreme, and intuition holds center in all things. When Luna is navigating this constellation, transformation is encouraged—hidden patterns and emotions emerge from the depths, becoming visible at long last.

The flavor of a Scorpio Moon: a rich chocolate torte drenched in warm dark chocolate sauce.

How to Connect with the Scorpio Moon

In classical astrology, Scorpio is ruled by Mars, and in modern astrology, it is ruled by Pluto. This is a powerful time to visit with your Shadow Self, to bring things up from the depths of your innermost parts and into the light for healing and integration. (See the next chapter for more about the Shadow Self.)

This transit can aid you in meeting your challenges or perhaps in challenging others in ways that you've been meaning to for some time. When guided by a kind and open heart, these frank, unvarnished energies can help you to connect with your inner truth and, based upon this knowledge, implement grand, beautiful changes.

The Moon in Sagittarius

The fiery Sagittarius Moon strides in to assist us in seeing and exploring just how wide the horizons are or could be. This courageous yet fun-loving transit brings us the energies of expansion, potential, freedom, and possibility. It encourages us to hold on to our bravery and walk firmly into the vast unknown, to learn and experience whatever it is we can learn and experience there.

Sagittarius Glyph

The Moon in Sagittarius is ruled by the planet Jupiter and therefore holds the energies of joviality even whilst being, at times, loudly opinionated and very direct in sharing those opinions. The energies are open and honest; there is never a need to worry about ulterior motives or hidden agendas here. It's all out in full view, like it or not!

The flavor of a Sagittarius Moon: a crisp, sharp gingersnap cookie!

How to Connect with the Sagittarius Moon

Under the auspices of the element of fire, you can connect with this lunar frequency by fanning your own inner flames. This is the Moon to begin a grand new adventure, to explore the world with sincere curiosity and playfulness—whether this happens squarely outside of your front door or requires you to embark upon a long plane ride.

Whatever increases your lived sense of freedom is well-supported during this time, too. This is the transit to let go of habits, objects, or relationships that are confining or unsupportive. Set down burdens to create the space that is needed for your current hopes and dreams to grow; walk away from the past and don't look back.

The Moon in Capricorn

Known for the earthy powers of patient diligence and humble dedication, Capricorn lunar energies are practical, pragmatic, and steady. When the Moon marches through this sign, we are encouraged to complete our due diligence in service to our highest ambitions for ourselves and our success.

♑

Capricorn Glyph

This is a cardinal Moon passage, providing anchoring energies, helping us to firmly root our keenest desires into the richness of the soil so that they may establish themselves and grow, especially in the arena of our careers and our worldly reputations.

The Moon in Capricorn loves to formulate firm plans for the future, defining dreams and creating systems and structures to build them into physical reality.

The flavor of a Capricorn Moon: freshly made pappardelle pasta with Bolognese sauce and grated Parmigiano-Reggiano.

How to Connect with the Capricorn Moon

The sign of Capricorn is governed by Saturn, the planet of discipline, ambition, productivity, and tenacity. With optimism, this is the transit to build and tend to foundations—both physical and metaphorical.

Practical projects having to do with resources (namely money) are specifically aided, including checking bank balances, paying bills, and laying concrete groundwork for getting out of debt. On the employment front, apply for your dream job or ask for that well-earned promotion.

The Moon in Aquarius

There is an air of crackling possibility when the Moon traverses idealist Aquarius, an electricity that fills the atmosphere and brings with it bolts of innovation, epiphany, and originality—a freshness that comes with the limitless promise of progress and evolution.

♒

Aquarius Glyph

Knowledge and learning—but not necessarily the intellectual kind—turns on the confident and clever Aquarius Moon. Expressing the marriage between intuition and information, the airy energies of this transit are hyper-progressive, often leading to sweeping change, chiefly in the collective, social environment. This energy is also decidedly idealistic, equitable, and gregarious.

Directed by the planet Uranus in the modern astrological system (Saturn in classical astrology), the Moon in Aquarius is the archetypal shapeshifter, able to fly on the wings of the wind, transmitting eagle-eyed information back to us on Earth. This Moon sees all of the possibilities with revolutionary, kaleidioscopic eyes.

The flavor of an Aquarius Moon: crispy double-fried salt and vinegar kettle chips.

How to Connect with the Aquarius Moon

When a fresh perspective is needed—one never before considered—petition this Moon for a new vision, a new dream, and an unconventional understanding. This is the time to imagine, to collaborate, to communicate candidly and deftly. What new beauty can you weave using empathic compassion to galvanize and fuel your far-reaching goals?

The Aquarian Moon inquires: What inspires you? What unshakeable hope do you hold deep within? This transit encourages you to apply yourself to your grandest goals now, now, *now*; to free yourself from all types of unconscious bondage; and to awaken into your Highest Self and your most-urgent purpose in living upon this beautiful Earth Mother.

The Moon in Pisces

This water-soaked sign is the final constellation of the zodiac, and it is ruled by the planet Neptune (Jupiter in classical astrology). As the Moon traverses creative and psychic Pisces, the frequencies are sensitive, adaptable, and emotional.

♓

Pisces Glyph

As Luna swims through Pisces, expect vivid and profound dreams combined with a sense of ethereal unreality. Big emotions may rise up from the depths, bringing about the revisiting of feelings we thought long-ago relieved to be worked through anew, ushering in profound and total healing.

The energies of the Piscean Moon are creative, generous, idealistic, psychic, sensitive, artistic, compassionate, dreamy, optimistic, loving, empathic, and intuitive.

The flavor of a Pisces Moon: a seaweed salad made with toasted sesame oil and sesame seeds.

How to Connect with the Pisces Moon

This lunar transit can help to activate your imagination and your self-understanding. Here, you can dive deeply into your emotions, that which is happening below the surface in your subconscious mind, and connect with your innate creativity and spirituality.

The Pisces Moon can inform you of your belonging, your infinity and eternity, your connection to all things everywhere throughout all space and time. Here you are reminded that we are all one and that approaching others—and yourself—with compassion, empathy, and sensitivity can help to make the world a better place.

This is a perfect Moon for soaking in hot springs, hot tubs, or a hot bath, adding Epsom salts and essential oils and herbs to support your heart and your deepest emotions.

Learning Zodiacal Symbols

If you haven't yet had the opportunity to learn the glyphs for the astrological signs and commit them to memory, now is the time to begin this study.

Pick up some 3 × 5–inch index cards and draw an old-fashioned set of flash cards. Play with them every day until you can recognize each glyph on sight. It can be helpful to carry them with you and look at them several times a day.

Your Natal Moon Phase

In addition to your natal Moon sign, your birthmoon is also created by your natal Moon phase. Your natal Moon phase is exactly what it sounds like: the phase that the Moon was in at the time of your birth.

This is the second and final component of your birthmoon, and this ingredient influences your temperament and how you interact with the world. Just as does each zodiacal sign, each lunar phase carries with it a different energetic signature. The phase of the Moon at the time of your birth exemplifies the tone or mood of your life and can offer insight into your innate personality.

Your natal lunar phase is another frequency you run in the background, and knowing this phase is additional information that can not only help you to actualize your full and complete Self and your highest mission but also to begin to truly discern your soul's purpose and journey in this lifetime.

Finding Your Natal Moon Phase

Discovering your natal Moon phase is ordinarily rather simple, as the Moon stays in most phases for several days. There are innumerable Moon phase calendars and calculators available online; once again it's best to have your birth time for this calculation, but it is not absolutely necessary.

If you type something like "natal Moon phase calculator" into a search engine, you will easily find a website where you can enter your birth information and quickly find yours.

What was the quality of light streaming down from the Moon at the moment of your birth? How much light was she—or wasn't she—beaming down onto your newborn human vessel?

What Does It Mean?

As Lunar Witches, we are always guided by her light and her dark, and our natal lunar phase not only supports us in creating the most momentous and expansive of magic, but it also helps us to understand our own personal baseline—our unique cosmic characteristics—revealing our depths and just how vast and strange and bizarre and galactic we truly are.

Here are some of the energies inherent in each phase as associated with our native lunar personalities:

- *New Moon:* The intrinsic energies of this phase are deliberate and unhurried with a strong intuitive sense.
- *Waxing Crescent Moon:* This phase brings a powerful desire to break free, to break through, to break chains both ancestral and of this lifetime.
- *Waxing Half Moon:* These are the energies of joyful building, of multitasking, of moving at a rapid pace.
- *Waxing Gibbous Moon:* The natural frequency here is one of curiosity, of seeking knowledge and understanding.
- *Full Moon:* Revelation and illumination are the energies most present in this natal phase.
- *Waning Gibbous Moon:* These energies are of quick-moving communication and the sharing of information.
- *Waning Half Moon:* This innate frequency is deliberate and dreamy, one of internal integration before moving outward again.
- *Waning Crescent Moon:* The vibrations of this phase center cleansing, clearing, endings, and closure.

Have you ever just been going about, minding your own business, and you have a sudden frisson or strange shiver come over you? This could be your monthly lunar phase return, when the Moon passes through the same phase it was in when you were born.

You return to your natal birth phase every single lunation—a monthly rebirth, an opportunity to ensure that you are living in alignment with your true Self.

This is your special moment of heightened inner wisdom, intuition, and sensitivity each lunation, and it's wise to mark this occurrence on your calendar every month so you are aware of what you are working with. You may experience more rawness or vulnerability during this time, more anxiety or overwhelm, or more creativity and inspiration. Try tracking your monthly lunar return to see how it manifests for you.

This monthly phasal return is also an invitation to break old patterns, to prioritize relevant healing, and to set better intentions for yourself for your personal "moonth" ahead. It can also be valuable to look at your natal chart in conjunction with the current transits to see what is occurring in your life, what flavors and energies are most prevalent—strong, helpful, or harmful.

If you haven't already done so, mark your everyday calendar with all of your upcoming monthly lunar phase returns. What do you notice about yourself each lunation when the Moon is in your birth phase? What is your energy level like? Your thoughts? Your feelings?

Your Birthmoon

Now you are aware of both your natal Moon sign and your natal Moon phase and how they combine to create your birthmoon. As an example, if you were born under the Waxing Gibbous Moon phase and that Moon was traveling through the constellation of Pisces at the moment of your birth, your birthmoon is the Waxing Gibbous Moon in Pisces.

Your internal realm was imprinted with this lunar information at the moment of your birthing, forming the bedrock of who you are—that unchangeable soul part of yourself that is always, always perfect and good—storing coded information, powers that can help you to better understand yourself, and powers that can be concentrated toward manifesting your desires.

Fathoming your personal pairing of astrological sign and phase assists in identifying your matchless gifts, composed of your inimitable vibrations, your singular talents, and your very individual personal cycles of growth, harvest, and dissolution.

Realization of who you are coupled with what the Moon is doing at any given moment, both astrologically and phasally, provides valuable knowledge. Depending upon the lunar transit you are experiencing (as well as the travels of other celestial bodies, of course), your personal energies can become amplified or diminished, more active or receptive. When you learn to dance with your own lunar rhythm, to master your own ebb and flow, you can appreciate when you are most productive, recognizing when it is best to take action and when to instead rest and replenish.

Your Lunar Birthday

Your lunar birthday is when Luna returns to the phase *and* sign she was in at the moment you entered this world. Note that this will rarely, if ever, happen in the same degree that the Moon was in on the day of your birth. Your lunar birthday is just as important as your solar birthday, and this is a beautiful day to celebrate *you*, to honor all you have accomplished over the past lunar year, and to do something special just for yourself.

To find your lunar birthday, simply look at your lunar calendar and turn to the pages nearest your calendar birthday. Look for the phase and sign of your birthmoon to discover when your lunar birthday falls in this particular calendar year. It may occur before or after your calendar birthday. Note how you feel when Luna returns to the sign and phase she was in when you were born. How will you celebrate yourself on this auspicious day?

Aligning Your Lunar Selves Ritual

This ritual practice can be done at any point of the lunar cycle.

To Gather

- Your Moon Journal and pen

The Process

Step 1: Note your personal birthmoon, composed of both your natal Moon phase and natal Moon sign. Familiarize yourself with the glyph that represents your sign.

Step 2: Ground, center, and open up a connection to your birthmoon. See-sense-feel this Moon and visualize the glyph that represents your Moon sign superimposed upon Luna.

Step 3: Think about your natal Moon sign. How does this energy make you feel? Is there a color or a scent or other sensory information you associate with it? Where do you perceive it in your body? How does it help you to better understand yourself? Breathe with your Moon sign and the cosmic energy it carries.

Step 4: Next, see-sense-feel Luna in your natal Moon phase. How does this energy make you feel? Is there a color or a scent or other sensory information you associate with it? Where do you perceive it in your body? How does it help you to better understand yourself? Breathe with your Moon phase and the cosmic energy it carries.

Step 5: Now see-sense-feel the vibrations of your lunar birthday, both sign and phase. Allow any wisdom or sensations that are there for you to crystalize into full consciousness. Stay here with the energetic imprint of your birthmoon for as long as you wish.

Step 6: When you are ready, say thank you to the Moon, take another deep breath, and return to regular awareness. Immediately write down your experiences in your Moon Journal.

Your Lunar Nature

Throughout each year, there are days that best harmonize with your distinctive lunar nature, helping you to both understand who you are as well as create a more fluid life filled with increasingly powerful magic.

As noted, the Moon's monthly passage through your natal Moon sign or natal Moon phase is infused with energies that will combine well to support your intentions. Your lunar birthday holds the greatest possibility for connecting with your Lunar Self and for performing magic and ritual toward your own goals and desires.

In addition to these uniquely personal optimal moments, there are also lesser occasions that present significant opportunities for magical and mundane workings. These include times when the Moon passes through certain Elements of Life or astrological modalities, and her interaction with the invisible push-pull that holds our Multiverse together.

You will discover that some of these occurrences are far more aligned than others. As a Lunar Witch, you will learn to identify these moments, to anticipate when they are coming, and to collaborate with them when they arrive to make the best use of the power available to you then.

The Elements of Life

Each astrological sign the Moon passes through also contains the energies of one of the Elements of Life—air, fire, water, or earth. At the most primary level, these elements animate us and all that lives: Air is our breath, fire is our Spirit, water is our blood, and earth is our body. As such, we already have an innate knowledge of how to dance and dream with them.

These elements contain the building blocks of all life and all magic and, like us, are interconnected. For example, fire needs earth and air to burn, and air is present within fire and water. The atmosphere of Earth is filled with air, her body is cloaked with water, and within her molten core we find fire.

Further, we can assign the energies of air to our intellect, the energies of fire to our ability to transform and create, the energies of water to our emotions and our feelings, and the energies of earth to our physical bodies, realms, and all that is of the Earth herself (i.e., all of the material world, which also includes the resources that support life).

We can use these elemental powers to further calibrate the timing and targets of our magic and of our everyday lives.

The astrological signs of air are Gemini, Libra, and Aquarius. During these moments, invoke the Moon with honeyed words, smoldering herbs, and an open mind.

The astrological signs of fire are Aries, Leo, and Sagittarius. When the Moon is in a fire sign, invoke her with bold actions, burning flames, and an expansive spirit.

The astrological signs of water are Cancer, Scorpio, and Pisces. When Luna floats through the water signs, invoke her with depth of sentiment, holy waters, and a pure heart.

The astrological signs of earth are Taurus, Virgo, and Capricorn. During these transits, invoke Luna with elegant movement, green witchery, and grounded service.

Astrological Modalities

Held within the four elemental designations of the astrological signs (sometimes named quadruplicities), we also find three more categories: cardinal, fixed, and mutable.

Each of these categories gives us more information about how a particular zodiacal sign behaves. In addition to understanding the Element of Life with which each sign collaborates, decoding how it functions can help us to power our spellwork and our rituals in richly fulfilling ways.

Cardinal

The cardinal signs usher in the beginning of each season on the zodiacal wheel and are also the first sign for their particular Element of Life. The four cardinal signs are Aries, Cancer, Libra, and Capricorn, and they are said to contain the primal power—the seed magic—for each of their respective elements.

Qualities and themes of cardinal signs include creation, innovation, leadership, initiation, imagination, enterprising, and pioneering.

These signs hold the vision of the greater picture and perspective; they are future focused and goal oriented. They move quickly, often leaping first and then building the bridge upon which to land after. They are the trailblazers, always pushing the limits of what is possible. They like to ask themselves—and others!—"What if?" and then try out their hypothesis.

Fixed

Fixed signs follow the cardinal signs, and they mark the midpoint of a given season. These signs—Taurus, Leo, Scorpio, and Aquarius—are said to solidify the energies of the cardinal signs, further ushering them into form, shape, and matter.

Qualities and themes of fixed signs include dedication, endurance, consistency, stability, preservation, consolidation, authority, tradition, and expertise.

These signs are often seen holding down the fort, making sure all is done in order and in the proper forms, that everything is up to code. These signs are grounded in the past and look to it to inform the present. They enjoy taking lessons from history, tradition, and the systems that have already been created and are in place, especially when they are working well.

Mutable

Mutable signs punctuate each season; they hold the energies of the transition between the conclusion of one season and the new beginning that will come again with a different cardinal sign. The mutable signs are Gemini, Virgo, Sagittarius, and Pisces.

Qualities and themes of mutable signs include adaptability, transformation, creativity, flexibility, and adroitness. They are the ambassadors, the diplomats, and the messengers.

These signs introduce a time of completion, employing the traits that help us to most gracefully transition as we move from one season into the next. They are intimately concerned with the present moment and work to facilitate the type of change that is easiest for the collective.

Projective or Receptive?

Finally, based upon the Element of Life each zodiacal sign falls within, it also carries the magical quality of either projective (sometimes named active) or receptive. In the past, this was once designated by gender with projective called masculine and receptive called feminine, but by far I prefer a non-gendered approach to this, as all beings contain the potential to express all energies, always.

These two types of energy are two sides of the same coin—the two forces necessary to create and sustain life. Without them, the Multiverse—and therefore our Earthrealm—would not exist. These powers exert a "push-pull," waltzing perpetually with one another, catalyzing harmony and balance together.

Projective energy is one of initiating. It includes the powers of push, heat, daytime, physicality, electricity, and the Sun. All of the zodiacal signs ruled by air (Gemini, Libra, and Aquarius) or ruled by fire (Aries, Leo, and Sagittarius) are projective.

Receptive energy is one of waiting to respond. It includes the powers of pull, cold, nighttime, spirituality, magnetism, and the Moon. All of the zodiacal signs ruled by water (Cancer, Scorpio, and Pisces) or ruled by earth (Taurus, Virgo, and Capricorn) are receptive.

Putting It All Together

Now that you have calculated your birthmoon and explored your lunar nature, go through your calendar and mark all of the occasions where the Moon will encounter similar conditions to the ones that existed at the time of your birth. You may want to use different color pens: one color for your lunar birthday, one for your monthly lunar phase return, one for your monthly lunar sign return, one for when she passes through your lunar birth element, and one for when she travels through your lunar birth modality.

Begin to pay particular attention to the times when the Moon traverses your natal Moon sign, Moon phase, Element of Life, and modality. Additionally, look for when the Moon travels through your natal Moon sign during a Full or New Moon and notice what arises for you then.

This activity isn't something to be done once and then set aside. Working continuously with your own personal astrological flavors can help you to reflect and refine upon what you know and what you don't know, leading to increased personal growth and emotional regulation, reminding you of your eternal connection with That Which Is Greater.

As you continue your own empirical research regarding the various powers of the ever-transforming Moon—how her vibrations of phase, sign, modality, and energetics interact with your own innate lunar nature—and as you develop your unique understanding that is based in your *own* body, mind, heart, and spirit, add to this simple chart, a beginning guidepost upon your journey of tuning into the Moon.

Review the energies of the phase and sign of the Moon on any given day, the Element of Life she is passing through, and then get finer and more descriptive as you consider, too, the astrological modality in play as well as the energy of push or pull that is assigned to each zodiac sign.

The following quick reference lists can then be used to plan and calibrate your timing for lunar magic and ritual as well as your day-to-day life.

The Moon in the element of...

- *Air feels:* fleeting, flighty, joyful, optimistic, buoyant, open, free, expansive, truthful, communicative, visionary, and insightful.
- *Fire feels:* rapid, quick, passionate, powerful, sweeping, external, illuminating, intense, transformational, confident, urgent, and vital.

- *Water feels:* internal, emotional, flowing, psychic, intuitive, authentic, perceptive, discerning, and sensitive.
- *Earth feels:* grounded, physical, wise, slow-moving, patient, enduring, foundational, committed, fertile, and embodied.

The Moon in the sign of…

- *Aries feels:* passionate, swift, and sparking.
- *Taurus feels:* grounded, solid, and luxurious.
- *Gemini feels:* curious, playful, and chatty.
- *Cancer feels:* nurturing, intuitive, and protective.
- *Leo feels:* sovereign, exuberant, and generous.
- *Virgo feels:* structured, centered, and analytical.
- *Libra feels:* collaborative, balanced, and egalitarian.
- *Scorpio feels:* deep, intense, and concentrated.
- *Sagittarius feels:* optimistic, adventurous, and rapid.
- *Capricorn feels:* steady, dedicated, and disciplined.
- *Aquarius feels:* inspiring, visionary, and expansive.
- *Pisces feels:* emotional, creative, and spiritual.

The energies of the Moon in the phase of…

- *New feel:* emergent, adventurous, visionary, spontaneous, and impulsive.
- *Waxing Crescent feel:* curious, hopeful, creative, connected, and instinctive.
- *Waxing Half feel:* tenacious, decisive, energized, focused, and dynamic.
- *Waxing Gibbous feel:* optimistic, vocal, active, passionate, and unorthodox.
- *Full feel:* euphoric, dramatic, ecstatic, clear, and aware.
- *Waning Gibbous feel:* crystallized, grateful, innovative, truthseeking, and teaching.
- *Waning Half feel:* integrating, spiritual, empathic, intuitive, and transformational.
- *Waning Crescent feel:* quiet, restful, dreamy, otherworldly, and introspective.

Allow the ever-changing energies and light of the Moon to become a rejuvenating beacon for your life, making space for your inherent lunar nature to anchor you more firmly into who you truly are at your very core, at your very center.

Chapter 4
The Shadow Side

The Moon Goddess Speaks

It is the Dark of the Moon, and from the Underworld, I arrive upon your doorstep to unlock the gate to That Which Is Hidden, that which you have hidden from others and from yourself.

Search your soul to unearth that which you must release, dissolve, or own. Be fearless now, knowing that I am guarding you, watching over you as you dig down into your own unconscious.

What boundaries must you set or shore up? What transitions or transformations must be made? You are an integral part of the infinite cycle of birth, death, and rebirth. Participate in it fully by making the changes that need to be made now. Wait no longer, for it is surely time for you to make the unconscious conscious, to bring forth and integrate all parts of yourself.

Here, in this place of murky, moonlit liminality, I will guide you with my blazing torch, and if you are brave enough to trust in my wisdom, you will emerge reborn by my hands and by my heart.

I am Hekate.

Journal Inquiries for This Gateway

What part or parts of myself do I hide from others? What am I denying or avoiding? What is one thing I can do today in support of building my self-love?

Affirmations for This Gateway

It is safe to transform. I accept my innate wholeness—my dark and my light. I honor all parts of myself.

As you walk the Path of Lunar Witchcraft, you will learn that the Shadow is a necessary piece of your magic and your medicine. The Moon is not only bright and full; she also diminishes and becomes dark, hiding away for several days each lunation.

When you accept her changing nature as a mirror of your own, you increase your understanding of the reality of this Earth realm: not everything is "white light." In fact, if it were, nothing would ever gestate and then be born. Darkness is where we all come from: the depths of the sea, the concealment of the womb, the reaches of the Cosmos, that mighty cauldron of birth and death and rebirth.

We, and all living creatures, grow in the dark from one single cell into many until it is time for us to enter the light that marks this particular lifetime. But we don't merely move from dark into light. We move from dark into light and into a ceaseless cycle of metamorphosis, one of conception, growth, peaking, and then diminishing—just as does the Moon's power and light during each and every lunation of our lives and hers.

Understanding this, accepting this, and yielding to this makes you a more dynamic Lunar Witch. It is important to acknowledge your Shadow, to learn to love and to accept it, and also to love and accept the Shadow times of the Moon and the Shadow that is inherent within each lunar transit.

Knowing who you are—fully and completely knowing your whole, true Self, your sacred, unique essence—means that you own and actualize your full story and your full Self. And this can be exceptionally empowering.

You are whole and holy throughout the entirety of your existence, just like the Moon. Even when we can't see her wholeness, she is still whole. As are you!

What Is the Shadow?

The Shadow—sometimes styled as the Hidden Self—is composed of those parts of us that we have concealed from view, sometimes even from ourselves. These are the little pieces we've tucked away over our time walking through life: those thoughts and feelings, actions and reactions, and little idiosyncrasies that we don't like, don't want, or don't feel are socially acceptable to display.

The Shadow is an aggregate of all the parts of ourselves we were told to hide, all those thoughts and behaviors we repress and suppress. This includes those things we were chastised for as children by parents, teachers, and other authority figures (e.g., "Boys don't cry!" "Don't rock the boat!" "Turn that frown upside down!"). The Shadow is also composed of emotions and traits commonly viewed as "unacceptable" by the culture or society we live (or lived!) in, and feelings that are uncomfortable or perceived as "wrong" (e.g., envy, anger, and grief). We may also tuck away our talents, gifts, and powers.

Over time, we learned to disguise all these things. The process of suppressing that which felt impermissible or unsafe to share became automated and then unconscious. Once buried away, all these components gathered together in our unconscious and created the Shadow Self, the repository of all the stories we have told ourselves—and the stories others have told us about ourselves—throughout our entire lives.

This Hidden Self is often tremendously unhappy because they have been camouflaged, stuffed down, forgotten, and isolated. And yet our Shadow is still very active in our lives, influencing and guiding our behaviors, thoughts, and actions without our conscious knowledge or consent. This often doesn't go well for us!

The Shadow Self is not "bad" or "negative," though. They are just misunderstood. These buried parts often contain profound wisdom, information, and knowledge, which, when properly integrated and directed, can help you to live your best life, a life of wholeness and full actualization of the person you *know* you are at your very center.

When you notice that things are not flowing well for you, this is a sign to stop and check in with your Hidden Self. When you experience big, forceful, extreme reactions to certain experiences, situations, or people, it is possible that your Shadow is at work—because these fierce reactions are usually a signal that what you are disliking outside of yourself is truthfully a reflection mirroring that which is going on within. (As Without, so Within!)

The stronger your reaction, the greater the need to sift and sort what is happening within, as this is where the healing begins.

Becoming aware of the shadowy phases of the Moon—as well as the shadow side of each astrological flavor—can be of formidable help on the Path of Lunar Witchcraft. Once you start observing your Shadow, opportunities for integration, mending, and even delight begin to emerge.

Shadow Connection Meditation

Here is a meditation to bring your Shadow Self out into view and to activate the wisdom they hold. Please read through all of the steps before beginning; perhaps you might record the meditation on your phone and play it back later or even ask a friend to read it for you. Create a cozy and quiet space for yourself in which you are free to completely relax.

The Dark of the Moon, when Luna is experiencing her own shadow, is an exemplary time to work with this practice.

To Prepare

– A quiet place where you will be left undisturbed

The Meditation

Breathe yourself into the holy moment of now, connecting with Earth below and Moon above.

Breathe lovingly into your heart center. When your heart is full, use your breath to reach out from this place of love and connect with your Shadow Self, filling this hidden part of yourself with loving sensations, too. Fill your Shadow Self with love from your heart.

Using breath and intention, invite your Shadow Self to connect with the Moon, with her energies of light and dark, of growth and dissolution. Allow your Shadow Self to receive these calming lunar energies.

Next, open your heart to the Moon, breathing her energies into your heart center.

When your heart is full of lunar energies, solidify this circuit of support, beauty, compassion, love, and transformation through breathing from your heart to Shadow, to Moon, to heart, and so on.

Within this circuit, consider that your Shadow has gathered certain experiences, information, and wisdoms to bring you to this place, to this singular, irreplaceable moment. Reflect on the fact that every single thing you have walked through is a necessary ingredient that resulted in who you are now, an exquisite, unique luminous being with so much to contribute to the world.

Affirm that you are whole and holy, exactly as you are in this and every moment. Blessed be!

The Lunar Nodes

As mentioned in the last chapter, there are two Nodes of the Moon: North (also called the True Node or the Ascending Node) and South (or the Descending Node). These are the two points where the orbit of the Moon crosses the ecliptic (the Sun's yearly travels across the sky as we perceive them from Earth), which is the geometric plane of the Earth orbiting around the Sun.

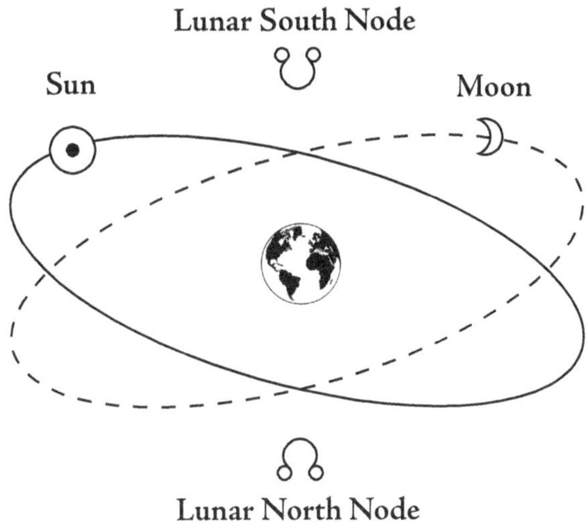

The Lunar Nodes

From a scientific, astronomical perspective, the Lunar Nodes are used to calculate when an eclipse will occur.

From a humanistic, evolutionary, astrological perspective, your natal Lunar Nodes can be used as clues to help you interpret where you came from and where you are headed. As the Nodes traverse the signs of the zodiac, they act as cosmic changemakers, ready to shake things up whenever you need to awaken once again or step into a new level of self-understanding.

Astrologer Sara Pastorius writes in the 2024 edition of the *We'Moon* annual datebook:

> Solar and Lunar Eclipses occur when the Earth, Sun and Moon align at the Moon's nodal axis, usually four times a year, during New and Full Moons, respectively. The South (past) and North (future) Nodes symbolize our evolutionary path. Eclipses catalyze destiny's calling. Use eclipse degrees in your birth chart to identify potential release points.[30]

The North and South Nodes of the Moon are always situated in opposing signs, located across from one another on the wheel of an astrological chart. The North Node is sometimes named the head of the dragon, with the South Node making up its tail.

30. "Solar and Lunar Eclipses That Are Coming up, and How They Influence Us."

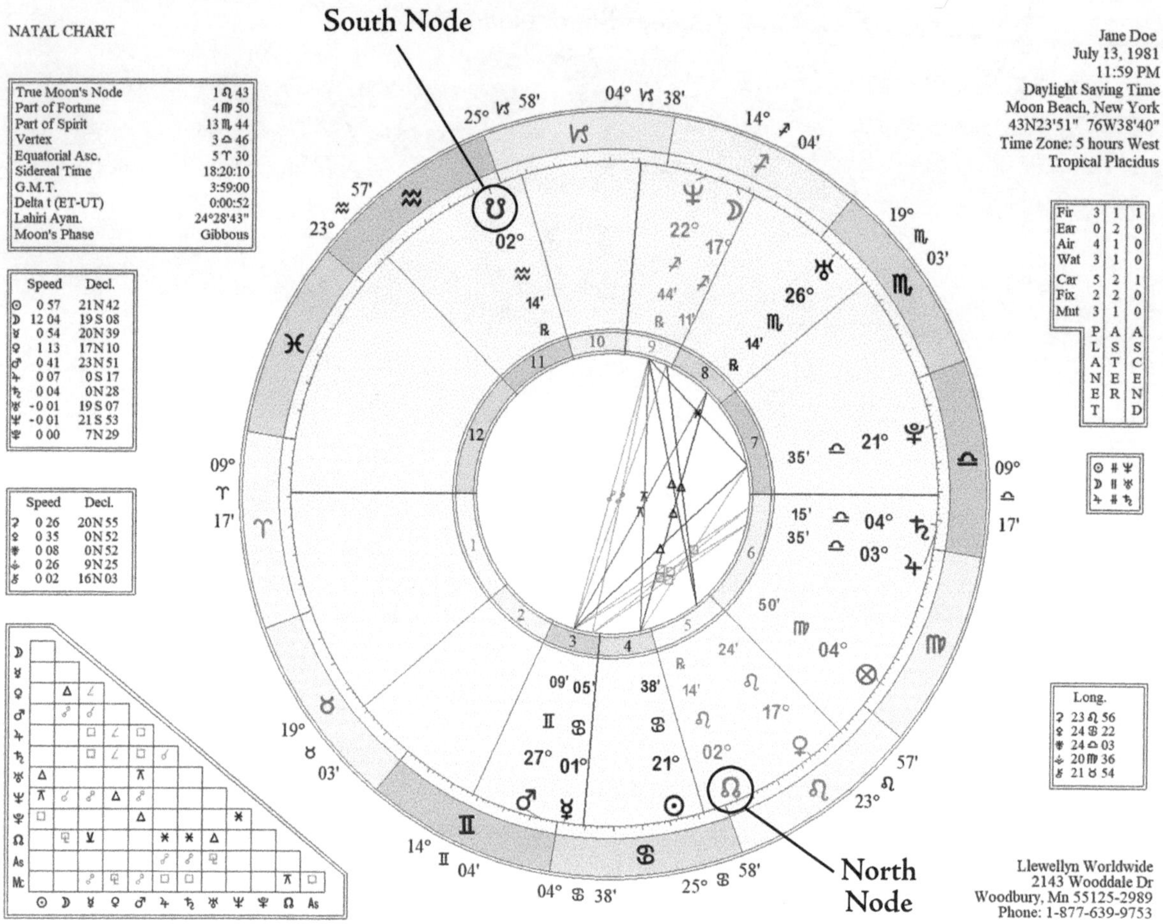

The Lunar Nodes in the Natal Chart

Your natal Lunar Nodes are clues that point to your soul's mission, with the South Node representing your past life (or lives) and the North Node representing your growth trajectory and mission for this particular incarnation, reminding you of your purpose and providing a map regarding the direction you are meant to go.

While your natal South Node is a comfort place, its opposite, your North Node, represents the unknown. It may, at times, feel a bit frightening, yet this Node holds the key to your core, which is eternal.

The Nodes of the Moon can function as our Sacred Guides, encouraging us to slow down and discover that which we've hidden from ourselves. Our Lunar Nodes are strong and gracious healers and mentors, creating a container and holding space for us to plumb our own depths, to merge our own personal Shadow with our Light, leading us into self-acceptance, self-compassion, self-love, and a greater sense of our own inherent wholeness.

The first step on the path of Shadow Self integration and healing is one of awareness, after which comes acceptance, and then, finally, welcome. When we use all of the tools available to us to develop an awareness of who we once were (South Node), who we are now (birthmoon), and the Self we are moving toward (North Node), we can create a space of safety and belonging for each and every part of ourselves.

There are many wonderful books and programs that can help you dive deeper into shadow work should you desire to do so. I especially appreciate the work of Debbie Ford (see "Recommended Reading" for a book suggestion).

Your Lunar Nodes

Look at your natal chart and answer the question: In which signs are your natal North and South Nodes?

Meditate upon the energies of your natal Lunar Nodes and then write in your Moon Journal about what possible messages they may hold for you. How do their astrological signatures resonate with what you know about yourself and your life's purpose at this moment in time?

The Shadow of the Signs

Our Shadow Selves invite us to retreat and reflect, to dream and incubate, and sometimes, to unravel and unwind that which has been woven. Each sign of the zodiac offers us a different perspective about what might need healing or attention, granting us new opportunities for self-knowledge and transformation.

The Shadow Side of the Moon in Aries

The shadow side of an Aries transit includes moving too fast—not dotting *i*'s, crossing *t*'s, or looking ahead to see what the possible results of words or actions could be—impatience, and a short fuse. This Moon runs into trouble with completion, although as the first sign of the zodiac, it is unequivocally the most skilled at beginnings and setting events into motion.

The Aries Moon sometimes sparks us to burn everything down so that we can start fresh. This burning everything down commonly includes relationships, much to my chagrin. Be mindful of when the Moon passes through this sign and consider if a fit of temper will actually be of service once the Moon moves on. The big problem with going "scorched earth" is that inevitably all we are left with are ashes.

Sometimes the impulsive, unthinking actions undertaken during the Moon in Aries cause tremendous harm. Words said in the flames of a moment cannot be unsaid, and sometimes our relationships suffer irreparably as a result. The competitive energies inspired by this Moon can also cause problems.

Due to a powerful drive, a fierce intensity, and the roller coaster of highs and lows, the Aries Moon can be aggressive, overambitious, and rushed, causing burnout and making us feel wrung out, spent, exhausted, and completely over everything.

Ways to Temper, Mitigate, or Shift This Shadow

When there is an overload of Aries Moon energy, you can temper this intensity and impulsivity through slowing your roll. Play hooky from work, rest, go on a long, leisurely hike, walk on the beach, or enjoy a meal that lasts for hours with no end in sight.

Put out that fire by playing in and around the water: Relax in a sacred bath, spend a whole day at the beach, or float down the river on a silly raft (I like a giant pink flamingo!).

Cultivating calmness through meditation and playing with creativity simply for its own sake (without trying to "produce" anything in particular) are also healthy outlets for moderating these sometimes wild and unpredictable energies. Breathwork to manage anxiety and stress can also be very helpful.

Affirmation: "Collaboration, not competition."

The Shadow Side of the Moon in Taurus

The shadow side of a Taurus transit includes heavy energies of stubbornness, grudge-holding, and an unhealthy territorial drive. The Taurus Moon, even though it is rich and fecund, will sometimes become overly worried about theft and will hoard resources—physical, yes, but also such things as knowledge and wisdom—refusing to share with others. This Moon can also provoke performative behaviors, with activities undertaken not out of joy or conscious choice but instead as a display: to be *seen* doing them.

When the Moon is traveling through this constellation, there can be a general undercurrent of stuckness or a fear of making any changes, a desire for softness beyond all else, an avoidance of overtly addressing anything that could potentially cause waves, and a choice to embrace what is already familiar above openness to new possibilities.

During a Taurus Moon transit, it is quite easy to check out of the Inner Self. Be very careful about repressing emotions or people-pleasing; instead remain connected to what is actually happening within.

A pull toward overindulgence as an escape mechanism—in food, drink, cannabis, drugs, social media, television, sex—may also be prevalent during this time, as well as compulsive buying sprees, often of unnecessary physical items that one can ill afford.

Ways to Temper, Mitigate, or Shift This Shadow

If the shadowy energies you are experiencing at this time are based in those things that are trapped and unmoving, relief develops through cultivating adaptability and flexibility through movement.

In the physical realm, yoga is advised as is ecstatic dance and even running. Physical activities that bring you completely into your own body and a willingness to experience all of the sensations and emotions that are happening for you within your own container can help get things moving again. Listening to what your body wants and then doing that can bring you back into balance.

In the mental realm, guided meditations and "brain dump" style journaling can be of assistance. And if what is needed is more connection with That Which Is Greater, perhaps adding a little something that is beautiful or even opulent to an altar or other sacrosanct place can inspire and shift the vibrations all around you.

Affirmation: "My inner resources are always available, accessible, and abundant."

The Shadow Side of the Moon in Gemini

The shadow side of the Gemini Moon is flakiness, flightiness, and a lack of grounding. During a Gemini Moon, we might find ourselves swirling around like a feather on the wind, flitting here and there, alighting and then flying off again without stopping or completely landing anywhere.

Too much movement, too many thoughts, and a resulting impression of haziness can come alongside this lunar transition. This can lead us into overcommitment and overextension, and the resulting overstimulation can leave us stressed, frazzled, nervous, restless, and even entirely disconnected.

Gossip and triangulation in community also seem to heighten while the Moon passes through Gemini. Once you accept that this is something that frequently happens throughout this transit, you can pledge to yourself that as a Lunar Witch you will not participate! When gossip knocks at your door, you can make the choice that it ends with you. And if you are truly curious about what you hear, you can go directly to the person(s) it concerns and ask them for the truth of the matter.

Ways to Temper, Mitigate, or Shift This Shadow

You can shake up and release yourself from the shadowy energetics of the Gemini Moon by spending time processing what is happening for you, either through slow conversations with a counselor or your beloveds or by bringing it to the page through uncensored writing or list-making.

Take care not to intellectualize this, though—the road through here is to get out of your head and into your heart, to feel your emotions instead of trying to categorize, analyze, or pathologize them. Processing can assist you in letting go of those energies that are unhelpful.

Resting deliberately in sacred silence—or if that is too big of a reach, listening to peaceful music (instrumental, try binaural beats)—and observing the thoughts that arise, blessing them, and then visualizing them floating away in a bubble can be valuable, too.

Affirmation: "I allow my thoughts to rest so my heart can be heard."

The Shadow Side of the Moon in Cancer

The shadow side of a Cancerian Moon is a magnificent moodiness, grouchiness, grumpiness, and inability to rise up out of the mud, or the bed. The Cancerian Moon has recorded and remembers the hurts of the past—often every single one of them, and in rich detail—and sometimes has difficulty surmounting these affronts.

The Moon in Cancer can feel strong, emotional, and quite overwhelming at times. Intuition is heightened like the waves of a King Tide crashing upon the rocky shore. These powers can smack us across the face, knock us off balance, and leave us gasping as though we are drowning and will never surface to breathe air again.

When Luna travels this constellation—her home base—we can become so involved with our own inner realms, our own emotions, that we forget to look up and out to see the beauty that surrounds us. Both beauty and horror coexist upon this human stage—they always have, and I believe they always will; it is entirely our choice where to place our focus.

Just as when the Moon passes through any water sign, a Cancerian transit can find us overcome with emotions, including those that do not belong to us personally. "Crying for the world" is something that may happen when the Moon traverses this most sensitive of signs.

Ways to Temper, Mitigate, or Shift This Shadow

To shift these energies, get outside your house or workplace, even if it is only for ten minutes. Take a walk in your current environment, and as you do so, notice as many things as possible. Feel the ground beneath the soles of your feet and truly take in and *see* what is growing on the Earth Mother. Notice any animals, wild or domestic. Look at every person you pass. Become super present with what is out there during each of these unrepeatable moments.

If you are inundated or hyperstimulated by social obligations, cancel or reschedule whatever you can and establish space for uninterrupted, quiet solitary time: Go within like a crab into their shell. Sip a restorative cup of tea or have a glass of your favorite wine. Read a book. Paint. Write. Draw.

Collage. Indulge in a leisurely bath. Whatever your inner introvert needs to recover themselves, give it to them. Refill your personal well instead of bulldozing yourself into a breakdown.

When hypersensitivity arrives with this transit, it brings a heavy burden. If you find yourself so overcome that you are unable to take action of any kind, you may need to simply pull those cozy covers up over your head and wait it out!

Affirmation: "Nurturing myself is self-love."

The Shadow Side of the Moon in Leo

The shadow side of the Moon transiting through Leo includes too-rapid movement, especially when it touches matters that surround the ego and the need to be seen and appreciated. We can act in ways that aren't aligned with our inner, true selves (think temper tantrums) to salve our pride, perhaps saying or doing things (loudly!) that we may later grow to regret.

As with other fire signs, we may feel too speedy, oblivious of what we are doing in the present moment because our heads have already moved on to the next task or big idea. The danger of the Leo lunar passage is a lack of full presence, one that can cause us to leave things incomplete without even realizing it because we've mindlessly pushed ourselves forward.

The Leo Moon can find us living in the future, disembodied and ungrounded. Additionally, we may often be motivated to overdo it, sometimes leading to extreme anxiety and even panic attacks and burnout. There can be a frantic vibe that arises during this transit, a notion that we are being driven—instead of being the driver—compelled, and compulsed into moving ever forward before observing where we have come from and integrating the lessons already learned.

Ways to Temper, Mitigate, or Shift This Shadow

Play (not competition!) is an excellent way to mitigate the blazing nature of the Moon traveling through Leo. Play helps us to move away from ego, channeling those fiery energies away from personal conceit and grandiosity and into that childlike state of exuberance, enthusiasm, and pure delight. Creative endeavors of all kinds can help shift the energies here, too.

What do you love to do most? What brings you the greatest of joy? Do that!

Under a Leo Moon, grounding and centering practices plus heart-healing guided meditations are useful endeavors to relax and come home into deep union with the Self. After connecting with Self, you can then connect with others, gifting yourself a felt sense of beauty and belonging with All That Is. I genuinely love practicing a loving-kindness meditation similar to that found in Buddhist traditions during this transit.

Affirmation: "Love easily flows into me, and I generously share it with the world."

The Shadow Side of the Moon in Virgo

The Moon treading through this sign can catch us up in perfectionism, micromanaging others, and an excessive need to control every situation. So focused upon every tiny detail surrounding what we think is "wrong" and the "right" way to do things, we may forget about ourselves—our feelings, our thoughts, our needs. While in service to others, we may try to fix things even if they haven't asked us to or don't want us to.

This transit can bring about exhaustion as we try to shapeshift into whatever we think is needed, repairing things that don't need to be repaired, hovering over others and henpecking them because we think we know more about their lives than they do.

The Moon in Virgo can bury us into our own perfectionistic high standards, pushing us to compulsively martyr ourselves without letting others experience or express their own sovereignty.

Ways to Temper, Mitigate, or Shift This Shadow

Taking a day off from life is a constructive tactic to mitigate these exacting energies. Everything is not life or death!

Allow someone else to decide: Let your housemate or child pack the dishwasher and don't go back in to rearrange it. Let your partner cook dinner or clean the house. Let your friends and family do things how they do them without helicoptering, making "helpful" comments, or redoing the task afterward.

And while you are allowing others the space to do things their way, do your own thing. What hobbies or crafts or projects are your favorite? Do those and focus completely on yourself while doing so. Observe your breath as it goes in and out of your body. Watch your hands move. Notice your feet on the Earth or your bottom on the chair. Be present in the moment.

Affirmation: "I find peace in the present moment."

The Shadow Side of the Moon in Libra

A lunar transit in Libra can lead us into a place where we overanalyze to the point of paralysis, where we can see all of the timelines that could possibly extend from any choice we make. This causes an inability to make any choice at all and an inability to trust our innate authority or intuition. A strong Libra transit can bring about an endless loop of helpless self-doubt where we end up stuck and unmoving.

Exacerbating these indecisive energies, we may also need to confront a compulsive draw toward people-pleasing, over-giving, and entering into unhealthy enmeshed and codependent dynamics with those who are closest to us. We can become agreeable to the point of dishonesty.

When the Moon is in Libra, we may define ourselves through others, not only taking on their preferences and their dislikes but treating them as extensions of who we are, projecting our own flaws and shortcomings upon them instead of taking ownership of ourselves.

Ways to Temper, Mitigate, or Shift This Shadow

If you find yourself mired in indecision during this transit because there are so many options, the best technique to move out of this current is to make a small decision that most likely won't have much, if any, of a lasting repercussion and follow through with it swiftly.

Any trivial, quick decision centering *yourself* and *your* wishes can help to reopen flow and ease here: Be the one who decides which restaurant the group should go to. Choose the first thing you like that you see on the menu. Make a spontaneous choice of what you want to do with your day.

Try making just one snappy, instinctive choice, then enact it without second-guessing yourself.

Affirmation: "I know what is best for me."

The Shadow Side of the Moon in Scorpio

When Luna is swimming through Scorpio, the energies can seem relentless, complex, and at times oppressive, as if we are being pulled under the surface and have been sucked unwillingly through the looking glass.

We may struggle with emotional congestion, cut off from our personal passions, secreting away our true thoughts and feelings and withdrawing completely from connection with others. We can become envious and jealous, competitive and possessive, perhaps even acting out in shifty, vindictive, dark ways because it feels like no one around us can be trusted.

All of our insecurities may arise at once from the very depths of our beings, activating our reptilian Primal Selves, making us believe we could drown in everything that is "wrong" with us, and convincing us to isolate even further. Self-sabotage can become a theme.

Ways to Temper, Mitigate, or Shift This Shadow

The antidote to an uncomfortable Scorpio Moon transit is truth-speaking. What feelings have you been concealing in your relationships with your closest people?

It may be scary, yet bringing these hidden energies to the surface and flushing them out of your body and your interactions with others will be transformational and, more often than not, profoundly healing. After all, everyone has probably been sensing the vibes anyway!

If you are feeling brave, delving into Shadow work is historically constructive at this time, revealing that which needs healing and helping you to integrate it in effectual ways. Seeking out a bodyworker, soaking in salty water, and/or playing with art supplies can also assist you in transmuting these intense and sometimes consuming energies.

Affirmation: "I am safely held within the depths of my emotions. This, too, shall pass."

The Shadow Side of the Moon in Sagittarius

This Moon invites us to adventure, but it also incites us to keep all of our options open at all times. Lacking commitment, we may miss out on those things we've longed for in the hopes that something better might come along. This highly opinionated vibration takes up a ton of space, which can also alienate us from those with whom we want to connect deeply.

As with all fire signs, we may hop from one thing to the next within a Sagittarian transit, neglecting to settle down to enable our roots to grow, therefore generating no future harvest. We can get caught up in our rugged, egotistical individualism, perhaps even thinking that we don't need anyone else in order to succeed.

When Luna is hanging out in Sagittarius, drama sometimes follows. Passionate, exuberant energies go sour when recklessness, thoughtlessness, and wild partying enters the equation. Preventable accidents can happen as we exhaust ourselves into complete collapse. We may find ourselves living outside of our hearts, out of touch with the beauty and sensitivity of who we truly are.

Ways to Temper, Mitigate, or Shift This Shadow

You can mitigate these shadowy Sagittarian lunar energies by coming home to yourself, by remembering that "wherever you go, there you are." Stop moving and allow yourself to catch up with *yourself*.

Earth is an invaluable remedy for the jagged experiences that this transit can sometimes bring. Go for a long, unhurried nature ramble. Walk on a beach and open to the invigorating ions of the waves. Repot a houseplant that is rootbound. Get those fingers in the holy dirt. Stop, breathe, observe.

Who are you in relationship to others? What reminds you that you belong, that you are already an important, integral part of a healthy, loving circle of like-minded people? Go there.

Affirmation: "I slow down and savor every moment of my life's journey."

The Shadow Side of the Moon in Capricorn

The Moon's journey through Capricorn can feel heavy, sluggish, slow, and even listless and lethargic. There's an "all work and no play" vibe in the air, with emotions buckled down and bound lest they get in the way of reaching that goal.

There is such a thing as too much dedication, too much discipline. When Luna passes through the sign of the goat, we may be quite rigid about our schedule, our methodologies, and that endless to-do list. The structures we created to control our lives are now in control of *us*, shrinking our domains and capping our creativity.

And all of this grasping tightness and resigned numbness further constricts our spirits, causing us to interact with life critically, pessimistically, and with cold detachment.

Ways to Temper, Mitigate, or Shift This Shadow

A different perspective is prescribed when you need to temper these overbearing, stolid, and passionless energies.

You can add a bit of sprightliness to a Cappy lunar transit by getting out and doing something atypical, something unexpected or exciting: Try out a new place for dinner, go dancing to live music of an unfamiliar genre, try running on a different trail, or gather some friends for a bonfire night on the beach. Get out of the office, get out of the house, step away from the computer, and have some fun already!

Affirmation: "I enthusiastically embrace joy; my playful spirit is a bright light for everyone I meet."

The Shadow Side of the Moon in Aquarius

The shadow side of an Aquarian Moon transit is a surplus of visions and an inability to usher any of them into manifestation. During this time, we can find ourselves lost as we try to wade through and organize all of our big ideas, epiphanies, and desires to create magnitudes of change.

When the Moon is flying through this constellation, we may find ourselves so seized with ideas that we have no idea how or where to start putting them into action. There are so many possibilities—like a "Choose Your Own Adventure" novel—that we just can't decide where to begin, and so we don't begin at all, staying lost in the gossamer clouds of potential.

Decision-making can sometimes be difficult, too. When there are so many wonderful and revolutionary options, how do we know we are choosing the right one? There are so many dreams to follow, so many puffy tails to chase, that narrowing things down and getting real and Earth realm about any of them can feel utterly impossible.

It's important to note that there can be a calculating, ruthless, emotionless vibe during this transit, too, a cold, clinical, and sometimes heartless view of reality that truly serves no one.

Ways to Temper, Mitigate, or Shift This Shadow

Stopping to check in with your body and your emotions is an informative way to mitigate overload. The simple act of connecting with your breath, with the Earth below and the Moon above, can provide a quick reset of your own energetic container, reminding you that you are part of the Oneness of all things that are, were, and ever shall be.

Talking about your big ideas with friends, colleagues, and mentors can also be supportive, even fun! Sometimes we really do need an outside perspective, especially when caught up in our own processes and patterns. Seek out interdependence and reminders that we are all in this together!

Affirmation: "My mind and heart lovingly embrace, and from this union, visionary beauty manifests."

The Shadow Side of the Moon in Pisces

When Luna swims through this sign, we can experience a tsunami of sentiments so strong that we are compelled to exorcise them in some way, to dull their sharpness. We may be unable to resist "acting out" emotionally, regressing into unhealthy patterns (primarily those that were formed in childhood as a result of trauma), or withdrawing, even dissociating.

If we have an existing propensity for them, and if we are not aware and prepared, addictive and compulsive behaviors are also likely to come into play now.

The Moon in Pisces can also have us forgetting our boundaries, forgetting that we have our own containers to care for, which, in turn, care for *us*. We can become lost to our own Selves, weakly floating without direction, motivation, or desire—lost in the trancelike depths of our emotional bodies.

Ways to Temper, Mitigate, or Shift This Shadow

Working with nervous system regulation exercises (see chapter 16) in conjunction with the Moon's travels through Pisces can be universally helpful, as is physical activity of all kinds.

Quiet, solitary, creative activities can also be satisfying, such as drawing, painting, and journaling. Try using an adult coloring book, a paint-by-numbers kit, or even a suncatcher set, where you add tiny plastic beads to each metal segment of a design and then bake it in the oven before hanging it up.

Pisces also adores all things spiritual, so try playing around with divination, dreamwork, journeying, scrying, and healing rituals to see what feels good.

Affirmation: "My dreams are a pathway to an embodied life."

The Shadow of the Signs

In this section, I shared some thoughts on the shadow side of each lunar transit. For each zodiacal sign, take these inquiries to your Moon Journal: What do you agree with? What do you disagree with? What would you add?

If you have worked with the shadowy aspects of the astrological transits before, have you found that there are ones more or less difficult for you? How does the shadow interact with your own natal Moon sign?

Legacy Work

I love how we can take what is classically considered the shadow side of the Moon passing through each of the signs of the zodiac and transform these transits into occasions to increase health—for ourselves, for others, and for the world in general. This is the Path of the Lunar Witch—one who makes beneficial shifts using awareness, mindfulness, and micromagic: a strategy of influencing the world through altering first ourselves, our own actions and reactions, creating change at the smallest possible level.

We don't have to be at the mercy of the swirling energies surrounding us. We can step up, grow up, and create containers for ourselves that are rich, healthy, and helpful.

We have both the authority and the responsibility to remedy our unhealthy ways of being, to break the chains from this lifetime or others. And may this all be done in the service of That Which Is Greater!

Chapter 5
Aligning with the Moon

The Moon Goddess Speaks

I am the Lady who bears the silver crescent, whole unto myself, fulfilled and joyful. If you dare, pluck up your courage and join me on an endless adventure of following the Moon through the starry skies, transforming alongside her, growing then fading, learning the secrets of her magic, mystery, and majesty.

These are moments of excitement and exhilaration, moments where everything can shift in the space between one breath and the next. These are the moments when you learn what you are made of.

Call upon me with a brave and pure heart, and I will take your hand, blessing all of your endeavors, granting you success and good fortune.

I am Diana.

Journal Inquiries for This Gateway

How can I deepen my trust in the guidance of the Moon? In which of Luna's phases do I feel most like myself? In what sign?

Affirmations for This Gateway

I transform with grace and ease. I trust in my relationship with the Moon. I am always in alignment with Luna's vibrations.

Aligning with the Moon can encompass and include all parts of our lives, from synchronizing our intentions, magic, and ritual with her phases and astrological passages to timing our everyday activities to proceed most effectively alongside her evolution, increasing the fluidity, ease, and efficiency of our daily routines.

To establish a solid connection and flow with Luna, it is paramount to internalize the nature of her cycling in such visceral ways that we instinctively know how to best combine our inner nature with her outer powers.

You already began this linking process when you started a daily practice of connecting with the Moon, integrated the energies contained within your birthmoon, and increased your self-awareness through acknowledging your Shadow Self.

The Path of Lunar Witchcraft is not one to visit once or twice a month—at Full and/or New Moons—but instead every single day. Lunar living is a consistent and constant path, an avenue of understanding and making sense of the cyclical nature of life, a wisdom that only proceeds from patient, unwavering commitment and care. This is a personal and spiritual discipline.

To become wise in the Craft is work; it is satisfying work, and yet it is work, nevertheless. Like any other healthy and enduring long-term relationship, your bond with the Moon will develop over a lengthy span of time, as you grow to truly appreciate one another. This is not something that happens instantly or overnight, and it cannot be rushed, purchased, or delegated to others.

The Path of the Moon Witch is different for each of us, although it is the same in that dedication, discipline, and devotion are all part of the journey and that the dedication, discipline, and devotion never end.

Here are some additional practical and magical approaches to cultivate the skill to follow and tap into the energies of the ever-changing lunar cycle, to attune yourself to the Moon with meaning and mindfulness.

Your Lunar Altar

Every person is Priest/ess/x of their own altar and the sovereign of their own realm. A lunar altar is an intentional place created in order to better sync ourselves and our surroundings with the Moon's rhythms, transforming our outer environments into vibrant reflections of our innermost selves, and our heartfelt desires for our lives.

Your lunar altar is a central focal point for your Moon work, serving as a microcosm of the greater world, of the Multiverse, and of your connection with Luna.

This altar should reflect your goals and desires for your personal relationship with the Moon. The level of complexity or simplicity is up to you, and your lunar altar should always be something you are happy to see, something that is pleasing to you and brings you joy.

For a permanent lunar altar, you might use the top of a dresser, a desk, a table, or even one shelf of a larger piece of furniture. Your lunar altar can face whichever direction is most comfortable to you or most aligned with your moonwork. My current lunar altar was once a rolling food prep island, and it is now situated at the entry point of my kitchen, where I can see and interact with it throughout my day.

If you are unable to have a permanent altar out in full view, try creating one in a box or tray that you can slip under your bed or into a drawer as necessary, pulling it out every morning and evening.

Your lunar altar can include anything that sings out to you as needful and sacred—it should be 100 percent meaningful to you and to you alone. For this altar, the only person you need to please is yourself. It is holy, belonging solely to you—it should not be shared with others. (You can certainly build shared altars with those whom you care about, but first, do have one place for your moonwork that is just yours.)

Use an altar cloth in a color that is resonant with the lunar energies: white, silver, or gray; even black, blue, or purple are sometimes appropriate. Include those items that correspond with the Moon's energies: silver platters and bowls; crystals such as selenite, moonstone, or clear quartz; images of the Moon; white or silver candles; clear vessels of water; your lunar scrying mirror or pendulum (see chapter 14)—whatever feels right.

Pay close attention to those things that naturally end up on your lunar altar—perhaps a shell from your trip to the sea, a forked stick found on a hike through the woods, a candle from your birthday cake, a round white stone acquired on a beach, a sprig of rosemary from your kitchen garden. The items that land on our altars reflect back to us our personal stories—where we have been, where we are at now, and even where we hope to be someday.

Update or reset your lunar altar whenever it feels right to do so. Some people keep to a strict schedule, cleaning and updating their altar at every New, Full, and/or Dark Moon, while some do so at every High Holyday, and some more, some less. This is a highly individual and intuitive process. Trust in your Moon Witch Within and you will know when it is time to cleanse, tidy, and refresh.

Once you have your altar set up as a focal point for your lunar practice, it can be easier to attune yourself to the phases of the Moon and to incorporate simple rituals and practical magics into your daily routines.

Include a place to make daily lunar offerings here, too. Will you burn incense or herbs for the Moon? Light a special candle? Pour her sacred water? (Water from your tap is sacred, and all water is one water!)

Lunar Altar Consecration Ritual

When you have finished composing this first iteration of your lunar altar, perform a short and simple ritual to formally consecrate and dedicate it in the name of the Moon. This is best done on or between the New and Full Moon, when Luna's energies are growing in power.

To Gather

- Something with which to energetically cleanse your altar, such as a pleasing incense, an herb bundle of pine, rosemary, or lavender, or salt
- Water contained in a small vessel
- A gift for the Moon (See the "Lunar Offerings" section below for ideas.)

The Rite

Step 1: Ground and center yourself, connect with the Earth beneath you and the Moon above. Invite the Moon to witness you and your work.

Step 2: Create sacred space around you and your altar. If it is part of your existent path, you may choose to cast a circle, or you could simply declare aloud that your space is sanctified.

Step 3: Using intention and perhaps words or sound, cleanse your altar with salt, smoldering herbs, or incense smoke. Visualize any energies that do not belong on or around your lunar altar drifting away into the Ethers, where they will be transformed into a neutral state. Do this until you no longer detect any energies that do not belong.

Step 4: Speak aloud your intentions for this sacred space. Perhaps you might say something like, "O Beloved Moon, here I will maintain a special place for us to connect with one another." Share with Luna whatever is in your heart.

Step 5: Lift your vessel of water up to the Moon and invite her blessing upon it. Then dip your fingers into the water, and bless all four corners and the center of the altar. Finally, bless yourself.

Step 6: With loving words, place your gift for the Moon upon your altar.

Step 7: Say thank you to all energies and entities you invited, and then bid them hail and farewell.

Step 8: Ground and center yourself again, releasing any extra energies from your body to the Earth and/or the Moon.

Meditate and journal at your lunar altar daily. Just as you would do with any good friend, share your joys and your troubles with the Moon. Ask for her advice and her wisdom.

Bless, reconsecrate, or rededicate your lunar altar in some way any time after you've cleaned it up or given it a fresh, new look.

As High Priestess Ffiona Morgan, creatrix of the Daughters of the Moon tarot writes, "The altar is a place for your Deep Self, a reflection of your internal landscape, and a home for the Goddess, inside and out."[31] Give yourself this gift!

Lunar Offerings

Making holy offerings at your lunar altar is a beautiful routine to connect with the Moon. Offerings can be made every lunation during a predetermined phase or astrological transit, on a certain day of each week, or daily. Daily is best!

Bring her fresh white flowers, fragrant herbs, holy waters, white and clear stones, silvery jewelry, and incense. Light a candle to her beauty and lift it up to the stillness of her orb. Hold a clear quartz stone in the rays of the Full Moon and gaze through it at her luminous roundness.

Catch her beams in your magic mirror or crystal ball. Capture her rays in the waters in a chalice or blessing bowl. Drink her rays in, making them a part of you—body, mind, heart, and spirit.

There are many ways that you can attune yourself with the lunar cycle that don't involve heavy or extensive ritual. Sometimes the word *ritual* insinuates a grandiose, extravagant hours-long ceremony, and yet daily rituals can be so short and so sweet, still replete with meaning and fulfillment.

The most important thing to remember is that there is no way to do this wrong. Your relationship with the Moon is your relationship with her; it doesn't need to look like the relationship anyone else has with her. As long as it feeds you and is healthy and supportive, it is the right relationship for you. There is no error in how you connect with Luna.

Water can be such a loving, gentle element to work with in this endeavor. Not only does it correspond to Luna's energies, but when you speak into water, it can record your prayers and your dreams. You can use this holy water to bless yourself, to bless others, and then pour it out with the objective that it carries your wishes down and across the Earth.

31. Morgan, *Goddess Spirituality Book*, 16.

Lunar Offerings Ritual

Start a simple daily ritual practice of making an offering of water to the Moon upon your lunar altar each morning (or evening). Read through the complete practice before commencing.

To Gather

- A special bowl or chalice to dedicate to this practice
- Water from your tap

The Rite

Step 1: Begin by filling your bowl or chalice with water.

Step 2: Check in with yourself and with the Moon, noting her sign and phase and how that feels for you; this is a tactic of simply tuning into the vibrations of that day without pressure or expectation.

Step 3: Using the water, bless yourself in the name of the phase and the sign of the Moon as you unreservedly *feel* into Luna's energies.

Step 4: Leave this water on your lunar altar overnight.

Step 5: The next morning, empty the bowl or chalice outdoors, or if there is a houseplant that thirsts for some special attention, feed it to that plant.

Alternative

You can store your daily water offerings in a large bottle (or other vessel with a cap or lid) over a period of days or weeks and then when it is full, convey it to an ocean, river, stream, or brook. Once you've arrived at the moving body of water, speak a blessing into this offering and pour it out into the living body of water as a heart-gift to the Moon and to the Earth Mother.

Experiment with your daily lunar offerings and see what brings you into the greatest alignment, understanding that this can evolve from day to day, month to month, or year to year. Be flexible and forgiving with yourself, too!

Remember: No one is watching you. This is about your connection with the Moon and how you choose to bring her energies down into your everyday life. These practices should always support and inspire you.

Tracking the Lunar Cycle

The Moon was one of humanity's first calendars, and even in these most modern times, I find that ordering and organizing my life around her endless transitions is exceedingly helpful in guiding my actions.

All people have their own monthly rhythms—times when they are up, down, mellow, passionate, wild, lethargic, and so on. Learn how the pull of the Moon activates you: She is the queen of emotions, regulating bodies of water as enormous as the largest ocean. Pay as close attention as possible to how you feel every day as she passes through each phase and each astrological sign.

Instead of merely reacting to the currents of the Moon, practice planning ahead and then working in concert with them, making better choices for yourself and the world.

There are a myriad of ways to track the cycling of the Moon, and it takes experimentation to learn which way or ways will work best for you. Here are three of my favorite methods:

Moon Journaling

If expressing yourself through words is your jam, try tracking Luna's cycle in your Moon Journal with these prompts and inquiries. Here is what that might look like:

Date:

Moon phase: In addition to writing the name of the lunar phase, draw a tiny representation of the Moon and then fill it in to match how Luna looks in the sky.

Moon sign: What sign(s) of the zodiac is she traveling through today? Is she void of course at any point?

Observation: Look for the Moon and write a word or two about what you see, think, or feel. (Remember: Often you will see her at night, other times she won't rise until after you've gone to bed, and sometimes she may be visible in the daytime sky instead of—or in addition to—the nighttime sky.)

Lunar offerings: What offering(s) did you make to her today?

Moon wisdom: Did you receive any messages from her today?

I like to start a fresh page for this practice each morning because some of these things (i.e., date, phase, sign) are ideally journaled upon waking. I complete my record in the evening as a bookend to my day.

Moonwheels

For a more visual way of tracking how my personal cycle corresponds to the lunar cycle, I use a circular lunar chart called a moonwheel, which I first learned about in Priestess Shekhinah Mountainwater's book *Ariadne's Thread*.

This is an excellent system for those who need something tactile, and it results in a vivid record of your relationship with Luna's travels throughout each lunation.

Begin by making a copy of the moonwheel below, then decide which part(s) of your life you would like to make more accessible and visible to yourself. You could track such things as your moods, energy levels, sleep patterns, dreams, diet, exercise, inspiration, menstrual cycle (if applicable), and more in conjunction with the sign and phase of the Moon.

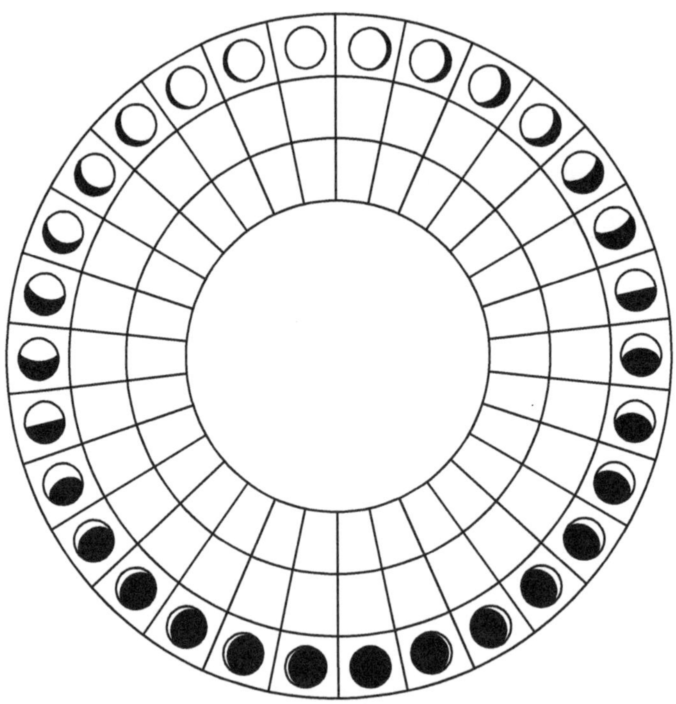

Moonwheel

At the beginning of each lunation, starting with the New Moon, fill in all of the phases on the wheel with the correct calendar dates. (Remember: The dates will not fit perfectly in the moonwheel because our modern calendar months are not aligned with the lunar months.)

As each new day arrives, add the glyph(s) for the astrological sign(s) the Moon is passing through on that date to the inner pane of the wheel.

Use different colored crayons, pencils, or markers to denote the element each sign is associated with so you can see at a glance what was powering the vibrations that day. Perhaps try yellow for air, red for fire, blue for water, and green for earth.

Include supplemental information such as when you are at your best and worst. Continue to add words and symbols, making notes each day about your experiences—emotional and otherwise—in conjunction with what is happening with the Moon.

Moonspotting

Moonspotting is a somatic practice, a form of lunar tracking that can help you to uncover knowledge through your actual firsthand experiences with the Moon.

Taking into account when Luna can be seen based upon the phase she is in (see chapter 2, "The Phases of the Moon"), go outside every day (or night) and look for her.

After locating Luna, spend a few moments connecting with her energies—her phase and her sign—noticing how your body reacts to the vibrations.

Become familiar with when each phase of the Moon can be seen from Earth, and keep a schedule of looking for Luna at approximately the same time every day or night. Witness her as she witnesses you, pledging her love, honor, and respect and receiving hers in turn.

Soon you'll intuit exactly where and when to look for her in the sky during each of her phases without needing to consult reference materials.

Make a simple commitment to following her cycle each and every day for at least three consecutive lunations (and better thirteen lunations; a full lunar year—or more!—is great).

When we keep track of the Moon and her moods, we begin to see how her tides not only affect us on an individual level but how they affect the entirety of how and where we live, our neighborhoods, our households, and our families and friends. The Moon is a key we can use to unlock the doors that are usually invisible, the doors of perception and of the unconscious.

Let's return to the remembrance of measuring time by the Moon as well as by the Sun!

Moon Tracking

Choose one (or more) of the three lunar tracking methods above, and as part of your daily Moon Witch practice, begin observing your personal cycle as it corresponds to the lunar cycle.

At the end of every day before going to bed, note how you felt throughout that twenty-four-hour period in conjunction with the Moon's changing nature—physically, mentally, emotionally, spiritually. Begin making connections between your emotions, thoughts, and energy levels and the pull the Moon is exerting upon them.

Once you've gained enough familiarity and data, you can tackle scheduling according to your natural energy patterns. As you do so, notice how your life shifts when your actions are aligned with your own cyclic nature and the cycling of the Moon.

Moon Meditation

Meditating with the vibrations of the Moon can be an eye-opening way of contacting your innate lunar nature. This can become an excellent method for grasping how each lunar phase and astrological sign impacts you in particular.

Spend five minutes each day (or night) opening yourself up to lunar energies and observing how they resonate in your body. Is there a particular body part in which you can more accurately sense specific lunar transits or phases?

You can also use the set of moon stones you created in chapter 2 to help you to focus during this practice. Simply hold the proper phase moon stone in your hand, rest it upon your body, or softly gaze at it.

Moongazing

Moongazing is just what it sounds like—gazing at the Moon. This daily practice can help increase your interrelation with Luna, interweaving your vibrations with hers.

Try moongazing at each phase and detect the differences. What do you notice when she is Dark? New? Waxing? Full? Waning? Get that beach blanket out, set it up in your backyard—or hike out in nature—and quietly revel in your connection with the Moon.

Become a moongazer, allowing yourself to fall in love with the Moon in all of her soul-stirring guises as she dances her orbit through the sky. You can hold your moon stones to augment your focus during this practice, too!

Moongazing

Begin by grounding and centering yourself by looking up at the Moon and breathing her beams into your body.

Using your breath, fill yourself up completely with her energies. Notice the sensation of her light (or her dark) upon your skin. Pause now, grounded and centered, and just breathe with her. Attune your breath to the Moon. How does she breathe? How deep or shallow is her breath? What temperature is it? Breathe until you feel every cell of your body vibrating with her energies.

Listen for the messages sent on her rays, the reflection of the Sun's light. What do you need to see or hear or know or be?

If you receive information from her, be sure to follow up. Don't dismiss these communications. If there is an action you were instructed to take, don't hesitate or procrastinate—do it!

Take her messages to your Moon Journal and see what else arises from them. Even if you receive only a word or an image—a flash of insight, ever so small—do not discount this detail as a figment of your imagination or a hopeful dream. When you follow the advice of the Moon, she is more likely to grant more wisdom to you when you are intentionally seeking it.

Moonletters

Writing moonletters is a practice I've been doing for myself for many years now, and it has never grown boring. As author Julia Cameron says, "Writing is one of the most powerful ways available to us not only to 'right' ourselves but also right the world."[32]

Moonletters stir up our connection with our Inner Lunar Witch, the Moon, and the Cosmos. They can help to remind us of who we are and what matters to us, to remind ourselves that we are part of something much greater.

There are two approaches for engaging with this practice: (1) writing letters to the Moon herself and (2) writing moonletters to yourself.

Writing Letters to the Moon

This can be a wonderful outlet for the overwhelming emotions some experience during certain lunar phases and transits, and in keeping these exaggerated emotions confined to the page, they tend not to overflow into our work and our relationships.

32. Cameron, *The Right to Write*, 97.

Write letters to Luna in your Moon Journal, especially when you are inspired by the sight of her or grateful for your connection. These letters may become free-form poetry as you permit images that speak to your sentiments to candidly spill onto the page without self-editing.

In your Moon Journal, also confide to Luna your hopes and dreams, perhaps even asking for her help in making the changes needed for them to become reality.

You can also write a love letter to the Moon or even a missive that shares your joy and accounts of the successes you've recently experienced while working with her energies. For letters like these, you may want to write on stationary and then ceremonially burn the letters with lunar herbs as an offering to her, sending your words up to her on wafts of sacred smoke.

I learned that there are seven towns named Moon in the United States; one each in Kentucky, Mississippi, Oklahoma, Pennsylvania, South Dakota, Virginia, and Wisconsin. I wonder what would happen if you mailed a moonletter to one of these post offices?

High strangeness: If you wanted to send an actual physical letter or other object to the Moon (and are prepared to pay to do so), you can check out Astrobotic. This company accepts "small mementos for missions to the Moon. These keepsakes will be stored on the Moon for centuries to come."[33]

Even though I can think of several exciting magical reasons I would like to send something to the Moon, adding objects to her surface just doesn't resonate with me. Maybe I will have a change of heart about this in the future, but for now, I am not comfortable participating.

Writing Moonletters to Your Future Self

Under the Moon, write a letter to your Future Self, your Future Lunar Witch. Try writing it alongside the New or Full Moon or another phase or sign that feels right.

What do you want them to know? What do you want them to remember? What do you want to remind them of?

At the Full Moon, you might write a letter reminding your Future Self of your best qualities, your successes, your accomplishments, what you've healed or transformed. What are you most proud of yourself for? This is a perfect opportunity to toot your own horn! No one will read this but you, so be earnest, unvarnished, and real.

At the New Moon, you could write a letter to your Future Self with reminders of your ultimate aspirations, your biggest dreams, and what you are looking to heal, clarify, or transform over the long haul.

Sometimes I will include a tarot or oracle reading I've done for my Present or Future Self. Sometimes I'll write about a dream (or dream fragment) that is unusually poignant. Sometimes

33. "DHL Moonbox."

I'll include a quote that felt resonant. Occasionally, I'll add some biodegradable glitter, a pressed leaf or flower, or something else that evokes deep feeling.

This letter is then folded and placed into an envelope. You may choose to scent it with an essential or magical oil like you would for a lover. You might even seal it with a big red—or black!—lipstick kiss.

Then hide the letter away somewhere where it will not be easily found. You can schedule an email to yourself to arrive at your own inbox one lunar year later, including information about where the letter is secreted away.

Or better yet—ask someone you love and trust to keep the letter for a lunar year and to mail it to you after this amount of time. (I have done this for my students, and it is an amazing honor to hold their missives for them for this year. I keep the letters in a dedicated place, sending them blessings and love whenever I pass by.)

Give your friend an envelope that is already sealed, stamped, and addressed to you, and ask them to schedule a reminder for themselves to send the letter to you at the one-lunar-year mark.

Ascending to the Moon

Ascending to the Moon is another pathway into discovering the phases and lunar frequencies that resonate most with you. This practice employs the art of astral travel, which is accessible to everyone. Even if you have not traveled astrally before, you are more than capable of doing so with the Moon as your guide.

Astral projection can be described as a purposeful out-of-body experience where the energy body purposefully journeys beyond the confinement of the physical vessel.

The astral realm is a fluid place that exists in all time and all space and outside of all time and all space. It is not bound by the same parameters that we are as Earth beings. This plane offers us the opportunity to survey those places that most of us, in our physical bodies, are unable to visit in this lifetime.

In an astral projection session, you voyage to and with your Deep Mind, seeking other planes of existence and the information and wisdom contained within them. In this particular practice, you will travel onto the body of the Moon.

A simple way to reach this state is to begin by grounding, centering, and opening the channel and then passing into this vortex using the river of meditation, moving easily from physical reality into astral reality.

It is important to note that you may or may not see anything. You may even feel like you are pretending, and there is nothing wrong with this! You may experience sound, color, emotion, texture, taste, scent. Allow yourself to sense or observe whatever is there for you. Do not hold on to expectations, and do not push. Instead, surrender and flow with What Is.

You can record yourself reading the following steps aloud and then use that as your guide, ask a friend to read for you, or just go through the steps mentally a few times and then use what you have learned as a jumping-off point.

Instrumental music played quietly in the background can be a significant aid for this practice. Tracks are readily available on the internet (try YouTube), and you can find instrumental 432 hertz compositions (the frequency of heart healing), ambient musical pieces specifically designed to accelerate lunar connection, as well as melodies created for each of Luna's different phases.

Ascending to the Moon Ritual

Ascending to the Moon can be performed in any of her phases. Try this practice during each phase of an entire lunation as it occurs. Or you could also select one zodiacal sign at the beginning of the year and then commit to Ascending to the Moon each time she enters that particular sign for an whole lunar year.

Be sure to note the phase and the different flavors and feelings you perceive in your Moon Journal each time you do this working.

There are thirteen steps to honor the potential total of Full or New Moons in any given calendar year.

To Gather

- An eye covering
- A plate of healthy, calorie-dense food
- A large glass of fresh drinking water
- Your Moon Journal and pen

To Prepare

Construct a journeying "nest" for yourself by creating a comfortable, cozy, and beautiful resting place within which to lie down, sit, or stand. You may want to line your nest with pillows, your favorite blanket, a special cloth, and so on. Have available some sort of cover for your eyes and your food, water, and journal nearby.

If you have specific things on your mind or heart about which you would like the Moon's counsel, formulate your questions in advance. Here are some broad inquiries to get you started: What is the Moon telling me? How does she affect my life? How does my personal connection with her overlap with the larger collective unconscious?

The Rite

Step 1: With words or action, create a circle of protection and magic, then make your body comfortable. You may lie down or sit in your journey nest or even stand (you can also switch between sitting and standing if you would like). Close your eyes and relax your body.

Step 2: Moving slowly and deliberately, begin to increase your connection with yourself through long, steady, slow breaths. Begin to deepen your connection with Earth by sending etheric roots down, down, down and across, across, across. Begin to expand your connection with the Moon and the Cosmos by sending branches up, up, up and out, out, out. Breathe in the power of the Earth Mother, the Moon, and the Cosmos.

Step 3: Once you are fully embodied in your own Moon Witch Self, rooted in the Earth, and connected to the Cosmos, give yourself over to the comforting blanket of gravity, resting as if asleep. Allow your human body to be held peacefully and securely upon the body of the Earth Mother, breathing slowly, your mind floating, empty, unseeing, relaxed, contented, untroubled, tranquil.

You are safe here, in connection with your own sweet Self, all parts of yourself whole, holy, and integrated. Allow the sacred darkness to flow over you and around you. Completely release yourself to the darkness, in trust and in surrender. Let the sacred darkness soothe you like a healing balm as you release your mind into the infinity of the void, the place of all potential and all possibility, the cauldron from which our dreams develop.

Step 4: Awaken your bindu chakra, your Moon Center, by making the sound of buzzing bees eight times upon your exhalations. As you buzz, envision your magical circle all around you like a bubble—a sphere of safety and protection in which to do your holy work. Envision the Elements of Life—air, fire, water, and earth—becoming more and more present, cascading in to support, protect, and witness your travels.

Step 5: Begin to breathe the energy of the Moon's light down, down, down into your human holy temple.

Step 6: Begin to count yourself up, up, up to meet her, beginning with the number one and ending with the number thirteen in this manner:

One. Feel your Astral Self gently moving up and out of your human body, rising slowly and deliberately toward the Moon. Use the vibrations of her rays as a pathway upon which to rise. See-sense-feel her with your inner eye, your third eye. You do not need to physically see her rays in order to detect them and ride them upward.

Two. Continue breathing in and out slowly. Begin to open your heart to the Moon. Feel her drawing you, your astral body, closer to her upon prismatic rays.

Three. Four. Breathe.

Step 7: Five. Six. You arrive onto the Moon, welcomed and loved by her. Make yourself at home here by sitting down.

Seven. Eight. Make your Astral Self comfortable, perched here upon our hospitable Moon. Allow your Astral Self to be completely held and embraced by her.

Step 8: Nine. Ten. Eleven. Twelve. With your physical eyes still closed, say aloud these words: "I am a Beloved of the Moon, a child of her silvery light." Pause here for a few moments and meld with the Moon, breathing her into your human vessel, your body, your mind, your heart, your spirit.

Thirteen. Notice how this particular lunar phase feels. Notice how the astrological sign she is dwelling within at this moment colors your feelings, your focus, your connection.

Step 9: Ask the Moon any questions you formulated earlier, or share those that are currently on your mind or in your heart.

Step 10: When you are complete, recognize that your work for this moment is done and that it is time to reverently return your astral body to your physical body. Count down now, as your astral body floats toward Earth, gently and tenderly. Count slowly in this manner:

Thirteen. Give Luna your gratitude. Say farewell to her for now, offering thankfulness for everything you discovered or learned.

Twelve, eleven, ten. Know that her energies are always with you, that she is always with you.

Step 11: Nine, eight, seven. See-sense-feel your physical body temple below you.

Six, five, four. Breathe into your human physical body. Still in your astral body, hover steadily and effortlessly directly above your physical body. Look at your human body and notice what it is like to look down upon it.

Step 12: Gently now, and slowly, sink back into your physical body. Become aware of what it is like to be in an astral body inside of your human body. Then shift your full awareness to your physical body, bringing all parts of yourself back into it.

Three, two, one. Open your eyes. Return, return, return. Wiggle your fingers and wiggle your toes; stretch out your arms and your legs, your hands and your feet; gently and slowly move your neck from side to side and all around.

Step 13: Ground and center yourself once again, feeling into your Earth roots and your sky branches. Slow your breath once again and take stock of your body. Gently pat and rub yourself all over, bringing yourself back, back, back into your body. Using one big, loud breath, retract your roots and your branches, bringing all parts of yourself fully back into your human body and into the richness of the present moment. Welcome back!

Slowly eat some food now, taking time to journal anything you would like to remember. This doesn't need to be anything more than an inkling, a feeling, and/or impression you may want to revisit later. Note that sometimes the physical body can become dehydrated after astral travel, so hydrate yourself now by drinking water, and then continue to drink an appropriate amount of water over the next few days.

A Caution

Do not permit yourself to become so caught up with the energies of "ascension" that you attempt to ascend yourself. This is a trap that has gained recent popularity, provoking people to "ascend" into higher dimensions and stay there.

In this particular lifetime, we are meant to live human lives learning human lessons. We are not meant to *ascend* and dwell in other dimensions now. This is spiritual bypassing and anathema to our purpose here and now on Mother Earth in this one brief, fleeting lifetime.

Walking the Path

Your relationship with the Moon will morph, fluctuate, and broaden over time, just as it does with every other being. Remember to treat the Moon as a cherished friend and beloved companion, and she will always have something with which to surprise you! Walking the Path of the Moon as a Lunar Witch is never boring, even when the discipline of it seems a shade tedious.

When you follow the calendar of the Moon, aligning your life with her sacred timing and with time itself as a sacred force, you will discover clarity around when you can do your best work, both magically and mundanely, and when it is advantageous for you to instead pause, dream, incubate, plan, and *then* take action.

The following is a simple and effective ritual, a calming and experiential quest to strengthen your partnership with the Moon and bring peace and restfulness into your own heart. In this rite, you will set an intention and then commune with the Moon in order to receive her wisdom, blessings, and/or healing.

Communing with the Moon Ritual

Before beginning the ritual, consider what you would like to bring to the lap of the Moon Mother. Some places to start: What is heaviest on your mind or in your heart? What is troubling you? What is just out of reach? What yearns to be revealed? What pain is burdening you? Where do you most need the blessing of the Moon?

Once you have chosen one single intention, look at your lunar calendar and determine the best phase and sign to support your rite. Select your date and time and then begin your preparations.

To Gather

- The items you would like to use to set your ritual altar. Choose colors, candles, herbs, crystals, and so on that correspond with your intention. Include any personal objects that are holy to you (also termed Sacreds) that you wish to charge upon your altar
- Something with which to magically cleanse your space (e.g., salt, water, an herb bundle of lavender, rosemary, juniper, or the like, sound)
- A symbol of what you are bringing to the Moon for healing, blessing, or illumination (e.g., a crystal or stone; an image of her; a representation of one of her correspondences; a picture, drawing, or sigil)
- An offering for the Moon, such as water, incense, flowers, or food
- Your Moon Journal and pen
- Cakes and Ale (i.e., a bit of food and a libation for yourself such as chocolate, fruit, or nuts and water, wine, or juice)

Optional

- Recorded instrumental music to support your work
- A drum, rattle, or other instrument for raising energy
- Poetry or invocations for the Moon

To Prepare

Familiarize yourself with the entire ritual in advance. If possible, do this several days ahead of time so your Inner Moon Witch is saturated with the energies before you begin. Additionally, you can use this time to unhurriedly collect your magical tools so you are ready when the time is right.

If desired, precede your ritual with a ceremonial shower or magical bath.

The Rite

Step 1: Set your working altar to please your Inner Moon Witch. Make this as artistic or as uncomplicated as you wish. Include the correspondences you chose earlier as well as the symbol of your focus.

Step 2: Cleanse yourself and your ritual space as guided by your intuition.

Step 3: Ground, center, and open the channel. Connect with your breath and then use it to link with the Earth below and the Moon above. From your body, send your spiritual roots down into the Earth Mother and etheric tendrils up to the Moon.

Extend gratitude to the Indigenous Ancestors of the land you are on and to the Moon for her witness of you and your life.

When you are grounded as the pillar between Earth and Sky, come into contact with your bindu chakra, third eye chakra, and your heart chakra, opening them up to give and receive Cosmic, Earth, and Divine Love.

Step 4: Invite the Elements of Life to join you: air, fire, water, and earth. Ask for their support and their protection.

Step 5: Breathe in the beauty of All That Is, watching your inhalations and exhalations slow and become full as you take in your innate belonging. Using your breath, increase this feeling until you are overflowing with it. Savor the sensation of peace that envelops you now.

Step 6: From your heart, ask the Moon to join you, naming her current phase and sign. Invite her into your ritual and into your life. You may desire to sing to her, dance for her, or channel poetry in her name. When you experience her presence, make your offering to her by placing it upon your altar.

Step 7: Welcome her serene, calming energies in your body, allowing her vibrations to fill you, streaming down first into your crown and then gently and slowly all the way down through the soles of your feet and into the Earth. Feel her light and/or her dark holding you lovingly and firmly.

Step 8: Make yourself comfortable at your altar and speak aloud to the Moon. Holding the symbol of your intention or need, tell her why you have invited her to join you in this rite. Share with her everything you want her to know. Do not hold back!

Step 9: Still holding your symbol, request her healing, her help, and/or her blessings.

Step 10: Return now to a quiet breath, slowing your inhalations and exhalations again if necessary. Breathe in peace, and breathe out anxiety. Breathe in stillness, and breathe out worry. Breathe in restfulness, and breathe out tension. Breathe in the medicine of the Moon.

Step 11: Listen, feel, sense, and see what the Moon holds for you now. Does she bestow wisdom upon you? Does she grant you a boon or blessing? Does she offer you healing? Permit whatever transmission the Moon extends to you to land in your body, mind, heart, and spirit.

Step 12: When this transmission from the Moon is complete, rest in the energies of your ritual, reflecting upon what Luna shared with you. Pause here and create space for whatever was transmitted to you to land in its entirety, integrating as much of it as you can in this here and now. Allow the vibrations of the Moon to saturate you with sensations of ease, grace, and serenity, permitting them to infuse your whole being. Stay in this moment for as long as you feel good.

Step 13: If you have any final requests regarding this matter, share them with Luna now, then hold your symbol up to her, thanking her for favor. Speak aloud your thankfulness for her aid.

Step 14: With gratitude, bless your Cakes and Ale in the name of the Moon. Whilst you partake of it, record your experiences in your Moon Journal.

Step 15: Thank the Moon and the Elements of Life for their presence in your ritual and in your life.

Step 16: Send any extra energies that were raised up to the Moon, then gently bring your cosmic tendrils and spiritual roots back into your body. Return fully to your physical vessel and the holy moment of now. Blessed be!

Chapter 6
The Moon in Magic

The Moon Goddess Speaks

Many are my guises, and many are my powers. Tonight, though, I come to you not as the Soft-Hearted One but as the Magic-Maker, the Silver Queen, the Night Queen, the Great Queen. I come to you as Moon Goddess, as Lady of the Otherworld, as the one who holds the transcendental power to combine mystical substances and create novel compounds.

Awaken inspiration! Awaken creativity! Your only limits are the ones you have set for yourself. You always have the ingredients you need to make power manifest into form. Match your intellect with your heart and you will discover fertile understandings of alchemical change.

Remember: The whole is always more mighty and more magnificent than the making of its material. Bring joy to your work; work with what you have.

I am Rhiannon.

Journal Inquiries for This Gateway

What magical allies already surround me? When do I feel most connected with my own magic? What makes my Inner Moon Witch happiest?

Affirmations for This Gateway

My magical work is in complete alignment with my highest good. I am attuned to the innate powers within all things. I hear and heed the wisdom of my Inner Moon Witch.

Each choice made for spellwork or ritual possesses an energetic signature that can be used to better align our energies with our intentions, which in turn can help to align the energies of Above and Below, with our human selves in the center.

When we include colors, herbs, oils, crystals, sounds, tools, and objects that "rhyme" and resonate with our aims, our intentions have a better chance of manifesting. Magical correspondences help to create links between our thoughts and desires and what we want to create or accomplish here in the physical Earth realm.

Correspondences function upon the Hermetic maxim "As Above, so Below; as Below, so Above"; the idea that we can assign certain components of the microcosm to affect and transform the macrocosm; that our internal reality is inextricably partnered with the greater collective, with external reality.

Magical correspondences can be crucial in successful spellcasting, as we can influence reality through the use of ingredients, objects, symbols, and timing that we know or sense are carrying the same vibrations and energies of what we want to realize into being and form.

Colors, crystals, days of the week, deities, essential and compounded oils, flowers, foods, herbs, High Holydays, lunar phases, metals, planets, planetary hours, plants, scents, and much more can help us to actualize our thoughts, visions, hopes, and dreams into form in outer reality.

Correspondences function like personal magical assistants. Their role is to help you to focus upon holding your unwavering intention whilst attracting into your field those things that mimic, match, or emulate their energetic signature.

So, is it better to choose a large quantity of correspondences or a few well-curated ingredients? This is entirely up to you! You will need to experiment to discover what combines best with *your* unique energetic frequency, what works best for *your* magic.

Some Lunar Witches carefully ensure that every single component of a spell or a ritual—from the time it begins (and sometimes even ends) to the color of an altar cloth to the type of incense burned—corresponds perfectly.

Some Lunar Witches have a magical number of correspondences they like to use (e.g., three, seven, nine, thirteen) and simply turn to what feels best for the rest. Some Moon Witches like to keep their work as simple as possible, curbing the number of lunar correspondences to under five or even under three. And yet other Moon Witches select one perfect lunar correspondence and build everything upon that one elegantly chosen color, object, or time.

The Correspondences of the Moon

Below you will find some beginning magical correspondences for your lunar spellwork. I will discuss lunar plants, herbs, and crystals in an upcoming chapter.

Colors

Color is a big part of magic of any kind (for sighted people) because it is an inseparable part of everything that is seen. Choosing altar cloths, ritual clothing, spell candles, and other spell components (such as ribbons, pouches, stones, herbs, and more) customarily involves color.

The primary color correspondences of the Moon are white, silver, and gray. Her secondary colors include black, blue, green, purple, and violet. For eclipses, you can try incorporating yellow, orange, or red.

Anatomy

The Moon is associated with the stomach, the digestive system, the chest, the breasts, and the uterus. She is related to the production and balance of the human body's hormones.

Mending and strengthening magic done in support of these body parts on behalf of the Self and others is well indicated as part of the Path of the Lunar Witch.

The Moon also rules over the subtle body: the first layer of the energy field, our psyche. It includes the etheric body, which is composed of thousands of energy channels, sometimes named the quasi-material aspect of the body or the body of light.

Creatures

The Moon is associated with numerous creatures, many of which are water creatures and naturally also correspond with the element of water.

These include alligators, barnacles, clams, crabs, dolphins, fish, frogs, lobsters, otters, plankton, porpoises, sand dollars, seagulls, sea urchins, sharks, shellfish, snails, turtles, walruses, and whales.

On land, she is associated with cats, deer, hares, nightingales, rabbits, and swans.

In general, all nocturnal beings belong with her.

Mythologically, she is connected with ghosts, mermaids, and undines.

Food

Food associated with Luna can be incorporated into your practice in several ways. It can be used as spell components, presented to the Moon or to a deity as ritual offerings, and/or ingested as part of the Cakes and Ale ceremony near the completion of many rites. Carefully chosen and prepared foods can add yet another vital layer to your magic.

Lunar foods include almonds, bamboo, blueberries, cheese, cherries, coconuts, dragon fruit, eggs, grapes, kiwis, lemons, lettuce, mangoes, milk, mooncakes, pancakes, passionfruit, pears, pomelos, pumpkins, tamarind, tapioca, turnips, watercress, watermelon, and yucca.

Sacred Tools

The sacred tools of the Moon are generally those that belong to the element of water. These include blessing bowls, cauldrons, scrying bowls, pools, and mirrors; ritual chalices (the blessed cup, the Holy Grail); sea salt; and shells.

All that reflects can be assigned to the Moon as a magical correspondence.

Tarot

In the major arcana, the High Priestess card, the Chariot card, and the Moon card best correspond with her energies. She can also be readily found in the suit of cups.

Tarot cards can be an excellent visual support for spellwork or add focal points when placed on a ritual altar. (I will cover divination and divination tools in chapter 14.)

The Moon as a Primary Correspondence

Because life as we know it most likely would not have formed without the Moon's gravitational pull upon all things on Earth, she can be viewed as prime mover, one who makes things happen.

She is the Muse of the Earth—and of Earth beings—inspiring us to creativity, to new ways of thinking, acting, and being. She continues to have an enormous effect upon all life within our biosphere and, as part of this, holds profound powers of manifestation. And what is manifestation but one of the primary purposes of ritual and spellwork?

The Moon is one of the most important magical partners we can have. As the Great Manifestor, our Lunar Lady can help to power our spells in ways that we could never do alone.

Unlike the constancy of the Sun's energy and light, the Moon's energy and light fluctuate depending upon her phase and the zodiacal sign she is inhabiting. This provides us larger opportunity for artistry in our channeling and direction of her energies.

The Moon is receptive, reflecting the Sun; the inner, personal, private, reflective world; our memories; our inner creativity and wisdom. She is the inward expression of light, ruling our emotions, our feelings, and our deep inner wisdom.

The Magical Realms of the Moon

When we yield to the cycling of the Moon, channeling her powers and strength into our workings, she becomes our primary magical correspondence, one we can depend upon as we do a longtime friend and trusted confidante. In turn, we increase our understanding of our own Self, magnifying the strength and power of our own innate lunar magic.

Her Powers and Provinces

Here are some categories where the Moon is most at home, places where you can direct your energies in concert with hers to achieve success:

- addictions
- administration
- the Akashic Records
- birth
- change
- children
- clairvoyance
- the collective
- connection
- cycles
- deliveries
- divination
- dreaming
- emotions
- epiphanies
- feelings
- fertility
- habits
- healing
- home
- illumination
- illusion
- the inner realm
- instinct
- intimacy
- introspection
- intuition
- love
- memory
- mothering/parenting
- mystery
- nurturing
- peace
- prophesy
- protection
- psychic ability
- psychic powers
- publicity
- rebirth
- secrets
- security
- sleep
- the subconscious
- telepathy
- transformation
- travel (by water)
- uncovering That Which Is Hidden
- visions
- women and women's issues

The Element of Water

Water is the Element of Life that corresponds most dynamically with the Moon and her energies. In the magical tradition in which I was raised, water is associated with the direction of west and with the energetic of *daring*.

Water—in your body, this is composed of your blood, your sweat, and your tears—is the element of receiving and abundance, and it falls under the auspices of the archetypes of the Sacred Sovereign, the Empowered King, and the Empowered Queen.

Experiences and powers associated with water often significantly overlap with the attributes of the Moon herself. These powers of water include abundance, adaptability, childbirth, cleansing, compassion, dissolving, divination, dreams, emotions, feelings, flexibility, flow, fluidity, gathering, healing, intuition, lactation, love, menstruation, moving (of energy), nurturing, peace, prosperity, psychic powers, purification, receptivity, reflection, secrecy, shamanic journeying, shaping, sleep, trance, and visions.

The astrological signs of Water are Cancer, Scorpio, and Pisces. Water is associated with our sense of taste. The time of day is sunset, and seasonally, it is related to autumn.

Places and experiences of water include baths and bathhouses, beaches, blood, brooks, creeks, fog, geysers, hail, harbors, hot springs, hot tubs, ice, lakes, mist, oceans, ponds, puddles, rain, ripples, rivers, rivulets, seas, showers, sleet, snow, steam, streams, saunas, sweat, swimming pools, tears, tidal waves, tsunamis, waterfalls, waves, wells, whirlpools, and wombs. What would you add to this?

Here are some descriptive words and phrases for the direction of west and the element of water, which you can use as or incorporate into invocations, prayers, or blessings when doing lunar rituals:

crystal clear waters
the cup runneth over
cycles
deep, dark waters
delving into the depths
diving in
flowing river, still pond
go with the flow
the Great Wave
the Lady of the Lake
leading like water
let your heart be your guide
the mists of the holy land of Avalon
oceans of our emotions
the path of least resistance
the Place of the Setting Sun
primordial womb

purify us
renewing life
the sacred blood that connects us all
stream of consciousness
swept away
wash over me
washing us clean
water wears away the stone
waters of the womb

An Energy Source for Ritual and Magic

Our magic and our ritual should never be fueled by our own energy bodies (unless it is in desperation—a life or death circumstance!—and there is no other option available).

You can use the Moon as an energy source for spellwork and ritual by sending your etheric branches into the Above, into the Star Body, into the Cosmos. Here you can draw down lunar energy through your etheric leaves and branches, then conduct that energy to power your magic.

As you have probably ascertained by now, many practices upon the Path of Lunar Witchcraft begin with a technique called "grounding, centering, and opening the channel." This process puts you first in touch with yourself through your breath, then with the Earth through the creation of etheric roots that go all the way down into her fiery center, her core of magma, and then with the Cosmos through the creation of etheric branches, including tendrils that go all the way up into the void, the cauldron of birth, death, and rebirth.

When practicing within a group setting, after you connect yourself with *yourself*, the Earth Mother, and the Cosmos, you are ready to connect with others. Come into resonance by entangling your roots and your branches with those of your circlemates, collaboratively using breath to develop a tapestry of sound (perhaps through a hum or the buzz of the hive). This in turn creates a distinctive frequency and vibration that will only be heard and felt during that particular rite, never to be heard or felt again after that ritual.

Thus connected, entangled, and energetically aligned with one another, turn your attention to synergistically creating an energy well at the center of the working altar. This is built first through synchronously envisioning a holy well that needs to be filled with energy to power the magic and the ritual.

Next, energy is drawn up through roots from the Earth, energy is drawn down through branches from the Cosmos, and then these Earth and Sky energies are channeled through your bodies and out your mouths using the sound "Ma" until the sound organically concludes because the energy well is full.

We use that power—not our own personal energies—to propel our magical and ritual workings.

This is something that I invite you to do by yourself—or with others—whenever you perform your moon magic or rituals.

Lunar Energy Practice

When filling an energy well, you can choose to use Moon energy in particular instead of utilizing general Cosmic energy. Try this out and feel for the differences!

Connect with your breath and then send your roots deep into the Earth Mother. Firmly grounded here, send your etheric branches up to the Moon. Bring the Moon's energies into your body now, and then channel it out to fill your energetic well.

Lunar Witches know lunar energies. As you work with this practice, take note: How does your body feel? What sensations do you experience? Is there an awareness of push or pull? Of expansion or contraction? Of slowness or quickness?

Understanding the Moon as a source of energy is not only about the sense of sight; it includes all of our senses: What does it look like, feel like, smell like, sound like? What temperature or texture or taste? What associations do you have with it—always or just today?

Magical Timing

Making the conscious choice to pay considerable attention to timing your lunar rituals and moonspells can result in your intended outcomes arriving with greater grace, ease, and dexterity. And since you've already begun to steep yourself in the cadence of the lunar cycle, your command of magical timing becomes easier and easier.

In its most elemental form, magical timing (what astrologers call electional astrology or event astrology) instructs us in determining the right time to do the right thing in magic, in ritual, and even in life.

There are many systems of astrological timing that you can use in conjunction with your magic, and most require rigorous study to comprehend. Do not become discouraged! Astrology is a complex field that takes lifelong examination and application to fully appreciate. Be kind and patient with yourself, and soon you will have a general understanding of when, where, and how to apply it.

The following are some foundational ideas you can use to calibrate your magic alongside the cycling and frequencies of not only the Moon herself but other aspects of life, power that you can learn to weave into your practice of Lunar Witchcraft.

Planetary correspondences and planetary magic are broad, far-reaching topics. Here, we make but a cursory foray into them.

Planetary Correspondences

Each planet rules its own domain, with its own authority, strengths, and specialties. You can use the energies of the planetary bodies to magnify your powers to fulfill your desires.

One important thing to note: Unlike planets and asteroids, the Moon and the Sun are never in retrograde.

Planetary Days

Each day of the week is assigned to one of the seven classical planets or one of the two luminaries. During their day, the powers of this particular planet or luminary are at the crest of their weekly cycle, and the influences they wield can assist (or impede) us in our endeavors that day.

I like to think of the planet (or luminary) who is having their day as being in charge of the happenings regarding the prevailing energetic impression for those twenty-four hours. They provide the vibrations, the ingredients, and the seasonings that are best used during that time to form what it is we want for ourselves.

Every planet and luminary contains energies that both inspire and challenge. Because these energetic signatures are not ours to create, it is generally in our best interest to ally with these cosmic forces instead of attempting to defy or fight them.

Each day, consider the attributes, values, and virtues of the planet or luminary guiding that day, and look for ways in which you can harmonize your own plans with them. You can consider, too, the shadow side of each and bring that into the light of your consciousness as well.

Some of the planetary rulerships should be obvious simply by the spelling and sound of the days in English (i.e., Sunday [Sun], Monday [Moon], and Saturday [Saturn]). In other languages, this also holds true (i.e., *martes* in Spanish and *mardi* in French are the words for Tuesday [Mars]).

Here are the days of the week and the planet or luminary that rules each:

Monday: Moon Day
Ruled by the Moon

Tuesday: Mars Day
Ruled by Mars

Wednesday: Mercury Day (*mercurii* in Latin; *mercredi* for our French speakers)
Ruled by Mercury

Thursday: Jupiter Day (*jovis* in Latin; *jeudi* for our French speakers)
Ruled by Jupiter

Friday: Venus Day (*veneris* in Latin; *vendredi* for our French speakers)
Ruled by Venus

Saturday: Saturn Day
Ruled by Saturn

Sunday: Sun Day
Ruled by the Sun

Not only does each planet rule a precise day of the week, it also rules a specific hour in both day and night. The times—and timing—of these planetary hours shift daily beginning with sunrise and beginning again at sunset.

Planetary Hours

The planetary hour correspondences are constructed from the Chaldean Order of the Planets, an ancient astrological system. This method of planetary sequencing is named the Chaldean Sequence, and it is rooted in ancient philosophy.[34]

The Chaldean Order of the Planets indicates the relative orbital velocity of the planets, the relative distance of the planets from the Sun, and the distance of the Moon from the Earth. In this sequence, the planets are ordered by their relative speed as observed from the Earth, the Moon being the fastest and Saturn the slowest. Planetary hours divide time using this order of the planets.

Just as it sounds, each planetary hour of each planetary day is associated with, and is ruled by, a different planet. And just as there are only seven days in the week, only the two luminaries and the five classical planets of the ancients are used for this system.

The first thing to notice when calculating planetary hours for your spellwork and ritual is that the planet ruling the first hour of the day is—without exception—the same as the planet that rules the entire day: The Moon is always the first planetary hour on Monday, the day of the Moon. Mars is always the first planetary hour on Tuesday, the day of Mars. When the Sun rises on a

34. Warnock, "Planetary Hours and Days."

Wednesday, it is always the day of Mercury and the planetary hour of Mercury—Mercury rules Wednesday. And so on, throughout each day of every week.

On the surface, planetary hours can seem analogous to the everyday hours to which we are accustomed: A planetary day is comprised of twenty-four planetary hours, and a regular day is comprised of twenty-four hours. This, however, is where the resemblance ends. Planetary hours are not the sixty-minute hours we use for our routine timing and daily scheduling.

When determining planetary hours, the day is split into two periods: daytime and nighttime. Sunrise to sunset is "daytime." Sunset to sunrise of the next day is "nighttime." These two periods are then each divided into twelve equal-length hours.

Regular, mundane hours always have the same sixty-minute continuum no matter the season. The length of each planetary hour, however, varies around the Wheel of the Year—daytime planetary hours and nighttime planetary hours are invariably of different duration except for twice a year, at the Spring Equinox and again at the Fall Equinox, when the dark and light are balanced and of equal length.

While a regular day begins at midnight and every regular day measures the same for all points in that time zone, a planetary day instead begins at the moment of sunrise in any given location. Since sunrise takes place at a different time in each place, every point on our planet has its very own planetary day: Because of our latitude and longitude, the Sun rises and sets at different times for each of us, even on the same day!

Using Planetary Hours

Planetary hours can be used to calibrate and fine-tune a magical or ritual working, harnessing the energetic tides that happen each day. After learning how to determine the planetary day that best supports your magic, planetary hours are an effective next step in further sharpening your magical proficiency.

In addition to all the other magical correspondences useful in carrying out a magical working, taking the planetary days and hours into account can boost the power when performing ritual and/or crafting magic, such as making candles, amulets, spell bags, talismans, and so on.

For example, if you want to perform a spell for prophetic dreams, you could cast it on Monday, which is ruled by our Lunar Lady; if you wanted to amplify this power even further, you could also time your spellwork on this same day during one of the planetary hours of the Moon.

Planetary hours can be extraordinarily helpful when you can't wait for the corresponding day and/or Moon phase to work your magic or perform your ritual. If you needed to pay your rent yesterday, and today is Tuesday, you can still do a money spell today and aid it along by carrying it out within one of the Sun's or Jupiter's planetary hours.

Planetary hours can also be of benefit when you are lacking energy or aren't feeling well and need some oomph in order to work a spell or ritual that must be done.

When you comprehend the symbolic associations of the planets, you will readily find an appropriate day and hour for any important decision, action, or event. The essential thing to keep in mind is that the planet that rules the day and the hour accelerates and activates those enterprises in its domain. Conversely, that planet can also hamper any activities opposite to its fundamental principles.

Begin your work with these subtle planetary energies by attuning your actions and decisions to the appropriate day and hour. Examine and learn how the energies of each planet feel and what happens in your life while they rule. You can also resolve to calculate the planetary hours by hand each day as a way to become familiar with this formula and the energies.

Calculating Planetary Hours

As earlier discussed, the first hour of any day is always ruled by the planet or luminary that governs that day. That first daytime planetary hour begins at the exact minute of sunrise in that location and corresponds to the ruling planet of the day.

Each planetary hour after this first one is ruled by one of the other planets in this sequence: Saturn, Jupiter, Mars, Sun, Venus, Mercury, Moon, then repeating endlessly, Saturn, Jupiter, Mars, and so on. (To identify which planet rules which day, please refer to the section above, "Planetary Days.")

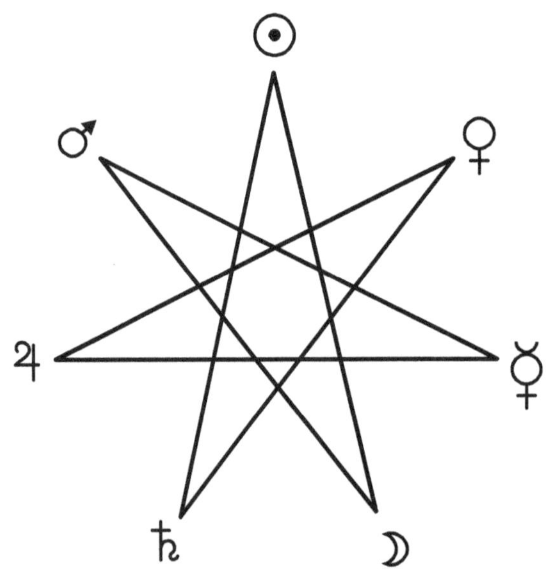

Star of the Magi: Days of the Week as Astrological Heptagram

The second planetary hour of the day begins when the first one ends, the third begins when the second one ends, and so on. Note that the shared minute between planetary hours is labeled as cusp—if at all possible, refrain from performing magic during this minute; when the planetary energies touch one another, the energy can be uncertain and/or erratic.

Begin by looking up the times of sunrise and sunset for the day you want to work with in a newspaper, almanac, or online. I like TimeandDate.com, but there are innumerable other websites you can use.

Now, to determine the length of one daytime planetary hour, add up the minutes from sunrise until sunset, then divide that number by twelve. If you want to be exact, you can calculate your planetary hours using both the minutes and the seconds, or if you are okay with having a bit of inexactitude, you can round up or down to the minute (whichever is closer). I'm not a math person by nature, so I round up or down to the closest minute.

Calculate now the length of one nighttime planetary hour by taking the period of time from sunset on this day to the following morning's sunrise and dividing that by twelve. Again, you can find the approximate times by rounding your minutes up or down, or you can be exact by using both minutes and seconds.

If you do choose to round up or down to the nearest whole minute, you'll notice that your minutes will be over or under the actual time of sunset or sunrise when you complete your calculations. One route around this is to schedule your magical activity closer to the middle of each planetary hour rather than at the very beginning or the very end.

Once you know the length of the daytime planetary hour and nighttime planetary hour for your given date and location, you can draw a table of the planetary hours, assigning each hour to the correct planet or luminary in the proper order based on the planetary day. Whew!

And now I'll tell you that you don't need to calculate planetary hours by hand. There are plenty of excellent planetary hour calculators online that will do the work for you. I prefer to use a planetary hours app, which I have on my phone and consult several times most days as I plan my activities.

Bringing It All Together

I believe that correspondences have been used for as long as the art of magic has existed within humanity. The following are some ideas for tying the various and vast number of lunar correspondences into your moonwork.

Lunar Adornment

An embodied way to incorporate mooncraft into your everyday life is through lunar adornment, a style of intentional, ceremonial dressing to honor the Moon. This is one of my favorite ways of connecting with her, and it can be even more powerful to do this on Mondays (Moon Day), her weekly holy day.

Wearing accessories or clothing in lunar colors and/or colors that match the astrological sign the Moon is passing through is an easy and entertaining way to amp up the energies when you are doing your moonspells or lunar ritual—or simply for the sake of connecting with the vibrations.

You could also dress to represent the Moon, a type of glamour magic. Envision the Moon as a character on a stage or in a film and get big with this. Consider ways in which you can embody the spirit of our Lunar Lady as an archetype, as the energy of the Moon.

Consider the powers of night, the unconscious, and the deep. Wear lunar jewelry and crystals, and clothing in white, silver, gray, navy, indigo, purple, violet, and/or black.

This is something that can be a lot of fun, especially when done by a group of Lunar Witches.

Cosmic Couture Practice

Here's a fun idea for employing color to enhance your lunar connection.

Buy or make something that you will wear only when working with the Moon and treat it as a holy well to hold the energies of her rays. This could be a full outfit (White? Silver? What catches your fancy?), a special robe or tunic, or something smaller like a scarf, a silver belt, or a silver circlet or crown that you put on each time you perform lunar magic or ritual.

I have a beautiful white cape that I prefer when it's cold outside. I also like to wear a special shawl that I've dedicated to my lunar path. My moonshawl!

Spellcasting with the Moon

To cast a powerful spell or perform a potent ritual, you can coordinate your work with as many correspondences as feel right: You could cast your spell on a day ruled by the planet whose influence is desired, during a phase and/or sign of the Moon and a planetary hour that harmonizes with your need, and use only ingredients and components that are in complete alignment with your intended result.

Here is an example:

Perhaps you would like to cast a spell to reinforce your alliance with the Moon. First, you would look at your lunar calendar and choose the best time for this working: A phase inside the waxing half of the lunation would be good, and if you can time it to coincide with the planetary hour of the Moon, that would be great. It would be even better if this lunar phase were on a Monday and if it were in the sign of Cancer or Taurus. If not Cancer or Taurus, then another other Water sign could be supportive.

You could cover your working altar with a white or silver cloth, place symbols of the Moon upon it, and include offerings such white flowers, a magic mirror, and a chalice of sacred water. Perhaps you would sip upon a lunar tea made of spearmint and rosehips and/or eat a food associated with her energies.

You might burn a compound of mugwort, jasmine, and rose; light a white or silver candle; bless yourself with sea or ocean water; and display upon your altar moonstone or selenite. You could also charge a piece of silver jewelry to later wear to remind you of your objectives.

Maybe you would also invoke a Moon Goddess: perhaps Artemis or Diana, Selene or Luna, or even Hekate.

A final word on lunar correspondences, which is something I've discovered: In a pinch, urgent necessity coupled with resolute focus can override all. Spontaneous magic done with considerable need can be exceptionally mighty.

Chapter 7
Lunar Magical Allies

The Moon Goddess Speaks

I hold in my hands the primordial power of magic, the power of life and death, connecting the entirety of all worlds. Through me, your desires blossom and are attained.

You are invited now into my bountiful garden. Here I will unveil before you the secrets of the holy plants and the sacred stones, their energies woven into all things, bringing both order and discord and all that lies in between.

I am the Holy Healer, and my powers of birth, death, and rebirth extend throughout all places, denied nowhere. I am the Great Lady of Magic, the Sacred Sorceress, the essential vibration of the Universe.

I am Isis.

Journal Inquiries for This Gateway

Who are my magical allies? What is one thing I can do to strengthen my commitment to their realm? How am I using my unique magical gifts?

Affirmations for This Gateway

I align my life with the seasons of growth and decay. I breathe deeply and connect with the natural world. I take comfort in nature.

Plants and stones, like everything else living on Earth, are individuals, each with their own characteristics and capabilities. And as humans are also singular, sovereign beings, we each have different plants and stones that resonate best and most advantageously with our personal frequencies. The plants and stones that harmonize most resonantly with our energies can become our allies, our spiritual guides and helpers, our special companions on this Earth Journey.

You may already have an affinity for and relationship with various plants, stones, crystals, metals, fossils, and other similar precious allies. These beings are part of the natural world, part of organic magic, and part of the Earth herself.

These elder beings may assist you and enhance your work with clearing and healing emotional and physical concerns; your spellwork and magic; the making of essences and potions for ritual and everyday life; and more.

Just like you, the Moon has her own allies that best correspond with her vibrations. Remember that stones, crystals, plants, and metals are of the Earth, and they, too, are impacted by the pull and tides of the Moon above.

You can connect with these plants, stones, crystals, and metals to deepen your relationship with the Moon, and they can also be used as magical correspondences in your lunar spellwork. In this chapter, you'll discover how to foster connection and cultivate relationships with these allies. In following chapters, we'll collaborate with these allyships through activities, projects, and recipes that will enhance your lunar magic and your mooncraft.

Lunar Plant Allies

The Moon has so many plant allies that you could create extensive gardens devoted solely to her. Lunar plant allies can be used to develop and uplevel the energies that you don't have access to in your natal chart. You could use an herb that is fiery, for example, if you are lacking fire in your chart or want to amp up warming or hot energies in your body, magic, and/or life.

In your search for the right plants, one easy guideline is that in addition to those specifically assigned to Luna, all plants silver or white are generally allies of the Moon. Here is a short list of plants which align with her energy.

General Plant Allies

agapanthus (*Agapanthus africanus*)
begonias (Begoniaceae family)
carnations (*Dianthus caryophyllus*)
gardenias (*Gardenia jasminoides*)
mushrooms of so many varieties

orchids (Orchidaceae family)
paperwhite (*Narcissus papyraceus*)
parsnip (*Pastinaca sativa*)
poppies (Papaveraceae family)
yarrow (*Achillea millefolium*)

Moonwort, also known as lunaria and the silver dollar money plant (*Lunaria annua*), which my grandfather would grow; the tropical white morning glory (*Ipomoea lacunosa*); and the moonflower (*Ipomoea alba*), quite obviously, belong to her as well.

Herbal Allies

The following are herbal allies, some common and some not. Have you ever harvested or wild-crafted herbs by moonlight? Try it out and see if the plant's power seems greater than those harvested by sunlight!

angelica (*Angelica archangelica*)
basil (*Ocimum basilicum*)
bay laurel (*Laurus nobilis*)
blue lotus (*Nymphaea nouchali* var. *caerulea*)
blue vervain (*Verbena hastata*)
camphor, also known as kapur and bhimseni Kapoor (*Cinnamomum camphora*)
catnip (*Nepeta cataria*)
clary sage (*Salvia sclarea*)
cannabis (Cannabaceae family)
chickweed (*Stellaria media*)
chrysanthemum (*Chrysanthemum morifolium* or *Chrysanthemum indicum*)
copal (*Protium copal*)
frankincense (*Boswellia sacra*)
ginger (*Zingiber officinale*)
hawthorn (genus *Crataegus*)
hibiscus (genus *Hibiscus*)
jasmine (*Jasminum officinale*)
kava kava (*Piper methysticum*)
lavender (*Lavandula angustifolia* or *Lavandula latifolia*)
lemon balm (*Melissa officinalis*)
meadowsweet (*Filipendula ulmaria*)

milk thistle (*Silybum marianum*)
milky oats (unripe seeds of *Avena sativa*)
motherwort (*Leonurus cardiaca*)
mugwort (*Artemisia vulgaris*)
mullein (*Verbascum thapsus*)
myrrh (*Commiphora myrrha*)
nutmeg (*Myristica fragrans*)
oat straw (*Avena sativa*)
peppermint (*Mentha piperita*)
plantain leaf (*Plantago major* or *Plantago lanceolata*)
poppies of all varieties (Papaveraceae family)
rose (*Rosa* spp.)
rose hips (*Rosa canina L.*)
rosemary (*Rosmarinus officinalis*)
rue (*Ruta graveolens*)
skullcap (*Scutellaria lateriflora*)
spearmint (*Mentha spicata*)
spikenard (*Nardostachys jatamansi*)
star anise (*Illicium verum*)
white sage (*Salvia apiana*)
wormwood (*Artemisia absinthium*)

Baneful Plant Allies

The following is a list of powerful, toxic, and poisonous lunar plant allies that are often used for hexing, cursing, and the like. Please use these allies only with extreme caution.

belladonna (*Atropa belladonna*)
black henbane (*Hyoscyamus niger*)
black nightshade (*Solanum nigrum L.*)
datura (*Datura stramonium*)
mandrake (*Mandragora officinarum*)

Watery Plant Allies

The Moon is also associated with all watery plants and plants of water.

all kelps and seaweeds
cucumbers (*Cucumis sativus*)
squash (genus *Cucurbita*)
lotus (genus *Nelumbo*)
melons (*Cucumis melo*)
reeds (*Phragmites australis*)
succulents (especially aloe and agave)
water lilies (Nymphaeaceae family)
watermelon (*Citrullus lanatus*)

Working with Lunar Herbs

It is my firm belief that plants are just as sentient as other beings—even without a central nervous system. Plants should be afforded the same amount of respect and care as any other being: This means offering them our awareness, appreciation, and gratitude as we harvest, chop, cook, prepare, consume, and/or use them in any way.

Cleansing Your Herbs

When you purchase herbs, it is advisable to energetically cleanse them before using in your medicine or magic. Just like anything else, plants pick up subtle debris from other things, including everyone who has handled them as they made their journey to you.

Here are few ideas to get you started with cleansing:

- Ask the Moon, a Moon Goddess, and/or your Spirit Helpers and Guides to purify them for you.
- Put them in a special container and leave them outdoors overnight during the Waning Moon phase to cleanse and purify or beneath a Full Moon to empower, much as you would crystals and sacred stones.
- Set a purifying crystal amongst them for a twenty-four-hour period. Try using amethyst, obsidian, smoky quartz, or another stone that beckons you.
- If using fresh herbs, give them a quick purifying bath with pristine running water before working with them. Be sure to dry them well! (If I'm in a hurry, I use a salad spinner.)
- Enchant the herbs. Enchanting is a tactic for activating your intentions within the herbs by adding and aligning your personal power with them. You can read more about this in

Scott Cunningham's books *Magical Herbalism: The Secret Craft of the Wise* and *Cunningham's Encyclopedia of Magical Herbs.*

These ideas can all be adapted to cleanse any other objects or ingredients you may use in your mooncraft.

Lunar Gardening

So many ancient (and modern) civilizations timed planting, pruning, and harvesting alongside the lunar phases. Green Witches appreciate the Moon as a helpful partner in the seeding, nurturing, pruning, and harvesting of plants, and it's true that you can time all gardening tasks by the lunar phase and zodiacal signs, maximizing the health and happiness of your beloved plants.

Generally speaking, plant and fertilize when the Moon is waxing; harvest, prune, and compost when the Moon is waning.

While the Sun is traditionally thought of as ruling the plant realm, Luna also has abundant sway over the health of plants. From the passage out of seed into leaf into fruit into harvest, you can work with the signs and phases of the Moon to encourage and support the well-being of your plant friends.

Since the Moon is most luminous and visible at night, one beautiful way to honor her is through creating a night garden, a hallowed place filled with plants that only bloom or are pollinated at night. Doesn't this sound gorgeous and ethereal and ever so witchy?

Whether by day or night, Moon gardens are absolutely stunning. If you have the time, land, and funds, planting one is a fantastic thing to do, and I stand in full support of these endeavors. Gardening by the Moon is an impactful and incredibly personal way to connect with her signs and phases.

That said, it may be far too ambitious for you to plant and attend to an entire lunar garden. If you want to connect with the Moon through the plant empire, you can choose one plant to nurture as part of your lunar devotional practice.

This involves dedicating yourself to nurturing, tending to, and observing this plant for the duration of its life cycle. Perhaps you have enough spaciousness in your life that beginning from a seed makes sense, or perhaps you need to instead adopt an already established plant from the local nursery. There is nothing wrong with that: We are modern Moon Witches, and we are not required to possess the capacity for everything!

If you don't have the time or space to create a full garden, simply choose an indoor or outdoor plant depending on where you live and what is practical for your life. Once you've selected your plant (or seed), tend to it. Nourish it. Fertilize it. Watch it grow. Prune it. If it produces fruit, harvest it and eat it. Share your love and energy with it.

Take notes in your Moon Journal about your new plant friend (future plant ally, perhaps?). How does it interact with you, your environment, and the different lunar phases and signs? How do you connect with it? What does it like and dislike?

In the name of the Moon, and as her hands and heart on Earth, give this plant being the best life it can possibly have.

Your Night Garden

If you do have the space for a garden, try designing a night garden. This requires research and planning, foresight and dreaming, and finally planting.

To Gather

- Your Moon Journal and pen
- Plants
- Gardening implements, such as shovels, hoses, watering cans, soil, and soil amendment as needed for your landscape

To Prepare

- Garden space

The Process

Step 1: First answer these questions: Which plants would be happy in the gardening zone where you live? Which plants are native and would provide the best sustenance for your local pollinators? How much space—and time—do you truly have to devote to your night garden?

Some lovely options for your garden might include night-blooming jasmine (*Cestrum nocturnum*) and tuberose (*Agave amica*)—my favorite scents! Evening primrose (*Oenothera biennis*) and angel's trumpet (*Brugmansia arborea*) also come to mind. Queen of the Night (*Epiphyllum oxypetalum*), with her showy white flowers, gardenias (*Gardenia jasminoides*), Casablanca lilies (*Lilium 'Casa Blanca'*), and mock orange (genus *Philadelphus*) are a few more delightful friends from whom to choose.

Step 2: Once you've discovered the answers to these questions, it's time to dream. In your Moon Journal, draw the shape of the land you are considering for your night garden, and plot it out a bit.

Step 3: Visit your local plant nursery to see what is available, what demands your attention, and what is native to your microclimate. But don't buy anything yet!

Step 4: Muse, dream, and journal again. What plants are you most connected to? What does the Moon want to see in your garden for her? What would you like to position here or there? Estimate how many plants you want to start with and who these plants are.

Step 5: Back to the research. How much space does each plant need when it grows to its fullness; how deep and wide does its roots grow? How much water does it need? How picky and precious is it? Is it potentially hazardous to humans, pets, or wildlife? How much time do you *really* have to take care of your night garden? Get real with yourself! Then head back to the nursery and ask your questions of the staff.

Step 6: Once your questions are answered, it's time to prepare the land for the Plant Beings you will bring home. Get everything ready for them: Clean the land and prepare the beds physically and spiritually; bring in bags of new (organic, pesticide-free) soil; acquire or replace hoses, watering cans, and other implements if necessary.

Step 7: And now it's time to bring home your new friends. Perhaps settle on just one or two to begin, and then go from there!

Step 8: Spend time communicating with each plant being and with the Moon. Do your lunar rituals out amongst them whenever you can. Cultivate your connection to these plant allies and to the Moon. Enjoy your night garden!

Lunar Stone, Crystal, and Metal Allies

Just as the Moon favors certain plants more than others, so does she have an affinity for and relationship with individual stones, crystals, and metals. You can develop closer relationships with these allies by placing them upon your lunar altar, holding them in your hands, and wearing them on your body.

General Allies

All translucent, luminescent, white, and/or glowing stones are historically said to be connected to the Moon.

amethyst
angelite
aquamarine
citrine
howlite
labradorite
lapis lazuli
opal
quartz

Cherished Allies

These allies have a unique link to the Moon through the element of water.

ammonite
coral
mother-of-pearl
pearls
sea salt
shells of all kinds (including crab and lobster shells)

Special Allies

These stones and crystals have a particularly strong connection to the Moon. Fun Fact: Moonstone is said to contain the energies of all the Moons it has lived through!

clear quartz
moonstone (white and rainbow)
selenite

Dark Phase Allies

Need a stone or crystal for your mooncraft during her dark phase? Here are a few that can work.

black moonstone
black tourmaline
jet
obsidian

Power Crystals by the Signs

There are many crystals that complement and correlate with each astrological sign. Here are some suggestions.

Moon in Aries: bloodstone, carnelian, red jasper
Moon in Taurus: green aventurine, rose quartz, selenite
Moon in Gemini: blue lace agate, orange calcite, yellow jasper
Moon in Cancer: moonstone, pearl, pink tourmaline
Moon in Leo: citrine, tiger's eye, sunstone
Moon in Virgo: moss agate, rhodonite, sodalite
Moon in Libra: blue chalcedony, lapis lazuli, white opal
Moon in Scorpio: black obsidian, celestite, malachite
Moon in Sagittarius: fire opal, turquoise, sodalite
Moon in Capricorn: black tourmaline, hematite, smoky quartz
Moon in Aquarius: aquamarine, labradorite, pyrite
Moon in Pisces: amethyst, fluorite, sugalite

Metal Allies

The Moon's metal is, of course, silver, and the attributes this metal carries includes the powers of heightening psychic powers and perception, spiritual cleansing, and purification as well as an ability to assist in stabilizing our emotions and our intuition.

Working with Your Stones

Just as you will do with all herbs, be sure to cleanse and clear your crystals, stones, and metals before using them.

Cleansing and Clearing

Clearing removes psychic dust, cleansing the subject of the energies and vibrations of all others who have come into contact with it before you. You want your magical allies to be attuned to your intrinsic vibrations, not those of others.

It is a good idea to cleanse your crystals not only when you first get them but after they have performed a specific task for you, prior to programming them for an express purpose, or if they feel "off." All stones will clear themselves if left alone over time, but you can also help the process along, especially if you need to work with a particular crystal at a particular time.

Stones that are worked with often will most likely need more frequent clearings than stones that are not—think of this as a reset of their vibrations. If you have done intense emotional work with your crystals, cleanse them directly after the session.

You will most likely be able to *feel* when they need cleansing.

You can adapt the methods shared above regarding cleansing herbs for these Healer Beings or even allow them to "go home" by burying them in the Earth for a period of time—perhaps an entire lunar cycle. Be sure to mark where you buried your stones so you can easily find them again!

Don't use this approach for stones that have iron as part of their composition, such as hematite, or ones that are water soluble, such as selenite. Research your stone before you cleanse.

You can also tuck your sacred stones and crystals in a safe place or in a special container and, as you might with herbal allies, leave them outdoors overnight beneath the Waning Moon to cleanse and purify or under a Full Moon to empower and charge.

Charging

Programming crystals, also termed charging, can be viewed as the opposite of clearing them. Instead of removing energies and vibrations, you are setting the crystals with the vibrations and intentions you want to absorb or manifest. You can charge your crystals in conjunction with different lunar phases for different purposes. As you program crystals with the lunar phases, you may also wish to match this vibrational work with the lunar sign, solar sign, and/or another astrological occurrence.

To change your perspective, hold a translucent crystal up at night and gaze through it at the Moon. Allow her light to fill the stone completely—to fill you completely.

Asteroids of the Moon Goddesses

While not necessary for success, working with the asteroids of the Moon Goddesses is another wonderful form of amplifying your magical pursuits through the inclusion of corresponding energies. There are virtually limitless asteroids in our solar system, both named and unnamed, and I like to use their powers to add another layer to my devotional work and to increase my magical potential.

Note that some of these asteroids move quickly, some considerably more slowly, and some are in retrograde throughout much of their existence.

As all of the following asteroids are named after Lunar Goddesses, they each bear many of the attributes, skills, and strengths of the Moon herself, as well as the more nuanced powers and magics of the particular Goddesses they are named after.

In the list below, I've included the asteroid numbers and some of the domains they preside over as well as a range of the diverse powers, energies, and realms they rule.

Artemis: Asteroid 105
Powers, energies, and realms: goal setting, shapeshifting, strength

Astarte: Asteroid 673
Powers, energies, and realms: fertility, love, sensuality

Diana: Asteroid 78
Powers, energies, and realms: birth, nature, protection

Dziewanna (Devana): Asteroid 471143
Powers, energies, and realms: freedom, growth, wit

Europa: Asteroid 52
Powers, energies, and realms: authority, beauty, power

Freia (Freya): Asteroid 76
Powers, energies, and realms: emotions, healing, magic

Hekate: Asteroid 100
Powers, energies, and realms: crossroads, divination, thresholds

Isis: Asteroid 42
Powers, energies, and realms: knowledge, protection, weather

Parvati: Asteroid 2847
Powers, energies, and realms: dignity, fertility, harmony

Rhiannon: Asteroid 16912
Powers, energies, and realms: dreams, forgiveness, song

Selene: Asteroid 580
Powers, energies, and realms: illumination, time, shadows

Tara: Asteroid 5863
Powers, energies, and realms: compassion, healing, liberation

Working with Asteroid Allies

Let it be known that I am not an astrologer, and the system I use to work with the Moon Goddess asteroids is quite simple and intuitive. You need not have any real grasp of astrology to try my methods. And if you do try them out, please let me know! I'd love to hear about how it goes for you, Moon Sibling.

If I hear a calling or require an extra *push* to ensure my magic manifests, I will do one of two things:

If I have time to plan my spellwork or ritual, I will choose a Moon Goddess with a named asteroid to help focus and magnify my work and then look to see what sign that asteroid is in to fine-tune my working (or look ahead at the transits to see when that asteroid might be in a sign that could be helpful).

If my spellwork or ritual needs to be done as soon as possible, as in *right now*, I begin by contemplating which astrological sign will best support my working and then look to see where the Moon Goddess asteroids are transiting, selecting one that is in my chosen sign.

When using either of these methods, I will generally cast a formal circle and invoke the Moon Goddess I have chosen as my central locus, incorporating correspondences and offerings for her on my working altar.

Your Natal Moon Goddess Asteroids

To discern where the Moon Goddess asteroids appear in your own natal chart, go to astro .com (or your preferred astrology site) and enter your birth time and place. Select then the option for creating an extended natal chart. In the "additional objects" section, input one or more of the Moon Goddess asteroids (by name or by number) from the list provided above. Run your chart now, and then print it out.

Look carefully at your chart to see where these Moon Goddesses appear, paying especial attention to their distance from—or closeness to—not only your natal Moon but your Sun, your Lunar Nodes, and all of the other planets that compose that snapshot the Multiverse created at the moment of your entry into this lifetime.

Spend time in meditation, journeying, and journaling with this enhanced version of your natal chart and then take these Moon Goddesses with you into ritual. Ask questions about the information and wisdom they hold for you. Ask why they dwell in a particular house or sign. Ask how they can help you navigate your everyday life and how they can help you with your magic and your connection with the Moon herself. Then listen with your whole being, and heed their teachings.

Chapter 8
Crafting by the Moon

The Moon Goddess Speaks

Ancient Creatrix am I, Lady of the Crescent Moon. I am here now to remind you of your own abundant creativity, your ability to think and then to turn those thoughts into form using your inventive mind and your generous heart. I can guide your hand in weaving beauty, in making precious things. I can heighten and brighten your expressivity, filling you with the impulse to bring more splendor into the world.

Just as the Moon grows, so now does your inspiration, your powers of vision, imagination, and ingenuity. Glide fearlessly and without pause upon the wings of your inner sight and innovate from there. Ride courageously with me upon my Sacred Lion across bright, brilliant land as we hunt the most wild and clever of insights.

Put your joyful hands to work now, all for the glory of the Moon. What makes your soul sing, beloved one?

I am Tanit.

Journal Inquiries for This Gateway

How can I better honor my innate creativity? What inspires me most? In which lunar phase do I feel most in flow with my ability to create?

Affirmations for This Gateway

I am a creative being. Expressing my creativity brings healing to the world. I cocreate with the cadences of the Moon.

In this chapter, I'll present some ideas for deepening your lunar partnership through crafts and creativity. I encourage you to sample all of these projects, identifying the ones with which you have the most rapport. They are great to play with alone or inside a coven, circle, or small group of friends. Enjoy an afternoon or evening in community sharing supplies, conversation, and Moon-inspired snacks and see what magic results.

Moon Medicine Basket

First, it is helpful to have a central location for all of your lunar projects and Sacreds. I keep mine in what I like to call my moon medicine basket. After much experimentation, I settled upon a very large handmade vessel woven by women in Ghana for my moon medicine basket. This basket is made of veta vera straw and is easily portable. As it is not rigid, but somewhat bendable, it's more like a round bag than a basket. In Ghana, it is used for marketing.

This basket is about twenty inches wide and just as tall with a fabric-wrapped handle for toting around. It is big enough to hold my drum, a rattle, my moonshawl, and other lunar objects. I love the ability to keep some of my moon magic portable and ready to go with me whenever I am headed out on the road.

Scout around on the internet or in a physical store, such as a crafting, import, or home goods shop, to see what type of vessel you might like to use as a moon medicine basket.

Think about the items you would like to store in this repository and how much room they will take up, then look for something that can contain all of those items and more over time. If you decide to go with a basket from Africa (or from any Indigenous source) like I did, please do your research and purchase it from a company that is part of the Fair Trade Federation, or from the artist themselves. Once you've obtained your basket, you will consecrate and dedicate it as a sacred object that supports you as a Moon Witch.

Consecrating, Activating, and Empowering Ritual

Consecration, activation, and empowerment is something you should do with every magical creation you make or Sacred you purchase. Going forward, use the following ritual for everything that you will place into service for your Lunar Witchcraft practice, from your moon medicine basket, lunar talismans, bath and body products, and magical tools to your lunar potions, libations, foods, and more.

Activated and empowered items tend to work better, and when my life is full, I've found it best to have things ready to go, especially that which supports my practice and supports my self-care. If something is already prepared, I'm far more apt to carve out the time to use it.

This process begins after your Sacred is brought home from the store or your creation is bottled, jarred, or otherwise complete. Before beginning, note the phase and astrological sign the Moon is in.

To Gather

- Your sacred item or creation

To Prepare

- A quiet space where you will not be disturbed

The Process

Step 1: Settle with your Sacred or creation in a quiet, private place.

Step 2: Hold your Sacred or completed item in your hands. Find your breath and deepen your connection with the Earth and Moon. Breathe here for a moment, inviting lunar and Earth energies to meet and become one within you.

Step 3: Connect with the essential nature of your Sacred or creation. Discern if there are any energies within it that do not support your intention. If you notice any, kindly ask them to leave or transform into vibrations that support your purpose.

Step 4: Now visualize yourself using your Sacred or creation. Feel the energies you want to have present within it and the energies you want to feel present within yourself when you use it. Utilizing your breath, amplify these sensations, feeling the magnitude of your purpose and your connection with the Moon.

Step 5: Build your lunar power-within as you continue to tune into your breath and your connection with the Moon. Now recall the phase Luna is in and the astrological sign, too. Bring all of this energy into your hands, noticing it tingling in your fingers.

Step 6: Visualize—see-sense-feel—these energies streaming easily into your Sacred or creation, possibly even envisioning the energies as rays of prismatic, silvery, or white light. You could also use another color that calls to you. Perhaps a color that echoes the phase or zodiacal sign elects to be present. Whatever arises for you, whether a color or not, is correct and perfect.

Step 7: In a strong voice, state your intention and *send* that energy, the vibration of your words, into your Sacred or creation.

Step 8: Now feel the Earth beneath you and the Moon above and take in one big breath. Hold it for a moment. See if you can take in a little bit more air. Now *send* that breath of Earth and Moon into your Sacred or creation. Send it *all* on your exhalation!

Step 9: When you have sent all of this energy into your Sacred or creation, set it aside and shake your hands vigorously to stop the current, freeing any extra energies into the Earth.

Step 10: Relax now, body, mind, heart, and spirit. Your Sacred or creation is consecrated, activated, and empowered; it is ready to be used, and it will stay this way unless you deactivate it. Blessed be!

Your Moonbox

A moonbox is a devotional implement of your own making; it is used every day to percolate dreams and let go of worries. I first heard about the concept of goddess boxes from GrannyMoon at the Goddess School a decade or more ago, and I adapted this learning into a practice that is used to increase lunar connection.

Through experience, I have learned that interacting with my moonbox is a lovely strategy for letting go of things that are out of my sphere of control and releasing everyday anxiety brought on by modern life. My moonbox lives on my lunar altar, so I remember that it is available for me whenever I have need of it.

Your Moonbox

Before beginning, recognize that this undertaking is not at all about being an artist or making fine art. It is about inspiring and engaging your Inner Lunar Witch, setting you up for future success. You are the only one who needs to be pleased by this project, so no self-judgment is allowed!

To Gather

- A durable round box or other container large enough to hold slips of paper and pocket-sized items yet small enough to secret away if the need arises. It should have a lid. Note

that this container can be composed of any material. If you can't find a round box, then a jar, coffee can, or even a plastic yogurt container will suffice.
- Things with which to decorate your container. Perhaps you want to paint it or draw on it with markers; affix pretty fabric to the inside or exterior; glue on ribbons, sequins, glitter, twigs, or shells; and/or add images of the Moon or a Moon Goddess.
- Something special to you—a stone or crystal, a dried flower, a personal trinket or keepsake—that will be dedicated to and kept inside the container.
- Small slips of paper
- A pen
- Your Moon Journal

The Process

Step 1: Decorate your container with the materials of your choosing.

Step 2: When your container is finished, inscribe these words on the inside of the lid or upon a piece of paper to place inside it, reading them aloud when you are done writing:

> *This is my moonbox. Whatever I place inside of this sacred vessel, I yield to the Moon Goddess. Here, I offer her my dreams and my desires, as well as my fears and my worries. When I close the lid, I know that what I have placed inside has been surrendered into her loving and competent hands. I will listen to her wisdom, trusting in myself and in my connection to All That Is Holy.*

Step 3: Consecrate, activate, and empower your moonbox using the process illustrated in the previous ritual, and then bless it using your own heartfelt words and/or gestures. Next, mindfully place your special item inside. Leave the slips of paper and pen near the box.

Step 4: Whenever something is heavy on your mind or in your heart, write it on one of the slips of paper and then add it to your moonbox. This could be a hope you have, a dream, a worry, an idea, or even a question. Use a different slip of paper for each notion. Remember to stay open to your own inner lunar wisdom and the hand of the Moon Goddess in your life.

Step 5: Within the Waning Crescent Moon phase—ideally during the Dark Moon—take out your papers and read them aloud. In your Moon Journal, note what has changed for you. Burn, bury, or compost the sentiments that you are ready to release, and return those that need more attention to your moonbox.

Moon Magic Candles

Working with candles is simple and enjoyable: Charging, blessing, dressing, or decorating candles to support your lunar practice is a satisfying—and incredibly easy—way to connect with the Moon. You can use whatever type of candles you prefer for your devotional work or magic: chime candles, tea lights, votives, tapers, pillar candles, jar candles, novenas, even birthday candles. Any candle you might use for moon magic or as a holy offering can be charged and blessed with the energies of our Lunar Lady.

Charging

Charging candles is simple. First, consider what they will be used for. You can charge candles under the Moon with the energy of a particular phase, a particular astrological sign or Element of Life, a particular frequency, or a specific occasion such as an eclipse, Blue Moon, Black Moon, Supermoon, Micromoon, and so on.

I like to charge sets of candles for the same purpose and reserve them for future use.

To charge your candles, you can set them outside to collect the desired lunar vibrations, perhaps even leaving them outside overnight to absorb more of the energy of the happening. If a lunar event will end before morning, bring the candles back inside before going to bed or set your alarm and go out to retrieve them.

If you live somewhere hot, be mindful of the outdoor temperature; if your candles sit out in the Sun, the wax could melt. Put them in a place that is as shady and cool as possible. I have heard from a Desert Witch who puts their candles outside on ice if it's going to be particularly warm!

Blessing

You can also bless your candles. Candle blessing can be done at any time: during a particular lunar phase, sign, or event (as in charging) or immediately before using them for ritual or spellwork.

Simply hold your candle up to the Moon and say something like, *Radiant Moon (or Mysterious Moon), please bless this tool of sacred fire with your gleaming (or veiled) brilliance.*

Or you can bless the candle or candles using improvised words that come from your heart in the moment. For the most part, it is my highest preference to do it in this manner, as it feels both current and organic, reminding me of my belonging in this life and my belonging as a Moon Witch.

Dressing

Candles are dressed to give them extra energy to hold and burn toward your intentions, to magnify your magic and your rituals.

Dressing candles is something that is most often done right before they are used for a particular purpose, although this can certainly be done in advance, especially when you want to "snapshot" a particular moment and store it for later use.

Unlike charging candles in advance of even knowing why you might use them in the future, though, when you dress a candle, you should already have a particular purpose and reason for its use in mind. For example: If you are dressing a candle for love, clarify the type of love you are seeking and contemplate that as you work.

Of course, if your plans change when you sit down to use your dressed candle in magic or ritual because you have another idea, go with it. We are always receiving new information, and oftentimes that new information is inspired information.

Dressing magical candles for moonwork is done by taking the energies that are present in the moment, connecting with them, and allowing them to flow through your body and into the candle, treating the candle as the magical tool it is—one whose purpose is to direct energy in the ways you desire toward your goals.

Whenever I dress a candle, it reminds me of how I might carefully dress my body for a particular event. When dressing with intention, I take time to choose each element I will wear, matching my outfit to the energetics of what I hope to experience. I also love to make secret magical commentary with my clothing, shoes, jewelry, and even the oils I anoint myself with. Even my undergarments and socks are generally chosen with purpose.

Dressing Uncontained Candles

Here is a means of dressing uncontained candles (such as chime, votive, pillar, and birthday). One warning: When burning dressed chime candles—votives, birthday candles, or any other candle that is not fully contained in a glass jar—be even more mindful than usual regarding fire safety! Sometimes herbs burn a bit wildly. Also, if you are creating your own oil, employ a less flammable oil as your base, such as olive oil, coconut oil, corn oil, soybean oil, or canola oil.

To Gather

- Procure or create a magical oil (see chapter 9)
- At least one dried herb that supports your magical purpose
- A mortar and pestle (if your herbs are in large pieces or are dried seeds, bark, or root)
- A plate or shallow dish that is longer than your candle is tall

The Process

Step 1: Ground, center, and open the channel. Connect with the Moon. Feel into her energies in whatever phase and sign she currently resides.

Step 2: Cleanse and clear your candle of all energies that are not yours and/or you do not want present. You can use water, salt, sound, burning herbs (such as cedar, pine, or lavender), and so on. If your magical oil and/or herbs haven't been cleansed and cleared yet, take care of this now, too.

Step 3: If your herbs are in large pieces, use your mortar and pestle to grind them into smaller bits. Focus on your intention while doing so! Transfer these small pieces to the plate or shallow dish when done.

Step 4: Rub your candle with your magical oil as you continue to hold your intention firmly in mind and heart. Permit the energies of your completed intention to seep out of your hands and into the wax. When anointing candles in this way, use a downward motion (from wick to base) when your intention is to bring things into manifestation (from Moon to Earth). Use an upward motion (from base to wick) when your intention is to release, banish, or let go of something (from Earth to Moon).

Step 5: Roll your candle in the plate or dish of herbs, continuing to hold your focus on your intention and send helpful energy toward your goal. You don't need to cover the whole candle with the herbs! Make sure there is still plenty of wax visible so your candle burns properly. Your candle is now dressed and ready for magic.

Alternatively

You can also dress candles simply by forgoing the herbs and anointing them with only a magical oil (or diluted essential oil) or moonwater (see chapter 10, "Lunar Potions").

Decorating Contained Candles

When dressing novena candles, sometimes called jar candles, I typically anoint only the interior of the glass and the wick. I then add herbs and sometimes glitter or even small curios depending upon my purpose. Since novena candles burn for many days, I like to take my creativity a step further and decorate them when preparing them for long-term moonwork.

If burned continually, novena candles can be used for nine-day spells (and sometimes even longer). Remember: Do not leave lit candles unattended, even if they are contained in glass! I knew a Priestess whose home burned because she thought it would be safe to leave a candle alight in the bathtub while she ran errands.

Here are some occasions you may wish to burn this type of moon candle:

- Once a week as part of your Moon Day devotions or specific lunar spellwork that you do only on Mondays.
- A few days a month when the Moon is transiting a certain astrological sign (for increase or decrease).
- Once per month during a certain lunar phase (depending upon your working).
- Once a year on the occasion of your birthmoon.
- Whenever you need lunar love and connection.

When the wax is gone, you don't have to recycle the glass right away. Buy a wax refill for the glass holder or simply use a tealight (wax or LED) to keep the magic going.

To Gather

- A novena (or other glass jar candle)
- Rubbing alcohol and paper towels
- A paper image of the Moon that speaks to your heart. (Find, draw, or otherwise create this; I like to play around with an online graphic design program.)
- Mod Podge or another gel medium
- Moon oil (bought or homemade; see chapter 9)
- Decorative items such as biodegradable glitter, sequins, ribbons, pipe cleaners, and/or additional images
- Magical items such as dried herbs and/or small (nonflammable!) curios

The Process

Step 1: Use a paper towel soaked with rubbing alcohol to clean away any factory goo from the exterior glass of your candle.

Step 2: Spiritually cleanse and clear your candle and all other objects of all energies that are not yours or you do not want present, however you wish (with sound, salt, herbs, blessed water, and so on).

Step 3: Glue the image of the Moon (and any other images you want) to the glass of the candle using Mod Podge or another gel medium.

Step 4: Decorate the jar in any other way you feel called.

Step 5: Add your herbs and/or nonflammable curios into the jar.

Step 6: Let your candle dry completely.

Step 7: Anoint your candle with moon oil, charging it and blessing it in the name of the Moon Mother and her wisdom. Your candle is now dressed and ready for magic.

Moon Mandalas

The Moon is a sphere that shows herself to us here on Earth as a circle, and circles represent wholeness, unity, and flow. This shape can help us to focus on our innermost Self and our ingrained truths all whilst connecting us to something bigger, greater, and far more vast than we ourselves are. Found throughout the natural world—as the Moon, Sun, Earth, and all the planets; in fruits and plants; in eggs and cells; and much, much more—circles remind us of the connection between all things.

Moon Mandala Project

Moon mandalas are round representations of the Moon herself and are also carriers of the wisdom she contains. In this work, you will create and meditate with one. Meditating with this esoteric device can help you to come into contact with yourself and the Moon.

To Gather

- Collect some markers or colored pencils in shades you like and then look around on the internet and find a round mandala to print out and color in. Or if you prefer a somatic experience, you can instead go out into nature and create a mandala there—of sand, chalk, flower petals, leaves, and/or other naturally found items.

The Process

Step 1: Color in or build your moon mandala from the materials you gathered.

Step 2: As you create the mandala, let the colors and the shapes draw you inward, becoming a journey into your inner realm as you observe the development of the colors and shapes.

Step 3: Once you have built or colored in your moon mandala, begin the meditation by taking in the entire mandala, without moving your eyes. See it as one complete whole.

Step 4: Now move your attention to the center of the mandala. Spend some moments here, slowing your breath and relaxing your whole body, bit by bit, moving down from the top of your head—your crown chakra—all the way to your root chakra and then down your legs to the bottom of your feet. Don't forget to relax your shoulders, arms, and hands, too.

Step 5: Allow the mandala to draw you further in, permitting your consciousness to focus upon whatever it is naturally called toward. It may seem as if the mandala is moving, shifting, and changing right before your eyes.

Don't push or force anything here. Your eyes should not strain to see anything in particular, and you should feel comfortable, your breath gentle and easy as it glides in and out of your body. If you notice any tension in your eyes or any other part of your body, stop and relax, using your breath to gently send away anything that is not of the here and now.

Step 6: Next, extend your field of vision whilst holding your eyes and head as stationary as is pleasantly possible. Continue to expand your field of vision as far as you possibly can without force or struggle. Allow yourself to become aware of whatever information you are meant to become aware of in the here and now.

Step 7: When you are complete with your process, begin to slowly draw your vision back toward the center of the mandala, releasing your larger field of vision.

Step 8: Now close your eyes and see-sense-feel it in your mind's eye (in addition to seeing, sensing, or feeling, you might also taste or smell) and then journey back out into shared reality, carrying with you this information and wisdom you were not even aware you were holding.

If this practice spoke to you, schedule another session with it on your lunar calendar now.

Lunar Talismans

Lunar talismans are meant to increase lunar alliance, lunar powers, and lunar good fortune. They can be worn on the body, often in the form of necklaces, bracelets, or rings; carried in pockets, wallets, and purses; hung in homes, cars, and places of work; buried at the corners of property; and more.

These talismans are created to hold and contain the energies of the Moon from a certain phase and/or sign.

Here is one idea to play with that falls within this broad category. It is a project that I began in 2015, and it continues to this day. Anyone who would like to join in is warmly invited to work this collaborative practice and hold this cooperative vision.

Seeds of Renewal Ritual

The Seeds of Renewal Ritual originated as a group practice done with the purpose of seeding the Earth with lunar magic for the benefit of ourselves and all beings—the magic of compassion and healing, of productive transformation, and of the reflective power of the Moon.

Additionally, Lunar Seeds of Renewal are meant to be a reminder of who we truly are, incorporating the understanding that we are constantly connected to That Which Is Greater. No matter what is happening in our human lives, we still hold the infinity and eternity of the One within us, and that can never be taken away.

To participate in this ongoing group ceremony, you will need at least two stones whose energies support the collective intention of this magic. Moonstone is an obvious favorite, yet other lunar stones also work well—clear quartz, obsidian, tourmaline, citrine, amethyst. I generally stay away from selenite, though, as it is rather soluble in water and will dissolve after a time. That said, there are definite pros to choosing a stone that will dissolve over time because you can leave it in a place where it will slowly release the energy it is holding back into the Earth or a body of water in a physical way.

To Gather

- One or more pairs of stones (e.g., two or four or six or even up to twelve or fourteen stones in total can work). Stones about the size of marbles or even smaller are perfect because they readily fit into closed hands. They do not need to be round. I prefer to work this magic batch-style, programming multiple sets of crystals at a time. (Note that for each pair, you will keep one stone and release the other.)
- A drawstring or other bag, small basket, or something similar in which to keep your stones throughout the process. I use a ritually painted dish that is kept solely for this purpose.

To Prepare

This ritual takes three lunations to complete, and this moonwork should only be done during the waxing half of each of the three lunations. You will program your crystals, which you can envision as the opposite of clearing them. Instead of removing energies and vibrations, you are setting the crystals with the vibrations and intentions you want to manifest.

Before beginning, mark your calendar with the three dates over the next three lunations upon which you will perform this ceremony. Match your work with the vibrations of a supportive lunar phase and/or astrological sign. Keep these dates holy, for you are doing holy work!

The Process: First Programming

Step 1: Ground, center, and open the channel, and then connect with the Moon or Moon Goddess. Create your sacred space and enter Ritual Mind in the manner you prefer, perhaps even casting a formal circle if it feels correct to do so.

Step 2: Sit comfortably, holding the stones in your hands, observing their energy. Ask if they have any messages for you. Listen to them with all of your senses, identifying what information they hold for you on this day, if any.

Step 3: Tell the stones that you are a Lunar Witch and you would like to program them to become Lunar Seeds of Renewal. Ask them if they are willing to undergo this transformation. If not, that is okay. Thank these stones and then release them to the work they are meant to do. End your ritual and try again with different stones at another time.

Step 4: If the stones are willing, offer them your gratitude. Through your hands and from your heart, send them the vibrations of our collective intention however it feels in your body, however you see it through your unique lens of viewing life. Our collective intention is: *Seeding the Earth with our lunar magic for the benefit of ourselves and all beings—the magic of compassion and healing, of productive transformation, and of the reflective power of the Moon.*

Step 5: When you are complete with this process, place the stones gently in the vessel you've chosen for them and then close down the energies and exit your ritual space.

Step 6: Interact with the stones as often as you can throughout the lunation. You may choose to keep them on your lunar altar and give them some love there every day. Or perhaps you will prefer to keep them with you. Some practitioners carry the stones with them each day in a pouch, purse, or even their pocket. Whatever feels respectful, connective, and correct to you is what you should do.

The Process: Second Programming

Step 1: After a lunar cycle has passed, bring your stones into ritual again. Ground, center, and open the channel, then connect with the Moon or Moon Goddess. Once again, create sacred space and enter ritual in the way you prefer.

Step 2: Sit comfortably holding your stones, empty your mind, and move into meditative space. Find your breath and inhale slowly, connecting as deeply as possible with the energies of the Earth below and the Moon above. Notice the resonance between you and the stones, and between the stones, which are creatures of Earth, and the Moon above, with whom they correspond magically.

Step 3: Once you and your stones have entered a calm, peaceful state, resonating with one another, hold the crystals in your open hands and gaze into them. Remain grounded and centered, your mind clear and your body as relaxed as possible.

Step 4: As you look into your stones, visualize our collective intention again, imagining that you can see it happening in front of you, inside the stones. As vibrantly as possible *see* and *sense* and *feel* our collective intention already manifest.

Step 5: Begin building energy in your body. Channel it up from the Earth and down from the Moon. Envision it coalescing inside of you.

Step 6: Now, holding the stones in your dominant hand (and positioning your nondominant hand atop it if necessary to keep the stones in place), see-sense-feel our collective intention, then release the energy you built up in your body out through your fingers and into the stones. Remember that this is the energy you are channeling from the Earth and Moon, and it is directed by your personal power. It does *not* originate in your body.

Step 7: Move this energy easily and effortlessly through your body and into the stones. See-sense-feel the power flowing through your body and out your dominant hand into the stones.

Step 8: Now charge the stones with the energy of our collective intention. When you *know* that the stones are vibrating with your energies and our intention, this part of the charging is complete.

Step 9: Create a precise phrase to describe the nature of the programming, such as "These Lunar Seeds of Renewal support the magic of compassion and healing, of productive transformation, and of the reflective power of the Moon." Speak it softly.

Step 10: Move the stones into your nondominant hand (covering it with your dominant hand if necessary) and relax. Find your breath again; find your connection with the Earth and Moon. Breathe slowly and steadily and ask for guidance, protection, and assistance from the Moon and/or Moon Goddess in this programming process. Open your consciousness to the natural flow that exists between your Inner Self, the Moon (and/or Moon Goddess), and the energies of the Multiverse.

Step 11: In a whisper or low voice, repeat your new phrase twenty to thirty times aloud into your stones while visualizing, sensing, and feeling the desired effect of our collective intention. Open yourself to higher assistance. As you repeat your phrase to your stones, you are building an energy field that matches our collective mission.

Step 12: Holding a conscious awareness of the energy field you've created with your words, hold your stones to your third eye, feeling a connection with them and our collective intention.

Step 13: Now conduct the energy you've raised into the crystals, allowing the program you created to be transferred into the stones. Trust your Inner Moon Witch regarding when this is complete, generally about thirty to sixty seconds.

Step 14: Seal our collective intention into the stones by visualizing light of whatever color feels right surrounding the stones, then witness that light radiating from within them in turn.

Step 15: Offer gratitude for all that has been brought to you, knowing it is already manifest. Repeat the thank you aloud three times. This can be quite simple; in fact, just stating "Thank you. Thank you. Thank you." from your heart is perfectly fine. Or you may wish to instead say something like "Thank you, Moon, for the beauty, magic, and healing you bring to my life." Follow the promptings of your heart.

Step 16: Release your ritual space when you are ready.

Step 17: Know that your stones will work with you, even when you are not focusing on them, helping make our collective intention become reality. Once again, spend time with the stones as often as you can throughout the lunation. Keep them on your lunar altar or carry them with you.

The Process: Third and Final Programming

Step 1: Prepare yourself and enter ritual space as for the past two programmings.

Step 2: Sit or lie comfortably with your stones in hand. Ground through your feet, sending roots down to grow deeply into the Earth. Allow your spine to lengthen as your crown opens to the Moon above. Breathe in and out slowly and fully. There is no rush.

Step 3: With (at least) one stone in each hand, raise your arms over your head, then place your palms flat against each other in a prayer position. Relax your shoulders. With your hands still in the prayer position, gently and slowly lower your arms to a comfortable place in front of your third eye.

Step 4: See-sense-feel your Lunar Witch power-within. See-sense-feel the blood of the Moon, of the Moon Goddess, flowing through your veins. This power-within you is not to be feared; it is your strength, your potential, your courage, your birthright. You can defend yourself with your strength if need be, and yet you can also use your strength for love, for caring, for changing the world. See-sense-feel inside of you the strength that is your Lunar Witch power-within.

Step 5: Now perceive the Moon's (and/or Moon Goddess's) presence in your life and open yourself up to these luminous energies. Listen for anything she wants to share with you or say to you. Offer her your gratitude.

Step 6: Read these words aloud, visualizing their vibrations going into your stones:

Beneath the loving Moon lies the Earth
She rests peacefully under this luminous power
The Earth herself, filled with strength
Overflowing with her own love
She offers her strength to all of the beings upon her splendorous lands
The Moon, ever-reflective, stores the gifts of healing, magic, and compassion
And she offers them back to us on Earth
Here is a place of both power and rest
One of protection and glory
Of learning and laughter
Of the stretching down and up
Of the truth of all things
May all beings be blessed
So mote it be.

Step 7: Sit with your stones for a few more moments, feeling your connection with them, feeling their connection with you, feeling your connection with the Moon, feeling their connection with the Moon. Know that you are in the flow of life. Know that serendipitous and synchronous experiences are happening for you every day—you are always in the right place at the right time doing the right thing. You are the embodiment of grand and vast creativity. You have so many things to create and share. Know and accept the value of what you—only you—have to bestow upon the world. See your individuality and your uniqueness as a huge gift that must be shared. Grow excited about life and all it has to offer. Your willingness to try new things, to go new places, to think new thoughts, expands. Life is a grand, awesome adventure for you.

If you desire them, rushes of excitement, passion, belonging, transformation, love, flow, and energy are all yours. You have a larger purpose in life than you ever knew before. You are here for a special and singular reason. Whatever your passion is becomes your legacy, and you are capable of dedicating and devoting yourself to this legacy.

You are part of the Moon, and you also carry the Moon within you—Within and Without. This is a sacred paradox and a Holy Mystery. Feel now that connection with all beings on this planet because they are all also part of the One.

Step 8: Now bless your stones and give them gratitude. Breathe with them. When you are ready, come back to this place and time. It is done, done, done!

Completion

For every two stones programmed, keep one and release the other somewhere—entrust it into the care of a willing person, a body of water, a holy place, or even into the Earth herself, whatever feels right to you.

Remember that there is no wrong way to program crystals or to work with them.

The programming you've done throughout this ceremony will stay active indefinitely unless you cancel it. From time to time, you might wish to refresh the intention by following the steps you just used or by doing something similar.

Thank you for being part of this holy work. Blessed be!

CHAPTER 9
Lunar Herbalism

The Moon Goddess Speaks

Many are my names, and many are my powers. Above all, though, I am the Lady of the Moon and the Sphere of the Green. All plants are my dear friends, and I will introduce you to them, if you sincerely wish to fathom their prescient, perceptive, beatific spirits.

Whose very nature draws you closer, stirring within you a yearning to better understand their essence? Is there a plant you long to meet, yet you feel too shy or apprehensive to approach? Who is lovingly whispering to your Moon Witch heart? If you are pure and genuine in your desire, I will help to foster these connections between the worlds for you, clearing the pathway of possibility.

You have greater instinctual power and ability within you than you have ever permitted yourself to know. I invite you to confidently enter this beautiful vortex with me and see.

I am Devana.

Journal Inquiries for This Gateway

How can I bring more meaning and closeness to my partnerships with my green allies? Where and why am I hiding my inner wildness? How can I establish space for my instinctual, intuitive Primal Self to become more present in my magical practice and in my life?

Affirmations for This Gateway

I glide through my world in joyful communion with the Green Realm. I accept my innate, untamed Self, and I allow space for full and confident expression. I find ways to honor and connect with my plant allies every day.

Magical herbalism is the art of working with the natural power and energies of plants, herbs, and flowers to bring about change, healing, inspiration, and wisdom through ritual, spellwork, divination, bathing, cooking, and other magical practices. As I shared in chapter 7, the Moon has relationships with certain plants, and you can cultivate your own relationships with these plants to enhance your work. Herbalism is integral to our Moon Witch magic.

From a potion brewed to bring on visions while scrying, to a spell bag made to manifest the biggest dreams, to a powdered incense burned in honor of a specific Lunar Goddess, to an oil used in a ceremonial bath or shower, we partner with our allied plants in some way in almost all of our spellcasting and rituals. In this chapter, we'll dive into the work itself.

Each plant has its own particular purpose, medicine, and magical correspondences. Herbal magic is sympathetic magic: like attracts like. Each plant emits its own unique vibrations, which can be used to draw what we desire closer to us or to send that which we don't away. When herbs are properly selected, they can assist us in realizing our goals.

Plants subconsciously remind us of, and join us to, the constantly changing Moon and the seasons, orienting us within the eternal cycle of birth, death, and rebirth. They are our teachers and guides. When we grow our own, we can follow along with them through the seasons and their life cycles, propagating and deepening these special relationships.

Herbal magic is practical magic. It requires no perfect ceremony, no complicated personal preparation, and, beyond gathering the necessary supplies, not much time. Herbal magic is multiversal, operating no matter the time, language, tradition, religion, and/or culture.

The herbs you choose for your mooncraft should transmit the vibrations that match your intent, whatever that may be. For example, you may use rose (*Rosa* spp.) for love, but you would probably employ something different to draw money; you may wish to use basil (*Ocimum basilicum*) for prosperity but not for healing; the energies of hops (*Humulus lupulus*) are appropriate for healing and sleep but not necessarily for protection or luck; and so on. This is why it is so necessary to research, experiment with, and develop your own relationship with the plants to learn their distinct powers and energies and how they interact with yours.

Plants partner with us in so many ways. From magic to food to medicine, there is a plant that can help us. From the mundane to the magical, they offer an astounding array of possibilities, countless applications and preparations to discover. Transforming earth, water, and sunlight, plants are our allies and our friends, sharing their life energies with us. We should always approach them with gratitude, reverence, and respect.

There are so many ways we can connect our body with the cycles and energies of the Moon. In this chapter, I'll share somatic practices as well as oil- and herb-based creations you can make to enhance your everyday affinity with Luna, increasing your magical bond with her.

Moon Magic Oils

Scents inspire us, awaken us, relax us, and even enchant us. And, because the sense of smell is tied to our emotional bodies as well as our physical ones, scents are also nostalgic: evocative aromas reminding us of certain events, feelings, and times in our lives, jogging memories and emotions—joyous, sad, and otherwise—both our own and those of the collective unconscious.[35] Plant fragrances have been used since antiquity to scent the body and home, and for ritual, magic, and offerings.

The power of moon magic oils reaches us through their vibrations, energies, and especially their scents. Scents stimulate and trigger different parts of our brains, opening and energizing us as we set about manifesting our desires. Further, each phase and sign of the Moon can also be tethered to a particular oil or oils.

You can use these oils in a number of ways. You could:

- Anoint your lunar ritual and moonspell candles
- Add to sacred waters
- Use in your lunar ritual baths or showers
- Bless yourself and others
- Incorporate into your moon charms, talismans, spell bags, and/or amulets
- Combine with your moon incense blends before burning on charcoal or shaping into cones
- Consecrate and/or cleanse your moon crystals and your divinatory and ritual tools

Essential oils (e.o.) are said to be the *blood* of a plant, holding its life force, carrying the very essence of that plant's life. They are produced through a distillation process utilizing a still and sometimes thousands upon thousands of pounds of plant matter. As an example: It takes about two hundred and fifty pounds of lavender to yield just one pound of lavender essential oil![36]

When purchasing essential oils, it is necessary to buy the real thing, not a synthetic or perfume substitute. Look for essential oils that are made from organically grown or wildcrafted plants and are sold in amber or cobalt glass bottles. Prices vary widely and are ordinarily dependent upon the availability and yield of the plant used.

Most essential oils are extremely irritating to the skin and/or have contraindications during pregnancy and lactation; for animal companions, children, and the elderly; in certain chronic and acute illnesses; and when exposed to sunlight. Always do your research before using any oil. Safety is primary; please observe all cautions and warnings. Be mindful when working with any part of the plants; they are powerful beings.

35. McDonough, "The Connections Between Smell, Memory, and Health."
36. "11 Essential Oils."

Virtually all essential oils *must* be diluted before topical use.

Blended magical oils typically consist of a combination of essential oils and a high-quality carrier oil, such as apricot seed oil, olive oil, grapeseed oil, jojoba oil, or another oil, and occasionally include other objects such as dried plants, resins, crystals, stones, metals, curios, glitter, and so on.

Designing and blending your own magical oils to connect with the Moon is both easy and fun.

Moon Magic Oils

To develop your blended moon magic oil, first consider your intention and then choose essential oils with matching frequencies. You can make a big batch in a "mother" bottle and decant later into smaller bottles, or you can simply make a smaller bottle each time. Be sure to keep comprehensive records so you can replicate your success and build upon those things that weren't as effective. Here are the basic steps for fashioning any magical moon oil.

To Gather

- A sterilized amber or other dark-colored glass bottle with a tight-fitting lid. Note: Do not use a plastic container. Many essential oils corrode plastic, and it will break down. This includes rubber bottle tops.
- A small funnel that fits into the mouth of your bottle(s)
- Essential oils of your choosing (6 to 33 drops of e.o. per ounce of carrier oil)
- Enough carrier oil (or oils) to fill your bottle(s). Try apricot seed, olive, grapeseed, jojoba, or fractionated coconut oil.
- Your Moon Journal
- Labels or paper and tape, paint pens, or other such implements

Optional

- Smaller bottles into which to decant your finished product. Glass bottles of all sizes and colors—spray, dropper, roller ball, and otherwise—are easily located online.
- Curios; dried plant seeds, bark, flowers, leaves, and/or resins; metals; small stones or crystals; glitter

The Process

Step 1: Physically and energetically cleanse and clear your bottle(s), funnel, and other supplies. Energetically cleanse and clear your carrier oil, essential oils and any optional ingredients you plan to use. You can use a method from chapter 7.

Step 2: Fit your funnel into the top of your bottle.

Step 3: Whilst visualizing your intention for your completed oil, begin adding essential oil(s), drop by drop, to your bottle.

As you build your desired scent with different essential oils, continue visualizing your intent with each addition. Be sure to write down how many drops of each e.o. you use!

Step 4: Close your bottle, swirl the oils together, then open and do a scent test, adding more essential oil if desired.

Step 5: Top your bottle off with carrier oil.

Step 6: Close your mother bottle and label it with the name of your blend, the Moon sign and phase, and your intention. Decant into smaller bottles should you wish. I like to pour my completed moon magic oils into cobalt blue half-ounce bottles.

Step 7: When you are complete, take a moment to consecrate, activate, and empower your finished moon magic oil. Use the method in chapter 8.

Be sure to cap your bottles tightly when not in use, always label your completed product, keep thorough magical records, and write down your recipes!

Store your oils away from light and extreme temperatures.

Lady Jesamyn's Moon Magick Oil

The best strategy to master almost anything is to learn by doing. Here is my favorite moon magic oil recipe to get you started.

To Gather

- 6 drops clary sage (*Salvia sclarea*) e.o.
- 4 drops jasmine (*Jasminum officinale*) e.o.
- 3 drops ylang-ylang (*Cananga odorata*) e.o.
- 3 drops juniper berry (*Juniperus communis*) e.o.
- A half-ounce bottle

- A small funnel that fits into the mouth of your bottle
- Jojoba oil

The Process

Step 1: Add the essential oils to the bottle.

Step 2: Fill to the top with jojoba oil and shake well to mix.

Step 3: Consecrate, activate, and empower as advised in chapter 8.

Aromatherapy for the Lunar Phases

Diluted essential oils and blended oils can also be combined with lunar affirmations and other modalities to increase our well-being and add vigor and reinforcement to our healing work.

Here are my favorite essential oils for each lunar phase. I invite you to experiment with them through inhalation, diffusion, or anointing (after mixing with a carrier oil, please) or as the basis for compounding the magical oils, sprays, or baths that best serve your unique situation. Add extra oomph to your work by blending your oils at the most supportive phase of the Moon.

- *New Moon:* clary sage (*Salvia sclarea*), cypress (*Cupressus*), lime (*Citrus aurantifolia*), lemon (*Citrus limon*), rosemary (*Rosmarinus officinalis*)
- *Waxing Crescent Moon:* basil (*Ocimum basilicum*), bergamot (*Citrus bergamia*), grapefruit (*Citrus paradisi*), tangerine (*Citrus reticulata*), spearmint (*Mentha spicata*)
- *Waxing Half Moon:* eucalyptus (*Eucalyptus*), fir (*Abies*), peppermint (*Mentha piperita*), thyme (*Thymus vulgaris*), wintergreen (*Gaultheria procumbens*)
- *Waxing Gibbous Moon:* cinnamon (*Cinnamomum verum*), coriander (*Coriandrum sativum*), clove (*Syzygium aromaticum*), ginger (*Zingiber officinale*), peppercorn (*Piper nigrum*)
- *Full Moon:* cardamom (*Elettaria cardamomum*), jasmine (*Jasminum officinale*), lemongrass (*Cymbopogon citratus*), rose absolute (*Rosa* spp.), sweet orange (*Citrus sinensis*)
- *Waning Gibbous Moon:* chamomile (*Matricaria chamomilla*), juniper berry (*Juniperus communis*), ravensara (*Ravensara aromatica*), rose geranium (*Pelargonium graveolens*), ylang-ylang (*Cananga odorata*)
- *Waning Half Moon:* cedarwood (*Cedrus*), copal (*Protium copal*), patchouli (*Pogostemon cablin*), sandalwood (*Santalum album*), vetiver (*Chrysopogon zizanioides*)
- *Waning Crescent Moon:* frankincense (*Boswellia sacra*), lavender (*Lavandula angustifolia* or *Lavandula latifolia*), mugwort (*Artemisia vulgaris*), myrrh (*Commiphora myrrha*), white sage (*Salvia apiana*)

Infused Oils

Making your own oils with herbal allies is a more involved operation, but it can be worth the time, and it is not at all difficult. Note, though, that you will rarely, if ever, have much of a scent. These oils are more generally indicated for medicinal functions, affecting the physical aspect of our bodies, yet I have also used them effectively over the years for anointing, charging, blessing, and more.

Infused oils can be used for culinary purposes as well as body care and magic depending upon the plant and base oil you partner with.

While you can make an infused oil with a combination of herbs, I prefer to use a single plant and then combine finished products when I want to work with more than one herbal ally.

To increase the magical power of an oil, you can create an infused oil and then add essential oils, dried plant matter, crystals, and/or curios to it, making the finished product both infused and blended.

Be mindful of your infused oils, as they can rapidly grow mold or become rancid. In general, they last about two to six months, perhaps longer when stored in the refrigerator. To prevent quick spoilage of your finished product, choose a base oil with a longer shelf life; I like olive oil or fractionated coconut oil (or MCT oil). You can also add some vitamin E to your finished oil to help preserve it (up to 1 percent). If you do this, though, note that you will not be able to use it for culinary purposes.

Be sure to sterilize the bottles in which you'll store your finished product and keep them in a cool, dark place. This will help to prevent quick spoilage. And for the same reason, it is often best to use dried plant matter for making infused oils. Of course, there are exceptions to this general rule, including St. John's Wort infused oil, which is best made with freshly picked flowers.

To add even more magic to this process, carefully choose your beginning lunar phase and sign, perhaps aligning your intentions with a planetary hour and/or astrological sign, too.

Making Infused Oils

Here are two techniques for making an infused oil, warm infusion and cold infusion. Cold infusions may be easier, but you'll need some patience and time. The warm infusion method gives you a completed product on the day you start it.

Try both of these approaches and see which you like best! Mugwort is a great herb to start with.

You can use your blended or infused oils by themselves or further compound them into salves. You will find instructions for making dream salves in chapter 15.

Wise Witch Method of Cold Infusion Oil-Making

Making a simple oil using the cold infusion method is much like the tincture-making process I will share in the next chapter.

To Gather

- One dried herb of your choosing
- A sterilized jar, such as a quart-sized mason-style jar, and its lid
- A base oil
- A chopstick, long spatula, or butter knife

To Complete the Process

- Cheesecloth
- A sterilized vessel into which you will strain the oil (I like to use a glass measuring cup.)
- A sterilized bottle (or bottles) to store your final product
- Labels or paper and tape, paint pens, or other such implements

The Process

Step 1: Pack your dried herb into the clean, sterilized glass jar. It should be about three-fourths full. Cover the herb completely with your base oil. Lid your jar tightly and give it a nice shake.

Step 2: Open your jar and use the chopstick, spatula, or butter knife to release any air bubbles. Add more oil if needed, making sure the plant matter is completely covered.

Step 3: Mark your calendar for one or two lunations from now and place your jar in a spot where it will receive the light of the Moon. It can be a warm place—but not hot! Shake your jar every couple of days. Add more oil whenever needed to keep your plant matter submerged.

Step 4: Strain your oil through the cheesecloth on the date you marked, making sure all plant matter has been removed from the infused oil. You may have to double or triple strain it.

Step 5: Pour the oil into sterilized glass bottles, label your finished product, and you are done, done, done!

Wise Witch Method of Warm Infusion Oil-Making

This method is the one to use when you need infused oil *today*. Making a warm infusion requires some equipment in addition to your herbs and base oil: a double boiler or small slow cooker. I've used both and each has its charm. With a slow cooker, though, you can start the project and walk away, letting your Crock-Pot do the work.

To Gather

- One dried herb of your choosing
- A base oil
- A small slow cooker or double boiler
- A spoon or other stirring utensil
- Cheesecloth
- A sterilized vessel into which you will strain the oil (I like to use a glass measuring cup.)
- A sterilized bottle (or bottles) to store your final product
- Labels or paper and tape, paint pens, or other such implement

The Process

Step 1: Place your dried herb in your slow cooker or double boiler and carefully pour in your base oil. Give everything a good stir, then add more base oil, covering the plant matter by about two inches.

Step 2: Heat the oil at the lowest possible temperature for one to six hours. You'll know your oil is done when it exhibits the hue and/or scent of the plant used. Turn off the heat and let the oil cool completely, then strain through cheesecloth. You may have to double or triple strain it to remove all the plant matter.

Step 3: Bottle the oil in sterilized glass vessels and label your finished product.

Moonmist Vibrational Sprays

Moonmists are vibrational sprays that can clear the energy field and raise your frequency to be more in tune with the Moon, reinforcing your emotional, physical, spiritual, and magical connection with her.

They are helpful when you need a quick energy shift—be it in your body, in your aura, in your home, workplace, or ritual space—dispersing unwanted energies and ushering in well-being and lunar rapport. They are ideal as part of preparation for—or during—lunar meditation, healing, or other energy work.

Vibrational sprays can be used for blessing, cleansing, consecrating, purifying, and sealing magical objectives; as offerings for the Moon or Moon Goddess; or simply for relaxation after a difficult or unsettling experience or a long day. They can also help you to unwind before entering the Dreamrealm.

Moonmist Vibrational Sprays

Moonmists are easy to create and even more enjoyable to use, an uncomplicated combination of water and essential oils. Here's how to make them.

To Gather

- A glass spray bottle (or bottles if you'd like to make a batch). Use one-ounce (or even half-ounce) bottles for travel and four-ounce—even up to even sixteen-ounce—bottles for spellwork, ritual, and home.
- Essential oils that correspond to the Moon and to your intentions. Refer to the suggestions earlier in this chapter.
- Water. Distilled water lasts the longest, but I've reliably had success with tap water or bottled culinary rose and orange waters as well as waters gathered from sacred sources that were strained and purified with alcohol.
- A small funnel that fits into the mouth of your bottle(s)
- Alcohol for preservation. Use vodka, grain alcohol, or another alcohol without scent.
- Labels or paper and tape, paint pens, or other such implements

Optional

- Small crystals or stones that correspond with the Moon and fit into the bottle
- Stickers to decorate the bottle. You could also use drawings or printed out pictures; use glue, Mod Podge, or transparent packing tape to attach these.

The Process

Step 1: Identify the lunar phase and/or sign that you would like to imprint upon your moonmist.

Step 2: Ground, center, and open the channel. Connect with the Moon, feeling into the energies of the phase and sign she is traversing.

Step 3: One by one, ask each essential oil and crystal (if using) you've selected for their permission to use them. Listen with your Moon Witch ears.

Step 4: Cleanse and clear your bottle of all energies that are not yours or that you do not want present in your finished mist. If your water, essential oils, and/or crystals haven't been cleansed and cleared yet, take care of this now, too. As always, intuit what is correct: water, salt, sound, burning herbs (such as cedar, pine, or rosemary), and so on.

Step 5: If using crystals, gently drop them into your bottle now.

Step 6: Insert the funnel and pause to reconnect with your breath and with the Moon. As strongly as you can, see-sense-feel your purpose whilst adding essential oils into your bottle, drop by drop.

Step 7: If you are making a one-ounce bottle, start with 3 to 21 drops *total* of one or a combination of essential oils as you feel called. If you are making a bottle that is larger or smaller, extrapolate the ratio.

Step 8: As you add each essential oil, connect with its unique vibration and its innate nature. See-sense-feel it responding to you and your desire.

More is not necessarily better! No matter what size bottle you are making, go slowly and build your scent—you can assuredly add more essential oil, but you cannot take any out. This is an art, not a science, so there is no way to do it wrong.

Step 9: Periodically close your bottle and give it a shake, then test the scent. Once you are satisfied, fill your bottle about one-sixteenth of the volume with your chosen alcohol to preserve your spray. You can simply eye and intuit this.

Step 10: Fill your bottle almost to the top with the water you selected. Give everything a big shake to incorporate all of the ingredients, then test the spray again. If necessary, add more essential oil to achieve a scent you—and the Moon—appreciate. When you are finished with your work, top off the bottle with water and close it tightly.

Step 11: Label your bottle, adding stickers, drawings, or other images as appeals to you. Be sure to include your magical intention on your bottle in name, words, or images. If you want, you can then cover your label and any additional images with a piece of packing tape to protect them in case the bottle gets damp.

Step 12: Consecrate, activate, and empower your vibrational spray. See directions in chapter 8.

Step 13: Be sure to shake your bottle well before each use, as essential oils don't actually mix with water; they tend to sit on the surface of it.

Moonbathing

We can relax ourselves, renew, and heal through bathing with the Moon both energetically within her rays as well as physically within a tub of water. Energetic moonbathing, much like the forest bathing that has become wildly popular over the past decade, presents a chance for you to pause and reset your systems: physical, etheric, emotional, intellectual, and spiritual. Physical moonbathing uses water and is another form of moonbathing that can be equally valuable. Let's look at both practices.

Energetic Moonbathing

As an energy practice, this type of moonbathing is simple and free. It requires only the light of the Moon in a phase and/or sign that is compatible with the frequencies you seek. To moonbathe, set yourself up comfortably outside or indoors (if you can receive moonlight there), perhaps with a special blanket or pillow.

You can enhance this practice with herbs and crystal allies. Maybe you'd like to hold your favorite lunar crystal or sip a lunar tea; perhaps you'd like to use a moonmist or anoint yourself with a moon magic oil; or maybe you'd like to simply show up as you are in the holy moment of now.

However you prepare, all you need to do is sit under her rays and open yourself to receiving her energies and any messages she may have for you. Calmly relax here or perhaps meditate. Allow whatever it is you need to receive from Luna to surface.

Bathing in moonlight is one of the simplest gifts of self-care you can offer to yourself. Set a monthly date to steep yourself in the Moon's rays and put it on your calendar now!

Physical Moonbathing

This is exactly what it sounds like: drawing a bath and immersing in it to connect with the Moon. This form of moonbathing can be a ritual in and of itself, can precede ceremony or moonwork, or can be done "just because." Moonbathing before bed can become an enchanting routine, preparing you for a night of restful sleep and good dreams.

Your moonbath can be simple. If all you can do is bless your tub full of water in the name of the Moon before slipping in, then that is enough. But it could also be more elaborate: You may opt to cast a formal circle, include lunar incense and candles, and/or set up a small altar with shells, mirrors, and other lunar symbols.

You can add special touches to your bath, too. Many of these only take a moment to gather and little, if any, prior planning. Here are some ideas:

- Waters collected from a sacred site
- Moonwater (see chapter 10 for instructions)
- A dropper full of a lunar flower and/or gem essence (see chapter 10)
- A spray or two of moonmist
- A few drops of moon oil
- A lunar crystal or two (If you do this, be sure the crystal is water safe.)
- Honey to sweeten the work at hand

You might also prepare magical and medicinal creations in advance. A strained lunar tea, an herbal Moon sachet, lunar bath salts, bath milks, and/or sugar scrubs (see recipes below) could each be a beautiful addition.

If you'd like, all of the correspondences you select could align with not only the Moon herself but also with her astrological transit and/or phase. If you want to work magic in the bath, coordinate your moonwork with the waning phases for releasing and transforming and the waxing phases for inviting and manifesting.

When you start your bath, invite the Moon (or a Moon Goddess) to join you, then soak for as long as you want.

Here are some projects and recipes to enhance your bath experience. If you don't have time for a full bath, the lunar sachets, salts, and milks can all be used in footbaths. Find a vessel big enough for both of your feet to comfortably rest on the bottom—a canning pot or stockpot work well for this purpose—put your sachet, salt, or milk in it, and then fill it with enough hot water to cover your feet once they are immersed.

Allow your magic to marinate until the water is cool enough to comfortably submerge your feet, then relax and enjoy!

Moonbath Sachets

An image from Scott Cunningham's excellent *The Complete Book of Incense, Oils & Brews* has always stuck with me; he likens a magical bath with a sachet to "a huge pot of herb tea in which the bather brews."[37]

When you want to moonbathe, you can simply toss your sachet into the tub and let it steep, or you can tie it to the waterspout so as the tub fills, the water runs through your herbal creation. Either way you do it, your magic will be activated by the water as it combines with the herbs.

Lunar Sachets Project and Recipes

This is an enjoyable, uncomplicated project, a wonderful starting place for your green witchery moon magic. I like to construct my lunar sachets in bulk, storing them in a big, lidded glass jar until I am ready to use them. I often keep them in a quart—or larger—canning jar.

After the basic instructions, you'll find specific some detailed recipes.

To Gather

- One or more herbs that correspond with the Moon in general (see chapter 7), with the zodiacal sign she is traveling through, and/or with your goals. For each sachet, you'll want about ¼ to ½ cup of dried plant matter.
- A large mixing bowl
- Cheesecloth and string or muslin drawstring bags. Muslin bags are available in many sizes and can be purchased in bulk relatively cheaply online.

The Process

Step 1: Once you've chosen your herbs, clear them of any unwanted energies and then add them to your bowl. Connect with the lunar powers and then, using clean hands, mix the herbs together as you request the Moon to imbue them with her energies.

Step 2: Place your herbal mixture in a piece of cheesecloth and tie with string or stuff it into a muslin bag, tying it closed when complete. That's it! This sachet is ready to go as is, or you

37. Cunningham, *The Complete Book of Incense, Oils & Brews.*

can spend a moment to consecrate, activate, and empower it to your purpose. Here are three recipes to get you started.

New Moon Bath Sachet

- 2 parts milky oats (unripe seeds of *Avena sativa*)
- 2 parts nettle (*Urtica dioica*)
- 1 part lemon balm (*Melissa officinalis*)

Full Moon Bath Sachet

- 3 parts rose petals (*Rosa* spp.)
- 1 part jasmine (*Jasminum officinale*)
- 1 part passionflower (*Passiflora incarnata*)

Dark Moon Bath Sachet

- 1 part mugwort (*Artemisia vulgaris*)
- 1 part skullcap (*Scutellaria lateriflora*)
- 1 part lavender (*Lavandula angustifolia* or *Lavandula latifolia*)

Lunar Bath Salts

Lunar bath salts offer another splendid form to connect with the Moon in the bath. A simple scoop of a previously prepared mixture can turn an everyday soak into a special occasion, deepening your understanding of yourself as a Moon Witch. Lunar bath salts can also be used as body scrubs in the bath or shower.

Lunar Bath Salts Project and Recipes

In the most straightforward form, you can create a beautiful bath experience using Epsom salt or sea salt (or a mixture of salts) combined with a few drops of diluted essential oils that are attuned with the Moon. Experiment with different combinations to figure out which recipes vibe best with your lunar nature. Here's an introductory recipe to adapt and improvise with. There are two dependable recipes included after these basic instructions.

To Gather

- 3 cups of Epsom salt
- 1 cup of coarse sea salt or Himalayan salt
- 20 to 60 drops of essential oil (or a combination of essential oils) diluted in ¼ cup of carrier oil. Preferred carrier oils for the bath include jojoba, olive, almond, avocado, and apricot kernel.
- A large glass or metal mixing bowl and a metal mixing spoon. (Because wood can be porous, I do not suggest using wooden tools when working with essential oils.) Consider having a large metal or glass bowl devoted solely to working with essential oils. I also keep a big, long metal spoon solely for this purpose.
- A large jar with a tight-fitting lid
- Labels or paper and tape, paint pens, or other such implements

Optional

- 1 to 2 tablespoons of white (or other) clay powder. I like white, as it corresponds well with the Moon.
- 1 cup of baking soda
- ½ to 2 cups of magnesium flakes
- 2 to 6 tablespoons of dried herbs. If you choose to add dried plant allies, grind them into powder. A coffee grinder is great for this (one which is dedicated solely to herbs), a mortar and pestle can work, or you can instead pop a fine-mesh sieve in your tub to catch the herbs when draining the water out once you're finished bathing. You could also make a separate herbal sachet and add that to your bath.

The Process

Step 1: Energetically cleanse all of your ingredients using your preferred method. See chapter 7 for options. Add all the dry ingredients (aside from the optional dried herbs) to your bowl, blessing each as you do so.

Step 2: Bless and add your blended essential oil(s). If you are using dried herbs, bless and incorporate them now. Then combine everything with your mixing spoon, using the back of it to completely break up any clumps. For added zing, stir clockwise for manifestation work or counterclockwise for releasing.

Step 3: Jar your mixture and label it with the Moon sign and phase and your particular goal (if you have one). Consecrate, activate, and empower your completed creation before storing, if you so choose.

Step 4: Store the mix in a cool, dark place.

If possible, leave time for all of the ingredients in your lunar bath salts to infuse and integrate—at least overnight or even longer. You can also try setting the completed jar out under the Moon to gather more of her vibrations before storing it.

To use the bath salts, start with ½ cup of mixture per bath, increasing to 1 cup if desired.

I like to gift people jelly jars of these salts complete with pretty labels, tied with a ribbon whose color corresponds to the magic within.

Waxing Moon Bath Salts

This recipe is meant to assist in integrating and conducting the enlivening energies of the Waxing Moon. When using these salts, you may also wish to include a sachet of herbs or a crystal in your bath that harmonizes with the vibrations. Be sure to dilute your essential oils first in a carrier oil. An easy rule of thumb is to use about ¼ cup of carrier oil per 20 to 60 drops of essential oil.

- 3 parts sweet orange (*Citrus sinensis*) e.o.
- 2 parts rose geranium (*Pelargonium graveolens*) e.o.
- 1 part rosemary (*Rosmarinus officinalis*) e.o.

Waning Moon Bath Salts

This recipe is designed to support you in flowing with the decreasing powers of the Waning Moon. Again, feel free to add to your bath a sachet of herbs or a crystal that harmonizes with the vibrations. Be sure to dilute your essential oils first in a carrier oil. A good rule of thumb is to use about ¼ cup of carrier oil per 20 to 60 drops of essential oil.

- 2 parts spikenard (*Nardostachys jatamansi*) e.o.
- 1 part clary sage (*Salvia sclarea*) e.o.
- 1 part white sage (*Salvia apiana*) e.o.

Lunar Milk Baths

Lunar milk baths are used in the same way as salt baths, but they use dry, powdered milk as their main component instead of salt. You don't have to use cow or goat milk; there are so many dry milks easily available now online, including donkey and camel!

Nondairy powdered milks are just as readily available. Try almond, cashew, coconut, oat, pea, rice, or soy. Experiment to see what your body likes best.

Lunar Milk Bath Project

This base recipe makes roughly four ½-cup baths; scale it up or down as per your preference.

To Gather

- 1½ cups of dried, powdered milk of any kind—or a combination thereof; I often use ½ cup of powdered oats and 1 cup of goat milk.
- ¼ cup baking soda
- ¼ cup cornstarch
- 10 to 15 drops of essential oil (or a combination of essential oils) diluted in ⅛ cup of carrier oil
- A large glass or metal mixing bowl and mixing spoon. Consider keeping a glass or metal bowl solely for working with essential oil projects.
- A large jar with a tight-fitting lid
- Labels or paper and tape, paint pens, or other such implements

Optional

- 2 to 5 tablespoons of dried herbs. As shared earlier, if you choose to add dried plant allies, grind them into powder. A coffee grinder is great for this (one which is dedicated solely to herbs), a mortar and pestle can work, or you can instead pop a fine-mesh sieve into your tub to catch the herbs when draining the water out once you're finished bathing. You could also fashion a separate herbal sachet and add that to your bath.

The Process

These steps are almost exactly the same as those for creating lunar bath salts.

Step 1: Begin by clearing and cleansing all ingredients, then add the dry ingredients to your mixing bowl. Bless and add your blended oils. If you are using dried herbs, bless and add them now, too.

Step 2: With the mixing spoon, stir everything together, using the back of the spoon to break up any clumps. Jar your mixture, labelling it with the Moon sign and phase and any intention you may be holding for your creation. Consecrate, activate, and empower it if you want.

Allow the ingredients to mingle in the jar for at least twenty-four hours before using. I sometimes place my jar(s) out under the Moon during this time.

These creations keep well in a cool, dark place for about a month or up to three months in the refrigerator.

Lunar Sugar Scrubs

While bath salts and milk baths are designed for soaking, sugar scrubs are, of course, made for scrubbing. A combination of a body-nourishing carrier oil and sugar crystals, they help to both exfoliate and moisturize the skin. I like to use these in both the bath and the shower, and I most often use them as part of my pre-ritual preparation.

Mundanely, sugar scrubs are used for exfoliation. Magically, scrubs can be used to dissipate those energies you don't want to carry with you, and conversely, they can also be used to scrub things *in*, into your bodies both physical and etheric. Depending upon your ritual intention, choose a scrub for either in *or* out, rarely, if ever, both.

One warning: I suggest *not* using a sugar scrub that contains essential oils on your face, especially if your skin is sensitive, like mine. If you would like to compound a sugar scrub for your face, simply leave out the essential oils and steep your mixture with your intentions. To amp it up, try including a crystal in the jar!

Lunar Sugar Scrub Project and Recipes

Like other moonbathing creations, I generally make my lunar sugar scrubs in advance—sometimes far in advance—in order to imprint the scrub with the particular lunar phase and frequency needed for a future rite. Here are general directions, which can be adapted to your preferences, along with some recipes.

To Gather

- 2 cups of sugar (brown, cane, turbinado, white—it's your choice!)
- 1 cup of skin-safe carrier oil (i.e., apricot kernel oil, avocado oil, coconut oil, grapeseed oil, jojoba oil, olive oil, or sweet almond oil. If using coconut oil, melt in the microwave or a double boiler, or use fractionated coconut oil.)
- 3 to 13 drops of essential oil or a combination of essential oils
- A large glass or metal mixing bowl and mixing spoon. Again, consider keeping a bowl solely for working with essential oils.
- A large jar with a tight-fitting lid
- Labels or paper and tape, paint pens, or other such implements

Optional

- 1 or more teaspoons of vitamin E
- 2 to 5 tablespoons of dried lunar herbs. If you choose to add dried plant allies, grind them into a fine powder so they don't hurt the skin.

The Process

Step 1: Cleanse and clear all the ingredients as you do. Bless your sugar and add it to your mixing bowl. Then, bless your carrier and essential oils. Mix the oils together, add them to the sugar, and then stir everything thoroughly. If adding ground herbs, do so now, blessing each.

Step 2: Using the mixing spoon, incorporate everything together, utilizing the back of the spoon to break up any clumps. Jar your mixture, labelling the container with the Moon sign and phase and any specific intention for your creation. Consecrate, activate, and empower your scrub if you want.

When stored in a cool, dark place in airtight containers, these creations last about two months.

Diana's Bow Sugar Scrub

Use this scrub near the beginning of a lunation to set your intentions for increase and expansion.

- 1 part cypress (*Cupressus*) e.o.
- 1 part lemon (*Citrus limon*) e.o.
- 1 part rosemary (*Rosmarinus officinalis*) e.o.

Hekate's Sickle Sugar Scrub

Use this scrub at the end of a lunation to release and reset yourself, body, mind, heart, and spirit.

- 1 part lavender (*Lavandula angustifolia* or *Lavandula latifolia*) e.o.
- 1 part bay or bay laurel (*Laurus nobilis*) e.o.
- 1 part yarrow (*Achillea millefolium*) e.o.

Chapter 10
Lunar Potions

The Moon Goddess Speaks

I am the Moon-Crowned Goddess of the Undying Flame, the bright arrow who maintains the burning blaze of inspiration, hearth, and forge. I am the Keeper of these Sacred Flames, the first spark of nature that births the fires of spring after the darkness of winter.

Yes, I am the Goddess of Solar Fire, and yet I bear, too, the powers of the Moon, and I am the Exalted Lady of All Fresh Waters. Guardian of sacred springs and wells, my powers purify you so that you may begin anew. My magic cleanses and emancipates, creating space for fresh beginnings, reminding you of your own potent gifts and enchantments.

You are the Blessed Alchemist, overflowing with the watery energies of transformation, healing, and creativity. Should you wish, I can amplify your arts—simply drink deeply of my holy elixir and feel my powers mingle with yours, flowing through your heart and out your hands as you conjure your own apothecary of artful lunar potions.

I am Brigid.

Journal Inquiries for This Gateway

How can I better saturate my moon magic with weave the powers of sacred water more deeply into my moon magic? What is my current relationship with the element of water, and what messages does it hold for me now? With which bodies of water does my magic feel most resonant?

Affirmations for This Gateway

I alchemize the mundane into the magical. I initiate only that which inspires me. I am always connected to the regenerative powers and healing magic of water.

We can further deepen our connection to Luna by creating any number of clever potions, combining the herbs, plants, and fruits that best correspond with her changing frequencies into delicious products we can eat and drink, serve as part of our Moon rituals, and even offer as gifts to our lunar kindred. From sacred waters and delicious teas to elixirs and cordials, lunar potions are both spiritually powerful and satisfying to make. Most of the recipes in this chapter are consumable; however, a few are not. I have provided details on usage and safety tips for you as you experiment with your lunar potion making.

Moonwaters

Moonwater is one of my most treasured things to create. It is a simple and extremely accessible magical product, a fabulous solution to concentrating and storing the energies of a particular lunar phase and/or astrological sign for future use. This sacred water is also a perfect medium for storing the particular vibrations that occur when the Moon is conjunct with other planetary bodies, during eclipses, and during other astrological events whose energies we may want to utilize later.

Moonwater enables us to capture the Moon's rays (or, in the case of a Dark Moon, the *lack* of rays) in water and then "fix" the vibrations with alcohol so the water doesn't spoil. Note that some moonwaters are potable and some are not. This depends on how you make them and with what. Please be cautious when creating these waters for drinking. I have included tips for safety in the following section.

On Sacred Waters

As you continue along your Lunar Witch Path, you may find yourself drawn to sacred waters, those that originate from significant and holy sites across the Earth. You might also discover an affinity for collecting them, using them in your mooncraft, and perhaps even mixing and creating your own.

All sacred waters may be used in whatever ways you are instinctively pulled toward—poured onto the Earth as a libation for Goddess; utilized for cleansing objects, people, and animals; employed in your spellwork; used in purification and blessings rites; and so on. The only thing limiting their use is your imagination.

I keep my sacred waters in various jars and other containers, sometimes even in plastic water bottles, usually when I am traveling by plane. For waters I will not immediately use, I add a small amount—about an ounce—of vodka, brandy, gin, or grain alcohol to preserve it from bacterial growth. Alcohol will prolong the longevity of sacred waters, often for years. I have waters that are decades-old and still as fresh as the day I collected them.

Be sure to label your sacred waters with pertinent information such as the place it was collected; the date; any astrological phenomena, such as Moon phase and sign, Sun sign, eclipses, retrogrades; and so on. Believe me—you will not remember what is in each bottle in the future, even if you think there is no possibility that you could ever forget!

On Tap Water

Be aware that whatever waters you use to make your moonwater will connect your magic not only to the Moon but to a precise place upon the Earth, which contains energies that are particular and unique to that location. When you use your own tap water, you are keying your creation to the energy signature where you (presumably) spend the majority of your time.

Do you know where your tap water comes from? This is a wonderful thing to research; knowing where my water comes from has helped me to connect closely with something I use every day, often without conscious thought.

Mayhap you are blessed with a well upon the land you live—about 15 percent of the United States population has private wells. Or like the other 85 percent of people in this country, maybe the tap water going into your home is from groundwater, lakes, and/or rivers.

The majority of my drinking water originates hundreds of miles away. My current home is served by the Mokelumne River watershed, and my drinking water is mostly composed of the melted winter snow of the Sierra Nevada Mountains. This water then flows into the Pardee Reservoir, about one hundred miles from my home. The water comes into my local area via gravity-powered aqueducts before being treated and sent through pipes into my tap.

Creating Moonwater

Use your moonwater whenever and however you want. Augment your moonwork by adding it to ceremonial baths or anointing candles, poppets, spells bags, talismans, amulets, or holy jewelry. Bless yourself, your home, your beloveds, your belongings, and your animal and plant companions. Anything you love or care about can be blessed with moonwater.

Use it on its own, as a standalone ingredient, or use it in place of essential or magical oils and perhaps even as a substitute for burning herbs or incense. Use it in your moonmists and your sacred baths.

How you work with moonwater depends on the ingredients you use, of course. moonwater is generally quite safe to be used for anointings. Since it doesn't have a scent, the majority of those who have scent allergies (as I do) will be able to tolerate it without issue.

Remember: Do not ingest moonwater that is not created with 100 percent drinkable ingredients. Mindfulness about this is essential, especially if you have preserved your moonwater with alcohol. See my tips about drinkable moonwater after this recipe.

To Gather

- A sterilized glass vessel
- Tap water
- Unbleached organic coffee filters (or a piece of clean muslin or cheesecloth)
- Alcohol for preservation: vodka, gin, brandy, grain alcohol, and so on. You will need 1 ounce of alcohol per cup of moonwater. If you don't want to use alcohol, you could use vinegar (apple cider vinegar is best), but do note that your moonwater will not last for very long.
- A sterilized glass jar or bottle for your final product
- Labels or paper and tape, paint pens, or other such implements

The Process

Step 1: Look at your Moon calendar and choose a lunar transit, phase, or other happening whose energies you would like to save.

Step 2: Energetically cleanse your glass vessel, and then fill it with water from your tap. Alternately, you can use water gathered from an ocean, river, lake, stream, or other natural source, or even from a holy place, such as a sacred well or spring. Remember: Whatever type of water you use possesses its own energy.

Step 3: After filling your container, set it outdoors for the chosen lunar event (perhaps even overnight) to collect the energies. If the happening is of short duration, you may want to stay with your vessel instead of leaving it unattended.

Step 4: After the lunar event is complete, bring your vessel back indoors and strain the water through the coffee filter, muslin, or cheesecloth to remove any debris. To preserve, add about 1 ounce of alcohol for every cup of liquid.

Step 5: After bottling, label your moonwater with the date, Moon sign and phase, and anything else you want to remember. Then store it in a cool, dark place.

Alternative: Enhanced Moonwater

Enhanced moonwater is simply basic moonwater enhanced with herbs. Before creating this version, identify a lunar phase and/or sign that you would like to preserve for future use, and one or more lunar herbs which resonate with those energies.

While under the Moon, add each herb to a sterilized glass vessel, blessing them one by one in her name and stating aloud their names and attributes. Cover the herbs with water from a sacrosanct place (this includes your tap!). Allow the herbs to soak in the water overnight or for the amount of time of the lunar event. Then strain the water through a coffee filter or a piece of muslin or cheesecloth, compost the plant matter, and add an alcohol preservative, bottling and labeling as usual.

Drinking Moonwater

You can use moonwater as a medium for tea, coffee, or other water-based libations. Moonwater can be frozen for later use; try freezing it as ice cubes to use in the drinks at your post-ritual feast! You will be blessed by the lunar energy present in the water.

Moonwater for drinking is created using the same procedure as basic moonwater: by leaving it out under the Moon for the night or throughout a particular lunar happening.

It can also be made far more quickly if needed. Pour some water into a chalice, hold it up to the Moon, and ask for the vibrations of her phase and sign to enter it. Request her blessings upon it. Raise your chalice up to her orb in honor, pour a splash out upon the Earth in appreciation, and then drink it as a sacrament.

Moonwater for drinking should be used rather quickly: within twenty-four hours if unrefrigerated and within six months if stored in the fridge. As with any consumable, if the water smells or looks weird or off, dispose of it immediately.

Remember to only use safely consumable additions when enhancing your drinkable moonwaters!

Portable Moonwater

You can create special, unique, once-in-a-lifetime blends of moonwater that can be used for blessing, anointing, or protection wherever you go. This practice also facilitates sacred, mindful exchange of moonwaters around the world, and it can help you to remember your belonging and your magic when you are far from home. This style of moonwater is not drinkable.

My current bottle contains waters from Chalice Well, the Mary Chapel at the Abbey, and the Red and White Springs in Glastonbury, United Kingdom; from the Leith River near the statue of Hygeia in Edinburgh, Scotland; from the Atlantic Ocean on the coast of Maine where I was raised; from the Reflecting Pool in Washington, D.C.; from the Pacific Ocean near my current home; and from the Russian River, amongst other holy places.

Creating your exclusive portable blend is simple. Wherever you go, carry with you a one-ounce glass dropper bottle of moonwater (perhaps in a purse, backpack, or briefcase). Try using one of the bottles that herbal tinctures are generally packaged in; they come in many colors, including amber, green, and purple. I mainly use cobalt-colored bottles for my portable moonwater because I favor the color correspondence, but you should choose a hue that speaks loudest to you.

Be sure your original moonwater has a bit of alcohol in it as a preservative. You may also want to decorate the bottle with words, images, sparkles, or more.

When you're out and about and find yourself near a source of water, ask permission of the water, express gratitude, and then use your bottle's dropper to make an offering of your moonwater. If you feel the water has granted permission to do so, you may collect some water from that source and add it to your moonwater bottle. You now have a bespoke blend of moonwater with the energies of places you have traveled. Again, this is for external use only.

Lunar Teas

Lunar teas are one of my everyday go-to potions to enhance my connection with the Moon. And this is even more true during the chilly and rainy months!

Over the years, I've been blessed with the space and capacity to maintain a fairly extensive herbal cabinet, and so I've been able to experiment with lots and lots of tea blends. I like matching my teas with the Moon phase, with my personal daily (or nightly) intentions, and sometimes with the sign through which Luna is traversing. While working on this book, my writing blend was crafted of hibiscus, rose hips, and spearmint.

Lunar Tea Recipes

As a general rule, when making tea use 1 to 3 teaspoons of dried herbs per cup of hot (not boiling!) water, and then steep your tea for about ten to fifteen minutes before straining and enjoying.

Here are some blends to get you started.

New Moon Tea

- 1 part red clover (*Trifolium pratense*)
- 1 part nettle (*Urtica dioica*)
- 1 part peppermint (*Mentha piperita*)

Waxing Crescent Moon Tea

- 2 parts lemon balm (*Melissa officinalis*)
- 1 part cardamom (*Elettaria cardamomum*)
- ½ part lemon peel or zest (*Citrus limon*)

Waxing Gibbous Moon Tea

- 2 parts lemon verbena (*Aloysia citrodora*)
- ½ part ginger (*Zingiber officinale*)
- ½ part cinnamon (*Cinnamomum verum*)

Waxing Half Moon Tea

- 1 part peppermint (*Mentha piperita*)
- 1 part spearmint (*Mentha spicata*)
- ½ part orange peel (*Citrus sinensis*)
- Optional: The freshly squeezed juice of a half or full orange

Full Moon Tea

- 3 parts jasmine (*Jasminum officinale*)
- 2 parts rose petals (*Rosa* spp.)
- 1 part lemon balm (*Melissa officinalis*)

Waning Gibbous Moon Tea

- 2 parts chamomile (*Matricaria chamomilla*)
- ½ part rosemary (*Rosmarinus officinalis*)
- ½ part rose petals (*Rosa* spp.)

Waning Half Moon Tea

- 2 parts chrysanthemum (*Chrysanthemum morifolium* or *Chrysanthemum indicum*)
- 1 part chamomile (*Matricaria chamomilla*)
- ½ part spearmint (*Mentha spicata*)

Waning Crescent Moon Tea

- 2 parts oat straw (*Avena sativa*)
- 2 parts milky oats (unripe seeds of *Avena sativa*)
- 1 part catnip (*Nepeta cataria*)

Blue Moon Tea

- 2 parts butterfly pea flowers (*Clitoria ternatea*)
- 1 part chamomile (*Matricaria chamomilla*)
- ½ part lavender (*Lavandula angustifolia* or *Lavandula latifolia*)

Black Moon Tea

- Black tea leaves (*Camellia sinensis assamica*)
- Vanilla bean (or vanilla bean simple syrup) to taste

Diana's Bow Tea

- 3 parts nettle (*Urtica dioica*)
- 1 part lemon balm (*Melissa officinalis*)
- 1 part lemon verbena (*Aloysia citrodora*)

Hekate's Sickle Tea

- 1 part mugwort (*Artemisia vulgaris*)
- 1 part rose petals (*Rosa* spp.)
- ½ part cinnamon (*Cinnamomum verum*)
- ½ part damiana (*Turnera diffusa*)

Dark Moon Tea

The following uses dried elderberries, which should be prepared as a decoction. Special instructions are below.

- 1 tablespoon elderberries (*Sambucus canadensis*)
- 1 tablespoon hibiscus (genus *Hibiscus*)
- 1 tablespoon passionflower (*Passiflora incarnata*)

Prepare the elderberries as a decoction by heating them to a boil with 1 cup of water in a covered pot; reduce the heat to low and simmer for thirty minutes. Leave the pot lidded and the mixture to sit for five minutes before straining. Prepare the hibiscus and passionflower together as a tisane in one cup of water. Add your elderberry decoction and stir.

Tea Additions by the Zodiac

To enhance your tea blends, you can add a magical link to the astrological sign the Moon is passing through. Just sprinkle these ground herbs or spices on top of your finished brew—or brew them alongside your other botanicals. Here is a list of corresponding ideas for each zodiacal sign.

- *Aries:* cinnamon (*Cinnamomum verum*)
- *Taurus:* vanilla (*Vanilla planifolia*)
- *Gemini:* fenugreek (*Trigonella foenum-graecum*)
- *Cancer:* jasmine (*Jasminum officinale*)
- *Leo:* ginger (*Zingiber officinale*)
- *Virgo:* lavender (*Lavandula angustifolia* or *Lavandula latifolia*)
- *Libra:* rose petals (*Rosa* spp.)
- *Scorpio:* hibiscus (genus *Hibiscus*)
- *Sagittarius:* nutmeg (*Myristica fragrans*)
- *Capricorn:* cloves (*Syzygium aromaticum*)
- *Aquarius:* chamomile (*Matricaria chamomilla*)
- *Pisces:* lemon balm (*Melissa officinalis*)

Moon Medicines

Creating herbal medicines—both physical and vibrational—can be done in conjunction with the Moon in several different ways. You can create remedies that employ the lunar phase and/or sign, you can steep your potions during specific phases or transits of the Moon, and/or you can set your potions out beneath the Moon to gather her rays and amplify your aims.

Lunar Tinctures

The process for creating lunar tinctures is similar to the one you learned for infused oils. I almost always have at least one lunar tincture percolating away in the back reaches of a kitchen cabinet, waiting on just the right lunar phase to fortify it with more zip.

For tincture-making, I like to follow a very simple process using the Wise Witch method. This method prioritizes intuition over precise measurements, which, for me, is perfect for connecting with the Moon.

Your tincture base, also called a solvent or menstruum, can be alcoholic or nonalcoholic depending upon your desires, the plant or plants you are tincturing, and how long you would like to be able to store your completed project.

Below are three solvents to experiment with. Note that alcohol-based tinctures will last far longer than nonalcoholic ones, as alcohol contains elements that help to best preserve the work. Because of this, alcohol is my go-to menstruum.

Alcohol

Alcohol such as brandy, vodka, rum, gin, tequila, and grain alcohol will help create a sturdy, durable tincture. You can also use cordials as your base, although do note that they will not last nearly as long, nor be as potent, as those made with a higher alcohol content. If you use grain alcohol, dilute it to decrease the strength.

Glycerin

Glycerin-based tinctures—also called glycerites—are quite yummy and excellent for those who cannot have alcohol for one reason or another. This is an excellent base to use with highly flavorful botanicals and, in and of itself, it is odorless and clear in color, viscous, and slightly sweet. Be sure to use only organic food-grade vegetable-based glycerin (sometimes labeled glycerol).

Because its ability to extract the chemical constituents of herbs and plants is not as strong as other menstruums such as vinegar or alcohol, your completed tinctures won't be as potent. But this can be fine depending upon your needs!

Vinegar

Vinegar-based tinctures—sometimes called infused vinegars or acetic tinctures—are another tasty option. I like to use raw apple cider vinegar for these tinctures, as not only is it tasty, but it has all manners of health benefits, too. Vinegar extracts more chemical constituents than glycerin does but still less than alcohol. They are made in the same manner as alcohol-based tinctures.

When stored in a cool, dark place, vinegar tinctures can last about one year, glycerin tinctures for about three to five years, and alcohol-based tinctures four to six years (or longer). You can often prolong the life of your tinctures by storing them in the fridge.

Magical

You can also create magical tinctures, which are not meant to be consumed. As in, do not *ever* consume them for any reason. They are designed to amplify your magic, consecrate your ritual tools, bless your home, and so on. These are generally made with an isopropyl alcohol (rubbing alcohol) base.

Wise Witch Method of Tincture-Making Using Alcohol

The following process is for a basic consumable alcohol-based tincture followed by some of my most-requested recipes. I also included tips for substituting glycerin for alcohol. An equal amount of apple cider vinegar can replace the alcohol in any of these recipes.

To Gather

- Dried food-grade botanicals *or* fresh botanicals (washed and cleaned)
- A sterilized glass jar, such as a quart-sized mason-style jar, and its lid
- Your alcohol menstruum (e.g, brandy, vodka, gin)
- If using dried herbs: a mortar and pestle; if using fresh herbs: a sharp knife and cutting board
- A chopstick, thin spatula, or butter knife
- Labels or paper and tape, paint pens, or other such implements
- Your Moon Journal and a pen
- Cheesecloth or muslin
- A fine-mesh sieve and a bowl

Optional

- Sterilized dropper bottles (½-ounce, 1-ounce, or even 2- or 4-ounce)

The Process

Step 1: In order to expose the maximum amount of surface area, which assists in extracting the most chemical constituents of the herbs, grind, tear, or chop your botanicals as finely as you can.

Step 2: Add your plant matter to the jar, filling it about three-quarters of the way, leaving ample room for your menstruum. Then fill the jar with your menstruum, pouring it over the plant matter, making sure everything is completely covered. Leave about an inch of headspace in your jar.

Step 3: Using your chopstick, thin spatula, or butter knife, carefully mix your botanicals with the liquid, releasing any air bubbles.

Step 4: Add more menstruum if needed. Remember: The liquid should completely cover all the botanicals with about one inch of headspace in the jar. If more liquid was added, use your chopstick, thin spatula, or butter knife to again release any air bubbles.

Step 5: Lid your jar, then label it with the date, Moon phase and sign, your intention, and all the ingredients you used. Also note your herbal formula in your Moon Journal. (Do not skip this step!)

Step 6: Give your jar a good shake, shake, shake, activating the mixture by saying or singing your intention aloud. Place your jar in a dark place for one lunation, shaking daily (or every few days) and speaking or singing your intention as you do so. Whenever needed, top off with more menstruum to keep your botanicals fully submerged in the liquid.

Step 7: After one lunation has passed, open your tincture and strain it through two to three layers of cheesecloth or muslin spread in a fine-mesh sieve set over a bowl. Don't be afraid to squeeze your cheesecloth (with clean hands!) to get every drop out. If you notice any sediment, which often happens with powdered or finely ground plant matter, repeat the straining procedure using an unbleached coffee filter.

Step 8: Bottle it. You can either return the tincture to your large jar or decant it into smaller dropper bottles for everyday use. I like to use cobalt, green, or amber 1-ounce dropper bottles for this. If you are storing your tincture in a clear glass jar, be sure to keep this "mother jar" somewhere dark (or in the fridge).

Step 9: Label your completed tincture with the date and Moon phase and sign, then give your potion a name.

Step 10: Consecrate, activate, and empower your bottle or bottles and then enjoy!

Ingesting Tinctures

There are several ways to ingest potable tinctures: They can be taken "neat," as in directly from the bottle, or you can partake of the drops mixed into hot tea, water, juice, or any other beverage of your choosing. For tinctures made of apple cider vinegar, you can even add them to your salad dressing! Remember: Never, ever ingest magical tinctures that have a rubbing alcohol base.

Optional

One idea for sweetening a completed alcoholic tincture is to mix it with glycerin. In a new 1-ounce dropper bottle, cleansed and sterilized, add 25 percent glycerin to 75 percent of your finished alcohol-based tincture. It is okay to eye this!

Alternative Methods and Tips

If you are using glycerin with fresh herbs, you don't need to add anything else. Do, however, muddle the heck out of your plants to release as much botanical information into the glycerin as possible. If you are using dried plant matter, you will need to include water to rehydrate your herbs. In this case, use a ratio of 75 percent glycerin to 25 percent distilled water.

If you would like to use glycerin but would prefer to create a more potent final product, you can use a ratio of 75 percent glycerin to 25 percent alcohol (like vodka, brandy, and so on) for your menstruum. Again, everything must be food grade, please! Using 25 percent alcohol in place of 25 percent distilled water will extend the shelf-life of your tincture, too.

Lunar Vision Elixir Tincture Recipe

Ingest this tincture before any type of lunar divination.

- 2 parts dried mugwort (*Artemisia vulgaris*)
- ½ part dried spearmint (*Mentha spicata*)
- ½ part dried peppermint (*Mentha piperita*)
- Brandy
- ¼ cup local honey

In a sterilized one-quart jar, add the dried mugwort, spearmint, and peppermint. Cover the herbs with brandy, leaving about an inch of headspace, and steep for a minimum of six weeks. Strain and add honey.

Moon Ritual Tincture

Take this potion before or at the beginning of your lunar rites.

- 2 parts of dried elderberries (*Sambucus canadensis*), prepared as a decoction; see the Dark Moon Tea recipe for the process.
- 1 part rose (*Rosa* spp.)
- 1 part jasmine (*Jasminum officinale*)
- A menstruum of your choosing

Moon Magic Tincture

Consume this tincture before beginning lunar spellwork.

- 1 part rosemary (*Rosmarinus officinalis*)
- 1 part lavender (*Lavandula angustifolia* or *Lavandula latifolia*)
- ½ part mugwort (*Artemisia vulgaris*)
- A menstruum of your choosing

Lunar Essences

Similar to enhanced moonwater yet purposefully made for consumption, lunar essences are liquid elixirs created during a chosen lunar happening or Moon phase and sign, and are made from diluted infusions of crystals and/or plants in water, which are then preserved (most often with brandy but occasionally—for children, animals, and those who cannot have alcohol—glycerin). The energetic frequencies of the plants and/or crystals are contained within the completed formula, imbuing it with their spirit.

In this elixir, water acts as a device that records the vibrations of the Moon (her phase and sign and/or other phenomena) and the plants and/or the gems used. These vibrations pass through the molecules of the water, "imprinting" each one until all of the liquid is resonating with the energies of the Moon and the plant and/or crystal beings involved.

While herbal tinctures are generally supportive of our physical bodies, lunar essences work on the vibrational level, supporting our emotional and etheric bodies, helping us to integrate our feelings and our experiences in helpful ways.

Lunar essences can deepen and strengthen our connection to ourselves and to the Moon, stimulating our subconscious awareness of this essential link. They also serve as a physical reminder of this connection, harmonizing our vibrations with hers each time we take our drops.

Lunar essences are gentle, nontoxic, and free of side effects; they are enjoyable and satisfying to create. They work well even though there is no logical reason why they should; in fact, it really makes no sense that they do! By the time a lunar essence has been diluted into a dosage bottle, there are only few—if any—actual plant or crystal constituents remaining.

Composing these essences in concert with the Moon, the plants, and/or our crystal friends is one of my absolute favorite things to concoct for my lunar apothecary. I invite you to experiment with them, keep precise records, and see how these lunar elixirs support you and your loved ones.

Creating Lunar Essences

Just the act of making a lunar essence can bring you into greater alignment with the Moon and the beauty that can be found in life on Earth.

Before beginning, look at your ephemeris and determine the lunar happening or Moon phase and sign you would like to record in your lunar essence. Once you have made this choice, gather your ingredients.

If you are unsure of which plant(s) and/or crystal(s) to use—or even which lunar sign or phase underneath which to formulate your essence—try using a pendulum to help discern what will be most helpful to your purpose.

To Gather

- A large clear glass bowl
- Water (purified or even tap)
- Organic, pesticide-free plant(s)—cut or still growing. Whenever possible, I prefer to use plants that are still growing.
- If you are using crystals, a small, sanitized jar, such as a mason jar, with a tight-fitting lid
- Tweezers or tongs
- Coffee filters
- A colander, fine-mesh sieve, or a pour-over coffee dripper
- A sterilized liquid measuring cup. One big enough for 2 or 4 cups is usually good.
- One or more large, sterilized bottle(s), depending upon how much essence you would like to preserve. I largely use quart-sized mason jars.
- Brandy (or vodka, gin, another alcohol, vinegar, or food-grade glycerin) for preserving your potion
- A small funnel

- As many sterilized bottles or jars with tight-fitting lids as you want to make stock. I often use just one 4- or 8-ounce dark glass bottle.
- As many small, sterilized dropper bottles as you want to make dosage bottles (½- or 1-ounce sizes are excellent)
- Purified water
- Labels or paper and tape, paint pens, or other such implements

Optional

- A pendulum or other divination tool
- Food-grade rose or orange water; these are common in Middle Eastern cooking (for dosage bottles)

The Process: Create Your Source

Step 1: Fill your bowl with water. Ground, center, and open the channel. Connect with your breath, with the Earth, and with the Moon. Open yourself to the lunar energies—her sign and phase—and see-sense-feel them streaming down into the water in your bowl.

Step 2: Sit and meditate with the plants and/or crystals you have chosen to work with today. See-sense-feel their vibrations. Allow yourself to receive any information from and about them. Ask the different plants and/or crystals to come into resonance with one another, with you, and with the lunar frequencies. When you are tuned into the energy of the plants and/or crystals, proceed to the next step.

Step 3: For the sake of safety, if you are using crystals as part of your essence, employ the indirect method for creating your potion. The indirect method is very simple: Sterilize a glass jar and its lid and place your stone(s) within it. Securely close the lid, and then add the jar to your main bowl, making sure your stone(s) will have no contact with the water. The vibration of the stone(s) will transfer into your essence whilst the jar prevents any of its actual physical molecules from doing so.

Step 4: Next, add your plants. If they are cut, gently rest them on top of the water. If your plants are still growing, gently bend their stems or stalks to submerge the flowers or leaves in your water. You may use your small jar to help keep them under water.

Step 5: Allow your bowl to sit out beneath the Moon throughout the astrological transit you have chosen, or overnight. Then, with gratitude, carefully remove the plants. If they are cut, you can set them in a vase upon your lunar altar or compost them. If they are still growing, thank them and help them to stand upright again. If you used a jar, remove it from the water and return your crystal(s) to their home.

Step 6: You now have your lunar essence source, and it is ready for bottling as your wellspring!

The Process: Create Your Wellspring

Step 1: To create your wellspring, you must first remove any sediment or impurities from your source. Do this by straining it through a coffee filter resting on a colander or fine-mesh sieve over another sterilized glass bowl or, as I do, through a coffee filter in a pour-over coffee dripper directly into a sterilized glass measuring cup.

Step 2: Once you see how much source you have, decide how much you would like to keep. You will add preservative to your source at a ratio of one to one. (I suggest brandy unless it needs to be nonalcoholic, then use glycerin.) For example, if you want to create a quart of wellspring, you will use 2 cups of source to 2 cups of preservative.

Any remaining source can be used as you wish—make an offering to the Earth with it, drink it, bathe in it, or use it in lunar ritual or moonwork. Do what feels right!

The Process: Create Your Stock Bottles

You can now make stock bottles from your wellspring. I usually make only one stock bottle and store the rest of my wellspring in a mason jar in a cool, dark place.

Step 1: To make a stock bottle, fill your bottle(s) halfway with brandy or glycerin, and then fill the rest it to the bottle's shoulder—almost to the top—with purified water.

Step 2: Shake your wellspring to wake it up, and then add seven to thirteen drops to each stock bottle. Shake to blend as you did with your wellspring. You can dose from this stock bottle or go down one more dilution to a dosage bottle.

The Process: Create Your Dosage Bottles

A dosage bottle can be composed of one lunar essence or a combination of many (traditionally two to thirteen, but this is entirely up to your discretion). Dosage bottles are most commonly employed when you would like to create a medicine that holds the energies of more than one lunar essence: Instead of taking drops from multiple bottles each day, you can compound one potion for your convenience and ease of use.

To decide which lunar essences to add to a dosage bottle and how many drops of each is best, use your intuition. If you would rather, you can instead use a pendulum (or another divination device with only yes or no as possible answers) and ask questions such as:

- Is this the right essence?
- Do I need to add one? More than one?
- Do I need to take any away?
- Do I need between one to four essences? Five to ten? Eleven to thirteen?

You can also try this method to determine the amount of lunar essences to combine into a dosage bottle: While counting up, beginning with the number one (one, two, three, four, five...), watch carefully for when the pendulum slows or stops.

Or, you can hold your pendulum over your bottles and use statements like "Show me the best essence for my highest good at this time."

Know, though, that the more lunar essences which are blended together, the more you are asking yourself (or another) to process and integrate at once. If you would like to go in this direction, trust in your Inner Moon Witch and your lunar magic and have faith in the outcome.

Step 1: To compound a dosage bottle, first create what is called a blank bottle. This is made by yet again blending half preservative (alcohol or glycerin) and half purified water—this time in your final bottle (ideally a ½- or 1-ounce dropper bottle). If you'd like to use rose or orange culinary water, substitute it for the purified water here or blend them together: I prefer to use about 25 percent culinary water to 75 percent purified water. Fill your bottle to the shoulder; it's okay to eye it.

Step 2: Now, if you are making a single lunar essence dosage bottle, add seven to thirteen drops from your stock bottle. If you are making a blended lunar essence, use the amount of drops of each single essence you earlier determined is proper.

Step 3: For both single and blended dosage bottles, shake, shake, shake to blend and integrate the vibrations. Your personal single or combined lunar essence dosage bottle is now ready!

Step 4: After creating your dosage bottle, spend some time with it. Shake it, hold it, sit with it, and see if anything surfaces: a word, a phrase, an idea, a thought, a feeling. Sometimes a lunar essence may tell you its name—and no matter how weird or silly the name may seem, this is the name it wishes to be called.

Step 5: Label your bottle. (If a name was given to you include that, and connect with this name each time you ingest your essence.) Energize your elixir as you wish; try using prayer, chant, song, or visualization.

Again, be sure to label all your bottles—wellspring, stock, and dosage—with name, date, Moon sign and phase, and all the ingredients you used, even if you think there is no way you will ever forget what they are.

Using Lunar Essences

Lunar essences do not impact or interfere with any other health modalities, so consider incorporating them into your daily practice. Generally, I only use one essence at a time so I can monitor its impact. On special occasions (say, a ritual evening), I may take a second essence in addition to my regular morning lunar essence practice.

To dose: Begin by shaking or tapping your bottle to wake up the energies. Lunar essences are most often taken three to five drops at a time. If you'd like, you can take them "neat" (undiluted): To keep from contaminating your dropper top, you can place the drops on your hand and lick them off. Or you can instead add them to your morning or evening beverage. I take mine in my first glass of water each morning.

Some Moon Witches take their lunar essences more often, perhaps three to four times a day: upon rising, before going to bed, and once or twice more each day independent of meals.

If you would like to intensify the effect of a particular essence, you can increase the frequency of your dosing schedule. Upping the quantity of drops ingested does not increase its effectiveness, yet upping the frequency might.

You can appoint a different essence to support you in your lunar connection daily—or every few days, weeks, months, or even years—as your situation, emotional state, or life changes.

Lunar Cordials

Lunar cordials are delicious beverages we can concoct to help us attune to the Moon and her vibrations, to use as magical helpers, ritual libations, or "just because."

You can even infuse herbal cordials to address specific health issues, such as the cold and flu, as well as compound those that are to be served by the dropperful to assist with magical practices, such as moonwork, dreaming, trance, ritual, and more.

The original etymology of the word *cordial* is from the Latin *cor*, which means heart. The formulations that bear a resemblance to our modern versions were first devised for medicinal purposes by fifteenth-century Italian apothecaries.[38] In fact, the word *cordial* can be translated as "that which invigorates."

The roots of cordials go back even further, as recipes for digestive liqueurs have been discovered in scrolls surviving from ancient Greece as well as within Egyptian tombs. Throughout the Middle Ages, cloistered monks continued to develop this medicine and art.[39]

The more modern cordials that we enjoy now became quite popular with the aristocratic class in Europe in the eighteenth century.

Even now cordials continue to be esteemed as appetite enhancers before a meal (e.g., Aperol, Campari, or Fernet-Branca), as digestifs after a meal (e.g., amaro, aquavit, or Chartreuse), and even as purported aphrodisiacs (i.e., absinthe and Bénédictine).

In addition to the plethora of herbs, roots, seeds, fruits, and spices, the original cordials contained some very interesting ingredients such as powdered pearls, gold flecks, and parts of snakes.

As any liquor can be used as the base for your cordial, it is wise to consider the energies you want it to convey once completed. For example, brandy and cognac are warming, so a cordial made with either can be wonderful for the dark, cold, wet, and/or snowy time of year, as they heat from the inside out.

Gin brings with it, depending upon the brand, the taste of the juniper bush and berry and other strongly flavored botanicals. Vodka can be made from many plants including wheat, potatoes, corn, sorghum, and even apples. Rum is generally made from sugar cane, and yes, you can use spiced or dark rum. Tequila is another great base, and the agave it is made from has a lunar correspondence, too!

Absinthe can be employed, which is particularly wonderful as it already contains botanicals with lunar correspondences such as wormwood, lemon balm, and/or angelica.

You can even choose to make a cordial using wine (red, white, or rosé) or commercially available liqueurs such as St-Germain, Chambord, Chartreuse, amaretto, Grand Marnier, and others, but do check the alcohol content and be mindful of mold or other spoilage that can form when the fruit and/or plant matter breaks down. As always, use caution and mindfulness when consuming anything homemade.

One note of import: The higher the quality of alcohol you begin with, the higher the quality your cordial will be at the end.

Making cordials is different than medicinal tincture-making, where the quality of the alcohol is not as important because the tincture is consumed in much smaller doses (i.e., drops instead of ounces).

38. Lee, "Grap & Grain."
39. Bethune, "The Medicinal Roots of Modern Liqueurs."

Cordials are either sipped alone in small glasses—I love seeking out vintage cordial glasses at charity shops and estate sales—or they can be diluted by employing them as ingredients in cocktails or simple two-ingredient drinks by mixing them with club soda, tonic, or a juice.

That said, while it's true that the better the quality of alcohol, the better the final taste will most likely be, don't worry overmuch about this. I've made perfectly wonderful lunar cordials with bottom-shelf brandy and have been quite pleased with the results.

As with herbal tinctures, you can also steep cordials using vinegar in place of alcohol. These finished products are styled "shrubs" and are used to flavor and sweeten cocktails and to formulate mocktails, marinades, sauces, and vinaigrettes.

Making a lunar cordial is a two-part process. You will first create a culinary tincture, decant it after a month or longer, and then complete it by sweetening it, which is what makes it a cordial.

Creating Lunar Cordials

Before beginning, visit your ephemeris and settle upon a day that corresponds with the energy signature of a particular lunar phase, sign, or happening that supports your working. If you want to get super fancy, begin your cordial during a planetary hour that further supports your purpose. Beginning at that planetary hour is enough; you don't need to finish your project during the same (or similar) planetary hour unless you want to. Once you've chosen the day, round up your supplies.

To Gather

- A sterilized 1-quart mason jar. You can certainly scale up, especially if you are already familiar with a recipe and are looking to replicate past success. Choose a jar that isn't too big, though, as you don't want much empty space once everything is added.
- Botanicals of your choice. See recipe ideas below or experiment. These can include herbs (fresh or dried), spices, citrus peels, fruit (dried, fresh, or frozen), and so on. A general rule of thumb is to use about half a jar full of dried herbs and/or fruits and about three-fourths the jar if using fresh herbs and/or fruit. Trust your Inner Wise Witch here! To extract the most possible goodness from your materials, finely chop up your fresh herbs and fruits and grind, tear, or chop up your dried herbs and fruits.
- A high-quality alcohol of your choice

- 1 cup honey (or even sugar) plus 1 cup water, a saucepan, and spoon, or you can try maple syrup, molasses, rice syrup, agave syrup, or even 100 percent fruit syrup
- Cheesecloth or muslin
- A colander or fine-mesh sieve
- A sterilized glass bowl
- A large spoon and/or a heavy pan, stone, or weight
- Labels or paper and tape, paint pens, or other such implements

Optional
- An attractive glass bottle (or bottles) for storing your finished cordial
- A funnel for filling your bottle(s)

The Process

Step 1: After gathering all of your supplies, spend some time considering your intention for your completed cordial.

Step 2: When the lunar phase, sign, and/or planetary hour is correct, magically cleanse and clear yourself, your workspace, and then, one by one, the jar, each of your botanicals, and your base alcohol. If you want to work within a ritual container or sacred circle, now is the time to create it.

Step 3: The first part of cordial-making is quite similar to our Wise Witch method of tincture-making, so you may already be familiar with this technique. One by one, bless and add each botanical separately into your clean, sterilized jar, charging them with your intention for the final cordial. When everything has been added, carefully pour enough alcohol into your jar to fill it nearly to the top, leaving about an inch of headspace, making sure all of your plant matter is covered in liquid by two inches, if not more.

Step 4: Next, close your jar tightly and give it a good shake to mix all the ingredients together. Label the top of your jar with the name of the cordial-to-be, the date, the lunar phase and sign, the planetary hour (if using), and any other astrological information you'd like to remember. You may also want to mark your everyday calendar with the date and time you made this potion. (If you cast a circle, open it now.)

Step 5: Place the jar in a dark place overnight. I like to use the kitchen cabinet farthest away from the stove. Twenty-four hours later, take the jar out and look to see if you need to add more alcohol. Sometimes dried botanicals will soak up so much of the liquid that more needs to be added. If more is needed, top off your jar, give it another good shake, and put it back in the dark place you've chosen.

Step 6: Mark your calendar for one lunation from today and also mark at least one day every week until then when you will take your jar out of the cool, dark spot and give it another good shake. I like to do this every day, infusing my lunar potion with my magical intentions each time. Because of the richness of some of your botanical ingredients, you will most likely notice that your potion has grown darker each time you take your cordial-to-be out.

Step 7: If at any time you notice your herbs are no longer covered in alcohol, top your jar off again. The plant material must remain covered with alcohol throughout the infusion process to prevent spoilage and foodborne illness: Add more alcohol if and whenever necessary throughout the infusion process.

Step 8: Remember: This is a magical act! Every time you shake your jar, you can speak affirmations toward your intentions for your completed cordial—or perhaps sing a song, chant a chant, or draw a sigil on the glass with your fingers.

Step 9: Once a lunation has passed, it is time to decant your tincture (see the "Lunar Tinctures" section earlier in this chapter) and add a sweetener. It is okay for it to infuse longer if you want—or need—to. Sometimes I allow months and months of time here.

When adding a sweetener, you have two choices: (1) create a simple syrup using one of the two methods indicated below or (2) simply add maple syrup, molasses, rice syrup, agave syrup, 100 percent fruit syrup, or another syrup of your choice ¼ cup at a time—shaking your jar to mix it well in between additions—until your cordial tastes delightsome.

The amount of sweetener is up to you—a traditional proportion for cordials is one-half part sweetener added to one part culinary tincture. You can pour your decanted tincture into a measuring cup to see how much you have, then divide that number in half for your sweetener measurement.

You can definitely start with less sweetener and then add more to taste. On the other hand, once you've added the sweetener to your tincture, you cannot remove it!

Create a simple syrup using 1 cup of water to 1 cup of local honey (you can certainly use sugar in place of the honey) in this manner. Pour your water and honey (or sugar) into a saucepan and place over medium heat. Stir occasionally, making sure the honey is completely dissolved in the water. When you notice a low simmer beginning, immediately remove the pan from the heat and set it aside to cool to room temperature.

If you would like your tincture to last longer and are pleased with its flavor and viscosity as is, you can sweeten your cordial in this manner. Heat 1 cup of honey with ½ cup of your tincture on super-low heat just until the honey and liquid are fully incorporated, and then remove the pan from the heat to cool. Use this method if your honey is particularly fluid as well.

When using honey—especially raw honey—in any of these methods and you want to keep the healthy bacteria alive, do not heat your syrup over 100 degrees Fahrenheit. This requires a special type of thermometer; I like to use one meant for candy-making. You can also scale this recipe up or down if you have made more or less than a quart jar of cordial tincture.

Step 10: Next, using cheesecloth or muslin spread in a colander over a bowl, a fine-mesh sieve set over a bowl, or both (I like to use a fine-mesh sieve lined with one ply of cheesecloth set over a quart-sized glass liquid measuring cup), open your cordial-to-be and gently—carefully!—pour out your jar, straining all of your herbal material from your alcohol.

Step 11: Press on the plant matter with the back of a spoon or place a clean, heavy pan, stone, or weight on it to release all of the alcohol that your herbs absorbed over the past month or more. This is where the good stuff is! I like to strain my potions twice to help filter out all of the little bits of plant that are left.

Treat these used herbs as holy relics of your magic and dispose of them with loving mindfulness in the compost. If you have used unbleached 100 percent cotton cheesecloth, that is compostable as well. You can also wash and dry it, saving it for reuse.

Step 12: Now, clean your mason jar and sterilize it again.

Step 13: This step is so fun, because it is about what tastes good to *you*! Begin adding your simple syrup to your alcohol base by quarter cups. Test after each quarter cup until you like the taste. After you complete this step, pour your cordial into your sterilized jar, placing it back in the dark cabinet for at least another week. This gives your cordial time to rest, "marrying" the flavors in impressive and memorable ways.

Step 14: Now it's time to drink it and/or bottle it! I like to decant my potions into ornate antique glass bottles from the thrift shop.

Using Your Cordial

Because herbal cordials can be high in alcohol content, they are meant to be sipped and served in small quantities only. A shot glass or special cordial glass, about an ounce or less, is perfect. You can also serve them on the rocks, shake them up with ice, and/or use them as a base to build delectable cocktails.

They can be drizzled over ice cream; added to hot tea, still or sparkling water, or fruit juice; used in baking as extracts (try substituting in place of vanilla extract); or added to muffin, quick bread, pancake, or waffle batter.

An easy recipe for fashioning a cordial into a cocktail is to add some ice to a pretty glass, pour 1 to 1½ ounces of your cordial over the ice, then top it off with some soda water. Garnish with a slice of fruit or a sprig of fresh herb that harmonizes with your potion and off you go! You can follow this same recipe using your lunar shrub to make a delicious and refreshing mocktail.

Herbal cordials generally keep for years due to their alcohol content. Your cordials made with fresh fruit will spoil first, with those made with dried herbs keeping the longest. Fresh fruit cordials usually last at least a year; cordials made with dried plant matter will likely keep for about two to three years, or more. As with all of your herbal products, be sure to label your finished cordials with their name, ingredients, and the date.

Simple Syrups

Simple syrups can be stored in airtight containers in the refrigerator for up to a month. A flavored simple syrup will last up to two weeks when stored in this manner. Be sure to look for mold and smell your stored syrup before using. If anything looks or smells "off," discard the syrup and start again.

You can easily infuse simple syrups with herbs—both fresh and dried. If you feel your lunar cordial-to-be is lacking something or you forgot to add an ingredient when making your alcohol base (don't ask me how I know that!), you can whip up a flavored simple syrup in this way:

As soon as you take your syrup off of the heat, add one or more ingredients before setting it aside to cool. Stir well, submerging the plant in the syrup. Cover the saucepan with a lid to keep the volatile plant oils inside and leave this potion to steep until the syrup has cooled.

Once it has cooled, remove the plant matter by straining or, for something like a cinnamon stick, rosemary sprig, or vanilla bean, just pluck it out with tongs. As an act of reverence and respect, be sure to compost with mindfulness. Refrigerate your syrup and then use it up before two weeks have passed.

Be brave and creative! Here are some ingredients to try: citrus rind (orange, lemon, lime, grapefruit), chiles (dried), cloves, ginger, oregano, jasmine, lavender, lemon balm, lemon verbena, marjoram, mints (peppermint, spearmint, wintergreen), nutmeg, peppercorns, rose petals, rosemary, vanilla beans.

Blue Moon Bounce Recipe

A bounce is a festive brandy-based cordial that was first popularized in the eighteenth century.[40] Brandy is macerated with fruit, herbs, spices, and sugar, then put away for at least three months (and often far longer).

The process for making a bounce is super easy, and it is very similar to the cordial-making procedure we followed earlier. Bounces are a bit simpler to compound because the sweetener is added alongside the botanicals during the first part of the process.

Either formulate this particular version under a Blue Moon or work in advance so that you can enjoy it during a Blue Moon—or give it as a gift to your lunar kindred!

To Gather

- 24 ounces of blueberries, moderately pulverized with a potato masher or the back of a big spoon. You can use fresh berries or frozen. If frozen, thaw, retaining the released juice for use.
- 5 cups of sugar (raw, turbinado, or white)
- 4 sticks of cinnamon
- 4 to 8 cardamom pods. Smash them up a bit with a mortar and pestle if dried; if fresh, use the side of a kitchen knife.
- 4 to 5 cloves, crushed slightly in your mortar and pestle
- 1 teaspoon ground nutmeg, ginger, or a combination of both
- Enough brandy to cover the herbal material (about 8 cups)
- A sterilized ½-gallon canning jar. If you'd prefer to make just a quart, simply half the recipe.
- A sterilized spoon
- Organic unbleached cotton cheesecloth, coffee filters, and/or a fine-mesh sieve for straining

Optional

- A sterilized bottle(s) for storing your completed bounce (or just reuse your canning jar)

40. Yarborough, "What Is Cherry Bounce?"

The Process

Step 1: Whatever you macerate your bounce in and however you store it, do be sure to thoroughly sanitize your vessels before using. You can dip them into boiling water and air dry or run through the hottest cycle of your dishwasher. Make sure they are completely dry before beginning.

Step 2: Follow the instructions for creating a cordial found earlier in this chapter, adding your sugar to the jar alongside your botanicals. Give everything a nice shake, set in a cool, dark place, and mark your calendar for three lunations from today.

Step 3: At the conclusion of the third lunation, have a taste, but be prepared to hate it. Be sure to use a sterilized spoon to collect your taste. Sample your bounce again at six lunations, and if it still doesn't taste ready, try once a lunation until it tastes good to you. Honestly, it's the patience it takes whilst waiting for it to be ready to drink that is the difficult part here. Some bounces are ready in as little as three lunations, but I like mine to rest for at least six lunations and often much longer.

Step 4: Strain well and bottle as you wish at this point.

Half a gallon is about 1.89 liters, if you prefer to use metric. As with the Wise Witch method of tincture-making, I generally use these recipes as stepping stones instead of hard-and-fast scientific instructions that will fail if not followed to the letter. I'll often use up whatever I have on hand and substitute for those things I don't. Play around and determine what tastes delicious to you.

Substitutions

You can also produce a Dark Moon Cherry Bounce by substituting cherries for the blueberries. I like to serve this one at Dark Moon esbats, as the cherry both corresponds to this lunar phase and matches the depth of darkness that is accessible then. Test out other fruits, herbs, and spices, too. Listen to your Inner Moon Witch and make all of this yours!

Other Lunar Cocktails and Moon Mocktails

Lunar cocktails and moon mocktails can be served as sacred libations during or after rituals, sipped to heighten your understanding of a particular phase or sign, or presented to friends and family for relaxation or celebration.

Here are some recipes that focus on those plants that correspond highly with Luna's energies. Unless otherwise indicated, the following recipes each make one drink. If you have a big crew, scale the recipe and make a pitcher!

Blue Moon Bounce Mojito Recipe

This is a refreshing drink, perfect for a hot summer day or moonlit night. This recipe is marvelous to experiment with: Try adding lemon juice and/or zest, fresh basil, rosemary, or lavender—even oregano, thyme, tarragon, marjoram, or (culinary) sage are not off-limits.

To Gather

- A cocktail shaker
- A muddler
- A pretty cocktail glass
- 5 to 10 washed mint leaves, plus more for garnish
- 1 to 2 ounces of Blue Moon Bounce
- 1 ounce of freshly squeezed lime (or other citrus) juice
- ½ ounce of simple syrup (or use 1 to 2 teaspoons of sugar, to taste)
- Ice
- ½ cup of club soda, seltzer, or sparkling water
- Lime (or other citrus) for garnish

The Process

Step 1: Gently muddle the mint in the cocktail shaker to release its aromatic oils. If you are using sugar, muddle it with the mint leaves. Add the Blue Moon Bounce, simple syrup (if using), the lime juice, and enough ice to fill your shaker about halfway. Shake, shake, shake!

Step 2: Strain into a pretty, ice-filled cocktail glass. Top with bubbly water and garnish with more mint and slice of citrus. Enjoy!

Moonshine Mocktail Simple Syrup Recipe

This mocktail uses a homemade nonalcoholic version of "gin" as the base. You can create this mocktail and use it as a lunar ritual libation, an offering to the Moon, or as something to sip whenever you'd like to heighten your connection to her energies.

This festive drink is lovely to share with friends and family, too!

Since this is a simple syrup and the completed beverage comes together quite quickly, you can easily tinker with the flavors to see what you and your loved ones prefer. Adjust the amount of juniper berries based on how piney you like your "gin" to taste.

You can also substitute some or all of these aromatic ingredients with botanicals you like better. For example, you could use cinnamon sticks for star anise, angelica for coriander, pomelo peel for lemon peel, rosehips instead of peppercorns, and so on.

To Gather

- A medium-sized saucepan with lid
- A spoon
- A sterilized glass quart jar
- Organic unbleached cotton cheesecloth and/or a fine-mesh sieve
- 2 cups of water
- 1 cup of cane sugar. You can substitute white sugar or honey if you desire; note: If you are using honey, incorporate it after your decoction is complete.
- ½ cup of dried juniper berries. This is where the main "gin" taste comes from.
- The peel of 1 lemon (or substitute an orange, lime, or grapefruit); set the juice aside!
- 13 coriander seeds
- 4 dried cardamom pods
- 7 peppercorns: black, pink, green, or a combination
- 1 star anise pod

Optional Additions or Substitution Ideas

- 7 dried cedar berries
- 1 tablespoon dried organic rose petals
- ½ to 1 tablespoon dried lavender flowers

- 1 to 2 cinnamon sticks
- 1 tablespoon dried elderberries, prepared as a decoction; see Dark Moon Tea for process.
- Rosehips
- Dried hibiscus petals
- Cranberries, blackberries, blueberries
- Bay leaves
- Pine needles
- Rosemary
- Licorice root
- Orris root
- Heather
- Milk thistle
- Saffron
- Bergamot

The Process

Step 1: Add all of your ingredients to the saucepan and place over medium heat, stirring often to dissolve the sugar. Do not leave it unattended, or it could burn. When your mixture reaches a boil, immediately turn the heat down to produce a low simmer. Cover your saucepan and simmer for thirty minutes. (Since many, if not all, of your ingredients here are dried seeds and pods, you are using a method termed decoction instead of making an infusion.)

Step 2: Next, keeping the lid on your saucepan, remove it from the heat and allow it to sit until it reaches room temperature. (If you are in a rush, you can wait fifteen minutes and then place the saucepan in the fridge to speed this process.)

Step 3: Once your syrup is cool, strain it through cheesecloth and/or a fine-mesh sieve into the sterilized jar. Compost your plant ingredients mindfully and with gratitude.

Step 4: Store your syrup in the fridge for up to two weeks (it may last for as long as three weeks) and use as desired.

Moonshine Mocktail Drink Recipe

Use the previous syrup to mix up the final drink. This recipe makes two drinks (or one big one).

To Gather

- Beautiful, chilled glasses (or a single big one)
- A cocktail shaker
- 1 ounce of citrus juice. You might echo whatever you used for your simple syrup: lemon, lime, orange, grapefruit, pomelo.
- 1 ounce of your Moonshine Mocktail syrup
- 4 ice cubes
- 4 ounces club soda or seltzer water

Optional

- 1 egg white

The Process

Step 1: Add your citrus juice, mocktail syrup, and egg white (if using) to your cocktail shaker and shake well for about twenty seconds. Next, add the ice and shake vigorously to chill.

Step 2: Strain into your chilled glasses and top with your club soda or seltzer water. Garnish with a citrus twist, serve, and enjoy.

You can treat this recipe as a suggestion, subbing out the soda or seltzer with flavored seltzer waters, tonic water ("gin" and tonic), and/or your favorite juice.

Moon Milks

Because of its color and nature, milk is a magnificent lunar correspondence, and as discussed regarding bath products, it is available in many forms, from dairy to plant-based.

Below are two recipes that feature coconut milk, as well as fruits that are sacred to the Moon and particularly correspond with her energies. You can replace the coconut milk with another milk, should you wish, yet be aware that the flavor will be drastically different.

Both of these recipes spotlight lemons—also tied to the Moon. They can be made alcoholic with the addition of an ounce or two of your favorite liquor.

Lemon-Coconut Refresher Recipe

Meyer lemons work best for this refreshing beverage, though you can substitute some or all of the lemon juice with regular lemon, lime, or another freshly squeezed citrus juice as desired.

To Gather

- A blender or food processor
- 4 cups of coconut water
- 1 can of unsweetened coconut milk (approximately 14 ounces)
- 1 cup of freshly squeezed lemon juice
- ¾ cup of simple syrup, honey, maple, or another syrup
- ¼ teaspoon of sea salt
- Cheesecloth or a fine-mesh sieve
- A pitcher for serving
- Pretty cocktail glasses
- Ice
- Lemon slices or twists for garnish

Optional

- 1 to 2 ounces per glass of your preferred liquor. I like limoncello, vodka, or rum in this one.

The Process

Step 1: Add the coconut water, coconut milk, lemon juice, syrup (or honey), and salt to your blender or food processor and blend on high for about one minute, until frothy. Strain into your serving pitcher through cheesecloth or a fine-mesh sieve.

Step 2: Serve in pretty cocktail glasses garnished with lemon slices or twists. If you'd like to make this alcoholic, add 1 to 2 ounces of your chosen liquor to the glass. Serve with a swizzle stick or straw.

Lemon-Coconut Pick-Me-Up Recipe

Here's another refreshingly yummy take on coconut and lemon. This recipe yields four beverages.

Note: You can substitute some or all of the lemon juice with lime or another freshly squeezed citrus juice; substitute the maple syrup with simple syrup or honey; and/or exchange the fizzy water for a flavored sparkling water.

To Gather

- 1 can of unsweetened coconut milk (approximately 14 ounces)
- 1 cup of freshly squeezed lemon juice
- ½ cup of maple syrup
- A pitcher for mixing
- Cocktail glasses
- Ice
- 1 liter of soda water, seltzer, tonic, or sparkling water
- Lemon slices or twists for garnish

Optional

- 1 to 2 ounces per glass of your preferred liquor

The Process

Step 1: Add the coconut milk, lemon juice, and syrup to your pitcher and mix until well combined.

Step 2: Fill the glasses with ice. Add liquor to the mix (if desired) and stir. Divide the contents of the pitcher between the glasses. Top with fizzy water, garnish, and enjoy!

I invite you to use all of the ideas in this chapter to fall even more in love with the Moon as a lunation unfolds!

Chapter 11
The Lunar Goddesses

The Moon Goddess Speaks

I sing of Moonbeams filtering through fleshy green leaves, the sound of them dry and crunching under my bare feet, their earthy, dark scents rising up all around me, just as does the Moon.

I am connected to all that is sacred as I stalk through the long-untread forest pathway with my Deer of the meadows and my Bear of the caves, soaking in the Moon's ivory rays as we make quiet, stealthy progress toward the secret place, the holy place where we hold our rites.

I can feel the power there, and I feel it within me, too. Her power. Moon power. Power I can wield when I need to, when I want to. Power to command. Power to protect. Power to direct as only I can, with silver bow and arrow, my aim, my directive, always—and only—true.

I can help you, too, to choose and achieve your goals. What is your target? What powers do you hold, inside? Is now the proper time? Call upon me when you see that first crescent in the sky, the opposite of Hekate's deathly sickle, and I will come. Call my name with courage and exuberance, and I will come.

I am Artemis.

Journal Inquiries for This Gateway

What do the limitless facets of the Lady of the Moon have to teach me about my own life? How can I deepen my connection to both her growth and her diminishment? What embodiment of the Moon Goddess most reflects the phase of life I am currently experiencing?

Affirmations for This Gateway

I open myself to the wisdom of the Lady of the Moon. I perceive life through lunar eyes. I activate the power of the Moon Goddess within me.

Our beloved Moon not only inspires modern people. She is also the seed from which multitudes of legends, myths, and folk stories grow. She has been long-beloved as a holy muse, guiding not only artists in creating great works. She also has led each and every person who has looked up at her face and felt a sense of boundlessness, of connection, of belonging, and of eternity.

On the Path of Lunar Witchcraft, the Moon is viewed as both a representation *and* a personification of the Divine, one who can manifest as a deity in and of herself.

Goddesses of the Moon exist in almost all cultures, and the Moon herself has been revered as a Goddess throughout time and space. Whilst she has many names and many powers, the Moon reminds us that we are all One. We are all gathered under her—no matter where we live or what we believe to be true. We are all under her luminous eye, held by her loving heart.

There are seemingly limitless methodologies we can use to develop personal relationships with the Moon Goddesses, ways in which we can work with their many guises and get to know them as individual entities—and to do this with honor and respect, with cognizance of what is ours to engage with and what is not.

Lunar Witchcraft is global, and it celebrates all cultures and ancestries. The Moon Goddesses have seemingly infinite names and faces, and it is my hope that we can collectively—as Moon Witches—call her forth in as many of these guises who wish to partner with us on the path, who wish to be present, recognized, or honored by us.

When we speak their names, we add our mana to their presence in this world. We help them to live in the modern era.

Calling Upon a Moon Goddess

To that purpose, we can call upon Moon Goddesses from all times and places in our personal rituals and invite them to be present with us *should they so wish*. We call upon these Moon Goddesses holding the never-ending resolve that we always do so in a respectful manner that does not appropriate, slight, or bring dishonor to any culture or tradition, living or of the past.

Before you call a Moon Goddess into a holy rite or begin to work with her, it is imperative that you spend a goodly amount of time researching, meditating upon, and connecting with that face of deity. It is imperative that you ask her for permission to invoke her—and heed her answer, whether you like it or not!

When you reclaim the Moon Goddesses of your ancestry, you reclaim more of your own authenticity, your personal and shared identity: This is your birthright. It is important to understand, too, that not all Moon Goddesses who reveal themselves may be of your blood lineage in this lifetime. This may be expressly true if you are adopted or do not have access to your DNA heritage.

Let us each be profoundly aware of our privilege as those who are free to practice our spirituality whilst remaining acutely conscious of the fact that not all people have this opportunity. And as such, let us strive to be mindful in all of our interactions with deity and with people from cultures that our bodies and bloodlines do not belong to in this incarnation.

It is my hope that the container of Lunar Witchcraft that we are cocreating and continuing to hold together be a sacred one in which every person upon this path feels comfortable to explore their own heritage and ancestry and the Moon Goddesses from those cultures, and to also experience the freedom necessary to discover and develop meaningful connections with those Moon Goddesses who call to us personally.

I encourage all Lunar Witches to explore their lineages of all kinds, to research how the Moon Goddesses were honored in cultures worldwide before the advent of Christianity—pre-patriarchy, pre-kyriarchy—and to bring their learnings back into their personal practices.

This includes researching Moon Goddess stories, folklore, and her-story; delving into archeology, anthropology, mythology, and art both ancient and modern; engaging in dreamwork, meditation, and ritual; celebrating feast days traditional and contemporary; and more.

The Moon Goddess is eternal. She may have been hidden away from our view for a while, but she never fully disappeared. In thousands of cultures the world over, she was the essential, original deity from which all else was birthed. As we Lunar Witches reawaken to our full potential, so does the Moon Goddess reawaken.

The Moon Goddesses

Some Lunar Witches work with a single Goddess or a cultural or personal pantheon of Goddesses for a lifetime. Some Moon Goddesses come into our lives for a specific period of time to address a specific need or deliver a certain message and then exit our lives after their work with us is done. It is up to you to discover and discern why a particular Goddess shows herself to you.

I invite you to become acquainted with each Moon Goddess who calls to you across no less than an entire lunar cycle. Longer is better! I prefer at least a lunar year to explore these partnerships. As you walk with the Goddess who has shown herself to you, pay close attention to what you experience with her as each lunar phase and sign passes in its turn.

Yes, this will most likely take many years, but remember: This is a path that never ends.

What can you learn about—and from—these Ancient Ones in concert with the rise and fall of the Moon's energies?

Each day, choose one of the practices outlined throughout this chapter and apply it to your growing relationship with a specific guise of the Moon Goddess. Jot down your observations in your Moon Journal and see what emerges.

Be very aware that it is your responsibility to engage with any Goddess you encounter in an ethical manner, with the full recognition that many deities are part of living religious traditions or perhaps even closed spiritual practices. As Lunar Witches, we always bring respect, mindfulness, and care to our work.

Here is a beginning group of Moon Goddesses and Goddesses of the Moon for your consideration. Who calls to you? Whose voice do you hear? Who are you pulled to learn more about?

African (Central): Jezanna
African (Dahomey Tribe): Mawu
Arabian/Chaldean: Al-lat
Aztec: Coyolxauhqui
Babylonian: Annuit, Ishtar
Basque: Ilargi, Mari
Buddhist: Quan Yin
Canaanite/Hebraic: Levannah
Celtic: Cerridwen, Morgana
Chinese: Chang Xi, Heng-o (or Ch'ang-o)
Columbian: Huitaca
Cretan: Britomartis
Egyptian: Bastet, Isis
Etruscan: Losna, Zirna
Filipino: Launsina (Alunsina)
Finnish: Kuu
Greek: Artemis, Hekate, Phoebe, Selene
Hawaiian: Hina
Hindu: Parvati
Incan: Mama Quilla
Indonesian: Ratih
Irish: Áine
Japanese: Izanami
Korean: Myeongwol
Lakota: Hanwi
Mayan: Ix Chel
Persian: Anahita
Phoenician: Tanit
Roman: Diana, Hecate, Luna

Slavic: Dziewanna/Devana, Myestas
Sumerian: Inanna
Tagalog: Mayari
Teutonic: Ursula
Thracian: Bendis
Vietnamese: Hằng Nga
Welsh: Arianrhod, Rhiannon
Yoruba: Yemọja (Yemaya) (Note: Yemaya is an *òrìṣà.*)

Research

Where does this Moon Goddess hail from and what are the stories told of her? Begin here, digging through scholarly books and articles, art, folklore, stories and legends, accounts of personal gnosis shared by others, and internet discussions.

Dig deeper any time you find a story where the Goddess is subjected to male rule, is dependent upon a male God, or is portrayed as something other than a whole and sovereign being in her own right, or whenever you find a story that paints her as evil, hostile, vengeful, or "just a love Goddess."

There is almost always an underlying, more ancient, and more accurate mythology hidden beneath the patriarchal overlay, her true story covered over (e.g., her actual genesis is before ancient Greece or Rome). For example, there is evidence that the origin of Athena is perhaps Minoan or North African, or she may even be an aspect of pre-patriarchal Inanna.[41]

Ancient Greece and Rome took the Goddesses from the cultures they dominated and twisted them to slot into their existent pantheons, forcing Goddesses into frameworks which depicted them as lesser than Gods, assigning them origin stories that fit into the new patriarchal narrative.

This information is often lost in time, yet as we develop a personal relationship with any particular deity, we can feel in our bodies if something is true or untrue, and this can lead us to that fragment of information that may help to uncover the truth. And sometimes Goddess will speak and tell us her true story if we but listen.

You may wish to approach a Moon Goddess by asking something like "Who was this Goddess before being cloaked by the patriarchy, before her powers were usurped to better fit the new paradigm? What would she look like without this mask?" You might then follow that thread as far as you can, using one or more of the ideas outlined below.

As you research her stories, you will organically discover her magical correspondences. What Moon phase or phases does she rule over or is most at home in? What powers does she hold? What qualities? What activities does she preside over? What are her functions?

41. "Cultural Objects Names AuthorityÒ Iconography Display."

What is her feast day or days or time of year? What offerings are customarily made to her? Are there any numbers associated with her? Is she connected with any planets, stars, or asteroids? What are her symbols?

What colors are best for ritual candles, cloths, and clothing? What crystals, metals, herbs, plants, or trees are her friends and allies? What animals, insects, or other creatures? What Element or Elements of Life? Is there a particular tarot card or cards that represent her energies and powers?

After all of this investigation, you may find yourself more open to personal gnosis. Because you have bathed in the flow of her energies as they have existed throughout time, your vibrations have become aligned with hers. As such, using meditation, journaling, journeying, and pathworking can often lead to insight and epiphany that you would not have reached without first diving into that good old-fashioned research.

Meditation

When you meditate with or about a Moon Goddess with the intent of learning more about her, your thoughts, your heart, your body, and the Goddess herself will lead you where you are meant to go. This requires a certain amount of yielding to That Which Is Greater, to surrendering to what is there for you in any given moment versus attempting to control or contrive a fixed outcome.

Set aside time—at least once a week is best—and sequester yourself away from all others to commune with your chosen Moon Goddess. Be sure to write in your Moon Journal—not only directly after each meditation experience but daily, especially in the morning when revelatory dreams may be closer to the surface and details easier to recall.

As with any meditation work, find a quiet place where you will be private and undisturbed for the duration. Tell those you cohabitate with that you will be in sacred space, usher animal companions to another room, shut off all electronic devices except any you may be using to time your session and/or to play music, and stop notifications and close all windows on that device so you are not disturbed. Here are two meditations to help facilitate your union with the Moon Goddess.

Embracing Her Essence Meditation

You can meditate with or on the Moon Goddess however you wish, are trained in, or want to experiment with. Here are two practices that I've created specifically for the Path of Lunar Witchcraft. As always, read through all of the instructions so that you are familiar with them before beginning any of the exercises.

To Gather

- A timer and/or a timed piece of music and something upon which to play it (such as your phone, or a tablet). If using music, select something soft, dreamy, and instrumental.
- Your Moon Journal and pen
- A glass of water to drink

Optional

- Incense that corresponds with the Moon Goddess you are connecting with. Incense can be purchased, or you can simply burn one or more of her herbs on a charcoal disk. For example, if you are working with Hekate, you might burn mugwort, or for Cerridwen, bay laurel. Alternately, you could diffuse a corresponding essential oil or anoint yourself with one that has been properly diluted.

To Prepare

- A comfortable space where you can completely relax

The Process

Step 1: Sit up comfortably with good posture. Don't lie down for this practice; you will be lying down for the journeying exercises outlined below. If you are in a chair, rest your feet flat on the floor. If your feet don't reach the floor, it may be better to sit on the floor, outdoors upon the Earth, or in another place where you can sit half-lotus style or crisscross applesauce if that is comfortable for you.

Step 2: Ground and center yourself, connecting first with your breath, then sending your roots down into the Earth and your branches up into the Sky.

Step 3: From this place of connection with Earth, Cosmos, and your sweet Self, return your focus to your breath. Now inhale slowly and mindfully on a count of five. Pause for a count of five. Now exhale at the same slow rate on a count of five. Go through this sequence at least five times or until you are settled and present within the holy moment of now.

Step 4: Start your timer or play the background music you selected: Try five minutes to start, and then expand your practice to ten, fifteen, twenty, and finally thirty minutes.

Step 5: Bring to mind the name of the Goddess you are working with and speak it aloud. As you do so, you may also find yourself experiencing her in other ways—perhaps an image, scent, sound, texture, color, or temperature change; however you experience her (or do *not* experience her) is perfect and wonderful.

Step 6: On your five-count inhalation, bring her essence into your body. Pause and hold for a five-count, holding her essence within your body. Exhale her essence out on another five-count. Say her name aloud on your exhalation.

Step 7: Continue this practice until your timer goes off or the music ends. Immediately write down everything you can remember in your Moon Journal for future reference and to build upon as the lunation unfolds.

Your journal entry may be pages, or it may be paragraphs, or it may even just be one word, one image, one sound, feeling, emotion, texture, color, temperature, or other sensation. Don't discount anything that comes through—write it all down and trust that more information may be revealed about your experience later, in the fullness of time.

Step 8: When you are complete with your journaling, draw your roots and branches back into your human body and release any extra energies into the Earth for her healing and up to the Moon Goddess in appreciation and gratitude.

Step 9: Shake off anything more, then pat your body gently all over. Wiggle fingers; wiggle toes. Open your eyes and look around. Drink the water you have set out for yourself.

Step 10: Be sure to return yourself to full presence before reentering everyday life. If you find yourself still spacing out and it's not time to sit down to a full meal, eat something with carbs or sugars. Touch the Earth and breathe with her until you are fully returned to yourself.

Decoding Her Disposition Meditation

Here is another meditation you can use to discover more about a particular Moon Goddess. Be sure to gather everything you need before beginning, and as above, create a space where you will be undisturbed and safe to meditate.

To Gather

- A picture of the Moon Goddess you are seeking connection with (printed out from the computer, a screenshot on your phone or tablet, or one you've drawn or painted)

- Music that is instrumental, soft, and soothing and something to play it upon. Ideally, the piece you choose should reflect the amount of time you will be in meditation (or you can set a timer for yourself).
- Your Moon Journal and pen

Optional

- Incense that corresponds with the Moon Goddess you are connecting with, or a corresponding essential oil to diffuse or dilute for anointing yourself.

The Process

Step 1: If you want to go all out, do so: create an altar, cast a formal magical circle, and so on.

Step 2: Sit comfortably and with good posture. (Don't lie down for this practice.) As noted in the previous practice, if you are in a chair, rest your feet flat on the floor. If your feet don't reach the floor, sit on the floor, outdoors upon the Earth, or in another place where you can sit in the lotus or half-lotus position if that is comfortable for you.

Step 3: Slowly and gently connect with your breath, with your roots and branches, and then link with Earth and Sky.

Step 4: Begin your music (and set a timer if necessary). For your first foray into the exercise, begin with five minutes, and then slowly over time increase by five-minute intervals until you are able to work this practice for thirty minutes or more.

Step 5: Using breath and visualization, relax each part of your body in succession. (If you'd prefer a vocal guide, a yoga nidra meditation recording can be helpful.)

Step 6: Now, look at the picture of the Goddess until you can see-sense-feel her in your mind's eye. Close your eyes, and ask the Moon Goddess to help you to know her. Allow whatever comes through to be present, trusting in the process. If nothing happens, that is fine, too. Now is not the right time, and you can revisit this practice later.

Step 7: When the music ends (or your timer goes off), thank the Moon Goddess by name and express gratitude for all she has shown or told you.

Step 8: Return to your breath and your body. Write everything that you remember in your Moon Journal without editing. It's necessary to get everything you discovered down as quickly as possible before you lose the details. You can refine everything later—or not!

Step 9: When you are complete, return yourself to full presence. Gently pat, touch, or hug yourself. Send extra energy down to the Earth Mother and up to the Moon Goddess. Return your roots and branches into your body. Drink water; eat food; touch the Earth. Continue exploring the best ways to bring yourself back to your body after meditation.

Journaling with the Moon Goddess

Journaling allows your Inner Self another place to connect with the Moon Goddess, and it can help you to discover information about her of which you were not consciously aware. The technique is simple. Begin by writing the name of the Lunar Goddess you are working with at the top of a fresh page in your Moon Journal.

Then, in the vein of morning pages as taught by author Julia Cameron, fill three pages with whatever comes to mind about that Goddess without pausing and without editing. Alternatively, instead of using a page count, you can set a timer for five or ten minutes and write as quickly as you can during that interval.

If you'd like to connect with the Moon Goddess more broadly, you can compose or select an inquiry for focus. Here are some of the prompts I regularly revisit; if you are working with a specific guise, replace the words *the Moon Goddess* with her name.

Morning

- What can I do today to better connect with the Moon Goddess?
- What qualities of the Moon Goddess do I want to embody during this day?
- What is standing in the way of my connection with the Moon Goddess today?
- What can I do to make more space for the Moon Goddess to express herself through me today?
- In what new way(s) would I like to connect with the Moon Goddess today? How would I like for her to appear in my life?
- What aspect of the Moon Goddess would I like to explore through the course of this day?
- What challenge(s) could the Moon Goddess possibly help me with today?
- What does the Moon Goddess want me to know and take with me today?

Evening

- In what ways did I connect with the Moon Goddess today?
- What qualities of the Moon Goddess did I express today?
- Where did I block my connection with the Moon Goddess today?
- How did I make space for the Moon Goddess to express herself through me today?
- In what new way(s) did I connect with the Moon Goddess today? How did she appear in my life?
- What aspect of the Moon Goddess did I learn about through the course of this day?
- What challenge(s) did the Moon Goddess help me to meet today?
- What wisdom did the Moon Goddess impart to me today?

General Prompts

- When I think of the Moon Goddess, what details do I see? Sense? Hear? Smell? Feel?
- What do I want my relationship with the Moon Goddess to look and feel like?
- What is one small step I can take to move toward making this a reality?
- What is the Moon Goddess most passionate about? What does she most value?
- What does the Moon Goddess like? What does she dislike?
- What does the Moon Goddess look like? What does she feel like?
- In what part of my body does the Moon Goddess dwell?
- With what would I like to ask the Moon Goddess to help?
- What offerings does the Moon Goddess want from me?
- What are the gifts of the Moon Goddess? What is her magic?
- What is most sacred to her?
- What Element(s) of Life is she most connected with? What is my personal connection with these element(s)? How can I deepen my connection with these element(s)?
- How can I walk in the truth that the Moon Goddess also dwells within me? How can I better express this as I move through my everyday life?
- What gifts of the Moon Goddess am I most grateful for today? Every day?
- What qualities does the Moon Goddess have that are already strong within me? Which of her qualities do I want to strengthen?
- What do I most appreciate about the Moon Goddess? How does this reflect self-love and self-appreciation?
- What evidence can I point to that shows that the Moon Goddess is active in my life?

Metacognitive Drawing and Automatic Writing

While these two tools look outwardly different from one another—one involving drawing and one involving writing—their inner function is so similar that I join them into a single practice. Here's a bit about each of them and then a practice that brings them together into one exercise. I use this exercise often to communicate with the Goddess, whether it be a named face of the Goddess or the Moon Goddess in her broadest expression.

Metacognitive drawing is a practice I learned from Shiloh Sophia McCloud, founder of the Musea Center for Intentional Creativity and the Intentional Creativity Foundation. In Intentional Creativity, this practice is generally used to free up space in the mind and heart for the Muse to arrive, and it is defined as "thinking about thinking with a pen in your hand."

Automatic writing, sometimes called psychography, is writing without using the conscious mind, creating a pathway that enables Goddess, Spirit, Guides, and/or our Inner Selves to use our human hands to speak through the written word. Some say this is a psychic art that can be used only by those who are innately gifted in it, but I don't agree. In my years of teaching, I have never met a student who was unable to achieve results with this uncomplicated process.

Pairing these two tools creates an effective means of merging both inner wisdom and the wisdom of the Divine, allowing messages that were buried or invisible to reveal themselves as they pass through the channel from the deepest part of ourselves—from the Oracular Self. Additionally, this practice can be easily applied to any of life's conundrums, and it has been astonishingly potent when I've felt stuck with any endeavor.

This is a method of information gathering that awakens the brain and our psychic capabilities in different and often unexpected ways. It moves us past what we already think we know into that holy space of Not Knowing—this is where the concept of "thinking outside the box" abides.

We may never ascertain exactly where the messages originate; some of the places oracular wisdom is thought to come from include our Ancestors (of blood, land, or choice), our Spiritual Guides and Guardians, Goddess herself, the Divine, and/or our Higher Selves.

Exploring the Unconscious

When playing with the following exercise, recognize that you may not receive any particular message at all but may simply find yourself able to move stagnant energies or obstacles. Whatever happens—or doesn't—is correct for you. When you engage in these practices without attachment or expectation of specific results, without comparison or competition, you will make space for what is most needed to arise for *you*.

I encourage you to become familiar with this tool and begin to use it in your own practice. It is a powerful way to alter energy and to get to the crux of what you are really, truly feeling and knowing in your core.

To Gather

- Three pieces of paper, a sketchbook, or journal. You may decide to dedicate a sketchbook just to this purpose. I did and I love having all of this work in one place. I decorated the cover of my sketchbook with a collage of the Moon.
- At least two pens or markers in varying colors that bring you joy
- A two(ish)-minute piece of instrumental music and a way to play it
- Your Moon Journal and pen

To Prepare

Create an inquiry, one that you will pose to yourself or to the Moon Goddess. Here are a few examples:

- What do I need to know about this Moon Goddess?
- What hidden aspect of this Moon Goddess wants to presence itself to me?
- What quality of this Moon Goddess would like to be present in my life right now?

The Process

Step 1: Start by writing your inquiry at the top of the page. This way, if you find that you've gotten "lost," it's easy to return to your inquiry without losing time. Throughout this exercise, hold your inquiry as gently as you can as you follow the pen or marker with your eyes and your body, allowing it to move as it does. Don't try to draw any recognizable shapes or objects. Don't try to write proper sentences or complete thoughts or words.

To keep out of self-judgment, try using your nondominant hand for both the metacognitive drawing and the automatic writing parts of this process.

Step 2: Once you have written your inquiry at the top of a blank page, take up your pen or marker and start up the two minutes of music. Allow the music to support you as you engage with metacognitive drawing. Permit the pen to move itself over the page, doing whatever it wants to do. Try to do this without lifting your marker, making one continuous line or shape.

Remember: You are not trying to draw anything here. You are freeing your body to free your mind and your Oracular Self.

Step 3: When the two minutes end, set your page aside and take up another blank paper or page. Once again, write your inquiry at the top. Start your music for another two-minute session, this time writing words. Just allow whatever words want to flow from your pen onto the paper. to do so Don't worry about making sentences, proper spelling or grammar or punctuation. It is best if the pen never lifts from the paper. Make space for your Oracular Self to emerge. Make space for the Goddess to speak to and through you.

Step 4: When the two minutes of music concludes, it is time to bring everything together into one impression on another blank sheet of paper. What did you learn, discover, and/or experience? Start your music again for two minutes and play with both words and drawing. If you are not finished when the music ends, keep going; spend as much time as you need.

Know, however, that this entire activity usually takes less than five minutes: One sentence, one concept, or one idea is a success.

Step 5: In your Moon Journal, write down the impression you arrived at with the knowledge that it will continue to percolate and grow within you. Revisit it whenever you want to. If you'd like, inscribe this impression on its own page in your Moon Journal so that you can add to it as new information presents itself.

Journeying

Pathworking, guided meditation, visualization, trance, and shamanic journeying are all closely related practices that accord us the opportunity to visit with the Moon Goddess. Here, we can ask any questions we may have, receive clarification on something we've already learned, request assistance with an issue wide-ranging or limited, or simply bask in her energies, connecting our hearts with hers on a more intimate level.

You can use journeying to unlock doors both practical and spiritual. For example, if you are stuck regarding a specific color you need to use for a ritual or spell, you can discover it here. Or if you need to receive heart-healing or divine unconditional love, you can find that here, too.

You can certainly journey without any agenda at all, and I often do this for the purpose of resting and communion with That Which Is Greater.

A Journey to the Moon Goddess

Choose a quiet place and time where you will be undisturbed by housemates, animal companions, and anything else. Turn off electronics. Be sure to read through the instructions before beginning and take the time to set up your space with loving mindfulness. I like to plan for journeying at least a few days in advance so I can go in prepared in all ways—body, mind, heart, and spirit.

To Gather

- An eye covering (a sleep mask, bandana, cloth, the arms of a soft sweatshirt, or something else)
- Recorded music and something on which to play it. Use your favorite instrumental music or find a shamanic drumming track; it's even better if you can find music from the culture of the Goddess you are working with or even music that was created in devotion to her. Twenty to forty-five minutes is an appropriate amount of time, depending on your intentions and desires. Note: If you choose a drumming track, it is best to select one with a call back sequence at the end.
- Your Moon Journal and pen

To Prepare

- A cozy and pleasant nest to lie down in during your journey. You may want to line your nest with pillows, your favorite blanket, a special cloth, and other comfort items.

The Process

Step 1: Choose the specific Moon Goddess you intend to connect with on this journey and replace the words *the Moon Goddess* with her name within the journey.

If you wish, you can record these words in advance, or you can simply look them over now and then allow whatever happens to happen, knowing that whatever does is right and good and that there is no way to do anything wrong. You can always journey again later.

Step 2: Start your music, lie down in your nest, and begin to slow your breath. Slow everything down. Notice the watery tidal energies of the Moon and the Moon Goddess holding you and supporting you in this holy work.

Step 3: Settle yourself even further into this sacred space now and make your body as comfortable as you can. Relax each muscle from the bottom of your toes to the top of your head in turn, release and let go, finding your breath and following it as it gently goes in and out, in and out, in and out of your body, this Holy Temple your soul resides in. With each breath, become more relaxed, more open, more expansive.

Step 4: Breathe slowly and gently. Feel yourself held by the Earth Mother below and supported by the Moon Goddess above. Feel the air of your breath, the fire of your spirit, the water of your blood, the earth of your body.

Step 5: Breathe in and breathe out, relaxing yourself on all levels—physical, intellectual, emotional, and spiritual. Each breath cleanses you. Each breath clears you. Each breath creates more space for expansion and understanding inside of your body. Each breath opens you to the energies and messages and guidance from the Moon Goddess.

Step 6: You are now ready to commune with the Moon Goddess and with your own sweet Self, to listen for and receive the messages that are ready to present themselves in your life, the messages that will free you from those things you hold that no longer serve your highest good. You are ready to listen and hear the voice of the Moon Goddess, to hear her wisdom and her truth.

Step 7: Breathe yourself now into a place of quiet in your inner landscape. Walk into a circle in that landscape and turn in the direction from which you know the Moon Goddess will approach. Hold in your outstretched hands a gift for her.

Step 8: She comes to you now and accepts your gift. What form does she take? Is she human? An animal? A symbol? A light? A color? An energy? Perhaps even a texture or a scent or a flavor? Look, listen, sense, and feel her holy and loving presence.

Step 9: The Moon Goddess invites you to sit with her in her favorite place, and you accept her offer. Spend time with her now, communicating with her in whatever way or ways seem honorable and correct. If it feels right to do so, ask her questions. Ask for her help.

Step 10: When your music comes to an end, it is time to express your gratitude and say farewell to the Lady of the Moon. Thank her for spending time with you, and thank her for any assistance, information, or gifts she offered to you.

Say farewell with the joyful awareness that you can return to this place—and to her—whenever you have need. As you say goodbye, the Moon Goddess turns and leaves this holy place. Watch her departure.

Step 11: Find your breath again and observe it moving gently in and out of your body. Begin to gently stretch your body, to wiggle fingers and toes. Lovingly pat your body all over.

Step 12: Take a deep breath in now, bringing your awareness to your physical body, fully, wholly, and completely returning. Bring your full, whole, and complete awareness to *this* here and *this* now.

Step 13: In your Moon Journal, note everything you can remember from your journey. Draw any symbols or imagery you experienced; write down the words and wisdom of the Moon Goddess. Chronicle your experience in words and in images.

Step 14: When you are done documenting, ground and center yourself. Feel the air of your breath, the fire of your spirit, the water of your blood, the earth of your body. Feel the Earth Mother beneath your body and touch the ground, sending any extra energy down to her for health and healing. Send extra energy up to the Moon Goddess with love and gratitude.

Move slowly and gently through the rest of your day or evening. Be sure to eat something healthy and to hydrate with blessed water.

Offerings for the Moon Goddess

Making offerings is an exceptional approach to honoring the Moon Goddess. This practice increases opportunity for connection, carving out priceless moments of intentional gratitude and respect that are woven seamlessly into our everyday lives. Much of my own daily lunar devotions involves making offerings to the Moon as Goddess, as luminary, and as a primary force in my life.

Offerings to the Moon as a heavenly body may be made in the form of any of her correspondences. When you are developing your relationship with a particular Moon Goddess, though, try to use her unique correspondences. You can certainly include those more conventional and traditional lunar correspondences, and most deities enjoy fruits, flowers, foods, herbs, incenses, sacred waters, and other libations. Do your research and mind your personal gnosis to discover what a particular Moon Goddess would like you to present to her.

Poetic offerings and prayers, either those you compile, write yourself, or read from outside sources are also beautiful ways to give honor to her many faces.

I like to write simple pieces of adoration and adulation by combining the forms, functions, and traditional titles and honorifics of a particular Goddess into appellations and then reading this list to her in grand and dramatic fashion.

Here is an example of appellations; I created this list for the Moon in her guise as Goddess Selene:

Horned Goddess of the Moon
The Moon Herself
Driver of the Chariot of the Moon
Crescent-Crowned Lady
Goddess Queen
Mother of Age
Fruit-Producing Moon
Lover of Horses
Fair Lamp of Night
Queen of the Stars
All-Wise Lady
Lover of Vigilance
The Foe of Strife
Splendid Queen of Night
White-Armed Goddess
Goddess of the Moon
Rich-Tressed Selene
The Eye of Night
Benevolent One
All-Seeing Lady

I also like to sing to her, be it a song I'm improvising or one that was written by others. Try it out and see what happens when you share your heart with her through words and sound.

Connecting with the Lady of the Moon Ritual

This is a ritual that can be used to solidify your kinship with the Moon Goddess in one of her individual guises. I suggest it be used once per lunation and, as always, to try it first exactly as written and then to make it your own.

Remember: The length of a ritual is not necessarily a sign of quality. Short and sweet is often indicated when we are practicing as solitary Lunar Witches.

I consistently do my best to either begin or end a devotion to a particular Goddess based upon the phase of the Moon she is most associated with. If she isn't associated with a particular phase, I'll check on her innate energies. Are they for increase or decrease? I may also gather more information by engaging with one of the practices I shared earlier. This helps me to make a decision regarding timing. If all else fails, I begin with the New Moon. It is entirely your choice as to exactly when within a lunation to use this ritual.

This rite can also be used for monthly reconnection with a Moon Goddess with whom you have a continuing devotion. I also like to use this ceremony (or a version of it) to reset my lunar practice or at any time I've lost my connection with the rhythms of the Moon or the Moon Goddess herself.

Before beginning, choose the Moon Goddess you would like to work with for at least one lunar cycle and get to know her using one or more of the methods discussed earlier in this chapter.

To Gather

- The objects you will use to create your ritual altar, including any personal Sacreds you wish to charge
- Something with which to ritually cleanse your space (e.g., herbs to burn such as lavender, eucalyptus, or rosemary, salt, water, or sound)
- A small symbol of the Moon Goddess you are connecting with (e.g., a crystal or stone; an image of her; a representation of one of her correspondences; a picture, drawing, or sigil)
- An unlit candle and a lighter or matches
- A length of white yarn, thread, or ribbon (or in a color that specifically corresponds to the Moon Goddess you are inviting into your life)
- Scissors with which to cut your yarn, thread, or ribbon
- Prepared Cakes and Ale (such as chocolate, fruit, or nuts and water, wine, or juice)
- Your Moon Journal and pen

Optional

- Recorded instrumental music to support your work
- A drum, rattle, or other instrument for raising energy

To Prepare

Be sure to read through the rite before beginning, ideally at least twenty-four hours before the time you have chosen to perform your ritual. I prefer to look rituals over three or more days in advance, and I use this time to begin slowly gathering the items needed. Additionally, you may immerse in a ceremonial bath or shower before beginning your ceremony.

The Rite

Step 1: Set a working altar—as simple or as elaborate as you wish. Include images, symbols, and offerings for the specific Moon Goddess to whom you are dedicating this ritual, including candles, incense, cloths, and crystals as appropriate.

Step 2: Cleanse and purify yourself and your ritual space. Always remember: Your visionary Inner Moon Witch already knows what to do.

Step 3: Ground, center, and open the channel. Connect with your breath, and then use your breath to connect with the Earth and Sky; from your body, send etheric roots down into the Earth Mother and etheric branches up into the Cosmos.

When you are grounded as the pillar between Earth and Sky, come into contact with your bindu chakra, third eye chakra, and heart chakra, opening them up to give and receive Cosmic, Earth, and Divine Love.

From this place of loving connection with All That Is, voice gratitude to the land you are on, its Indigenous Ancestors, and your own Benevolent Ancestors of blood and/or choice.

Pause here and enjoy the sensation of belonging and connection for as long as it feels supportive, powerful, and good.

Step 4: Call in the lunar energies. Drum, rattle, sing, and/or chant as inspired, communing with the energy, phase, and sign of the Moon, her eternal cycle, and the energies of growth, harvest, and decay.

Now, slowly and with elevated consciousness, open yourself up to the powers, energies, and qualities of the Moon Goddess you will invite to join you throughout this lunation.

Step 5: Connect with the ritual intent. Spontaneously speak aloud your purpose for this rite. You may also wish to say something like "With honor and with respect, I request that Moon Goddess (speak her name) walk with me throughout this lunation. With pleasure and with humility, I ask to learn your wisdom, O (speak her name)."

Step 6: Create an energy well. Using the sound of "Ma" or "Om" or another tone that resonates with you, create an etheric well of energy to draw upon for your ritual.

Step 7: Step Between the Worlds. Separate your ritual space from the everyday world using whatever method(s) work for you. You may decide to cast a formal circle, offering invocations to the elements or directions and your Guardians or Guides, and/or whatever else your personal spiritual path calls for.

The one thing that is important to do during this step is to invite the Moon Goddess to join you by name. You can do this through a formal invocation that you have written in advance or one that comes through you in the moment, using an invocation someone else has written, or through poetry, sound, dance, or other art. Do speak her name, though, and ask (Ask! Please do not demand.) for her presence in your circle and in your life.

A loving reminder that experimentation is beautiful, and it is always okay. We learn through trying new things, and our innocent willingness is far more important than any calculated attempt at flawlessness.

When you are finished with this step, you may wish to announce: "The circle is cast, and I am Between the Worlds."

Step 8: Seat yourself comfortably before your altar in such a way that you can easily see and touch the object you have designated to represent the Moon Goddess. If you have chosen recorded music to support your work, this is the time to turn it on.

Now, think about the Moon Goddess you have called to join you for this lunation. Experience her energies, consider her attributes and powers, and begin opening yourself to greater communion with her.

With gratitude and love, light your candle in the name of this Moon Goddess, and in heartfelt welcome.

When you are ready, begin speaking to her from your heart. Tell her who you are and why you have asked her to join you and for how long you would like her companionship. Share with her what you hope to explore, learn, and achieve. Whatever is on your mind, say it to her. And yes, speak aloud!

When you are complete with your words, touch the object you have chosen, and ask her that it remind you of the relationship you are exploring with her whenever you see it. Feel her energies moving through your body as you conduct them outward through your hand, awakening and infusing the object with your purpose.

When the object feels filled with her energies, say aloud, "It is done".

Step 9: To further enhance your connection with her, wrap your yarn, thread, or ribbon around your wrist, blessing it with these words:

> *Moon Goddess (say her name), Beloved of Humanity*
> *For this next lunation I pledge myself to knowing you*
> *To learning your ways*

To hearing your wisdom
May your visions color my perception
May your inspiration ripple through my body
May your love flow through my heart
May my hands do your good work on Earth
And may this thread remind me every day
Of this sacred commitment
So mote it be!

When this is done, you may tie your thread and cut it so it is comfortable upon your wrist (or wait and ask a trusted loved one to do so for you after your circle is open).

Step 10: With joy, empower and seal your magic. Use your arms to gather up all of the energies from the center of your circle—and from the etheric well you created in step 6—and send these energies up to the Moon in thankfulness using a "Ma," "Om," or another tone.

Step 11: With exuberance, chant these words aloud three times: *It is done, it is done, it is done, done, done!* You may wish to shake a rattle or bang a drum or dance to move these energies through your body and your ritual space.

Step 12: Enjoy your Cakes and Ale. Bless your sacramental food and libation in the name of the Moon Goddess and then eat and drink with reverence. If you would like, you may journal about your experiences now, within your sacred circle, whilst eating and drinking.

Step 13: Open the circle. Speak your gratitude to the Moon Goddess, thanking her by name, and to any other energies or entities you invoked, sending them lovingly on their way.

Step 14: Ground and center yourself. Release any extra energies from your body down into the Earth Mother for her health and healing. Carefully retract your etheric roots and branches, restoring them steadily and firmly into your physical body.

Step 15: Give yourself and the Moon Goddess your appreciation and gratitude for work well done. Blessed be!

If you did not journal while within your circle, do so now, committing as many details as you can remember to the page. Include any thoughts, feelings, or insights you gained so that you can reference them again later.

Place your blessed object where you will see it daily throughout the lunation—your lunar altar is an excellent place for this.

Keep your thread on your wrist for the lunation or longer, if you are working with her for more than one lunar cycle. Ritually cut the thread from your wrist when your time with this Moon Goddess concludes and then release the thread, treating it as the holy relic it is by placing it somewhere hallowed to you or disposing of it in a sacred manner.

Working with these guises of the Moon has helped me to form profound connections with the Goddess, She of Infinite Names. It is my hope that you will find the same sense of belonging, comfort, and guidance that I have received into my life over the years of tending to these relationships with the various faces of the Divine.

Chapter 12
Moon Magic and Lunar Rites

The Moon Goddess Speaks

I am the Moon, my magic cyclical, transforming with the tides. I come to remind you that you, too, hold an untouchable, singular force within, one which can shift fate and change the world should you but believe in yourself.

My powers are instinctual, natural, transformational, just as are yours. I am creative and creating, inspirational and inspiring, soft, sharp, and stirring. Light for me a white candle and fill with seawater a clear vessel and then look up, visiting me with your eyes.

I am your silvery mirror. Look within me to see a reflection of your most luminous Self.

I am Luna.

Journal Inquiries for This Gateway

What is my favorite lunar phase in which to work magic? How can I best connect my innate magic with the powers of the Moon? What would my life look like if I completely and shamelessly embraced my own singular magic?

Affirmations for This Gateway

I am a Moon Witch. My magic flows with the Moon. I fully embrace my power.

In its simplest form, Lunar Witchcraft is working magic and ritual in conjunction with the phases and astrological travels of the Moon. It is really that uncomplicated.

The Moon can support us in whatever we do, but especially in our magic. She grows and diminishes, over and over and over again, just like our own human energies do. When we partner with her and her energies, our magic takes flight.

When we walk with the Moon, entrusted with her secrets, we are able to wield the powers of alchemy and transformation, placing them in service to our own spirituality, our belonging, and our connection to All That Is, all that was, and all that will ever be.

Lunar Spellwork Fundamentals

Working hand in hand with the Moon to perform magic awakens our Primal Selves to the remembrance that there is a hidden force of creativity behind all things, that there is a fathomless depth to our own potential and the potential of all of our fellow humans.

Simple spellcasting might be composed of lighting a candle of a certain color, writing down your intentions, speaking to the wind or to the ocean, creating an amulet to wear, constructing a poppet, or burning something in a fire.

There is rarely a need to work a complicated spell requiring archaic, expensive, and/or hard-to-find ingredients in order to manifest successful results. All you truly ever need is you—magic comes from within, and your kinship with the Moon enhances and magnifies your innate powers.

Form Follows Idea

Our thoughts are the quickest and most volatile form of energy. They are here, and then they are gone just as quickly, distinct from those things that have already taken the form of matter.

When you want to manifest something, you first create it in your mind. Epiphanies, inspirations, ideas, and thoughts are always the initial step in manifesting anything, from the most mundane to the most magical.

For example, when you realize you are hungry, your thought is the spark that precedes you getting up and making something to eat.

According to author Shakti Gawain, "The idea is like a blueprint; it creates an image of the form, which then magnetizes and guides the physical energy to flow into that form and eventually manifests it on the physical plane."[42]

42. Gawain, *Creative Visualization*, 19.

A new home is built by first thinking about it, then finalizing a blueprint, then purchasing the materials, then preparing the land, and only then do the builders arrive on the site to begin bringing the dream into physical reality.

Unwavering Intention

The potency of spellwork is determined by unwavering intention, where your will and your consciousness intersect. To accomplish your goal, you must hold it with clarity of purpose—this means that prior to beginning, you have already examined your emotions around your need, deliberately put aside all thoughts and feelings that don't serve your objective, and focused your energies alone upon your intention.

The amount of emotional connection to your goal that you can bring forth into your spellcasting helps to determine the results. The more powerfully you are able to recognize and connect with your need, the more likely you are to manifest it.

Spellwork Preparation

Before beginning your lunar magic, it is necessary to prepare. You must set up your magical space, gather the components needed, and ready yourself.

Prepare the Space

No matter where you do your magic, the most important quality of the space is that it feels safe, protected, and private, permitting you to easily step Between the Worlds, into an altered state of consciousness.

Your magical space may be a dedicated place where you consistently do your moonwork (e.g., at your lunar altar), or it may be something you set up each time you perform your spellwork or ritual and take down after. If you are not using your lunar altar for your spellwork, for example, it's best to create a temporary altar where you will do your moonwork and assemble there all of the necessary tools or ingredients for your next spell or ritual.

If possible, do your magic in the same location each time—this helps you to slip into Ritual Mind more rapidly; naturally fosters a sustained energetic container over time; and, on the practical level, is convenient in that all of your lunar tools and correspondences can be stored there together.

Deal with Distractions

Before beginning any spell or rite, you will also take care of any mundane tasks that could cause distraction. Here are some ideas for your checklist:

- Is your door (or doors) locked?
- If you live with others, have you told them that you will be unavailable and/or placed a sign on your door?
- Are your electronic devices turned off, set to silent or, even better, left outside of your sacred space?
- Is everything that may need your attention handled in the mundane arena (e.g., children and animals fed, food put away, trash taken out)?
- Is your working space comfortable, including lighting, temperature, and seating?
- Have you gathered all of the necessary tools and ingredients (including such things as lighters or matches) and set up your altar?
- Do you have a written version of your spell or script on hand? (If using)
- Have you identified the location of cardinal directions in your space? (If inviting the directions)

Prepare Your Tools

Tools are never essential for lunar magic or ritual—you and your link with the Moon are all that is truly needed. Combined with a quiet, safe space, your concentration and will can manifest successful results.

That said, ritual tools and other ingredients are often quite helpful. These components assist you in opening to greater psychic and magical receptivity, and tools store power, helping to remind you and your inner Slothperson—the Ancient One Within, that most primal part of yourself—that something exciting, different, and magical is happening.

Preparing Yourself

Always purify and cleanse, ground and center before beginning any ritual or spell. You may wish to take a magical bath or shower. (See chapter 9 for ideas.) Or you may wish to wear your lunar clothing and jewelry or go moonclad (i.e., without clothing). How you prepare is entirely your choice, based upon your energy level, purpose, and what brings you joy.

You can quickly prepare your mind and body by first getting in touch with yourself through your breath and then with the Earth. When you are connected with your Inner Lunar Witch and the Earth, open up your connection with the Moon and step into flow with her.

Magical Timing

Lunar timing is one of the simplest things around which to build a spell or ritual.

When crafting your lunar rituals and moonspells, determine first the phase of the Moon that will be most favorable for your working. Next, consider the sign the Moon will be in and the relationship between that sign and the sign the Sun will be in. Then bring in the energetics of your own natal Moon sign and your natal Sun sign. Do these energies combine pleasantly, or could they be at odds? Could you add or subtract magical ingredients that would help to ease connection, create greater harmony, and/or negate differences?

Depending upon your working, you may also want to choose a specific planetary day and/or hour to support your aims.

You can also use the Elements of Life as a foundation for your decision-making:

- When the Moon is transiting an air sign, perform magic regarding the mind, the intellect, and communication. Spellwork for clarity, decision-making, inspiration, and freedom are most supported during these times, especially when a new beginning, a new perspective, and/or a new vision is needed.
- When Luna is transiting a fire sign, make magic for creativity, transformation, and quick results. These are the moments to build moonspells to enhance courage, strength, and determination, to increase health and personal power-within.
- The Moon is most at home when flowing through the watery parts of the zodiac. While she traverses these signs, it's time to work magic regarding emotions and feelings. Relationship spells for connection, love, and self-love are supported, as are those centered in psychic abilities, dreaming, and intuition. Cleansing and purifying magic is also well done during these transits.
- When the Moon is moving through the earth signs, incorporate the energies of fertility, prosperity, and growth into your workings. If money is tight and resources are low, this is the transit to do spellwork to remediate these struggles—whether you are seeking a new job, a new home, or an influx of cash. Healing of all kinds is appropriate during this time, as is working with the soil of life.

Energy Projection and Storage

Power is energy, effort, force, drive, vigor, zip! The power that drives spellwork and powers ritual can be found and stored in various places.

An Important Reminder: You are a channel for these energies, not their originator. Even though you generate power in your body, the fuel for your ritual and magic should be channeled from other sources—first through your body and then directed outward using the power of your mind, your will, your consciousness. Strive to remember that while this power channels through your body and is focused by you, you are not using the energy from your own cells. This keeps you healthy and strong, your personal power intact and sustained.

Power from Earth and Sky

When you ground yourself before ritual and/or magic, you connect first with your breath, then with the Earth beneath and the Sky above. Connecting with the Earth includes the Earth Herself—she who is a caring Mother, who loves and nurtures unconditionally—and the Below: the Benevolent Ancestors and the Holy Magma of the Earth's core.

Connecting with the Sky—including the Moon—encompasses all of those energies existing Above: the sky itself, all of the celestial bodies, and the Luminous Void where all potential and possibility resides.

Power from the Moon Alone

As a Moon Witch, you can draw upon the energies of the Moon alone to power your magic, further enhanced by her phases and travels through the astrological signs.

Power from the Moon Goddess

When you call upon a Moon Goddess to guide your ritual and magic, you ask for her presence, assistance, guidance, and wisdom. You ask her to grant your wishes, to meet your needs, and to help you to manifest your goals and desires for your highest good and that of all involved.

Power from the Elements, Elementals, Nature Spirits, Guides, Allies, and Others

When you call upon the elements and/or the directions, you also welcome their inherent powers and energies; for example: the winds of change, the fires of transformation, the quick flowing river, those of hoof and paw, and so on, or less distinctly, wind, ocean, mountain, stone, tree. Nature spirits, plant devas, elementals, your personal Spiritual Guides (human, animal, and other), and more can also be entreated for magical support and power.

Storing Power

When you drain excess power from your body at the end of ritual or any magical undertaking, you may choose to drain it into the Earth for her healing, trusting in her infinite wisdom that it be used where it is most needed, or you may send it up to the Moon as an offering of gratitude.

You can also use your lunar ritual tools or other Sacreds to store some of this energy, releasing the excess energy first through the object—so that it becomes a *well*—and then into the Earth. The power held in a well builds over time and can be accessed and later used in other spellwork or ritual; it can be exceedingly helpful when you need to perform magic but do not feel 100 percent physically, mentally, emotionally, or etherically healthy.

Most often, I use a moonstone and/or a dedicated quartz crystal for this practice, yet anything that holds meaning for you can be used: your athame, a stone, your chalice, or another object or tool.

See-Sense-Feeling

You can send power to your workings through see-sense-feeling the energies you gathered and then projecting them outward. This see-sense-feel skill is one that everyone has, and the more you practice using it, the better your short- and long-term results.

Magical Documentation

This may come as a surprise. Working lunar magic involves paperwork. There are a myriad of reasons for keeping these valuable records—they will benefit you now and also those who may come after you in the future. Magical records help you to document your progress, your successes and failures, and assist you in honing your abilities through removing conjecture and assumptions; you can plainly read what happened in the written (or typed!) word.

Just as a biologist meticulously records the conditions and results of her experiments, a chef documents and files their new recipes, and an artist makes careful notes of how to achieve an exclusive color, recording your magical exercises helps you to later improve upon your spellwork through repeating the results, identifying where you went wrong, or figuring out what might have worked better.

Over time you can look back and answer questions such as: Am I more successful when my spells use herbs or crystals? Does candle magic or do talismans work better for me? What phase was the Moon in when I cast that money spell that worked so magnificently? On what planetary day and hour was that love spell cast that backfired so spectacularly? What was the chant I used over that healing poppet? Was that spell I did for a promotion two years ago performed on the Full Moon or the New Moon?

Few—if any—of us have flawless memories. Even if you do, using your sense of sight and surveying your past work written down in front of you can help you to notice patterns, to see where there are connections that you may have missed.

Your moon magic records can be organized in your Moon Journal, your Book of Shadows, in a book specific to recordkeeping, in a three-ring binder, or even in an electronic file (this option allows for easy searching). The most important part of magical recordkeeping is that you do it; to facilitate this, you must create a system that works for *you.*

Recordkeeping Example

Below is a sample record for moon magic, with examples of the types of things you might include in your own documentation. Use this as a beginning point. Adapt it and make it your own.

Do not be afraid to experiment. Keep excellent and detailed magical records and soon you will discover what works best for you and what does not work at all. Take the time to note what you did and how you did it, and then revisit your record once the spell has manifested (or not). This will help you to troubleshoot any problems or later replicate your success.

Date: Knowing the date a spell or ritual was performed will help you to understand where it falls in the greater flow of the arc of your life.

Purpose: Why are you doing this working?

Moon Phase and Sign: When doing Lunar Witchcraft—whether planned in advance or done spontaneously—always note the Moon phase and sign. When you go back to reread notes about your work later, you may find resonance, seeing the hand of the Moon at work.

Waxing or Waning Moon: What is her exact phase? Within which astrological sign is she traveling? In what degree? If it is a Micromoon or Supermoon, you may want to note that. Eclipses should always be documented.

Time: This is useful as a historical record and for analysis of your development over time. In other words, at what time of day/night are you most magically skilled as a Lunar Witch?

Sun Sign: What sign is the Sun in?

Other Astrological Happenings: Is a celestial body in retrograde? Are you making use of a particular conjunction, opposition, or other relationship? Are you working with a particular Moon Goddess asteroid?

Day and Planet: What is the day of the week and the planet that rules it?

Planetary Hour(s): Document this even if you haven't planned your working with it as a consideration. Remember: You can easily find this information using an app or online calculator—no matter how many days it is after the fact.

Location: Where are you performing your working? At your lunar altar? At an altar you set up specifically and only for this particular objective? In your home or elsewhere? Indoors? Outdoors?

Weather: Is it sunny? Rainy? Cloudy? Snowy? Windy? Did you notice the weather impacting your personal energy, your sacred space, or your working in any way, big or small?

Health and Emotions: Keep this brief and don't include explanations of why you feel how you do. One or two words are best (e.g., relaxed, tense, angry, happy, anxious, excited). If applicable, you may also want to record where you are in your menstrual cycle.

Type of Working: Are you employing water magic, crystal magic, candle magic, herbal magic? Are you creating an amulet or talisman or potion? Are you scrying or divining?

Participant(s): Are you alone? Are you performing the working with others?

Tools/Ingredients/Supplies: List here all of the magical tools, herbs, oils, crystals, candles, and other supplies that you are using. Be as detailed as possible and include your color correspondences and the creators of products (if purchased). More information is better than less here.

Moon Goddess Invoked: Are you calling upon a specific face or guise of the Moon Goddess?

Chants/Songs/Charms: What are you chanting or singing? If something new emerges while you are working, document it. Write down the words you used, perhaps even record yourself singing or chanting into your phone.

Instructions/Composition: If you are the originator of a working, be sure to include what you wrote or did (either your step-by-step process or a general outline). If you are following a spell or ritual written by another, note this here. Include any book titles or websites referenced (the exact address plus the date accessed) if used. After your working, be sure to note any changes or adaptations you spontaneously made.

Notes/Comments/Observations: This is a general—quick!—immediate reflection upon the working as you experienced it. Try to do this right away, as details tend to be lost rapidly when we emerge from our time Between the Worlds.

Approximate Length: After the working is complete, document how long it took. You could note your beginning and ending times, or just write something like "thirty minutes."

Results: Stay open to observing your results. Note any changes regarding the purpose of your moonwork: big, small, or in-between. When did you see results? What were your results? Did the spell work?

Date and How of Manifestation: Note the date that your working was a total and complete success. Include how it manifested in your life.

A Note on Substitutions

When baking a cake, it is almost always necessary to follow the recipe exactly as it is written in order for the cake to rise. Lunar spells, however, are *not* like this type of recipe, one where if the instructions are followed to the letter, the intended results will presumably occur.

Think of lunar spells more like guidelines. When making another type of food, say a soup or stew, a recipe is most commonly a set of ideas, guideposts that you can choose to follow, or not. Substitutions in ingredients can be made easily, and sometimes the results of a substitution will even surpass the original recipe.

Just as in cooking, though, be sure that you comprehend why you are making a substitution. You wouldn't add sugar in the place of salt in a recipe or a banana in place of a potato. So should your moonspell substitutions "rhyme" in some way. All of your ingredients should resonate peacefully and amicably together.

The purpose of magical correspondences is to add power to your work, not take it away. Sometimes it is for the best to simply leave out an ingredient you don't have than to try to replace it. Other times it is advisable to wait until you have everything called for on hand before beginning. And yet other times it is more advantageous to write your own recipe, your own spell, based upon your own needs, environment, energies, perceptions, research, and desires.

The Components of a Lunar Spell

Lunar magic is quite similar to all other spellwork; the difference is that the working is optimized by the Moon, her phases, and her frequencies.

Almost all lunar magic consists of these ten components, typically applied in this order:

1. The knowledge of an intention, goal, target, or desire you wish to bring into being.
2. A decision regarding the best strategy to reach this intention, goal, target, or desire. (What type of spell will you cast?)
3. Choosing the timing of the spell based upon the lunar phase, sign, and/or additional phenomena.

4. Gathering the magical correspondences (ingredients such as candles, herbs, crystals) and setting up a working altar.
5. Purifying your sacred space and requesting the Moon's protection, guidance, and witness.
6. Grounding, centering, and opening the channel.
7. Raising power through connecting with the energies of the Moon and/or other sources.
8. Directing this power to shift the odds in your favor and sending it to the intention.
9. Offering gratitude to the Moon and releasing any extra energies from your body (to Earth, Moon, a well, or all).
10. Denouement: Finishing the working through properly attending to the remnants of each of the spell ingredients as necessary (this includes such things as burning a spell paper, burying a crystal, tossing flowers into the sea, burning a candle down, and pouring out libations).

Moonspells are not about avoiding mistakes—this work includes trial and error, a willingness to fail, and an open and curious heart that is excited to learn.

Magic for All Her Phases

As Luna passes through the phases and frequencies of her never-ending journey, we see that she mirrors our own human lives. When we align ourselves with these energies, we organically deepen our relationship with her, to the Divine both Within and Without, to the Goddess herself.

The constant changing of the Moon reminds us that we are constantly changing, that life itself is a state of perpetual transformation. Here, we can find the courage to evolve with grace, to ebb and flow alongside the Moon.

Here is a selection of moonspells for each of the phases of the Moon to help you find that alignment and realize that change. I invite you to try them all out.

New Moon

The point of transmutation has passed, and something new is coming to be. During this phase, make wishes, pray, and perform magic for what you want to bring into your life and grow. Take action to usher your dreams into reality, and gather the resources that will be needed to implement your lunar spellwork and ritual.

New Moon Dreamseed Spell

In this moonspell, you will meditate and journal about what is awakening for you. Then you will open your eyes, ears, and heart to the power of lunar inspiration.

To Gather

- Your Moon Journal and pen
- A timer
- Loose Paper
- Matches
- A fireproof container

To Prepare

Sit down with your Moon Journal and set a timer for ten minutes. Now write—without overthinking or pausing or self-editing—about those dreams that you brought Earthside but then neglected. Just draft a list here, no judgment, no self-recrimination, no guilt.

When the timer goes off, peruse your list and separate your musings into two categories:

- The dreams you are ready to release. On a piece of loose paper, transcribe all of those dreams that you are ready to let go of. Once you've written them down, fold this piece of paper three times *away* from you, turning the paper counterclockwise in between each folding. Place this paper on your lunar altar.
- The dreams you *truly* want to nurture into completion (it may be none of them). On a fresh page of your journal, list those dreams that you are ready to interact with and tend, no matter what.

Now follow the process, reading through all of the instructions before beginning.

The Process

Step 1: Mark your calendar for the next Hekate's Sickle Dark Moon phase.

Step 2: Look at the list of dreams that you are ready to nurture and choose one of them. If there aren't any on your list, choose now a new dream. This needn't be some huge desire—perhaps you'd like to opt for something simple to move toward over this next lunar cycle.

Step 3: On another piece of loose paper, draw a circle to represent the Full Moon. Inside of it, write your dream in present-tense, affirmation form, as if it is already manifested. Here is an example that highlights dedication to the Path of the Lunar Witch: "I interact with the Moon every day."

Step 4: Place this paper where you can see it daily, ideally upon your lunar altar. At least once a day, say your affirmation aloud and perhaps even take one small step toward your goal. Pay exquisite attention to your affirmation and your goal throughout the entire lunar cycle, interacting with it daily.

Step 5: When the date you have marked in your calendar arrives, go back to your Moon Journal and write about any changes you've affected in your life over this last cycle that are related to your affirmation.

Step 6: Then burn your released dreams paper in a sacred manner, offering love and blessings to these dreams that are not meant to be (At least in this here and now. They may return later, in different forms.).

Step 7: After you've burned this paper of released dreams, bury or compost your affirmation dream paper so that the energies you've dedicated to your dream over this cycle will continue to nourish your goal. Blessed be!

Moon Map Vision Board

Moon map vision boards—also called treasure maps and spirit maps—are valuable, effective partners for increased clarity and manifestation. As an oracular activity, creating a vision board can help you to access and develop your personal power-within and connect it with the power of the Moon.

The objective of a moon map is to create a visual image, a collage depicting what you want to birth into being. These magical objects—created from cut-outs from magazines, old greeting cards, photos, computer printouts, and other items that are glued to a piece of poster board, cardboard, or pasted in a special book—are made for several different purposes.

You can make a vision board for a defined goal (such as a better job, a new car, a vacation), or you can craft one as a shamanic process and practice of sacred art, letting the Moon, the Moon Goddess, and/or your Spirit Guide(s) lead you into cognizance of your innermost desires. You can then use your completed board as a focus to attract to you the energies and things you want.

Moon maps work on an elemental level, speaking to your Slothperson in their own primary language of images. There is no right or wrong way to make a moon map. You may wish to work with more than one map—an overview, big vision, channeled piece followed by many smaller maps, one for each part of your life, such as health, work, spirituality, relationships, and such.

Here are some guidelines that I have developed over the years.

To Gather

- Poster board. Your map can be of any size or shape that suits you; decide what you would like to make now. Some of my vision boards are created on huge pieces of poster board, some on smaller pieces of cardboard; I have an old scrapbook that I craft smaller spirit maps in as the Moon calls. You can even make a tiny map to carry in your wallet, purse, or pocket.
- Markers, pens, or other writing devices in any colors
- Magazines, old greeting cards, photos, computer printouts, and other images

Optional

- A photo of yourself. Ideally this is a powerful image, portraying you doing, having, or being what you want to manifest

The Process

Step 1: Choose your intention. Do you wish to make a moon map for a specific goal or part of your life? Or is this to be a ritual act and a surrender to what is deep inside of you? Neither choice is better than the other—select what calls to you now.

Step 2: Casting a circle or otherwise creating a sacred space to work in can be helpful. Invite the Moon to join you in this holy place.

Step 3: If you have chosen to include a representation of yourself, glue it onto your board first.

Step 4: Next, thumb quickly through the magazines, cards, and pictures you selected. Without intellectualizing, pull out images which support your intentions, those which are beneficial, optimistic, and ideal. There is no need to worry about or to illustrate in any way *how* the situation, object, or feeling will manifest. Leave anything undesirable, unsatisfactory, or unwanted off your map.

Step 5: Include something that evokes the Moon or the Moon Goddess as a reminder of your infinite connection to your path such as an image of her, a symbol, a color; whatever speaks to you and reminds you that you are One with the Oneness of the Moon.

You can include affirmations or other positive phrases, too. In addition to including your words, author Shakti Gawain suggests writing this cosmic phrase on your finished board: *"This or something better is now manifesting for me in totally satisfying and harmonious ways, for the highest good of all concerned."*[43]

Step 6: When you are finished creating your moon map, bless and consecrate it as you would any other magical tool. Give thanks to Luna and to the Muses for cocreating with you.

Step 7: Hang your moon map in a place where you will see it often and watch for what happens. Sometimes the manifestation of your goals will commence immediately. At other times, it may take years for your goal to become present in your life.

Observe and practice patience. I once found a map six years after I created it and had hidden it away; I was shocked that everything I had put on it was now present in my life!

As things begin to materialize, you can use stickers to mark the images. I like using hearts, Moon stickers, or even gold stars. This is a beautiful offering of thanks to the Moon and to yourself for your cocreations.

It can be a fun experiment to place at least one "wildest desires" image on your vision board to see what seemingly outlandish dreams can come true when you partner with the Moon. Blessed be!

Waxing Crescent Moon

This is the phase to do magic and ritual pertaining to attracting or increasing those things you want; it is best for growing, planting, happiness, harmony, reaching for goals, and positive transformation.

Rituals for health, good luck, abundance, success, and love are typically performed now. This is also an auspicious time to begin magic that you will complete at your Full Moon esbat.

This lunar phase is marvelous for moonwork to boost resources and prosperity, especially when she is transiting an earth sign. Here is one of my favorite ideas for you to try:

43. Gawain, *Creative Visualization*, 136.

Lunar Prosperity Charm Bag

Utilize the growing energies of this phase to craft a charm bag that you will tend until the Full Moon, when you will release its contents back into the Multiverse.

Decide on one intention for your prosperity—it is best to choose just one for this magic so you can focus all of your energies upon that desire without diluting it with another purpose—then collect your ingredients. Ensure they are all biodegradable, Earth and animal friendly.

Before beginning, be sure Luna is not void of course, and if possible, time your magic with the planetary hour of the Moon and a congruent zodiacal sign.

To Gather

- A small piece of cloth and a length of yarn, ribbon, or string in a color that corresponds to and supports your desire (or purchase a ready-made drawstring bag)
- A small white stone to represent the Moon. It needs to fit into your cloth or pouch. This could be one of her magical crystals or a white or gray pebble or rock.
- A pinch of one to nine herbs that correspond to the manifestation of your intention
- A diluted essential oil or magical oil blend that is also supportive
- A small piece of paper and a pen or marker. If possible, utilize a favorable color for this, too.
- Cleansing lunar herbs in a fireproof vessel
- A lighter or matches

The Process

Step 1: Ground, center, and open the channel.

Step 2: If desired, cast a magical circle—preferably under her light.

Step 3: In your magical circle, speak to the Moon Mother. Speak from your heart, as you would to a loving friend or caring mentor. Spill your guts! What is it you seek? Why do you seek it? What will your life look like when this goal manifests?

Allow yourself to really *feel* into these energies. Feel and see and sense your life as if your magic is already complete and manifest.

Step 4: With smoldering herbs, cleanse your paper and marker of unwanted energies. Then write *one* word or draw *one* symbol that represents what you are casting for.

Step 5: Using the burning herbs, cleanse your cloth and yarn, ribbon, or string (or pouch) and attune it to you. This becomes a "womb," a place for your dream to grow and be nurtured as the Moon grows in power.

Step 6: With reverence, place your paper inside of the cloth or pouch.

Step 7: Now, cleanse each of your other items with the smoldering herbs, one by one, placing each gently and lovingly into the pouch after doing so.

You may want to include something to link the bag to you alone: a piece of hair, a fingernail, blood, spit. This helps to optimize the coherence between your magic and your unique energetic signature.

Step 8: Once all of your items are inside, tie your cloth into a bundle (or tie the bag closed). With each knot, whisper your intention. You may want to tie your knots in groups of three: three, six, nine. If you are working longer magic, try tying thirteen knots to represent the number of lunations in a typical calendar year.

Step 9: Hold your completed pouch to your heart and once again tap into the energies around your dreams. *Feel* it, see it, be it, and then send this energy into the bag.

Step 10: Stand and hold your pouch up to Luna, asking for her blessings upon your will and your desires. Anoint the pouch and yourself with your oil.

Step 11: Open your magical circle, and either carry your pouch on your person, or place it on your lunar altar.

Step 12: When the Moon is Full, bring your pouch outdoors under her light. If you wish, cast a magical circle. Speak your intention aloud again, three times. Now untie your bag and scatter its contents onto the Earth Mother. It is done, it is done, it is done, done, done!

Step 13: Open your circle and go on with your life. Keep accurate magical records and note when your working manifests.

Waxing Half Moon

During this phase, you may need to make some decisions: Do you carry on with the intention(s) set at the New Moon, or is this, in reality, not the correct time? If it's necessary to cut an intention free, do so with self-compassion and radical self-love. Should you decide to continue pursuit of your goal, double down on your diligence and determination and implement any necessary adjustments, fine-tuning your plans to reach your destination.

Moonwork to support continued long-term focus (or for clarity, if you are still undecided) can be beneficial now. This is also a perfect time to work with attraction magic: What do you want to magnetize into your life?

Waxing Half Moon Container Spell

Container spells are a perfect fit for this stage of a lunation. Start by getting very explicit about what it is you desire to manifest and commit to one target for your spell. If you want to call in, magnetize, or amplify more than one thing, do more than one spell. You want each target to remain clear.

To Gather

- A container. You can build a magical container using a bottle, a jar, a box, or anything that has a lid, stopper, or top.
- Paper. Use what is right for you: You can try colored paper, parchment paper, a leaf (dried bay leaves are excellent for spellwork), a page you pull out of your journal, or even just a piece of printer paper. Make sure to choose paper that will fit comfortably inside the vessel once it's folded up.
- Something to write with. You can use a fancy pen, a quill, a colored marker (match the color to your intention), or simply your favorite everyday pen.
- Something for cleansing. This could be a smoldering herb bundle such as rosemary or lavender, incense, a stone such as obsidian, salt, water, sound, or anything else that resonates with your practice.
- One or more crystals that match your goal
- Dried herb(s) that match your intention. Always use dried plant matter in your manifesting spellwork because fresh plants will die and rot, and these are definitely not energies compatible with growing your intentions into reality. You can certainly use fresh plant matter when working on banishing. Some suggestions: Rose (attraction, beauty, success), chamomile (abundance, luck, prosperity), and bay leaves (good fortune, luck, protection of your work and of you and yours) are great choices for any manifestation work.

- A diluted essential oil or magical oil that aligns with your purpose. See chapter 9 for ideas.
- Items that represent your dream: curios, charms, photographs, drawings—whatever fits the moment. If you have a particular job in mind, a photo of someone working in that profession is marvelous. If there is a location that you would like to go to for your vacation, a picture of that place torn out of a magazine is brilliant. The more precise you can get, the better. Other things to consider are twigs, metals, and even small toys; photocopies of tarot or oracle cards that represent your desire are also excellent additions.

Optional

- Candles, incense, and anything else that supports the magic at hand
- Music that echoes your intentions

The Process

Step 1: Set up your space. You can cast a circle, or not, as you wish. I usually do so in order to better hold the energies I will raise and direct into the moonspell and the container itself. The cast circle mirrors the container that will be used in the spell.

Step 2: When you are ready, cleanse and clear your container, your paper, and your writing implement.

Step 3: Write your desire on your paper.

Step 4: Holding your paper in your hands, consider how you will feel when your dream comes true. Picture your life and see-sense-feel yourself within it as if your desire has already landed. Bring substantial emotions to this moment, feeling into it as powerfully as you can. The Moon can help you to access your Big Feelings!

Step 5: Next, fold your paper *toward* your body (toward yourself for attraction) at least three times, turning it clockwise (the direction of increase) in between each fold, then tuck it into your container.

Step 6: One by one, cleanse each of the items you chose, making sure all of the energies and vibrations are aligned with you and you alone. Once purified, place each object into your container with intention, speaking aloud if you would like.

Step 7: After everything is in your container, consecrate, activate, and empower this holy instrument.

Step 8: Place your container where it will be bathed in the light of the Moon as she continues to wax toward her fullness—perhaps on a windowsill, or if possible, bring it outdoors every evening and bring it back inside every morning.

The Moon's vibrations will activate and magnify the energies you have contained in your vessel, increasing the power aimed toward your intention alongside her growing light.

Something that is often true of any type of magic is that the greater the thing desired, the longer the amount of time needed for manifestation. So don't lose hope or patience!

Always act in kind. You are not doing magic in a vacuum, and you must be a full participant. You can't call forth your dream job and expect it to pop out of thin air. Work on your résumé, network, do all of the mundane things you possibly can in conjunction with your moonwork.

Step 9: When the Full Moon arrives, sit down with your container spell and assess where you are with realizing your goal.

If your desire has not yet arrived, wrap your container in a dark cloth (preferably black) and hide it away until the Moon begins to wax again. You want this sacred container to hold on to the energies of the Waxing and Full Moon phases.

Store your wrapped container spell safely away (do not look at it) until the Moon is born anew again. When the New Moon arrives, sit down and consider your intention and decide if you want to reactivate your spell beneath the Waxing Moon.

Step 10: When your spell is complete—either your dream has manifested or you have determined that you no longer want to continue on with it—gratefully deconstruct your container by removing each item. Burn your paper and your herbs, release other items back to the Earth, and/or cleanse and deactivate your crystals, curios, toys, and any other objects you have used.

For advanced practitioners: If you are skilled at holding and working with multiple goals at one time, you can instead designate a lidded container to encompass continual magical workings, adding components to represent new intentions and removing, deactivating, and discarding components that you no longer need, either because they came true or because you are no longer interested in them.

Waxing Gibbous Moon

Spells to direct energy toward your desires in conjunction with the Moon's increasing light may be helpful now. Some candle magic to give a bit more oomph to past spellwork may serve, and yet be careful not to overdo it! A big part of magic is to do the working and then to let the working do what needs to be done, without interference.

Trust and yield here, believing that what you want is coming to you if it is for your highest good. The Moon—and the Moon Goddess—knows best. Recognize that as Luna holds more and more light, things that were hidden become visible. You may be surprised by something you didn't see coming emerging, sometimes from others and sometimes from deep inside your own Self.

A Waxing Gibbous Moon Spell

If you can get outside in a place without buildings or artificial light on a cloudless night when the Moon is moving toward fullness, try this seemingly simple spell.

To Gather

- Your Moon Journal and pen

The Process

Step 1: Walk toward the Moon's rays and chant aloud thirteen times: "Just as the Moon waxes, I walk toward my destiny."

Step 2: Open your heart and your mind's eye to any images or sensations that arise within you as you do so. Note them in your Moon Journal. That's it!

Full Moon

When the Moon is Full, spellwork and ritual that energizes, empowers, transforms, and fulfills is best carried out. Luna channels tremendous cosmic fuel during this phase, offering the optimal moment to send off the energies that have been coalescing since the New Moon to do their work both Above and Below, pushing you and your dreams over the hump. Time your work to take advantage of this giant rush of energy, raising your own vibrations to match those of the Moon in all her bright glory. Up, up, up!

This is also the prime lunar phase to do magic to discover what needs illumination and to shine a lantern into the cave where your Shadow Self dwells, inviting them to step out into the moonlight with you and share what is ready for integration.

Full Moon Gratitude Magic

Offering the Moon gratitude for everything you have learned and accomplished since she was last Full is a marvelous way to honor this phase. Here is an easy means of professing thankfulness to the Moon; it is a remarkably impactive and moving—yet fun!—spell to practice in a circle of Lunar Witches.

Ideally, this rite is performed outdoors upon the Earth, under her rays. If you will be indoors, you will need a large vessel into which you will pour the water.

To Gather

- A pitcher or large vase filled with blessed water

Optional

- A large vessel. This is only necessary if you are doing this ritual indoors.

The Process

Step 1: Ground, center, and open the channel. Open yourself up to the energies of the Full Moon.

Step 2: Cast a sacred circle if you so desire.

Step 3: Make yourself comfortable and amplify your inner gratitude. Pull on this feeling of thankfulness, expanding it within your body using your breath. Do this until you are overflowing with appreciation for yourself, your life, and All That Is.

Step 4: Raise your pitcher or vase up to Luna so that the water can take on the vibrations of her Full Moon light.

Step 5: Now it's time to pour out libations of blessed water in the name of the Moon. Standing, pour a bit of water out onto the Earth (or into your large vessel or bowl).

With each offering of water, name aloud something that you have experienced or felt since the last Full Moon, something that you are appreciative of, from silly to serious and everything in between.

Do this until your vase or pitcher is empty.

Step 6: Speak now any further words of gratitude you have for the Moon.

Step 7: Open your circle, sending any extra energies from your body up to the Moon with love and thankfulness. Say: "It is done, done, done!"

Waning Gibbous Moon

When the Moon is waning to darkness, make wishes, pray, and perform magic concerning what you want to release from your life. This is an ideal time to tie up any loose ends and wrap up any last matters that you have left hanging from your waxing phase moonwork, setting yourself up for future success.

For the rest of this lunation, focus upon endings, diligently and mindfully closing chapters—or even books—that you are complete with or, in all honesty, no longer have interest in pursuing. Cord cutting spells and rituals can be well indicated now. Here is a ceremony to get you started:

Cord Cutting Ceremony

Cord cutting is a ritual of magical release, a way of unhooking yourself from those things that are unhealthy and/or draining through the severing of energetic cords.

These etheric cords—which are not unhealthy in and of themselves—are formed whenever an attachment to or with someone or something is developed, creating a route for energy to travel. Cords connect you to people, places, objects, behaviors, memories, and/or relationships.

Sometimes these energetic cords are—or become—unstable, dysfunctional, even toxic and injurious. These are the cords that are no longer of good service and must be cut away or replaced.

A cord cutting ceremony can be done each lunation to help you to anchor into the life you want versus the unsupportive and sometimes unsafe patterns and situations in which you may have become mired.

Before any cord cutting ceremony, sit down with your journal and assess those places where you feel overwhelmed, trapped, inauthentic, controlled, captive, or unsafe.

Is there a place or a situation where there is always some sort of unwelcome intensity or high drama? Perhaps there is a place or situation where you have no choice but to diminish yourself, muting or hiding your light, your true thoughts, your true feelings? Or are there places or situations where things just seem "off," icky, sticky, and/or uncomfortable?

These are all signals indicating that something significant is going on, that a cord or cords need to be acknowledged and most likely cut.

You'll need a quiet place and time where you are safe to complete this ceremony.

To Gather

- A candle
- An herb bundle or incense for cleansing such as cedar, eucalyptus, or pine
- A lighter or matches
- An athame or ritual knife, even a kitchen knife can work in a pinch
- A supportive diluted essential oil or blended lunar oil (See chapter 9 for recipes.)
- Your Moon Journal and pen

The Rite

Step 1: Burn your incense or herbs to cleanse and clear your working space.

Step 2: Light your candle, speaking aloud your intention to cut unhealthy and/or unwelcome cords.

Step 3: Find a comfortable position for your body, either sitting or lying down. In loving and gentle inquiry, consider the cord(s) that you will cut in this ceremony. What—specifically—is the cord or cords you will cut embedded in? What has brought you to this moment? What has shifted for you?

Observe the sensations, thoughts, and feelings that reveal themselves to you.

Step 4: Bring your awareness to your breath and take at least four deep inhalations and exhalations as you inhabit your physical body as completely as possible.

Step 5: Ground yourself and root into the Earth below. Send branches up to the Moon, connecting with her energies above.

Step 6: With loving curiosity, run gentle hands over your body, beginning at your crown and moving slowly downward, stopping at each part. Allow your fingers to see-sense-feel what is happening for you—where inside of your body is this cord or these cords situated?

Step 7: Search out the cords that need to be cut and take mental notes of where they are located. Look for those cords that block, freeze, or cut off your sense of self-love and self-compassion, those that obstruct or constrict your natural flow of expression, love, creativity, power, intuition. You may see-sense-feel these places as voids or vacuums or tangles or knots or even hooks.

Step 8: For every cord you discover, pause and endeavor to trace it back to its origin. With whom or what did it begin? With whom or what is it connected?

Step 9: With the knowing that all loving connections remain forever, ready yourself to cut the unhealthy cords you found.

Step 10: With a joyful heart, speak aloud this intention: "In the name of the Moon, I reclaim myself and free my power-within."

Step 11: Invite the Moon or Moon Goddess to join you now, to help you to reclaim that which is already yours.

Step 12: Use your athame or ritual knife to energetically cut each etheric cord from your body, mind, heart, and spirit, liberating yourself from all that binds. As you cut each cord, say aloud, "I now cut this cord throughout all realms, throughout all time and all space, freeing myself from all control, coercion, and interference."

There is no need to rush. Progress deliberately and slowly without overdoing it, stopping as soon as you feel finished. If there is a need, you can certainly go back and do this ceremony again at another time.

Step 13: When you are finished cutting cords, anoint yourself with your oil and say aloud, "Through the witness and power of the Moon, I have reclaimed myself and my power-within. I am liberated and filled with love, and this is for the highest good."

Step 14: Say aloud three times, "It is done; it is done; it is done, done, done!" followed by, "And so it is."

Step 15: When you are ready, thank the Moon (and/or Moon Goddess) for her witness and support. Ground yourself fully, sending any extra energy up to the Moon with gratitude. Bring your roots and branches completely back into yourself.

Step 16: Immediately spend some time journaling about your experience.

Waning Half Moon

This is the moment to turn your attention—your magic and ritual—toward bringing things to as graceful a conclusion as you can manage, to finishing up your moonwork for this particular lunar cycle.

During this phase, earnestly clear the land of your life, speeding up your process, working diligently and quickly to remove and discharge all of the remaining obstacles from your path, making space for what is to come.

Wrap up anything that you haven't taken care of from the Waning Gibbous phase. Pay your bills—physical and metaphorical—clean up any messes that need to be handled, do what needs to be done to mindfully close this particular lunation, considering what you want to keep for the next cycle and what you would like to set down and leave behind.

Here is a powerful spell to partner your body and your feelings with the darkening of the Moon and the energies of release:

Decomposition Cauldron Spell

This is a helpful idea for using the essential energies of what you are releasing to fertilize your heart for future dreams. Everyone and everything on Earth participates in the eternal cycle of birth, death, and rebirth, and not everything is meant to continue. Things end, and we also are responsible for ending things—this is part of the reality of this human lifetime. The Decomposition Cauldron moonwork assists us in letting go in healthy, constructive ways.

Decomposition Cauldrons can be approached as parallels to moon map vision boards—these magical objects concerned with what you are releasing versus what you are magnetizing into being.

The following practice begins at the Waning Half Moon and concludes with the Waning Crescent or Dark Moon.

To Gather

- A small box or other biodegradable container. Alternately, you can use your physical magical cauldron as a repository for this moonspell.
- Paper and pen

Optional

- Pictures, symbols, herbs, crystals, curios, and other such items that represent what you are releasing.

Note that if you intend to release the whole "cauldron" into the compost bin or into the fire, be sure everything is biodegradable and Earth-safe. If you are releasing items that are not Earth-safe, your cauldron will need to be disposed alongside landfill-destined trash.

The Process

Step 1: Set out in front of you upon your altar your "cauldron," whether it be a biodegradable vessel that you will dispense with at the end of the lunation or your own magical tool that you will cleanse and reuse after the working is done.

Step 2: In a soft, kind, and self-loving manner, consider one or all of these inquiries (or one or more of your own), allowing images, feelings, and sensations to arise for you in an organic fashion:

- What do you need to release into the Great Unknown for your transformation, for your healing?
- What is holding you back from expressing the fullness of your being?
- What is standing in the way of your owning yourself as sacred, as sovereign?
- Where are you giving away your power?
- Where are you refusing your responsibility or abdicating your authority?
- Where are you forgetting that you already know what is best for you?
- Where have you forgotten that you are whole and holy, exactly as you are in this and every moment?
- Have you forgotten that you matter?
- Have you rejected your belonging?
- Are you embracing love as the center of your life?
- What needs to go?

You can write down your answers on small pieces of paper or make use of the items you have collected.

Step 3: When you are ready, begin to toss your words, objects, symbols, and so on into your vessel. You can do this all at once and be done with it or leave this spell out where you will see it, continuing to add things as Luna wanes.

Step 4: When you are finished, write an affirmation to support your release, to make space for the relief of release.

Step 5: Near or at the end of the lunar cycle, burn, bury, or compost your vessel or that which is contained within it. Be sure to acknowledge the work you did and to feel into the spaciousness you created for yourself.

Step 6: After letting go, be sure to name that which will fill the void lest the Multiverse do it for you! Or, if you are feeling very brave and very trusting, ask the Moon to fill the space you created and see what presents itself in your life.

Waning Crescent Moon

As Luna's light defers to her darkness, the last phase of each lunation begins, providing final moments to work with the energies of the Moon to set free those things that need to be taken down, broken into their smallest pieces to later be reconstructed into something new, or released back to the Earth for her health and her healing.

All mooncraft focused upon decrease is best carried out at this time. This is the appropriate lunar phase during which to cast spells and perform rituals involving such things as countermagic, healing, self-liberation, maturity, overcoming challenges, the selling or gifting of resources (especially real estate), reversing, protection, wisdom, and the breaking of addictions, unhealthy habits, and streaks of bad luck.

Banishings, bindings, exorcisms, and both the casting and the breaking of curses and hexes are also traditionally performed throughout the Waning Crescent Moon phase.

This is a great time for cleaning altars in preparation for New Moon resets; cleansing and clearing cars, homes, and workplaces; releasing the old through magical baths; and magical floorwashes done to mop up the old in anticipation of the new beginning to come.

Home Blessing and Energy Reset Spell

I like to do an energy cleanse and blessing of my home (car, workplace, and such) during this phase to remove any stale, unwelcome energetic signatures or forms that developed throughout the lunation.

You can remove the energies of arguments, frustrations, ill health, creative blockages, poor sleeping, unhealthy eating, and any other stagnant vibrations that have been clouding up your sacred space. And yes, your home is a sacred space—it houses you, and you are both holy and sacred.

To Gather

- The supplies and equipment you normally use for cleaning your home
- A bundle of cleansing herbs such as eucalyptus, lavender, or rosemary. If you would rather not use smoke for this cleansing, you can instead use water, moonmist, salt, or sound for this same purpose.
- A lighter or matches

Optional

- Moonwater
- A magical oil

The Process

Step 1: Clean your home before beginning any energy cleansing. Remove trash and recycling, tidy any clutter, wash windows, dust, sweep, vacuum, and so on. If there are items that don't feel good to have around, clothes that don't fit, or unused or unneeded objects, get rid of these now, too. Set them aside for a charity shop.

Step 2: Whenever possible, open all of the windows and doors.

Step 3: Walk through your home counterclockwise with a smoldering bundle of cleansing herbs three times, naming aloud those things and those energies that you want gone from your space.

Step 4: After circling counterclockwise—the direction of release—thrice, move once in a clockwise pattern, naming aloud those things that you would like present in your home (car, workplace, and so on) for that lunation, those things that you are inviting in with an open heart, an open mind, and an open door.

Step 5: If you have time and are motivated, you can follow this reset and blessing with a magical floorwash, incorporating moonwater and/or an appropriate blended oil to seal in all of your intentions.

Dark Moon

The Dark Moon, Hekate's Sickle, is concerned with secrecy, sorcery, prophecy, healing, and the most profound Mysteries of the Multiverse—this phase contains all that cannot be seen with the waking eye or the rational mind, that which can be sought and seen only through the potency of psychic gifts, oracle, and divination; the energies are drawn tightly inward, spiraling into the innermost Self.

This is a time of messages arising from the deep, dark places, the caves in the center of the Earth, the Sybil, the Pythia, the Oracle speaking in tongues. A place of liminality, the doorway between the old and the new, the death and the rebirth, this is the territory of that which *isn't quite*... isn't quite gone, isn't quite here, that sacred place.

Many Moon Witches avoid spellcasting until this lunar phase passes, waiting instead until the New Moon to again initiate magical activities. This time is spent in self-reflection, facilitating self-understanding to bubble up to the surface of consciousness where it can be retrieved and placed into service alongside the new cycle. There is also a natural calling toward resting, recuperating, and engaging in self-care.

If you choose not to perform spellwork during this phase, you don't need to close down all of your spiritual activities, though: This is an ideal time for meditation, dream incubation, shadow work, vision-questing, divination, scrying, studying, journaling, journeying, and designing future moonwork including calendaring goals and ritual plans.

This is also a perfect phase to consider what you will seed into the next lunar cycle, about to begin. I like working with black candles, black stones and crystals, and sipping on dark herbal blends during these moments.

If you do desire to perform magic, the powers of disintegration, which rule this time, can support you in performing robust banishing work, including intense cleansings, hex- and curse-breaking, and protection and self-defense magic (physical and spiritual).

Letting go and never looking back are also appropriate. Transformational healings, the releasing of old, entrenched trauma, and the breaking of epigenetic chains can also be indicated, if the situation is correct and the right amount of professional support is available.

I also love to engage with micromagic throughout the Dark Moon phase. These are beneficial shifts we make inside ourselves that then reverberate out to all of those around us, which then continues changing the world, as each of those people touch others, which then further extends out into the next circle of people, which continues changing the world, and so on, ad infinitum.

Micromagic involves tending to our own "house" first instead of looking into others' homes and casting judgment or trying to help or fix or heal things, unasked. The empowered Lunar Witch puts on their own oxygen mask before assisting others, lovingly interdependent and yet never codependent.

One small pebble can change the entire environment of a smooth, quiet pond. I invite you to change the world by becoming that cosmic pebble!

Dissolve Old Energies Spell

As you move into her darkness, it can be valuable for your Primal Self for you to perform a working to dissolve old ways of thinking, being, doing; old habits and addictions; old patterns of behavior; and/or tired old beliefs. My favorite time to work this magic is the night before the New Moon.

To Gather

- Soil, sand, or salt contained in a small vessel
- A bowl of water

The Process

Step 1: Ground, center, and open the channel. Connect with the Moon or Moon Goddess. Cast a circle if so desired.

Step 2: Sit with yourself in the darkness and become certain about what it is you are ready to dissolve from your life. Listen to the wisdom of your Inner Moon Witch and the wisdom of the Moon.

Step 3: When you are ready, speak into the soil, sand, or salt, naming all of those things that you will leave behind with the ending lunation. Speak from your heart; you may be surprised by what rises up and out of your body.

Step 4: When you are complete, pour your soil, sand, or salt into the bowl of water. Watch carefully as the water interacts with that which you are releasing. Change is already here!

Feel the change that is here; feel the transformation that has already happened. Notice the relief you feel and the spaciousness that comes with it.

Step 5: Give gratitude and open your circle.

Step 6: After your circle is open, empty your bowl of water outdoors or set it aside to bring with you and empty when you are next in a place where this is possible, perhaps in running water. For a big release and to be done with it forever, you can alternately flush it down the toilet. Say: "It is done, done, done!"

A Reminder: Magic and the Void of Course Moon

When the Moon is void of course, it is well-advised to take a break from magic and ritual as experience shows that spellwork done at this time will most likely fail or backfire.

These are powerful and precious moments organically built into every lunation, moments of sacred pause that are ideal for quietness and gestation, meditation and pathworking, divination and dreamwork, and self-care.

Esbat Rituals

Most basically, an esbat is a lunar rite comprised of ceremony and/or magic. Margaret Murray, author of *The Witch Cult in Western Europe,* borrowed this term from the Old French *s'esbattre* (Modern French *ébat*), meaning "to frolic and amuse oneself, diversion."

When you hear the word *esbat* and it is not preceded by the name of a lunar phase, you can assume that the celebration is Full Moon esbat, a popular time for Witches to gather. The very definition of *esbat* in some traditions is that it is a ritual taking place at the Full Moon.

It is my opinion, though, that an esbat need only be a lunar rite, and it need not be held at a specific lunar phase. Celebrating all of the phases of the Moon can greatly help us in reclaiming and honoring ourselves as the holy, priceless beings we are.

On the Path of Lunar Witchcraft, we follow the cycling of the Moon closely and every one of her aspects holds meaning for us in magic, ritual, and all that we do. Therefore, an esbat can take place during any of her phases—Full Moon esbat, Dark Moon esbat, New Moon esbat, and so on.

A Lunar Self-Blessing Rite

This rite is meant to be enacted once per lunation for an entire lunar year and then begun again. If you are only able to incorporate one monthly lunar rite into your life, here it is.

This ritual will assist you in renewing—and deepening—your connection with the Moon each cycle. For your first lunar year, I suggest it be performed at every New Moon. If you don't have an affinity for the New Moon, you can adapt this rite and perform it during a different phase; I suggest the Diana's Bow Moon, Waxing Half Moon, or Full Moon. The power of the Waxing Moon will better serve this magic than her waning energies.

Ideally this ritual is performed within the same phase every lunation; however, it is understood that this may not be possible. Just do your best. If a month arrives and your only choices are to do it during Luna's waning or to not do it at all, do it during her waning. Completing this rite once per lunar cycle is far more important than being perfect. If the best you can do is once a lunation irrespective of phase, then that is excellent work!

You may want to buy or decorate a small notebook or journal to dedicate solely to your experiences with this ritual or block off at least thirteen pages in your Moon Journal, one for each cycle.

To Gather

- All of those things you would like present upon your ritual altar, including any particular Sacreds that you want to charge. Match your correspondences to the phase and sign of the Moon you will be working within, including your colors, crystal and plant allies, candles, incense, and so on.
- Herbs, incense, salt, water, sound, or something else to use to cleanse your ritual space. Cedar, rosemary, or lavender bundles are good options.
- An offering for the Moon, such as a small bowl of water, a candle in a color that honors her, or some lunar incense
- A small vessel filled with moonwater (see chapter 10) or moon oil (see chapter 9)
- A lighter or matches
- Your Moon Journal (or dedicated notebook for this rite) and pen
- A bit of food and a libation for yourself for Cakes and Ale (e.g., chocolate, fruit, or nuts and water, wine, or juice)

Optional

- Recorded instrumental music to support your work
- A drum, rattle, or other instrument for energy raising
- Poetry or invocations for the Moon

To Prepare

Since you will complete this ritual each lunation for thirteen Moons, you should first write on your everyday calendar all of the dates on which you will perform this rite over the next year and a day.

In advance of each of the ritual dates, read through the outline so you know how to prepare yourself and what to expect. As before any holy rite, you may want to take a magical shower or bath before beginning.

If you are not yet aware of the Indigenous Ancestors of the land upon which you live, research their name(s) and make a note.

The Rite

Step 1: Create your working altar—or reset your lunar altar—in a visually and sensually pleasing way. Include all of the items on the "To Gather" list.

Step 2: Cleanse and clear your working space using whatever method you have chosen.

Step 3: Ground, center, and open the channel. Slowly and fully connect with your Inner Lunar Witch through your breath, then extend that connection down to the Earth and up to the Moon, sending roots down and branches up. Spend a few moments here with closed eyes focusing upon your breath, noticing it gently coming in and going out of your body.

Notice the Earth Mother underneath you and the Moon above. You are the Holy Pillar between Earth and Sky, composed of the venerable energies of both. Breathe with the powers of Self, Earth, and Moon, welcoming them into your physical vessel.

Step 4: Acknowledge the Indigenous Ancestors of the land you are on. You may invite them to join or witness you and/or to invite your own Ancestors of blood or choice.

Step 5: Honor the Elements of Life: air, fire, water, and earth. You may wish to invite them to join or witness you and/or to cast a formal ritual circle. Follow your intuition.

Step 6: Make your body as comfortable as possible—standing or seated—grounded and centered in preparation for your holy work.

Take a long breath in, hold it for a moment, then let it out slowly, activating your channel to the Moon, see-sense-feeling it swirling around behind you, below you, above you, all around you, bringing your consciousness together with the Moon like a welcome and gentle hug.

Bring your consciousness to the phase and sign the Moon is currently traversing.

Step 7: Make now your offering to the Moon, presenting the water or lighting your candle or incense and saying aloud:

> *I make this sacred offering to you, O Beloved Moon, you who contains the*
> *Infinity of the All, from giving to receiving, from dark to light and back again.*
> *Maiden Moon, Sister Moon, Warrior Moon; I, (speak your name), salute you.*
> *Mother Moon, Queen Moon, Crone Moon; I, (speak your name), salute you.*

Step 8: Seat yourself comfortably at your altar, closing your eyes and finding your breath again. Shift your connection with the Moon into the forefront of your consciousness. See-sense-feel into the phase the Moon is in, allowing these energies to fill you completely.

Feel how your energies mirror these lunar energies. Breathe into those places in your body that need more of that particular energy.

Step 9: Feel now the power of the astrological sign the Moon is transiting, and feel the power of the particular Element of Life (air, fire, water, or earth) that rules it.

Feel how your energies mirror this lunar frequency today. Breathe into those places in your body that need more of that particular frequency.

Step 10: Now feel into the Moon's completeness, feel into the combination of her phase and her sign. Seek now those places inside your own body that are resonating with the vibration and frequency that is happening for our Lunar Lady. Breathe into these places; lean into these places.

Step 11: Now, with your moonwater or moon oil, speak the following words aloud, lovingly anointing each part of yourself named with the energies of the Moon:

> *With the power of the Moon, I bless my crown, my connection with the Cosmos, with divinity, and with myself as sacred. The Moon dwells within me.*
>
> *With the power of the Moon, I bless my brow, my third eye, my connection with the Unseen Realm, my intuition, and my sacred vision. I expand my perception of what is possible.*
>
> *With the power of the Moon, I bless my eyes and my sight, both internal and external. May I be open to new perspectives, and may I always see the Truth.*
>
> *With the power of the Moon, I bless my nose and my sense of smell, both physical and nonphysical. May I be aware of all of the scents of beauty that surround me. May I always smell the harmony of life.*
>
> *With the power of the Moon, I bless my lips. May the honey of the Moon sweeten my words that they be received with love.*
>
> *With the power of the Moon, I bless my throat, my connection to knowledge and self-expression. May I speak my Truth with compassion.*
>
> *With the power of the Moon, I bless my heart, my connection with my emotions, what I love, and my love for myself. May my heart expand to accept love in all healthy forms.*
>
> *With the power of the Moon, I bless my solar plexus, my connection with the astral realm and my power-within. I am a sovereign being, and I know what is best for me.*
>
> *With the power of the Moon, I bless my sacral chakra, my connection to all things pleasurable and sensual. All acts of love and pleasure are my rituals.*
>
> *With the power of the Moon, I bless my roots, my connection with the Earth, and all things physical. May my body be healthy.*
>
> *May the gifts of the Moon fill me with health, support, protection, and joy!*

Pause for a few moments to take in all of these energies, integrating them within your body, mind, heart, and spirit.

Step 12: As you receive and activate the powers of the Moon say these words:

> *I invoke the power of the Moon within me.*
> *Her constant transformation mirrors my own.*
> *Her surrender to flow inspires mine.*
> *O Brilliant Moon, may your light and your darkness be my guide, now and always.*
> *So mote it be.*

Step 13: Now kiss the back of your dominant hand three times and raise it up to her.

Step 14: Take one more big, slow, long breath in. With your exhalation, send energies of love and gratitude up to the Moon with thankfulness and appreciation for her support and her witness of every moment of your life.

Step 15: Bless now your food and libation in the name of Luna, and consume them with gratitude. Whilst enjoying your Cakes and Ale, write your thoughts and feelings in your Moon Journal (or dedicated notebook for this rite).

Step 16: Give the Moon and the Elements of Life your gratitude for their witness of your rite and your existence. If you cast a formal circle, now is the time to open it and to say hail and farewell to all of the entities and frequencies that were present for you throughout your ritual.

Step 17: Send any extra energies from your body down to the Earth and up to the Moon, slowly returning your roots and branches fully into your own vessel as you do so. Return to your regular consciousness using breath and slow, gentle movement. Blessed be!

Chapter 13
Chakras and the Moon

The Moon Goddess Speaks

I am the keeper of lunar perception, the sacred repository of the wisdom of each of the phases of the Moon, the holder of occult knowledge.

I carry the soft peace of the night, my gentleness the very balm of her silvery rays. I am the creative force that sustains all, the bringer of fertility and divine power.

Tonight I come to teach you of the glorious power that already lives within you, a power that is waiting to be discovered, freed, and wielded in the name of love and beauty. I come to activate and energize your connection to the endless cycling of the Moon, the endless cycling of you. I come to awaken you to the mystery of creation and your role within it.

I am Parvati.

Journal Inquiries for This Gateway

What does my Lunar Self want me to know about my psychic sensitivities? What synchronicities and signs surround me? How can I practice trusting my inner wisdom?

Affirmations for This Gateway

I am connected to my Lunar Self. I trust my intuition to guide me. The Moon speaks through me in powerful ways.

Chakras—often described as perpetually spinning wheels of energy or energetic vortexes—are those parts of our etheric bodies that draw in vibrations, process them, and then, hopefully, send whatever is unhelpful or unneeded back out of our bodies again.

They are called by different names in different traditions, but we will use the word *chakra* here, as it is almost universally understood as the system of energy centers that range throughout the body. Whilst many use the basic seven-chakra system, it is important to recognize that there are actually hundreds, if not thousands, of energy vortexes in your body, each with its own function.[44]

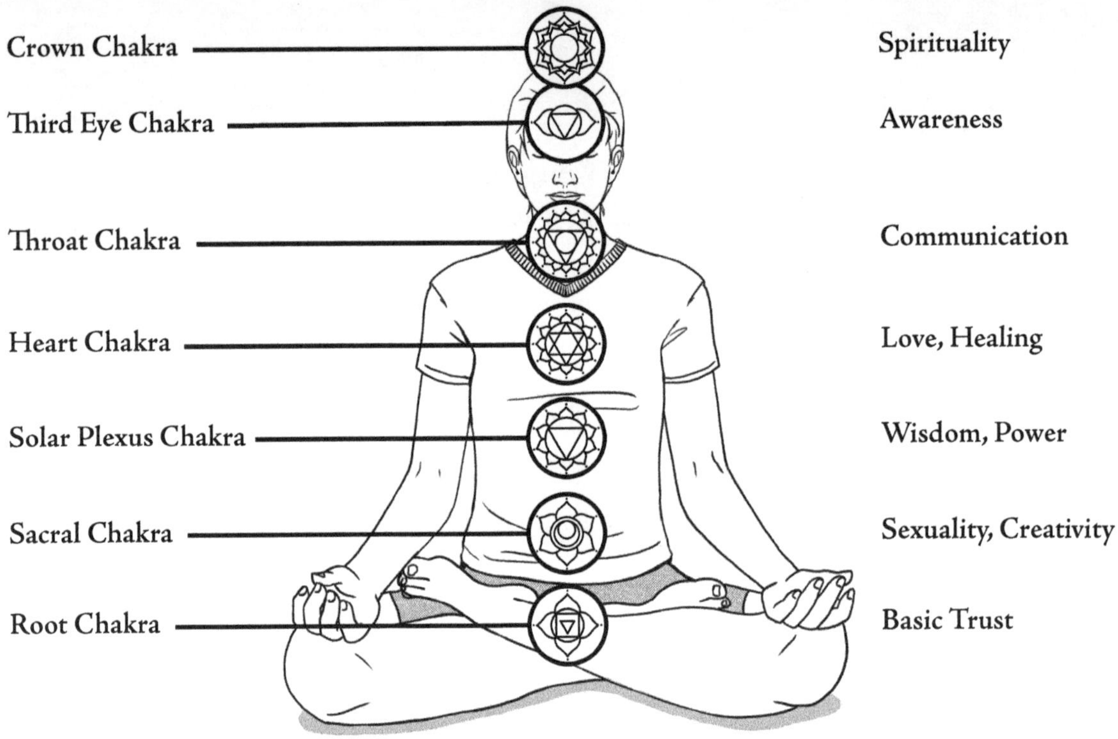

The Seven-Chakra System

As in the manifestation of all things, Lunar Witchcraft requires energy: energy to keep our bodies healthy, energy to fuel our magic, and energy to power our rituals. The brighter and more radiant our chakras are, the more pure energy they have available for us to direct toward our desires. We can collaborate with specific chakras—those located in the upper parts of our energetic bodies—to refine and strengthen our connection with the Moon and to augment our own natural psychic potential and proficiency.

44. Novak, "The Science Behind Your Chakras."

Psychic sensitivity is our birthright, and it is inextricably connected to our lunar nature. These supersensory powers help us to relate to the larger patterns of life as well as the energetics outside of this particular incarnation, connecting us with the Moon as well as the Multiverse and our place within it.

As we increase the integrity and coherence of these whirling energy centers, so do we increase the clarity and power of our lunar divination, lunar magic, and lunar ritual.

The Upper Chakras

There are three upper chakras most involved with intuitive abilities, located in and around the head. When strengthened, they can specifically help us to connect more strongly with the Moon and, therefore, with our own psychic nature. They are the ajna, sahasrara, and bindu chakras.

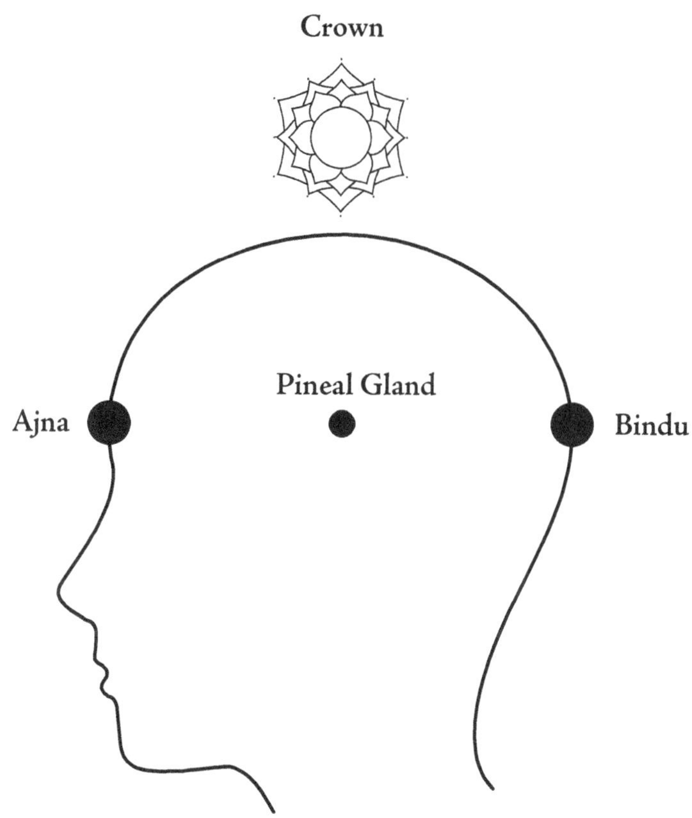

Upper Chakras

Of these three chakras, the one most associated with psychic abilities is the ajna chakra, also named the third eye chakra or the sixth chakra. Unbound by the constraints and constructs of time and space, this energy center is concerned with veiled wisdom, and it is active whenever we use the tool of visualization. It is connected to our intuition, as is the Moon.

The third eye chakra is the storehouse for all of the images we each hold within—a comprehensive catalog of symbols from both the tangible, physical outer realm and the untouchable, private inner realm—our outer sight and our inner sight. This chakra acts as a translator of what we are feeling, doing, and thinking inside so that we can share it with the outside world.

The color this energy center is most often assigned is indigo blue.

The seventh chakra, also termed the sahasrara chakra and better known in Western culture as the crown chakra, is our connection to the Divine, to multiversal consciousness, to That Which Is Greater. A primary function of this chakra is to recall that we are all One and that we are perpetually connected to this Oneness.

Interestingly, the crown chakra is seated on the top of the head, not actually inside it. It is located right above the head, reaching out upward and sideways.

The color most often associated with this vortex is the color violet.

The final chakra of this set is the bindu chakra, also called the Moon Center and sometimes known as the eighth chakra. The bindu chakra is a secondary chakra; it is not part of the primary seven that are arranged in a column up and down the body.

The bindu chakra is related to the upleveling of consciousness. Located at the back of the head, above the third eye and below the crown, it is pictured as a twenty-three-petaled lotus and is symbolized by the Moon. The bindu chakra is represented by a crescent Moon and a drop, and it is ascribed to the color white or pearl.

Bindu Chakra Symbol

When we practice bringing the various powers of these three chakras together—the powers of intuition, Oneness, and higher consciousness—linking them into a freely moving yet predictable circuit of energy, we organically increase our access to insight, precognition, vision, and pattern recognition, further unlocking our connection to the fundamental essence of the Moon.

The Pineal Gland

Every chakra in the human body informs the functioning of a specific gland. The ajna, crown, and bindu chakras are all connected to the pineal gland, which helps to regulate the transmission of hormonal messages and the human circadian rhythm, our body's internal clock and our progression through the cycles of light and dark.

This tiny pinecone-shaped gland is the size of a grain of rice, and it is also styled as the Seat of the Soul, the Mind's Eye, and the Heavenly Eye. In ancient Egyptian cosmology, it is the Eye of Horus, also related to the Moon.

The pineal gland both secretes and synthesizes melatonin, which is related to serotonin, which introduces a relaxing effect upon the nervous system. Melatonin shares several chemical constructs with entheogens—visionary, sometimes hallucinogenic plants—assisting with dreaming, visioning, and intuiting, making the pineal gland itself the throne of our native clairvoyance and psychic powers.[45]

Because it acts as a translator between light and our bodies—completely independent of external clocks, calendars, and our modern human modes of measuring time—this gland connects us to nature, to the cycling of the seasons and the cycling of the Moon. It grants us a type of perception that can open up our intuition and clarify our psychic sight, assisting in greater spiritual awakening, empathy, and accuracy in divination.

When you work with the Moon as a support for intuition and prophesy, a cleansed and activated pineal gland will move you into more meaningful rapport with Luna—with her vibrations, her frequencies, and the messages and wisdom she holds for you at any given time.

Here is a short cleansing and activation practice to clear these three upper chakras and activate the pineal gland, unifying these distinct energies so that they work in concert with one another, increasing psychic strength, insight, and intuitive abilities.

Pineal Gland Cleansing and Activation

When engaging with this practice, allow whatever happens for you to happen, with the understanding that whatever you experience is correct for you in that particular moment. There are no special supplies needed for this exercise.

45. Luke, "Psychoactive Substances and Paranormal Phenomena."

The Process

Step 1: Begin in a seated position, making your body as comfortable as possible.

Step 2: Close your eyes and allow your jaw to gently drop.

Step 3: Use your breath to relax your body even further.

Step 4: Generate the sound of "Om" (or another relaxing sound that you prefer, such as "Ma" or another tone) six times.

Step 5: Slow your breath, inhaling and exhaling deeply and mindfully. Observe your breath without forcing it to do anything in particular.

Step 6: Bring your attention to your third eye chakra, and breathe a healing, silvery light into it three times.

Step 7: Bring your attention to your crown chakra, and breathe that same healing, silvery light into it three times.

Step 8: Now bring your attention to your bindu chakra (located at the back of your head, where many people have a cowlick or whirl of hair), and breathe a healing, silvery light into it three times.

Step 9: You may experience a light, comforting sensation or gentle pulsating in your head, shifting your perception of reality.

Step 10: When you are ready, return your consciousness to your body. Stretch your muscles and pat yourself gently all over to come fully back.

Your Body's Moon Center

The formal name for the Moon Center is the bindu visarga chakra, which is translated as "the falling of the drop" or simply as "tiny drop." Historically, this chakra is associated with the Fountain of Eternal Youth, and it is sometimes titled the "Gateway to Expansive Possibilities."

The Moon Center is situated near or underneath the whirl of hair that grows at the back of the head, almost opposite the ajna chakra in the center of the forehead.

This whirl of hair is the location of what was the posterior fontanelle—one of those "soft spots" on a newborn baby's head where the bones of the sides of the back of the skull (the occiput and the parietal bones) are found, unfused so that we can enter the world through the birth canal. Later they completely come together, with all skull bones generally fused by the age of eighteen months.

The bindu chakra is governed by the Moon. Its symbols include "dot," "point," and "pearl." The senses that help to stimulate it include taste, sound, touch, and sight. In meditation, many experience this chakra as emitting a glowing light, just like the Full Moon, or a luminous darkness, like the Dark Moon.

When the bindu chakra is asleep, it looks like a dot. However, when it is awake, it is said that the energy contained within it drips into our bodies, both physical and etheric.

When this energy center is awakened, the pineal gland is activated, and when the pineal gland is activated, it is said to release *amrita,* the golden nectar of immortality that flows through all consciousness, granting genuine peace and unequivocal well-being, harmonizing and balancing all of our chakras, connecting us in Oneness with All That Is.

The bindu chakra is a healer, bringing gifts of lasting contentment and delight in all that life has to offer and the calm and peace that appears alongside expanded possibility and potential. When your bindu chakra is activated, open, and healthy, not only do you reap the benefits but all you come into contact with does, too, especially those closest: your family, your friends, your animal and plant companions.

An unobstructed and open bindu chakra is one of the most helpful devices on the Path of the Lunar Witch. This energy center is a bridge you can use to connect not only with your own full power but with the full power of the Moon herself. Activating this chakra with mindfulness within various lunar phases can also be helpful in strengthening your bond with the Moon.

Here are several keys you can use to build your connection with your bindu chakra; experiment with them as you wish, yet please try each practice at least three times before discarding it as not for you. When journaling after these practices, be sure to note for future reference the lunar phase and sign alongside your experiences.

Bindu Massage

If possible, try this practice with your head turned or tilted so that the Moon is facing your bindu chakra.

During the massage, you may discover why this chakra is called the Bliss Point. This is a lovely practice to perform for others, or to have others perform for you, perhaps in a lunar ritual.

You can deepen this practice by using a few drops of a (diluted) essential oil or a blended oil, maybe one associated with the lunar phase or sign you are experiencing (see chapter 9 for a list of oils associated with each lunar phase).

The Practice

Step 1: Begin by grounding and centering, sending roots into the Earth and branches up to the Sky.

Step 2: Draw Earth energy up from your roots, carrying it up through all seven primary chakras, beginning with your root chakra.

Step 3: When you reach the top of your head—your crown chakra—allow the energy to slide downward over the back of the head, touching and activating the bindu point.

Step 4: Now, with gentle fingers, touch that point and massage it carefully and lovingly. When you feel a sense of bliss and connection with All That Is, you know that you are working the right point.

Step 5: When you feel complete, end the massage, bringing your etheric roots and branches gently back into your body.

Bindu Chakra Connection

Stillness will aid in magnifying your connection with the Moon. Have you ever gone outside on a quiet night and been filled with awe at the sight of her silent presence hanging brightly in the nighttime sky? You can fill yourself with this same sense of unification, possibility, and wonder by opening the bindu chakra in meditation and breathing moonlight into it.

Note that when meditating with your Moon Center, you may notice a vibration, a tingling, or even a gentle rhythmic pulsing at the point of this chakra inside or directly above it. What do you notice when meditating with bindu? Note this in your Moon Journal each time so you can track your progress through your own lived experiences.

The Practice

Step 1: Begin by allowing yourself to receive a breath from the Moon, accepting it steadily into your lungs, savoring it for a moment, and then releasing it back up to Luna.

Step 2: Inhale the light (or dark) of the Moon, breathing it deep into your bindu chakra. Feel the peace, calm, and clarity that accompanies this lunar light (or darkness).

Step 3: Feel her light (or dark) filling your bindu chakra, then flowing through your entire body, the nectar of amrita soaking you with its healing and loving properties, cleansing and clearing you, chakra by chakra by chakra, until your entire body is saturated with beauty, relaxation, harmony, and joy. Feel yourself as part of All That Is and take your rightful place here.

Step 4: Rest and relax.

Step 5: Fill yourself with moonlight (or moondark), the silence of deep space and the innermost Self. Observe your bindu chakra and connect with it in conjunction with the Moon.

Step 6: When you are ready, return to this here and now.

Activating the Bindu

There are other means of strengthening your connection to your bindu chakra and activating its energy, including through melody, breath, and physical action.

Every person experiences a different sound, frequency, or melody when linked with their bindu chakra, one that is exclusive to them—because every person has a unique etheric body composed of uniquely tuned chakras.

Spend time seeking within to hear, feel, or sense your individual melody, your individual vibrational kinship with Luna. Gently rock back and forth as you move to the harmonious energies of the melody of your singular bindu chakra.

Yet another way to activate the bindu chakra is through the bridge pose. If you do yoga, Pilates, or strength training, this pose is one you may already use.

One of the best things about this pose is that you don't need a lot of space to do it. Another benefit is that it can feel really good as it gently stretches out your back muscles, especially after sitting at the computer for a long stretch or when you get out of bed in the morning.

Bindu Bridge Pose

Before trying this activation exercise, warm up your body: Slowly stretching your neck, arms, shoulders, wrists, and legs is great. Adding on a bit of very light cardio at the end, such as a slow march, can also be helpful in awakening your body and getting it ready for what is to come. If you'd like to use other poses before the bridge, try experimenting with child's pose, cat into cow, and cobra.

Over time, become familiar with this bindu bridge pose, perhaps even trying it daily until it becomes part of your everyday Moon Witch practice. If you are called to go further, there are more advanced poses that also activate bindu, including the shoulder stand.

To Gather

- Modification props as needed, such as a pillow, yoga block, or exercise ball, to support your hips and spine

Optional

- A yoga mat

The Practice

Step 1: Begin by lying down on your back carefully and gradually, one vertebra at a time. Open your arms wide and rest the back of your hands softly upon the ground, palms facing up toward the Cosmos.

Step 2: Pause here to connect with the Earth Mother: Focus on your abdominal muscles, inhaling as you draw these muscles down toward the ground or floor. Notice how this naturally tilts your pelvis upward, moving it barely off of the ground.

Step 3: Stay here for a few moments, feeling your Oneness with the Earth Mother. Exhale slowly and completely, feeling how your body rests naturally in this neutral position.

Step 4: Concentrate on increasing your feeling of connection with the Earth, the Sky, and with All That Is. Do this process three or more times, whatever seems right to you.

Step 5: Now, move into the bridge pose. Bend your legs and draw them in toward your body, as close as you can without any pain or discomfort, in line with your hips. Keeping your feet and your shoulders firmly planted flat on the ground, push up from your heels. The majority of your weight should rest in your heels and shoulders; you should be able to lift up and wiggle your toes.

Step 6: Extend your arms toward your heels. If you can reach your heels, use the tips of your fingers to touch them. If not, just rest your hands, palms down, as close to your heels as is comfortable.

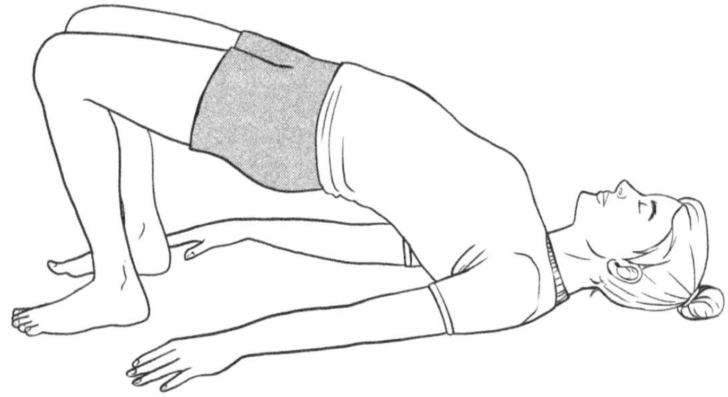

The Bridge Pose

Step 7: Inhale fully, press your heels into the ground, and exhale, lifting only your hips up toward the ceiling or sky. If necessary, adjust your knees so that they remain in line with your hips. To create a strong foundation for your body, roll your shoulders underneath and lengthen your neck. Allow the majority of your weight to rest on your shoulders and your arms as you raise your chest upward toward the ceiling or sky. Use modification props when needed.

Engage your core, pulling your belly button down toward your spinal column. Engage your butt muscles, tightening them alongside your core.

You should feel safe and solid here, connected with the Earth Mother through the bottom of your feet and your shoulders. Your abdomen and buttocks should feel strong and stable. Notice that the part of your head where the bindu chakra is located is in natural contact with the ground when performing this pose.

Step 8: Relax the muscles in your neck and lift your hips as high as you can without discomfort. You should not feel uncomfortable in any way. You should not feel any compression, pressure, or pain in any part of your body. This should feel good!

Step 9: Breathe slowly and intentionally and relax as thoroughly as you can. Find a soothing pattern of inhalations and exhalations. With your body still in this pose, breathe in and out gently for a cycle of thirteen breaths.

You may need to begin with a cycle of three breaths and work your way up over time to thirteen. Don't overextend yourself! If you need to take only one inhalation and one exhalation before releasing this pose, listen to your body and follow its needs. This is a practice you are working with, not an end result.

Step 10: To finish the pose, exhale whilst gently and mindfully bringing your hips back down to the ground, rolling down flat on the ground vertebrae by vertebrae, until your spine is once again resting, relaxed and easy, upon it.

Step 11: Bring your knees as far as you can into your chest, hugging them, leaning into a nice, slow, easy stretch. Then open your arms wide once more, palms open to the Cosmos above, stretching your legs out flat on the ground.

Bindu Breathwork

Finally, you can also deepen your connection with the Moon and your bindu chakra through this simple breathwork practice.

The Practice

Step 1: If it's comfortable for you, begin by kneeling with your hands resting on your thighs; if not, try sitting with your legs folded in a half-lotus position or sitting in a chair with the soles of your feet resting firmly on the ground.

Step 2: Breathe, ground, center, and open the channel; send roots into the Earth and branches into the Cosmos.

Step 3: With your eyes closed, inhale your breath up, up, up from your roots, through your spinal column whilst tilting your head gently backward so that your chin is pointing skyward.

Step 4: Exhale whilst tilting your head gently forward so that your chin is tucked into your neck, sending that breath and those energies back down, down, down your spinal column, through your roots, and out into the Earth Mother.

Only tilt your head as far back and as far forward as is enjoyable! Do not push or force the range of motion. This should feel pleasant—in both directions. Go slowly and carefully so as not to pull or overstretch these tender muscles.

Step 5: Monitor your breath closely as you inhale and exhale. Do this process at least three times before moving on.

Step 6: On your next inhalation, gracefully raise your arms, up, up, up, fully extended, opening them high and wide in the shape of a chalice, collecting the energies of the Moon as you breathe in.

Step 7: On your exhalation, bring your fully extended arms straight forward in front of you, bending at the waist. If you are kneeling, you will end up with your arms fully extended on the ground, your third eye touching the ground in front of you.

Again, don't overextend yourself. Make sure your neck and shoulders are relaxed; do not hold tension in them. You should feel completely at ease, and your body should feel relaxed and happy.

Step 8: Stay in this comfortable position for at least three cycles of inhalation and exhalation.

Step 9: Now, inhale once again, moving yourself back into kneeling (or sitting), one slow vertebrae at a time, ending with your hands resting on your thighs.

Exhale completely, then begin this cycle once again.

Step 10: Inhale fully, lifting your arms up to the Moon in the shape of a living chalice, receiving her energies as you breathe in. Exhale, slowly bending at the waist, placing extended arms and palms and third eye upon the ground in front of you.

Complete at least three more cycles of inhalation and exhalation here before moving slowly and mindfully back into kneeling with hands on thighs.

Building a Rapport Between Chakras

After you have become familiar with your bindu chakra and learned to activate it, you can try building a rapport between all your of these upper chakras to increase energy, reinforce the strength of your lunar channel, and further open your psychic ability, which can then be applied to divination, dreaming, magic, healing, ritual, and more.

Here are two practices to help you build those connections; try playing with them every day until they are routine, then integrate them into your Moon Witch Path as desired.

Upper Chakra Breathwork

I like to move into this practice directly after completing the Bindu Breathwork practice. If you'd like to do it separately, begin as such:

The Practice

Step 1: As in the Bindu Breathwork practice, begin by kneeling with your hands on your thighs if comfortable for you; if not, sitting with legs folded crisscross applesauce is a lovely pose for this work, as is sitting comfortably in a chair with the soles of your feet resting firmly on the ground.

Breathe, ground, center, and open the channel, sending your etheric roots down and sending your etheric tendrils up.

Step 2: Now bring the breath all the way up your body with short, pulsing inhalations. Using your hands to help the energies move up, up, up from your root chakra, up your central channel, take this energy and draw it up in front of your third eye, sweeping it up to your crown, and then use your hands to pour the energy from your crown up and over your bindu chakra, see-sense-feeling it flowing down over the back of your head as you exhale.

Do this at least two more times.

Step 3: Breathe upward fluidly as you fully extend your arms. As you exhale, place your hands in prayer position, drawing them up over your third eye, and then up to your crown, tilting your hands backward over the back of your head over your bindu (your hands face downward at this point).

Do this at least two more times.

Step 4: To complete, inhale fluidly, extending arms fully outward, and then exhale, wrapping your arms around your body, giving yourself a tight, loving hug.

Upper Chakra Connection

Here is another route to connect the three upper chakras:

The Process

Step 1: Stand or seat yourself as seems best, then inhale. On your exhalation, send your breath as far out into the Multiverse as you possibly can—out, out, out into eternity, into infinity, into the very cauldron of birth and death and rebirth, that place where all potential resides.

Step 2: As you inhale again, see-sense-feel yourself receiving your breath back from this far away place. Breathe these holy energies into your own human vessel, expanding what is possible for you, in this here and this now, in this lifetime. Fill yourself up with these multiversal energies now.

Step 3: As you exhale again, completely empty yourself, your lungs, your breath into the cauldron of birth, death, and rebirth. Release and let go now; there is no need to hold on.

See-sense-feel your human breath going into the cauldron, into this holy place—your breath a special ingredient that only you can add to this delicious cosmic recipe. Let your breath become mist or fog or even rain, whatever comes to you. Notice what color it is and whether there is a scent or sound that goes along with your exhalation. Gift your breath to the multiversal cauldron of hope, magic, and possibility. Share your breath with the Multiverse—your breath, which only you can offer. Feel how you are a part of all things, now and always.

Step 4: Inhale again from the cauldron, this time holding this breath of infinity within your human body for as long as you possibly can. Top off your breath with as many little sips of air as you can take in. Experience the breath of infinity filling you, swirling all around your body, healing you, connecting you with yourself, with the Earth, and with the Multiverse—with All That Is.

Step 5: When you are ready, move calmly back into slow, full, easy exhalations and inhalations.

Step 6: Connect with the Moon, with the Lunar Lady. Ask her to help you to connect with your bindu chakra. Open yourself to receive the gift of communication from the Moon. Allow her divine energies to course fully through you now.

Step 7: Ask the Moon to help strengthen your relationship with her and your Moon Center. Feel her light (or dark) streaming into your bindu chakra. Feel her energies clearing, cleansing, and opening your crown and ajna chakras, clearing your pineal gland, gently creating a continuous pathway between your crown, your third eye, and your bindu.

Step 8: Breathe in your own divinity now and feel divinity all around you. Feel the Moon's light (or the Moon's dark) settling like a warm and welcome cloak around your shoulders, holding you with unconditional, divine mother's love.

Step 9: Open yourself to blissful energies, to bliss itself. Feel the energies of bliss permeating every cell. Continue to take in lunar energies with every inhalation. With every exhalation, empty yourself of all that does not serve: all energies, emotions, and judgments that keep you from your Oneness with the Moon, your Oneness with all things.

Step 10: Ask the Moon to connect you with her, with her knowledge and wisdom, and with your own knowledge and wisdom. Ask that all your upper chakras function in harmony with one another. As Above, so Below.

Step 11: When you are ready, return to this time and place.

Receiving Information

Once you are familiar with opening your bindu chakra and linking it with your ajna and crown chakras so that they are all operating together, take this next step, which will help you to receive information through these energy centers with ease and efficiency.

Quick Activation

After following this protocol, you can use your mudra combined with your phrase to quickly open and link these three energy centers in advance of lunar rituals, moonspells, or divination or whenever you are called.

The Practice

Step 1: Begin by taking a few generous breaths in and out, connecting with the Earth below and the Sky above. Connect with the Moon and your bindu chakra, breathing moonlight into this energy center.

Step 2: Consider now a hand position (sometimes termed mudra) that you can use to immediately open and activate all three chakras. This need not be complicated; whatever first comes to mind is right.

Step 3: Create a phrase that you will use in concert with this hand position. (I like "These three chakras are open, locked, and in harmony.")

Step 4: Once you have decided on your phrase, hold your hand position and speak your words into it three times.

Step 5: Still holding your mudra, create a different phrase designed to close those chakras and unlock them from one another.

Step 6: Speak this phrase into your mudra once, releasing your hands as you do so. Shake off any extra energy.

Chapter 14
Divination

The Moon Goddess Speaks

Sorceress, Enchantress, Witch—these are all names I have been called, I who hold the mirror upon which others project their fears. I do command these powers, yes, and yet, I am so much more.

I walk the night, coursing with the Moon, directing the energies of transformation with my holy hands.

I can sense beyond the veil, and I can touch the infinite with my fingers. I can see the swirling of the cosmic energies, and I can choose where to insert my will. I control all of the tides—the tides of the sea and the tides of life.

I am Morgana, Morgan le Fay.

Journal Inquiries for This Gateway

When do I feel most connected to my intuition? What practices help me to free the voice of my Oracular Self? What divinatory practice am I meant to explore next?

Affirmations for This Gateway

My connection to the Moon increases my intuitive abilities. I hear the voice of my Lunar Oracular Self. I am open to uncovering that which has been hidden.

Divination, prophesy, foretelling—all have been practiced in one fashion or another by all cultures since archaic times. Predictive guidance is accessible to all of us, furnishing a route upon which we can seek from within, a channeling of information from something bigger than ourselves—Divinity Within and Divinity Without.

When a Seer probes into what is cloaked, they first tune into the Deep Mind. The everyday rational mind is suspended so that the timeless other side may surface. This process utilizes the sixth sense, the same faculty with which we cast spells, perform banishments, read the subconscious, and create miracles of healing.

Our minds can be compared to an iceberg, the conscious, rational part visible above the surface of the sea. The broader, deeper aspects are immeasurable, far beyond our intellectual awareness. Although all humans are in some way sixth sensories, the patriarchal approach to life requires a suppression of the Deep Mind, and we are taught to dwell exclusively in the rational, using only the evidence of the remaining five senses.

All divinatory systems perform the same function: They provide a point of focus to help us relax, concentrate, and make contact with that other mind, that sixth sense. In this shadowy sanctuary, past, present, and future exist simultaneously, and it is possible to see any aspect.

Foretelling works because all time is one time; all time is *this* time. It is only the conscious waking mind that needs the linear progression of *nows*, a brilliantly clever illusion that we collectively create so that we may have a common ground for experiencing this dimension, this reality. Linear time is really just a construct that we have put in place to help us to navigate this three-dimensional world.

Divination can be used every day, helping us to become aware of the energies surrounding us at a particular moment, the possible steps we can take to resolve a given situation, even acting as a guide in creating an action plan for something that is worrying us.

It can be used for prediction but also to support everyday living: for finding answers, delivering divine counseling, guiding shadow work. There is no one "right way" to use divination. Each of us will approach it through the lens of our own unique gifts, talents, and personality.

Your Inner Moon Witch already knows how to do this. The real skill involved in opening the gateway to your intuition originates in surrendering and trusting, in allowing the space needed for insight and awareness to simply be present without pushing or forcing anything to the surface. The art of divination is more about practice and yielding than anything else.

Divining with the Moon

The Moon can serve as oracle in her own right, a source of oracular wisdom, and as an activator of the Oracular Self.

Always remember that the real skill here is believing in yourself—in your own intuition, power-within, and innate connection with the Moon and the Moon Goddess. Any divinatory method is simply a tool; any successful reading requires you to trust in your abilities as a sacred channel and the understanding that all the skills you need are already inside you (although they endlessly require sharpening).

Practice is central, and you can best hone your skills through hands-on work combined with time and perseverance. As your practice unfolds, you will develop your own style of divining, bringing your own unique oracular gifts to the world.

The Basic Divinatory Process

Before beginning your divinatory work, apprise yourself of the phase and sign the Moon is in. Is there a particular tool that you prefer to use based upon this information? What works best for you during each lunar sign or phase? To illustrate: I like to scry with a mirror, chalice, or bowl when Luna is in a water sign or when she is Full, and I prefer tarot when she is in an earth sign or when she is New.

Once you've chosen the tool you will use for your session, prepare your space. Even if you do not cast a circle before engaging in any divination, ground and center yourself. This can be as brief as taking a moment to align with your breath, your body, the Earth, and the Moon.

You may elect to create and light a special incense or candle, perhaps even set an altar to assist your focus. Ensure that your body is as comfortable as possible—sitting while divining is ideal.

Next, connect with your breath, then with your tool, attuning your energies with each other. Invite the wisdom of the Moon to enter you and your tool as well. Quiet your mind and open your awareness.

If you have a specific question or situation to address, bring it forth by speaking it aloud whenever possible. It is at this point you begin to confer with your tool, permitting whatever wants or needs to come through to reveal itself to you. Be ever courageous!

As you tap into the eternal cycling of the Moon as an inspiration for your oracular work, you will learn what best works for you and when. Always use your Moon Journal to record your experiences.

Lunar Tarot

Lunar tarot reading is, at its very core, channeled storytelling, using the cards as a guide. Tarot cards can be viewed as special keys that unlock the various doors we must walk through in order to properly tell the tale of what is happening—or the tale of the possibilities that could happen. Our intuition is what guides us in following the correct path from door to door.

The meaning of the cards vary: Interpretations can be traditional, deck-based, intuitive, and those that happen only once in one unrepeatable moment. In the book *Secrets of the Waite-Smith Tarot,* Marcus Katz and Tali Goodwin write, "The oracular moment is sacrosanct."[46] What the Seer says a card means in that moment is what it means.

The crux of being a good tarot reader is to rely upon your intuition no matter what, including when things don't seem to make rational sense or when a message is difficult to give. To be a good reader, you must be willing to take a risk, to leap, to embody the Fool.

The tarot is ever accurate on some level—it perceives the root of whatever is present—although you might not discern the how or the why until time unwinds and things shake out into resolution.

How this works is a mystery, and your only job is to become a steady, open channel, a vessel and a voice for the energies to speak through the cards. It is not your responsibility to worry about how this works or to try to control how this happens.

Before considering the traditional meaning of a card that shows up in a reading, take a moment to engage with the image. How does it make you feel in *this* moment? Do you catch any flashes of insight? What symbols on the card most draw your attention? Is there a dominant color? Does the expression on a character's face resonate with the inquiry?

If you are reading for yourself, you may wish to engage in a dialogue with the card's character or characters—internally, aloud, or through automatic writing—or try to connect with the character through meditation and/or on the astral plane.

There is a wealth of gorgeous mooncentric tarot and oracle decks available, and you may wish to seek out a new one to dedicate to your lunar divination practice. Consecrate these tools purely for your Lunar Witchcraft Path, inviting the magic of the Moon to partner with you in your oracular work.

Lunar Tarot Activation

Before beginning this exercise, you may wish to use one of the bindu activation practices from the previous chapter to open up your psychic skills and strengthen your connection to the Moon.

To Gather

- Your tarot deck

46. Katz and Goodwin, *Secrets of the Waite-Smith Tarot,* xiv.

The Process

Step 1: Hold your tarot deck in your hands and breathe with it. When your energies are resonating with your cards, ask the Moon to fill you and your deck with her energies and her wisdom.

Step 2: See-sense-feel your body filling with her brilliance. Permit the Moon's energy to overflow from within you, and then direct these energies out of your palms and fingertips into your deck. See-sense-feel your tarot cards vibrating with these cooling, wise lunar energies.

Step 3: When you sense your cards are completely filled up with the Moon's powers, say aloud, "It is done. Luna is here." You may notice your fingers tingling, see or sense a glowing or an aura around your cards, or experience a sense of stillness or something else—or you just may have a knowing it is complete.

Step 4: Give the Moon your gratitude and stop drawing her energy down. Allow your channel to the Moon through your crown, third eye, and bindu chakras to remain open and clear.

Step 5: Now, do your reading.

Step 6: When your reading is complete, thank the Moon again, and then gently close your chakras almost completely, like a sheer drape pulled across a window.

Lunar Tarot and Oracle Card Spreads

For the following spreads, it is your choice to use tarot or oracle cards. Oracle cards are similar to tarot, but they do not rely upon its traditional system or symbolism. You can also try using both at once: Sometimes I pull cards from a tarot deck to create the spread on one side and then shuffle and pull oracle cards, setting up the exact same spread next to it. Then I look at what is reflected in the mirrored readings, just as the Moon mirrors the Sun's light.

Remember: Sometimes it takes time for a spread to make sense, time for the energies to settle down and then play out. When a spread seems extraordinarily confusing, take thorough notes (or use your phone to take a picture or create an audio file) and mark your calendar to revisit the information later—perhaps in three months, six months, twelve months, or even longer.

For each practice, you need a deck of cards—tarot or oracle (or both)—and your Moon Journal (or a journal you dedicate solely to your lunar divinatory practice).

Daily Draw Divination

If you don't already do so, try pulling a card for yourself every morning. As you shuffle your deck, ask the Moon, "What do I need to know today?" or "What do I need to do (or *not* do) today?" Examine the card's images, symbols, and colors; note your first impressions and how the card makes you feel. As you go about your day, notice: What is the meaning of this card? How is it showing up in my day?

Record what you observed in your Moon Journal each evening. Don't get bogged down; a few quick moments spent each night is perfect.

Lunation Spread

This spread covers an entire lunar cycle, beginning with the New Moon phase. Shuffle your cards and then set them up as follows, in the round shape of the Moon:

- *Card 1 (bottom center):* New Moon
- *Card 2 (bottom left):* Waxing Crescent
- *Card 3 (middle left):* Waxing Half
- *Card 4 (top left):* Waxing Gibbous
- *Card 5 (top center):* Full Moon
- *Card 6 (top right):* Waning Gibbous
- *Card 7 (middle right):* Waning Half
- *Card 8 (bottom right):* Waning Crescent

After arranging your layout, view the cards as one whole picture. Are there any themes, symbols, colors, or suits prevalent, or do the cards seem to be disparate and all over the place?

Feel into the cards as one complete story, as the general energies and pattern of the lunation you are about to experience. Do some journaling and compare the cards to your everyday calendar. What is on your schedule for the cycle ahead and how does it match—or not match—the energies of the cards present?

Next look at each card one at a time, viewing each as a representation of the energy or happenings of each upcoming phase. Do some more journaling and perhaps mark the dates on your everyday calendar with their matching cards. As your month plays out, observe how each card resonates with what occurs.

Lunar Phase Return Spread

This is a spread to use each lunation when you would like a sense of what your personal cycle ahead will *feel* like. Begin this reading with the phase of your natal Moon, with card 1 illustrating the energies of that week.

Shuffle your deck and draw four cards, with each card more or less representing one week, one quarter of the lunar cycle.

- *Card 1*: Your place of beginning; your reset
  Inquiry: What are the prevailing energies as I begin my new personal lunation?
- *Card 2:* Your place of waxing
  Inquiry: What is coalescing in my life or around me?
- *Card 3:* Your place of waning
  Inquiry: What is dissolving in my life or around me?
- *Card 4:* Your card of ending
  Inquiry: What is concluding as I end this personal lunation and prepare to begin a new one?

This spread presents an excellent opportunity to try out the mirroring reading option suggested above. Create the spread on one side with tarot cards, and then set down the same spread next to it using your oracle cards. What is the same? What is different?

Lunar Year Spread

Thirteen cards are used for this reading, each one representing a Full or New Moon (your choice) for the given lunar year—or you can instead use this spread to mark your monthly lunar phase returns throughout the year.

Shuffle your deck and draw one card for each lunation, laying your cards out in the form of a circle—the shape of the Moon as seen from Earth. Explore the reading as a whole, observing any themes that pop out to you.

Document your spread with a quick snap on your phone and/or draw it in your Moon Journal. On your personal calendar, note the date each month when you will check in with your card for that lunation.

Observe how the reading plays out for you throughout the lunar year, then begin again.

Triple Moon Spread

The Triple Moon spread is a simple three-card layout that can be easily adapted to whatever situation you are facing; it can be as cursory or as in-depth as appropriate. When performing a three-card spread, draw a fourth card when clarification is needed. This fourth card may indicate an action you can take or might provide greater illumination if the original message is incomplete, ambiguous, or nebulous.

You can experiment with Triple Moon spreads that show the general vibrations surrounding you during different parts of a lunation:

- New Moon ~ Waxing Moon ~ Full Moon
- Full Moon ~ Waning Moon ~ Dark Moon
- Waxing Crescent Moon ~ Full Moon ~ Waning Crescent Moon

Or you can try various other related ideas. Here are some themes for this simple layout for you to play with:

- Yourself ~ The Surrounding Energies ~ The Lesson
- Yourself ~ Your Current Path ~ Your Potential
- Your Current Challenge ~ Your Aspirations ~ The Outcome
- Stop ~ Start ~ Continue
- Your Situation ~ Your Goal ~ The Best Action to Take
- That Which Hinders ~ That Which Helps ~ That Which is Hidden
- You ~ The Energies Surrounding You ~ How to Work with Them

Spreads by Lunar Phase

You can use the Moon's phase to enhance your divination practice, either as a one-card reading or in full spreads. When doing one-card readings for various Moon phases, try centering these themes:

- New Moon: Where must I begin again?
- Waxing Crescent: What is germinating?
- Waxing Half Moon: What is my progress report for reaching my goals for this lunation?
- Waxing Gibbous: What energies should I add to what is growing?
- Full Moon: What should I honor and celebrate?
- Waning Gibbous: What needs appreciation and gratitude?
- Waning Half Moon: What is falling away and needs to be released?
- Waning Crescent: What needs healing?
- Dark Moon: What has died and needs to be composted?

Here are some ideas for full spreads. Attempt them as is or modify as desired to suit your needs.

Lunar Phase Spreads

For the following layouts, use the instructions found earlier in this chapter. Once again, you may use either a tarot or oracle deck, or both.

New Moon Spread

Card 1: What new opportunity is waiting in the wings?
Card 2: What do I need to know about this opportunity?
Card 3: What step or steps should I take toward manifestation?
Card 4 (optional): Message from the Maiden Moon Goddess

Full Moon Spread

Card 1: What hidden knowledge is now illuminating?
Card 2: What is culminating in my life?
Card 3: What can I celebrate myself for completing?
Card 4 (optional): Message from the Mother Moon Goddess

Dark Moon Spread

Card 1: What is dying or dead?
Card 2: What aspect of my life needs more spaciousness?
Card 3: What do I need to get rid of?
Card 4 (optional): Message from the Crone Moon Goddess

Blue Moon Spread

Card 1: My emotions and energies
Card 2: The emotions and energies of those who surround me
Card 3: How to stay centered

Lunar Eclipse Spread

Card 1 (placed in center): What are the overarching energies or themes playing out in my life right now?
Card 2: (left): Body
Card 3: (top): Mind
Card 4: (right): Heart
Card 5: (bottom): Spirit

Solar Eclipse Spread

This is an elemental reading. What does each Element of Life want me to know?

Card 1 (center): You
Card 2 (left): West: Feelings, emotions, ebb and flow
Card 3 (right): East: Intellect, vision, beginnings, bird's-eye overview
Card 4: (bottom): South: Passion, creation, destruction, protection
Card 5: (top): North: Wisdom, health, physical reality and resources

Black Moon Spread

Card 1: What part of my Shadow Self wants to be acknowledged now?
Card 2: What healing does my Shadow Self need?
Card 3: How can I best integrate this part of my Shadow Self?

Supermoon Spread

Card 1: What energies are rising?
Card 2: What energies are diminishing?
Card 3: How can I harmonize these two poles?

Micromoon Spread

Card 1: What is slowly moving into place for me?
Card 2: What do I need to understand about my role in this?
Card 3: What action should I take?

Lunar Scrying

Scrying is another form of the divinatory arts; lunar scrying uses moonlight (and moondark) as the focalizer of this practice.

Like tarot, divination through scrying need not only concern foretelling the future. Scrying for everyday life inspiration, creative innovation, and self-awareness can be immensely helpful to the Lunar Witch, too.

When scrying, do not expect to see scenes unfolding in front of you as if a movie is playing. It is far more common to experience flashes of insight, words, sounds, images, or symbols in your scrying tool or to see-sense-feel things in your mind's eye. In fact, you may not see-sense-feel anything at all, receiving information instead as if by telepathy or epiphany.

Full understanding is often revealed later, sometimes years later, and even while engaging in other activities, such as through dreams when sleeping, while meditating, or during journeying.

Scrying in the Moon

Before we delve into scrying tools, here is a framework for scrying with the Moon. It can be adapted to work with any scrying method or tool you choose, and it is meant to be a springboard. Practice it as you experiment with the various tools and processes shared throughout this chapter, then tailor them to fit your life.

To Gather

- Your scrying tools
- Your Moon Journal and pen
- A plate of healthy, calorie-dense food

Optional

- Instrumental music or binaural beats tracks

To Prepare

Before you start, select your scrying location and your scrying method (see the next section) and be aware of the sign and phase of the Moon.

It is my preference to cast a sacred circle around myself before scrying, especially when I am outdoors, but it is up to you whether or not you want to take this step.

Some people like to play instrumental music or a binaural beats track in the background whilst scrying. This is not for me, but it may be of help to you. Experiment with both natural sounds (or silence, depending on where you live and how loud it is there) and music (either played ambiently or through earbuds).

The Process

Step 1: Make your body comfortable; sitting or kneeling is generally best unless you prefer to stand. Ensure your scrying object is near enough that you will be able to gaze into it for a significant period of time and that your body will be okay in the position you choose throughout this time.

Step 2: Close your eyes, contact the Earth Mother and the Cosmos. Slow your breathing.

Step 3: Connect with your ajna, crown, and bindu chakras, opening and activating them however works best for you. You can use one of the longer practices from the previous chapter or try the "Quick Activation" hand position and phrase you created.

Step 4: Attune yourself to your surroundings. Using your senses, feel into what is happening around you: Close your eyes and notice the breeze on your skin, let the Earth take your weight, smell the scent of flowers upon the air, hear the wings of bats or birds beating overhead as they hunt their nightly quarry.

Step 5: Once you are in tune with both your own body and the body of the Earth, raise your arms up to the Lunar Lady and open your eyes. Call her attention to you; invite her to join you in your scrying tool.

Delight your Slothperson here, that most primal part of yourself who has no words, only sensations. For example, if you are using a scrying bowl, you might pour your moonwater into it in dramatic fashion.

Step 6: Envision the wisdom of the Moon filling your scrying tool, then begin to gaze into it. Allow all of your senses to broaden, including your thoughts. What comes through? Do you see a symbol in your tool? A picture? Do you receive a particular impression or smell a familiar scent? Do you hear a word or a sound that holds meaning for you?

Stay here, receptive and in communion with the Moon, for as long as you want.

Step 7: When the rush of information concludes, thank the Moon. Ground and center yourself.

Step 8: Write about your experience in your Moon Journal, including every detail you can remember, recognizing that you may not identify what it means for your reality until much, much later.

Step 9: Eat some healthy, calorie-dense food to help you completely return to shared reality.

Alternative

Try scrying in the Moon directly. This is exactly what it sounds like: gazing into her luminous body with the goal of receiving information. This requires no gear whatsoever—nothing but a clear night (or day, if she is visible then). Follow the same steps as with any other form of scrying.

Lunar Scrying Tools

There are many tools that are used for scrying. Here are a few options for you to try.

Lunar Scrying Crystals

One of the simplest of scrying tools is a crystal or stone, especially one that is dark and shiny. There are many possibilities; I love to use the slick side of a palm-sized chunk of rough obsidian for this purpose.

Ideally, select a crystal with some sort of glossiness so it can catch and reflect the light of the Moon. However, if you have a strong affinity for a particular stone and it is not shiny, you may be able to find one in the same family that has been cut and polished to serve as your scrying stone.

The traditional crystal ball falls into this category. These are attainable in all sizes, colors, and materials. I love my large clear crystal ball just as much as my tiny green glass one.

Try using the previous scrying exercise with a reflective crystal, stone, or ball to view the moonlight. What do you see-sense-feel as Luna beams her wisdom into your sacred tool?

Lunar Scrying Vessels

Scrying vessels must be watertight and are generally used in one of two ways: (1) to catch the light of the Moon in water so you can scry from the reflected rays and (2) to gaze directly into moonwater (or another holy liquid) to receive lunar information from the water itself.

For divination using moonlight, it is not necessary to use something expensive or ornate; for example, a clear glass bowl, a silver goblet, or even a large shell work equally well.

For water divination (with or without moonlight), black lunar scrying bowls or goblets are often used; these can be bought online or at local metaphysical shops or created by painting the exterior of a clear bowl with black paint.

In a pinch, any bowl, goblet, or cup can be used!

Decide if you'd like to first try scrying in water by catching the light of the Moon on its surface or if you'd like to simply gaze into moonwater and see-sense-feel what materializes for you there.

Once again, use the process described above and explore the messages you receive when utilizing water, the most lunar of the elements.

Scrying Tool Activation

No matter what tool you use for your lunar scrying, it should be activated to your purpose immediately before use, each and every time. Here is one way in which to do this:

To Gather

- Your scrying tool

The Process

Step 1: Relax yourself—body, mind, heart, and spirit—making yourself as comfortable as you can.

Step 2: Hold your scrying tool in both hands and connect with your breath, slowing and deepening it.

Step 3: Begin to attune your Lunar Self with your scrying tool by breathing with it. Take the time to sync your breath with that of your tool, whatever that is like for you.

Step 4: Softly gaze into your scrying tool, enhancing your connection with it through your hands and your eyes. Be kind with yourself; there is nothing to do but gently hold the aspiration of attunement and relationship.

Step 5: When you are connected, ask your tool if it is willing to work with you at this time. Heed the answer you receive. Sometimes it is not the correct time to work with a particular device, and you must choose another tool or choose another time. No matter the answer you receive, thank your scrying tool.

Step 6: Return to this here and now and proceed with your intentions for scrying if it is the correct time to do so.

Lunar Magic Mirrors

Magic mirrors are another scrying device, and they are excellent for lunar divination, corresponding perfectly with the reflective nature of the Moon. You can purchase one ready-made or design your own. Creating your own lunar magic mirror is an excellent project to deepen your connection to your Inner Moon Witch. Here are some basic instructions.

Creating Your Magic Mirror

For this project, you will need to find an inexpensive wooden or metal picture frame that summons you at a garage sale, charity shop, or another store. Maybe you already have one tucked away! Look for a frame that is muted and dark in color, as bright and shiny frames can reflect in your finished mirror. The glass should be in perfect condition, intact and unmarked.

Some Moon Witches prefer a round or oval frame, yet rectangular or square frames are fine as well. Whatever works for you! The frame should not be too big; you should be able to carry your mirror with you if you want to—definitely no more than twelve inches across, no matter which shape you choose.

To carry out this project, pick a place with proper ventilation—outdoors is highly preferable—and ideally on a sunny, windless day so nothing unintended blows onto the wet paint. If crafting outdoors is not an option, use black high-gloss acrylic paint and apply it with a foam brush.

To Gather

- A picture frame with a glass insert (dark-colored frames are better for scrying than light)
- Glass cleaner and a microfiber cloth or paper towels
- Newspaper or a large piece of cardboard (larger than your frame)
- Black high-gloss enamel spray paint (or even a dark blue or purple) that is made for use on glass. Read the label. (Use black high-gloss acrylic paint and a foam brush if you must paint indoors.)
- Eye protection
- Clothing protection

Optional

- Embellishments for decorating the frame (such as glitter, markers, sequins)

The Process

Step 1: Carefully remove the glass from the frame and place it on a flat surface. Clean it well on one side with glass cleaner or a vinegar and water solution. Be sure it is completely dry, then repeat this procedure on the other side.

Step 2: Place the clean glass on the large sheet of newspaper or cardboard, handling it only by the edges so you do not cause fingerprints on the surface. Be sure your work area and your person will be protected from the spray paint; you may wish to wear old clothes, gloves, and/or face and eye protection.

Step 3: Spray the paint on the glass, going back and forth with quick, light, even passes until the glass is completely covered. Do not permit the paint to run or bubble.

Let the paint dry completely; this might take quite a few hours.

Step 4: You may need to apply two or more additional coats, until no visible light streams through the glass. Be certain to let the glass dry completely in between coats; this could take several days depending upon the humidity and temperature in your location. Don't rush—allow your paint time to cure.

Step 5: While you wait for the paint to dry, you could decorate your frame with symbols, your name, and/or other embellishments.

Step 6: Place the fully dry glass back into the completed frame, painted side facing the back. Your lunar scrying mirror is complete and ready to be consecrated for your use!

Consecrating Your Magic Mirror

Now you will consecrate your mirror as you would any other Sacred. Before beginning, look at your lunar calendar or ephemeris and identify a phase and/or sign to perform this moonwork.

To Gather

- Your magic mirror

The Process

Step 1: Ground, center, and open the channel, moving yourself gently into Ritual Mind. Cast a formal circle if it is your desire to do so.

Step 2: Find a comfortable position; sitting is probably best. Hold your scrying mirror with both hands and close your eyes. Allow your Inner Moon Witch, your lunar consciousness, to open to your mirror.

Step 3: Your magic mirror will tell you a word, a secret word that is just for the two of you.

Step 4: Open your eyes and place your most dominant finger upon the center of your magic mirror, then whisper the secret word into your mirror. Remove your finger now and send a big breath into the spot where you were touching your scrying mirror.

Step 5: Do this two more times (for a total of three times), allowing your lunar consciousness and your psychic energies to mingle with that of your mirror.

Step 6: Leave your scrying mirror out in the Moon's light (or dark) for three nights.

Whenever you use your magic mirror, bring it to a place where you can see the Moon and awaken it by simply holding your hands over its surface and whispering your secret word into it three times. Then use the scrying process from earlier in the chapter. Catch the light of the Moon in your mirror and see-sense-feel what is there for you!

Magic Mirror Wells

Another way to store the energy of a single lunar phase is within your magic mirror. You can work this activation process once or over a long period of time: Try every lunation throughout an entire lunar year or even longer—over thirteen or more years!

For example, perhaps you would like to devote your scrying mirror to the New Moon phase. You can create a New Moon–specific magic mirror, charged only during this phase to record only this particular frequency.

What happens when you use your magic mirror outside of this time and phase, though? You will use up the energies—maybe all at once or maybe more gradually. But the reality is that it will become drained of this energy, and usually rapidly, because it has only been charged with it once.

Here is an introductory practice.

Magic Mirror Energy Wells

This is the quickest way to create this type of well; it takes only a brief elapsing of time.

To Gather

- Your magic mirror
- Cloth, which will be used to cover your mirror, in a color that supports your intention

The Process

Step 1: Determine a lunar happening that you would like to save or record in your well. For your first foray, perhaps select just a phase or zodiacal sign.

Step 2: Bring your magic mirror out under this phase or sign and expose it to the Moon during this time only, verbally inviting this one vibration to dwell within it.

Step 3: Cover your mirror with your cloth and bring it indoors before the Moon moves into the next phase, sign, or happening. Now you have a mirror that is holding the energies of this particular lunar moment, saved and ready for you to use whenever you desire.

Advanced Work with Mirror Wells

To spark your imagination, here are three ideas to experiment with storing energy in your mirror. These practices take more planning and devotion than the quick practice yet can be very rewarding.

Charged with a Particular Phase

This course of action is carried out for an entire lunar year as the desired Moon phase marches through each of the twelve astrological signs. For example, perhaps I'd like to make a well containing New Moon energies, and I began with the New Moon in Cancer. At the beginning of the following lunation, I will repeat the above steps with the New Moon in Leo. During the next lunation, I will again repeat this process, this time under the New Moon in Virgo. And I will continue this until I have exposed my magic mirror to all of the New Moons in succession, each sign following the next.

This magic would be completed beneath the New Moon in Gemini the following year. Alternately, you could seal your work by completing the process alongside the same New Moon you began in. In my example, I would consecrate my mirror under the New Moon in Cancer that would occur one lunar year after I began.

Be aware that this is a big enterprise, and if the practice doesn't progress in the proper order (i.e., you are on vacation and miss a New Moon, forget, or don't complete it for whatever reason), you will need to scrap your work and start again from the beginning. This takes a lot of discipline, and over a year of moonwork, but if you are so called, it is well worth it.

Charged with a Particular Sign

This is helpful when you want to easily access a certain zodiacal sign for your scrying work. Perhaps you've discovered that your psychic abilities are heightened, for example, when the Moon is in Pisces, and so you'd like to have a lunar scrying mirror that is keyed to the particular energies of the Piscean Moon. This procedure, like the Moon phase process, takes at least one year to complete. You will expose your mirror to the Moon whilst she is dwelling within the sign of Pisces *during every lunation.*

After the Moon progresses through this sign throughout an entire lunar year, you might like to seal the energies by exposing the mirror once again to the Moon when that sign returns to the phase it was in when you began this process the year prior.

For example: Say I wanted a magic mirror keyed to the vibrations of the Moon in Aries. I might begin this process with the New Moon in that sign, an excellent starting point as Aries is the first sign in the zodiac and a New Moon is the first phase in a lunation.

I would start by setting my mirror under this New Moon in Aries, removing it before Luna switches into the sign of Taurus. (Note that I would further remove my magic mirror before the Moon goes void of course, but following this guideline is wholly up to you.)

I would then cover my mirror with a cloth, store it in a safe place, and look ahead in my lunar calendar to see when Luna is next in the sign of Aries. During that time, I would put the mirror out again. This will most likely be during the Waning Crescent phase. That timing complete, I will cover the mirror and tuck it away yet again, marking my calendar for the next time Luna enters Aries.

We move backward yet again, and when I look, I see that in the next month she is still in the Waning Crescent, but this time very close to the Waning Half Moon. The next lunation, she is in Aries beginning on the Waning Half and moving toward Waning Gibbous.

The following lunation finds her in Waning Gibbous moving toward the Full Moon. The next lunation finds her still in Waning Gibbous, missing the Aries Full Moon by a very small margin, and so I know that the next lunation will bring me to the Aries Full Moon, about halfway through this working.

I continue on until she reaches the Dark Moon in Aries. When the New Moon in Aries returns yet again one lunar year later, the mirror is fully charged and ready for consecration and activation. It will hold this record forever (although you can keep going with the process if you want or recharge it at any time when the Moon returns to Aries in the phase under which you are moved to reenergize it).

Charged with a Particular Sign *and* Phase, Concurrently

This is an exceptionally long process and requires an immense amount of planning, patience, and time. If there is a particular Moon sign and phase that you wish to strongly imbue into your magic mirror, you can work to do this over a period of years. I suggest thirteen.

One of the most advantageous magical times for you is your birthmoon, and so if this project calls to you, this would be a perfect first attempt.

As an illustration, let's say your birthmoon is a Waxing Gibbous Moon in the sign of Capricorn.

Begin the process at the correct time as outlined above, carefully wrapping your mirror when finished and putting it safely away. If you stow your mirror somewhere strange (i.e., in a place that you have never stored a magical tool before) note where you put it in your Moon Journal so you know where it is when you need it again.

Now, you'll need to go to a lunar calendar for the following year to find out when the Moon will next be in that phase and sign. Mark your calendar for the following year, and when that time arrives, perform this entire practice again.

Like the yearlong version of saving the Moon's light, energies, and vibrations outlined above, it is best to go through a full cycle. The length of that cycle is up to you; I chose thirteen years as this is a magical sum and a lunar number to boot. Your mileage may vary, though. Perhaps three years is enough!

You could instead use your mirror without waiting until you are finished charging it, still continuing with this process every year on your birthmoon (or whatever phase and sign you chose).

Remember: You can imbue your magic mirror with any phase, any sign, or any combination of a particular sign and phase. If there is a particular astronomical event occurring and you think you'll want to use those energies later, get charging!

Moon Pendulums

Sometimes the only thing we want is a simple answer, a straightforward yes or no regarding a choice or decision that must be made—and made quickly. A moon pendulum supplies a simple way of connecting with the Moon to predict the yes or no of any situation.

In *Ariadne's Thread*, Shekhinah Mountainwater writes that pendulums work "with auric vibrations, or the energy field that surrounds the person who holds the pendulum."[47]

Another explanation of how pendulums work is that they deliver messages from our subconscious by a process named ideomotor action—our instinctive thoughts are transmitted into patterns of muscular activity, directly accessing information held by the subconscious, bypassing the conscious mind or ego. Muscle testing, automatic writing, spirit boards, dowsing, and other forms of divination have also been attributed to this phenomenon.

Lunar pendulums can be made of any material. Ideally, though, a moon pendulum is made from a string or chain and an object that corresponds with lunar energies: a stone, metal, or crystal; a wood, seed, or herb bundle; a necklace, ring, or bracelet.

For me, this historically means a silver chain and a piece of moonstone.

A pendulum is held by its diviner with as steady a hand as possible, allowing the weight to freely swing, with one direction indicating a yes answer and the other direction no. A yes or no (or maybe) question is asked and the moon pendulum begins to swing in the direction of the answer.

Pendulum Boards

If you haven't used a pendulum board before, I invite you to try it out. Pendulum boards do not need to be purchased or created by a professional; in a fix, you can draw one for yourself with a simple piece of paper and a pen. I prefer making my own because I can readily compost or burn them when I am finished with my divination.

Pendulum boards are predominantly circular and include the words (or symbols for the energies of the words) *yes*, *no*, and *maybe*. Some boards also include the word *unclear*. *Yes* and *no* are indicated on

47. Mountainwater, *Ariadne's Thread*, 231.

opposite sides of the board with *maybe* (or *unclear*) often written on the bottom and the word *rephrase* on the top.

Sound familiar? Yes, they can be quite similar to the Ouija boards that many of us experimented with as young people.

I like to draw my pendulum boards as a round representation of the Moon, request that she join me, and then get to asking!

Moon Pendulum Consecration

Cleanse, clear, and attune your pendulum before its initial use, and do so at least monthly after that for as long as it is in service. As with any sacred tool, take the time to develop a relationship with your pendulum before moving forward with it for divination.

Many people have a secret word they use to awaken their pendulums before using. Follow the steps in the earlier practice: Consecrating Your Magic Mirror.

I like to cleanse my lunar pendulums in conjunction with a Waning or Dark Moon and charge them during a Waxing or Full Moon. Some choose to cleanse and charge their pendulums before each session.

Additionally, a moon pendulum is best consecrated before its first use. This is one way to do it.

To Gather

- Your moon pendulum
- Something to represent each Element of Life: air, fire, water, and earth (for example: smoldering incense for air, a lit candle for fire, a small bowl of water for water, and a stone for earth)

The Process

Step 1: Ground, center, and open the channel.

Step 2: Cleanse your moon pendulum by the powers of air, fire, water, and earth using the symbols you gathered.

Step 3: Breathe into your pendulum three times.

Step 4: Speak this charm aloud three times:

> *I consecrate and charge this pendulum in the name of the Moon.*
> *May our energies blend and harmonize.*
> *May all answers offered be true and for my highest good.*
> *It is done!*

Your moon pendulum is now consecrated.

Moon Pendulum Attunement

Before each use, it is imperative to check in with your moon pendulum and reattune yourself with it. Strangely, the directions that indicate yes and no sometimes change! Each time you use this sacred tool, take a moment to check in with it to see which direction is which. Oftentimes, spinning or moving in a clockwise direction indicates yes and counterclockwise no. When it doesn't move, I accept the answer as maybe, or perhaps there is not enough information at this time.

To Gather

- Your moon pendulum

The Process

Step 1: Start this attunement by grounding, centering, and opening the channel. Connect with your breath, with the Earth, and with the Moon. When you are sufficiently plugged in, ask the Moon to visit your pendulum and help you.

Step 2: Close your eyes and suspend the pendulum in front of you. Speaking aloud or not, your choice, ask it to move in a clockwise direction. Now open your eyes to see this happening, then tell it to stop movement.

Step 3: When the movement stops, close your eyes again, and ask your moon pendulum to move counterclockwise. Again, open your eyes to see this, then tell it to stop its movement, observing as it does.

Step 4: To discover which direction is yes and which is no on any given day, hold the pendulum in your dominant hand and ask it to answer an easy question to which you already know the answer. Then do the same thing but use the opposite hand to see if that feels more natural.

Step 5: Now you are ready to use your pendulum for lunar divination.

Chapter 15
Dreaming

The Moon Goddess Speaks

Just when you think you have my measure, another aspect of my Deep Self emerges. I am Protectress and Guardian. I am Creatrix and Mage. I am Mother and Gardener. I am Queen and Goddess. Every phase of the Moon carries my essence, from dark to bright and everything in between.

With deft fingers I knit the silvery beams into dreams for you: prophetic dreams, healing dreams, dreams of wholeness and power. And then I send them to your sleeping form. Will you welcome them?

What do you want to dream of? Here, in this dark and shadowy land, I will bring you a vision that will support you. Rest assured that I will always come to you when you have need of me, and in the proper form.

I am Hina.

Journal Inquiries for This Gateway

Do I trust my inner Dreamer? What is my most enduring, perhaps even secret, dream for this lifetime? What is one step I can take toward bringing this into being?

Affirmations for This Gateway

My intuition is strong, and I dream truly and powerfully. It is safe to follow my dreams. I trust the wisdom that surfaces from the Dreamrealm.

Not only is our waking life profoundly affected by Luna's dance through her phases and the signs of the zodiac, so is our dreaming life. The Moon rules the Realm of Dreams, where we spend about one-third of our lives. We can connect with her for deeper sleep, more profound and meaningful dreams, and prophetic messages.

If our conscious, rational, active, physical body is our Solar Self, then our subconscious, reflective, receptive, emotional body is our Lunar Self. Most alive in the holy darkness and richness of our inner existence, the Lunar Self is the part that dreams, storing all of our memories, feelings, and emotions, striving to sort, categorize, and organize all of the experiences of our waking lives.

Intrinsically connected to the cycling of the Moon, your dreamlife is subject to her perpetual shifts. Once you have deciphered your own distinct lunar energy cycle, you can in turn master how it affects your sleep and your dreaming, hearing and absorbing the divine nighttime messages you receive.

Exploring the Dreamworld

Here are some ideas, both esoteric and earthly, for exploring the lunar Dreamworld and growing your understanding of its terrain and purpose. These strategies are meant to help you to approach dreams as divine teachers, increasing the synthesis between your dreamlife and the energies of the Moon as a path to personal power.

Dream Tracking

Recording your dreams is an important first step in dream recollection and can provide a valuable source of insight into your personal Dreamrealm.

Through the eyes of a lunar Dreamer, begin looking for connections between your emotions, your dreams, and your sleep quality, paying close attention not only to how you feel but how you dream as the Moon moves through each phase and astrological sign.

If you haven't already done so, create a section in your Moon Journal for your lunar dreamwork or begin a separate notebook—a Dream Diary—that is dedicated solely to this practice. To set yourself up for success keep this, along with a pen, beside your bed.

You need not remember the minutiae of a dream in order to record it, and you need not spend a significant amount of time documenting it either. Although it may be helpful later, there is no obligation to write a step-by-step, blow-by-blow account of your dreams unless you are so called.

Each morning, try writing down something simple and quick: a keyword or phrase; an image or two; a symbol, emotion, color, or scent; the setting; and/or the people, plants, or animals involved. If a fuller dream recollection emerges later in the day, log that as soon as you can.

In doing your disciplined best to record something each day, even merely jotting down one word, you are collecting data that can, over time, reveal the recurring themes of your life and how your singular nature interacts with Luna.

Of particular interest is when the Moon journeys through your natal Moon sign, your natal Moon phase, and/or your natal Sun sign. Notice if you dream differently during these special times.

Try adding this piece to your daily lunar tracking practice: Spend a few minutes writing brief notes about your dreams every morning promptly upon waking, paying particular attention to your dream in relationship to the changing Moon sign and phase. Don't wait until later; even vivid dreams tend to fade quickly once we arrive back in the ordinary world.

When engaging with this devotional practice of dream logging, you will learn not only how to translate your dreams and dream fragments in helpful ways but when you tend to dream more deeply, sharply, or not at all.

Every so often, go back through your Moon Journal or Dream Diary and read it from cover to cover, taking note of any patterns you see, including those that appear to be seasonal. I like to do this quarterly, within the restful period of the Dark Moon.

When you awaken and can't remember any dreams or dream fragments, try working with the following inquiries. Whether or not they jog your memory is moot—so long as you are writing something about your dreams every morning, you are doing great.

Morning Dream Diary inquiries:

- What is my mood this morning?
- Do I have any feelings or energies that I am bringing to my waking life from the Dreamrealm?
- Did I sleep well or poorly?
- How long did I sleep for?

Dream Recollection

The best system I have found to remember my dreams is to simply tell myself that I will remember them!

Try it. Right before falling asleep, ask the Moon to send you a dream, then write this sentence at the top of a blank page in your Moon Journal or Dream Diary, simultaneously saying it aloud: "Tonight I will dream vividly, and when I wake up, I will remember my dreams and write them down."

In the morning, record your dreams directly under that phrase in your Moon Journal or Dream Diary, noting the sign or signs and lunar phase that you dreamed through overnight.

Dream Interpretation

When interpreting dreams, trust your Inner Moon Witch and first go within; don't get bogged down by seeking out someone else's interpretation in books or online. Your dreams are yours—they belong to no one else. What an object or location means to you may be entirely different from what they mean to anyone else.

A valid dream interpretation may be as simple as identifying the emotion behind the dream or the personal significance of a particular symbol.

A simple daily dream interpretation practice—a way to find meaning in your nightly dreams—can look like this:

Note a dream or dream fragment alongside the lunar phase and sign. Then spend a few minutes in your Moon Journal or Dream Diary answering such questions as:

- What meaning does this hold for me?
- What feelings, experiences, and associations does it evoke?
- What does it remind me of?

Freewrite, allowing everything to flow forth without self-censoring.

Dreams About the Moon

When you dream about the Moon, your subconscious is seeking your attention. It is a signal to evaluate what is happening beneath the surface of your life. When you have such a dream, light some lunar incense or a candle, get out your Moon Journal or Dream Diary, and play with the following inquiries:

- What has been my baseline emotional state over the past days (or weeks)?
- What part of my life would be well served by some illumination?
- What intuitive "hit" have I had of late that I may be ignoring or suppressing?
- What hidden places, thoughts, feelings want to be brought out into the world and fully expressed?
- What message is trying to rise up from within my own Inner Self?

Dream Protection

As everything everywhere is connected, we are all subject to the emotions, energies, and desires of others. The antidote to this is constructing a strong and safe everyday container for your own energy field, strengthening your energetic boundaries and bringing awareness to the energies you allow into your life.

If you notice that you are chronically tired, your life seems to move from one chaotic situation into another, you are often ill, or you feel angry, heavy, sluggish, lifeless, or dull, it is highly likely that your container needs some attention, that it is leaking and needs to be shored up.

True well-being happens when your personal energetic container is maintained with loving attention daily. When your life is flowing, vibrant, and inspiring, you know that your personal energetic container is sturdy, stable, and effective.

It is always good to create additional layers of etheric security for yourself, not out of fear but for the finest possible care and advisable of your own priceless energies. No matter how robust and healthy your personal container feels, part of lunar sleep hygiene includes some form of nightly dream warding. This protection should be part of your daily, foundational Moon Witch practice—it is part of your psychic self-care.

Dream warding can help to dispel nightmares as well as the energies of other people and entities—and it can be as simple as charging a sacred object to promote a safe dream space. Amulets, charm bags, crystals or crystal grids, dream pillows, magical oils, mirrors, and warding stones are all excellent objects to use.

Creating Dream Protection Bottles

Here is a protection vessel you can assemble, then place near or under your bed and perhaps even bring with you when you travel.

In this project, you will use selenite, mugwort, and rosemary. Selenite is used in this spell in its capacity as a protector, peacekeeper, and stress reliever. This crystal can transmute unwanted vibrations into the helpful frequencies of love and serenity, enhancing healthy spiritual connections, aligning our energy bodies, and creating clarity and expansion in our understanding of the spiritual world and our place within it.

Selenite is wonderful for invoking protection from the Divine and helps in dispersing unwanted energies, removing energetic blocks from both our etheric (auric) bodies and our physical bodies. It is often used to create grids for protection and shielding in the home.

Mugwort is included to help us balance and harmonize our psychic potential and integrate the Dreamworld with everyday life, reinforcing the power of our intuition during sleep and bringing greater awareness of our dreams into conscious presence.

Rosemary is employed here to dispel, repel, and ward off nightmares and unhelpful spirits. It is also good for grounding and helps to amp up any spell it is used in by energizing all the other ingredients present.

To Gather

- A small glass vessel with a top. Try a 1- or 2-ounce bottle with a cork, a 2-ounce jelly jar, or even a 4-ounce canning jar.
- A piece of plain paper to use as a funnel
- A piece of selenite that fits inside your vessel.
- Mugwort (dried)
- Rosemary (dried)
- A wax stick or a drippy candle for sealing (ideally in a color that supports your purpose)
- Something for cleansing. This could be a smoldering herb bundle such as rosemary or lavender, incense, a stone such as obsidian, salt, water, sound, or anything else that resonates with your practice.
- A lighter or matches

Optional

- A protection oil (purchased or one you create) or diluted e.o. of your choice

The Process

Step 1: Ground, center, and open the channel. Connect with the Moon. Feel into her energies in whatever phase and sign she is currently traveling.

Step 2: Cast a circle if you wish.

Step 3: Invite your Inner Dream Self to join you. Connect this part of yourself with the Moon.

Step 4: Cleanse and clear your vessel, selenite, mugwort, and rosemary (and oil if using) of all energies that are not yours and/or you do not want present. (If your wax stick or candle needs cleansing and clearing, take care of this now, too.)

Step 5: Now construct your Dream Protection Bottle. Make contact with the spirit of your selenite before placing it into the jar. Whisper to it, imbue it with your purpose, and ask it to aid you.

Step 6: Roll up your paper, and using it as a funnel, mindfully add the mugwort and rosemary to your vessel, filling it to the top.

Step 7: When your bottle is filled, close it and activate it with a heartfelt kiss. If using a magical oil, anoint your vessel (and yourself, if you'd like) now.

Step 8: Light the wax stick or candle and drip the wax all over the lid or cork to seal your bottle.

Step 9: Now empower your bottle by chanting the following charm until you feel intuitively finished, holding the vessel in your hands and channeling supportive and restful energies into it:

> *Ruler of Sleep, Beloved Moon,*
> *Protect my nights, grant this boon.*
> *Beloved Moon, Ruler of Sleep,*
> *From my dreams, harsh energies sweep.*

Step 10: Store your protection bottle beneath or next to your bed. Blessed be, Dear Dreamer!

Dream Shields

Alongside the physical objects that can protect your Dreaming Self, you can also utilize mental shielding techniques to safeguard yourself or bolster your work.

If you only have a moment, a quick and simple method of dream shielding is to tender a heartfelt request to the Moon, the Moon Goddess, or a Benevolent Ancestor, Guardian, or Guide to watch over you while you sleep. If you go this route, choose one with whom you already have a relationship, and be sure to present offerings of gratitude upon awakening.

You can also connect with your personal Sleep Guardian, a Spirit Guide who works on your behalf in the Dreamrealm. See the next section for more about this.

Creating Dream Shields

I like to create the following shield while I am lying in bed, immediately before sleep. It dissolves upon awakening. You need do nothing to make this happen!

To Prepare

- Your bed and yourself

The Process

Step 1: Begin by getting comfortable in your body. With eyes closed, return to your inner realm, to yourself. Find your breath. Check on your connection with the Earth below and the Moon above, with your roots and branches. Slow your breath—slow, easy, big, full breaths.

Step 2: As you relax all parts of your body, breathing slowly and steadily, release any stress or tension into the hot, molten core of the Earth, into the Holy Magma.

Step 3: Using light from the Moon or Moon Goddess, focus on forming an expansive, luminous field around your entire body in the shape of an egg.

Step 4: Stretch this shield out to include not only your physical body but your etheric body, your auric body. You may want to incorporate colored light—perhaps indigo from the sixth chakra, violet from the seventh, or a pearly, prismatic white from your bindu chakra.

Step 5: Now use the powers of your mind to set an intention, such as: "This is my shield created of lunar love and light, which protects me from all harm. Here I am securely connected to the Moon (or Moon Goddess), to the wisdom of her light and her dark."

Step 6: See-sense-feel this glowing inner shield now surrounded by a seamless wall of mirrors, facing outward. Here, all of your parts, physical and etheric, dwell in peace and safety. As you rest within this field of energetic protection, know that if any unwanted energies come toward you, they will be instantly reflected away.

Step 7: Affirm now that only love passes through your shield, in all directions.

Step 8: Breathe here, feeling into the serene sanctuary that exists within your inner sacred space.

Step 9: Using your hands, seal this feeling into your body. This will help you to quickly form your dream shield again on future nights.

Step 10: Sleep well!

Practice creating this dream shield every night for several weeks and soon it will manifest as quickly as you bring it to mind.

Dream Guides, Sleep Guardians, and Dreamrealm Protectors

Spirit Guides are altruistic, multidimensional, nonphysical beings who watch over us, assisting us throughout our lives in both the spiritual and the material dimensions. They can be solicited for guidance, advice, and help. As our soul's special teachers, healers, guardians, and protectors, they are devoted to our growth, helping us to fulfill the spiritual contracts we made for this lifetime. Spirit Guides bless us throughout our lives—we are never alone!

Some people believe that they are our personal Guardian Angels, assigned to us or chosen by us before birth. Others think that they are Benevolent Ancestors, Saints, Goddesses, Ascended Masters, other Angels, Light or Energy Beings, Nature Spirits, or something else.

In addition to our primary Spirit Guide(s), we each have at least one companion specific to the Dreamrealm, a member of our spiritual team who is skilled in navigating this particular world. Known as Dream Guides, Sleep Guardians, or Dreamrealm Protectors, many of these beings specialize in the phases of the Moon and/or the energies of the various zodiacal transits.

Meeting Your Dream Guide

You do not need any formal training to contact and communicate with your personal Dream Guide, only a heartfelt desire for relationship with them. You already have the ability to do this.

To find your Dream Guide, simply set a firm intention that you will meet them. Right before turning in for the night, speak your intention aloud, saying something like "I wish to meet my Dream Guide." Then release any expectations or preconceived notions of how this might happen, ground and center, and drift off to sleep.

Once you have met your Dream Guide, ask their name. Learn their preferences and continue to develop your relationship with them—honor them, talk with them, bring them gifts, heed their advice.

Once you have become better acquainted with your Dream Guide, you can ask for even more help.

Before going to bed, speak to them, saying something along the lines of "Dream Guide (if you know their name, use that instead), please help me to dream deep and true tonight. Please bring me a meaningful dream. Help me to remember what I have learned and to bring all helpful wisdom back into my waking life."

Then watch your Dream Guide get into a little boat and sail out upon the nighttime waters, the rays of the Moon illuminating their path.

Once you have awakened, note any information received in your Moon Journal or Dream Diary.

Any time you have questions, you can ask your Dream Guide to take you to a dream or a place in the Dreamrealm where these questions will be answered. You may want to add the caveat "for my highest good and with harm to none" to any request you make.

Sleep Hygiene

In order to dream, we must experience quality sleep—and the older we get, the more elusive sleep can become.

As we age, the pineal gland can atrophy, producing less and less melatonin as time goes on. From diet to our sleep environment, there are many things we can adjust, though, to help ourselves get the rest we need.

Making sleep hygiene a priority can help you to get better rest. Experiment with such things as reducing the amount of light in your bedroom, using blackout curtains and a blackout eye mask to block light from outside sources. Be mindful, too, of the blue light that is emitted by electronic screens.

While blue wavelengths can be beneficial during waking daylight hours, after dark, this type of light becomes troublesome. Once the Sun sets, blue light wavelengths disrupt your circadian rhythms, causing the pineal gland to suppress the production of melatonin for several hours, resetting the sleep cycle in unhelpful ways.

You can minimize the effects of these wavelengths by keeping your electronics in night mode and as dim as possible (automate this, if possible) and/or wearing blue light blocking glasses.

Daily Sleep and Dream Hygiene Help

Here are some ideas of things to consume or practice that can assuage both acute and chronic sleeping concerns. As always, please check with a medical professional before beginning any new health programs or ingesting any new supplements.

Supplements

Cannabis-derived edibles
Magnesium
Melatonin
Vitamin B complex
Vitamin C
Vitamin D

When it comes to cannabis-derived edibles, CBN is best, followed by CBD. If you decide to try THC, microdose. Start with two milligrams of an indica-type strain about thirty minutes to two hours before you'd like to fall sleep. Trial and error is often necessary to discover what works best. Note that some people experience anxiety with THC use. Please also be aware of local laws regarding the use of THC and other cannabis-derived products.

Foods

Almonds
Apple cider vinegar
Bananas
Cherries or cherry juice (unsweetened)
Dark chocolate
Greek yogurt
Kiwi fruit
Oats
Raw cacao
Seaweeds and kelps
Turkey
Walnuts

Here is a tip: Drink more water! Many people are chronically dehydrated. A simple way to estimate per day water intake for optimal hydration is to divide your body weight in half—that number in ounces is a ballpark measure for the amount of water to try to drink each day. (Of course, this is just a helpful guideline! Your needs may vary based on activity level, health, season, and climate.)

Herbs

California poppy (*Eschscholzia californica*)
Chamomile (*Matricaria chamomilla*)
Hops (*Humulus lupulus*)
Lavender (*Lavandula angustifolia* and *Lavandula latifolia*)
Lemon balm (*Melissa officinalis*)
Passionflower (*Passiflora incarnata*)
Valerian root (*Valeriana officinalis*) (Note that it can cause sleeplessness or anxiety in some.)

Spiritual Activities

Banishing
Chanting: Try "Om" to activate the sixth chakra.
Chi circulation: Check out qigong, tai chi, acupressure, acupuncture, tapping (EFT).
Guided sleep meditations including yoga nidra
Grounding and centering

Journaling: Try doing a brain dump before sleeping; write without stopping for three pages, letting everything flood out of your mind and body. If you wake in the night and your mind is racing, do another brain dump. Get it all out on the page!
Meditating: Try this practice in various positions or forms, such as sitting, walking, or standing.
Ritual baths or soaks
Shielding: Try the previous shielding exercises.
Sound: Try binaural beats and isochronic tones.
Visualization: Try relaxing every part of your body step-by-step, from head to toe, from Moon to Earth, envisioning yourself being gently and lovingly cleansed inside and out with water or with a specific color of light.

Everyday Activities

Blue light: Try reducing exposure and keep electronics as dim as possible at night.
Caffeine: Don't have any after midafternoon. Or, if you are a night owl like me, try not to drink it after three in the afternoon.
Darkness: Sleep in complete darkness by wearing a blackout mask, using blackout shades, covering lights, or doing whatever is appropriate for your sleep environment.
Exercise (daytime)
Massage
Sunshine: Soak in five to ten minutes of sun a day; it is a mood booster, helps the body produce vitamin D, and is helpful for melatonin production.
Reduce or eliminate alcohol consumption.
Yoga (day or night)

Here is another tip: If you awaken in the middle of the night, approach it without distress and name it as the preindustrial biphasic sleep pattern. Try reading, meditating, or doing yoga for thirty to sixty minutes before returning to sleep.

Lunar Dream Divination

Dream divination, foretelling, and interpretation has a rich and venerable foundation with evidence of its importance in ancient Mesopotamia, Egypt, Greece, and other cultures.[48] Called oneiromancy, this practice is derived from two Greek words meaning dream and prophesy.

The information gathered through dreaming can be viewed as messages from deity, ancestors, spirits, and other guides. As Lunar Witches, we can practice oneiromancy in concert with the

48. Prema and Joshi, "Dream Interpretation."

Moon by treating dreams as a form of divination, using the information gleaned to meet challenges, answer questions, and even provide solutions to long-standing problems.

Lunar dream divination is a process by which the sleeping, subconscious, intuitive Self is programed to remember an intention, to gather the needed information in the Dreamrealm, and to bring it back for application in the waking world.

Lunar Dream Divination Method

Look at your lunar calendar and choose a Moon phase that would best support you in uncovering the information you seek. This night should be at least half a lunar cycle (i.e., about two weeks or thirteen nights) away.

To Gather

- Your Moon Journal or Dream Diary and pen

The Process

Step 1: Before bed every night between now and then, write these words and then say them aloud three times before retiring for the night:

> *At the time of Luna's _____ (fill in the blank with a word or words such as newness, fullness, waxing half, darkness), I ask to know ______ (fill in the blank). I open myself to the magic and the mystery of the answer I seek.*

Step 2: On the night of the lunar phase you chose, update the words to:

> *Tonight, at the time of Luna's ______ (fill in your chosen phase), I receive the perfect dream about _____ (fill in the blank). I am now completely open to the magic and the mystery of receiving this answer tonight.*

Step 3: As soon as you wake up, write down everything you remember from your night of dreaming: sights, sounds, scents, objects, symbols, and locations—even textures, temperatures, and anything else.

Do not be upset if your question is not answered immediately or straightforwardly; sometimes the conscious mind takes a while to catch up with the subconscious. Continue to explore whatever you remember through automatic writing or metacognitive drawing, perhaps acting out any snippets of a remembered scene (with a trusted partner, if you can), eating any foods that appeared in the dream, making a vision board of its images, meditating, moving, or through anything else you feel is right. Allow the information you received to ripen over the next two weeks.

If you still haven't received the information you seek, begin the process again. (It is also possible that you are not ready to hear the information gleaned.)

Tarot Dream Divination

An easy way to link lunar divination and dreaming is to draw a tarot or oracle card directly before going to sleep.

To Gather

- A tarot or oracle deck
- Your Moon Journal or Dream Diary and pen

The Process

Step 1: While in bed, draw a card and look at it closely, taking in every aspect you can see or sense or feel. Look at the card until you can see-sense-feel it in your mind's eye with your physical eyes closed. Set the card next to your bed on your nightstand, or slip it into your pillowcase, and go to sleep.

Step 2: If you awaken in the night, try to see-sense-feel the card again as you drift back off into slumber.

Step 3: Write down anything you remember upon waking in the morning.

Lucid Dreaming

Lucid dreaming involves the awareness that you are dreaming, coupled with the ability to control the dream itself. The practical applications of this discipline include helping to release fears or phobias and resolve nightmares; heal emotional wounds; inspire creativity; practice real-life skills; solve real-life problems; reduce stress; sleep better; discover who you really are and what you really want by engaging with your subconscious; and to just have fun!

The felt experiences of lucid dreaming and astral projection (see chapter 5) can be exceptionally similar. In fact, some choose to define them as the same thing.

They *are* distinct—but perhaps not by much. It is more of an energetic variance, a slight nuance that differentiates these two states. Lucid dreaming takes place in the Dreamrealm. Astral projection takes place on the astral plane (sometimes styled as the Deep Mind). Our abilities—and our ability to discover needful information—can happen in either dimension.

This type of dreaming, also called dream meditation, facilitates an altered state of consciousness, imparting access to your inner wisdom and the deepest planes of your essential nature, where you have some control over what you are experiencing—and what you want to experience. Engaging with this practice can also effect powerful change in your waking life.

Opportunity for extraordinary healing, alchemical transformation, and vigorous growth are already latent within you, and lucid dreaming can help you to peel back the layers that have grown up over time to hide away those shadowy parts of your own Self. The deeper you go and the more you interact with the Realm of Dreams and your inner world, the more healed you become, the more peace available to you in your day-to-day experience.

General Lucid Dreaming Tips

If it feels right to you, charge a special stone (such as a lapis, moonstone, selenite, or clear quartz crystal, or see the "Dream Stones" section later in this chapter) to use as a focus whenever you are lucid dreaming. Use this particular crystal only at this time, though, to continue increasing its potency and power.

For all lunar lucid dreaming sessions, set up a restful, quiet, calm space that is sacred and safe, ensuring that you will not be disturbed by anyone or anything during your practice. Wear loose (or no) clothing, making sure your body is adequately warm or cool.

Create an intention for yourself. What do you want to learn in the Dreamworld? What answer are you seeking? What problem do you need to untangle?

Begin, as always, with grounding, centering, and opening the channel, then settle your body into a comfortable position.

Throughout the exercise, hold the aspiration of bringing awareness and mindfulness to your travels through the Dreamrealm; of remembering what you see, hear, feel, and experience; and to interact with this dimension only in ways that are beneficial, helpful, and respectful.

Here are two lunar lucid dreaming exercises to explore.

Lunar Lucid Dreaming Doorways

This method of lunar lucid dreaming begins with crossing through a portal or doorway. Before beginning, read through the previous tips to prepare yourself for the dreaming experience.

To Prepare

- A dark, comfortable space

Optional

- Your lucid dreaming crystal

The Process

Step 1: Begin by envisioning the phase the Moon is in, then imagine a doorway that looks like that phase.

Step 2: Emblazoned upon the door is the astrological sign the Moon is in, scribed in the color of the Element of Life to which it belongs to (i.e., air may be yellow or white; fire may be red or orange; water may be blue or gray; earth may be brown, green, or black). Speak a secret word to the portal and watch the door swing open.

Step 3: Safe in your dream body, step through the portal and into the vortex. While you are here, do the work you settled upon for this session.

Step 4: When complete, leave through the doorway, speaking the same secret word to close the portal and using your hand to emblazon the astrological sign upon it, which locks the door firmly behind you.

A Lunar Lucid Dreaming Practice

The intention of this exercise is to reenter a poignant dream or dream fragment. This practice works best when you are lying down, fully prone and completely comfortable. You can either do this in your bed or create for yourself a nest using a yoga or other mat, a blanket or sleeping bag that covers your whole body, a favorite pillow, fuzzy socks, a sleeping mask or other eye covering, and so on. Use whatever feels right and good to you!

To Gather

- Your Moon Journal or Dream Diary and pen
- A timer or soft music
- A sleep mask or other cover for your eyes

Optional

- Your lucid dreaming crystal
- A small sachet of mugwort
- A cup of mugwort tea (recipe can be found later in the chapter)

To Prepare

Read through the practice before beginning. After familiarizing yourself with the process, decide how long you wish to be in the Dreamrealm, and then ascertain some sort of cue to bring you back into ordinary reality when you are finished: perhaps a subtle alarm or a timed piece of soothing, calm instrumental music playing in the background.

Go through your Moon Journal or Dream Diary and find a dream or dream fragment that you would like to resolve, release, explore, or discover new opportunities within.

The Process

Step 1: Start your music or set your alarm and lie down comfortably on your bed or in your nest. It is best to move as little as possible throughout this practice, ideally staying in the same position throughout the session.

Step 2: Cover your eyes and relax into your cozy position. Find your breath. Rest your muscles, giving your weight completely over to gravity, to Mother Earth. Make contact with the Earth, with your roots within her. Make contact with your branches, stretching up to the Moon. Breathe slowly in and out with the Earth and with the Moon.

If you are using a dreaming crystal or herb, make contact with it now, with its eternal spirit. Breathe with it. Everything is slow, restful, and unhurried.

Step 3: Allow your mind to become completely free. Focus on the darkness behind your closed eyes; focus on your breathing. Allow any thoughts to simply float past you and away. With every breath, you are accentuating the relaxation of your mind and your body.

Step 4: Become aware now of the dream you wish to explore, the dream or dream fragment you've chosen to work with during this session.

Step 5: And now you easily find something that looks like a portal, like a window, a door, a hole, or even an energy bubble. It is easy to find because it is lit up by a moonbeam. Follow the Moon's rays, enter this portal, and find yourself in the dream or fragment that you chose.

Allow your Lunar Self to arrive effortlessly into your dream, whatever that looks or feels like to you. You may not see anything at all; you may experience sound, color, emotion, texture, taste, or something else. Allow yourself to sense whatever is there for you. Don't push, force, or struggle. Instead, surrender and flow.

Surrender and flow...

Spend as long as you planned to in your lucid dream.

Step 6: When it is time to return, say farewell to the Dreamrealm, giving gratitude to the Moon and gratitude for all you've discovered and learned. Return fully into your physical body, shifting your awareness to your physical body and physical reality. Return, return, return; wiggling fingers and toes, stretching, and gently rubbing and patting your body.

Spend some moments recording your experiences in your Moon Journal or Dream Diary.

Lunar Dream Incubation

Dream incubation, sometimes described as shamanic dreaming, is a method of dream divination where an intention is set before sleeping, either to answer a question, seek out specific wisdom needed for decision-making, or just for pleasure.

In ancient times, prophetic and divinatory dreams that arose from dream incubation rituals were viewed as messages from deity, and both clergy members and laypeople would descend into caves—the wombs of the Earth—seeking these visionary dreams for themselves, their loved ones, and their communities.[49]

In Crete, dream incubation was done in the temples, oftentimes taken on by a Priestess who was working on behalf of another at their request.[50] Offerings were made both before dreaming and upon awakening, usually symbolizing the message received.

49. Laios et al.,"Dreams in Ancient Greek Medicine."

50. Gadon, *The Once and Future Goddess.*

Dream Incubation Ritual

In this Dream Incubation Ritual, you connect with the Moon immediately before sleeping, focusing upon your question or goal while gently holding the objective of receiving guidance or answers within the Realm of Dreams. Here, you surf the waves of what is possible, connecting with your dreams as priceless gifts from your Inner Lunar Witch, your infinite soul, and the benevolent powers of the Moon.

To Gather

- An eye mask or other eye covering
- Your Moon Journal or Dream Diary and pen

Optional

- Soft music

To Prepare

It is best to take a purifying magical bath or shower shortly before beginning this rite. As you immerse yourself in the healing waters, consider the question or situation you would like to incubate in your night's dreams.

You may also opt to play instrumental music quietly in the background. If you do so, make certain that when the music ends there will be no disrupting sounds that could waken you from your rest.

Tell everyone you live with that you are not to be disturbed. Firmly close your window shades and wear an eye mask.

The Rite

Step 1: Begin the ritual in your bed, ready for sleep, your space quiet and dark.

Step 2: Activate first your dream shield and/or invite your Dream Guide to join you and watch over you.

Step 3: Relax your breath and relax your body, slowly and gently, part by part by part, from head to toe, from Moon to Earth. Allow any excess energy from your body to ground into the body of the Earth.

Step 4: Bring to mind now your intention for this incubation session. Either aloud or in your mind, share your intention with the Moon. Ask for her assistance and her wisdom in the discovery of what you need to know, and may it be only that which will serve your highest good.

Step 5: Breathe yourself into as great a state of restfulness as you can as you prepare to journey far into the Dreamrealm.

Step 6: Visualize now the light of the Moon illuminating an opening in the Earth: a cave, a crack, a passageway. Know that this opening will lead you where you need to go. Follow the moonbeam and enter that opening now.

Step 7: Become aware once again of the question or concern you wish to explore, the energies you've chosen to work with tonight. Using your breath, allow yourself to slip fully into the Dreamrealm, whatever that looks or feels like for you. Remember: You may not see anything. You may experience sound, color, emotion, texture, taste, or something else. Allow yourself to sense whatever is there for you this night. Don't press or push; instead, surrender and flow.

Step 8: Follow your breath, and permit yourself to surrender and flow, drifting into the Dreamrealm, where you will spend your night's rest.

Step 9: When you awaken, write down every single thing you can remember, whether it seems meaningful or not. Give gratitude to your Dream Protectors, the Realm of Dreams, and any beings you met there for anything you discovered and learned. Shift your awareness to your physical body. Come back completely into your physical body now, wiggling fingers and toes, stretching, and gently rubbing and patting your body before arising from your bed.

Dreamy Materia

Here are some Dreamworld helpers and allies to attune with as you work with these practices.

Dream Stones

Pi stones, also referred to as donut stones, shaman stones, or torus stones, can be designated as dream stones, bolstering dream recall and dreaming true.

These sacred assistants are created from various stones and can reinforce your relationship with your bindu chakra. They are formed to be flat, smooth, and round and have a hole in the middle.

You may have seen someone wearing one as a necklace; they are usually bound with a cord that is then tied about the neck.

Pi stones are representative of wholeness (both Within and Without), of the energies of the Multiverse, and of our eternal luminous energy bodies. They are also the physical representation of the ouroboros, the serpent who eats its own tail, signifying the eternal cycle of birth, death, and rebirth as well as the Oneness of All That Is.

Since pi stones are made from numerous and diverse crystals, you have options. If you are intrigued and want to work with one, what type of crystal speaks to you? Be certain it is sourced ethically, perhaps made by an Indigenous shaman. There are many stones called "pi stones" that have been mass-produced in China or the like, and these products most likely do not hold the energies needed to help activate your bindu.

Pi stones can be used as magical device, as keys to help you to unlock the mysteries. They can be utilized as interdimensional portals or gateways for journeywork and healing from this dimension and others, both forward and backward in time and space.

Activating Your Dream Stone

Once you've sourced your pi stone, it's time to empower it with your purpose. This magical partner is best activated under the Full Moon.

To Gather

- Your pi stone
- Something for cleansing. This could be a smoldering herb bundle such as rosemary, eucalyptus, or lavender, incense, a stone such as obsidian, salt, water, sound, or anything else that resonates with your practice.

The Process

Step 1: When you are ready to activate your pi stone, sit with it, feeling into its nature. Cleanse and clear it in a way pleasing to you. Next, attune it to your frequency by breathing into it three times, see-sense-feeling it connecting with your own unique energetic signature and with your heart energy.

Step 2: Once your dream stone is activated, hold it to your heart chakra. Once you are calm, relaxed, and connected with the Self, Earth, and Cosmos, exhale three times through the hole in the stone, activating your bindu chakra and opening up your channel and connection to the Moon Mother.

Step 3: Slowly and intentionally bring your stone up from your heart to your third eye, over your crown chakra, then down to your bindu chakra, holding it gently to this sacred spot.

Step 4: Breathe here as long as you wish, see-sense-feeling the energies of the Moon entering your body through this gateway and gently dripping or cascading throughout your entire body, mind, heart, and spirit. Feel your blissful bond with the Moon strengthening as you connect with All That Is. Blessed be!

Herbal Dream Allies

As discussed in previous chapters, there are a plethora of herbal products you can create to help facilitate a more meaningful connection with the Moon and your lunar nature.

There are also any number of herbs that are associated with dream divination, dream incubation, and lucid dreaming. The easiest fashion to consume these herbs is to prepare a tea to drink before retiring, using one teaspoonful of dried herb per cup of hot water. Herbs can be combined, so investigate and discover what formula works best for your Lunar Self.

Here are some commonly available green allies that can be helpful when traveling the Dreamrealm:

Borage (*Borago officinalis*)
Burdock (*Arctium lappa L.*)
California poppy (*Eschscholzia californica*)
Catnip (*Nepeta cataria*)
Chamomile (*Matricaria chamomilla*)
Cinnamon (*Cinnamomum verum*)
Damiana (*Turnera diffusa*)
Elderberries (*Sambucus canadensis*)
Ginkgo (*Ginkgo biloba*)
Hibiscus (genus *Hibiscus*)
Hops (*Humulus lupulus*)
Jasmine (*Jasminum officinale*)
Kava kava (*Piper methysticum*)
Lavender (*Lavandula angustifolia* and *Lavandula latifolia*)

Lemon balm (*Melissa officinalis*)
Mugwort (*Artemisia vulgaris*)
Mullein (*Verbascum thapsus*)
Nettle (*Urtica dioica*)
Passionflower (*Passiflora incarnata*)
Peppermint (*Mentha piperita*)
Raspberry leaf (*Rubus idaeus*)
Rosemary (*Rosmarinus officinalis*)
Roses (*Rosa* spp.)
Sage, culinary (*Salvia officinalis*)
Skullcap (*Scutellaria lateriflora*)
Valerian (*Valeriana officinalis*)
Vervain (*Verbena officinalis*)
Wood betony (*Betonica officinalis*)
Yarrow (*Achillea millefolium*)

Look through this list and intuitively choose some dreaming herbs to work with, or experiment with some or all of the tried-and-true recipes that follow. Remember to always consult a medical professional before ingesting any herbs.

Mugwort—the Dream Herb

Ruled by the planet Venus and yet also powerfully linked to the Moon, mugwort (*Artemisia vulgaris*) is a formidable ally for the Realm of Dreams. Mugwort is an herb that can enhance your lucid dreaming abilities, make dreams more vivid, improve dream recall, and grant access to divine visions and other significant information. It is sometimes nicknamed the travelers' protection herb, and what is dreaming but traveling!

Also called sailor's-tobacco, mugwort can be smoked, burned as incense, drunk as a tea, used in magical baths, and more. Note that mugwort is highly contraindicated during pregnancy and lactation, so please do not work with it in those seasons of life. Here are some recipes, projects, and rituals that use mugwort for dreaming.

Mugwort Dream Bag

A mugwort dream bag is an uncomplicated yet powerful magical item to create to enhance your dreamwork as well as your dream spells and rituals.

To Gather

- Dried mugwort
- A small organza drawstring bag (or you can use a piece of cloth and ribbon or string with which to tie it). I like to match the color of the bag to my intent, so I prefer white, gray, silver, or black for the Moon or even pearly white for the bindu chakra, violet for the crown chakra, and/or indigo for the ajna chakra.
- Something for cleansing. This could be a smoldering herb bundle such as rosemary, lavender, or pine, incense, a stone such as obsidian, salt, water, sound, or anything else that resonates with your practice.
- Dream oil (See the section later in this chapter.)

The Process

Step 1: Ground, center, and open the channel.

Step 2: Cleanse your bag (or cloth and ribbon or string) with smoke, sound, or something else to your liking. Next, cleanse and clear your mugwort of any energies that do not belong in your working.

Step 3: Bless and charge all of the components for dream augmentation and support now, then stuff your bag (or cloth) full of the dried mugwort. Mindfully pull the bag closed (or tie the ribbon or string at least three times), speaking aloud your intention.

Step 4: Consecrate, activate, and empower your finished bag, charging it for dreaming.

You may opt to nourish your bag with a dream oil, placing a drop or two on your fingers and then, with reverence, rubbing the oil gently all over your completed bag. It is a smart practice to nurture your bag by offering it some dream oil every lunation for as long as you are working with it. Be sure to mark your calendar so you remember to do this!

Once your work with your dream bag is complete, deactivate it by removing the mugwort and offering it to the Earth (or into fire or water) and then clear the bag or cloth of the energies, setting it aside for a future purpose (or, if you do not want to use it again, disposing of it in a respectful manner).

Mugwort Dreaming Ritual

Here is a simple ceremony to connect with the powers of mugwort and amplify your work in the Dreamrealm. I particularly like to perform this rite during Diana's Bow or Hekate's Sickle.

To Gather

- Dried mugwort in a teaball or a bag of mugwort tea
- Sweetener, if desired
- Hot (not boiling) water to steep your tea
- A mug
- A form of mugwort for the ritual bath, perhaps a bath salt or a sachet. You can also add a few drops of mugwort essential oil to a diffuser in your bathroom.
- Mugwort salve or diluted mugwort essential oil for anointing
- Your mugwort dream bag
- Your Moon Journal or Dream Diary and pen
- A sleep mask

To Prepare

Before enacting this ritual, first decide on your goals for your night in the Dreamworld.

Prepare a strong cup of mugwort tea and keep it warm: to 1 cup of hot water add 1 tablespoon of dried herb. Add your favorite sweetener if you find it too bitter. Agave syrup and honey are both lovely choices.

The Rite

Step 1: Begin your ritual by taking a magical bath or shower, incorporating mugwort in some manner. Perhaps add a sachet or bath salt, or maybe diffuse some mugwort essential oil.

Step 2: When you are done bathing, anoint yourself in a sacred manner with mugwort salve or diluted mugwort essential oil, paying particular attention to your ajna, crown, and bindu chakras.

Step 3: Dress yourself comfortably, either in a loose robe or pajamas, or go moonclad. Make yourself cozy in your bed. While sipping your tea, write your intentions for your night's sleep in your Moon Journal or Dream Diary.

Step 4: When you have finished your tea, snuggle up with your mugwort dream bag and go directly to sleep. Wear a blackout mask and calm your body from Moon to Earth, from crown to root. Surrender yourself to the power of restful insight.

Step 5: As soon as you awaken, write everything you can remember in your Moon Journal or Dream Diary and observe any further insights that arise for you throughout the day.

Dream Potions

Through the power of our plant allies, dream potions can help to activate our powers in the Dreamrealm just as they can when working with the Moon in general. Here are some of my favorite potable potions that I've used over the years.

Dreaming with the Moon Cordial

This cordial is at its best when it is left to macerate for at least an entire quarter (e.g., Summer Solstice to Fall Equinox) before straining and sweetening. I love this recipe, which I developed through trial and error. I like to pour this finished cordial into little cobalt blue dropper bottles. I give these as gifts to other Lunar Witches, and I enjoy a few drops out of my own right before bed to help facilitate dreaming.

To Gather

- 1 cup of dried elderberries (*Sambucus canadensis*)
- 4 cups of water
- A medium saucepan with a lid
- 2 sticks of cinnamon (*Cinnamomum verum*)
- 4 tablespoons dried chamomile (*Matricaria chamomilla*)

- 2 tablespoons dried jasmine (*Jasminum officinale*)
- 1 tablespoon dried California poppy (*Eschscholzia californica*)
- Brandy
- 1 cup of local honey to sweeten

The Process

Step 1: Prepare the elderberries as a decoction. Combine the elderberries and water in a saucepan, cover and bring to a boil, then reduce the heat, simmering for thirty minutes. Allow the covered pot to sit for five minutes, strain, and then set the liquid aside to cool completely.

Step 2: Once the decoction has cooled, follow the general cordial-making procedure outlined in chapter 10.

Dream Tea Recipes

Teas are another yummy, accessible route to deepening your connection with your Dream Self, the Dreamrealm, and the work that you wish to do there. At least once over this next lunation (and better, three nights in a row), formulate a tea with a dreaming herb or herbs and consume it immediately before retiring. Note your experiences in your Moon Journal or Dream Diary the next morning. Here are some combinations.

Sweet Dreams Tea

3 parts chamomile (*Matricaria chamomilla*)
1 part passionflower (*Passiflora incarnata*)
1 part rose petals (*Rosa* spp.)

Deep Dreams Tea

3 parts skullcap (*Scutellaria lateriflora*)
3 parts chamomile (*Matricaria chamomilla*)
1 part mugwort (*Artemisia vulgaris*)
1 part catnip (*Nepeta cataria*)
1 part California poppy (*Eschscholzia californica*)

Lucid Dreaming Tea

2 parts mugwort (*Artemisia vulgaris*)
1 part lavender (*Lavandula angustifolia* or *Lavandula latifolia*)
1 part damiana (*Turnera diffusa*)

Dream Recall Tea

2 parts peppermint (*Mentha piperita*)
2 parts lemon balm (*Melissa officinalis*)
1 part passionflower (*Passiflora incarnata*)
½ part orange rind (*Citrus sinensis*)
½ part cinnamon (*Cinnamomum verum*)

Dream Incubation Tea

2 parts hibiscus (genus *Hibiscus*)
2 parts nettle (*Urtica dioica*)
1 part mugwort (*Artemisia vulgaris*)
½ part borage (*Borago officinalis*)
½ part wood betony (*Betonica officinalis*)

Dream Oil Recipes

You can concoct your own dream oils by steeping a carrier oil with herbal allies or, if it is scent that you are going for, with essential oils. As you learned in chapter 9, it is exceedingly easy to make blended magical oils. For dream oils, I like using almond oil for my base. Almonds correspond with lunar energies, and their oil is sweet and fragrant, generally hypoallergenic and safe for sensitive skin. Including 1 percent vitamin E oil in your finished products can help to preserve them longer.

Here are some recipes for simple dream oils that can be used for anointing yourself, others, and your dreaming tools. Play around with these ideas and see what you think, then create your own recipes! For the highest quality results, be sure to use pure essential oils (not synthetic fragrance or perfume oils).

Lucid Dreaming Oil

3 parts mugwort (*Artemisia vulgaris*) e.o.
2 parts lavender (*Lavandula angustifolia* or *Lavandula latifolia*) e.o.
1 part patchouli (*Pogostemon patchouli*) e.o.

Good Sleep Oil

3 parts helichrysum (*Helichrysum italicum*) e.o.
2 parts chamomile (*Matricaria chamomilla*) e.o.
1 part rose (*Rosa* spp.) or rose geranium (*Pelargonium graveolens*) e.o.

Dream Divination Oil

2 parts mugwort (*Artemisia vulgaris*) e.o.
2 parts clary sage (*Salvia sclarea*) e.o.
1 part cinnamon (*Cinnamomum verum*) e.o.
1 part lavender (*Lavandula angustifolia* or *Lavandula latifolia*) e.o.

Creating Dream Salves

Salve-making is one my favorite Lunar Witch projects; these products can be made from a base oil plus essential oils, an infused oil, or an infused oil plus essential oils, which is my favorite method. To prepare your salve, use a base oil or a previously infused oil (see chapter 9) of your choice and then experiment with the recipes for blended dream oils, or create your own.

To Gather

- A double boiler
- A spoon or spatula for stirring (be sure your spatula is heat resistant)
- 4 ounces of infused oil or carrier oil
- 10 to 30 drops of an essential oil or oils
- 1 ounce of beeswax or carnauba wax (vegan)
- Small sterilized containers to hold your completed salve. Little tins, tiny glass jars, and even lip balm tubes work great.

Optional

- Curios, seeds, resins, dried flowers or leaves

Note: If using these optional ingredients, add them to your prepared containers before beginning the process of creating your salve.

The Process

Step 1: Melt your wax over very low heat in a double boiler. It is often easier to do this if the wax is broken into smaller pieces before beginning. To do this, you can wrap the wax in a kitchen towel and whack at it with a rolling pin, hammer, or meat pounder. This can be incredibly satisfying!

Step 2: Once the wax has completely melted, slowly and carefully pour in your infused or base oil, heating all the ingredients and stirring well to incorporate them.

Step 3: Remove the wax from the heat and stir in your essential oil(s).

Step 4: Working quickly, pour the mixture into your prepared containers. Let it cool completely.

Step 5: Consecrate, activate, and empower your salve under the Moon.

Note that this recipe can easily be scaled up or down in quantity, and you can adjust the texture to your preference. Test the consistency during your creation process by scooping up a bit of warm salve with a cold spoon and placing the spoon in the freezer for a few minutes to see what your finished product will be like. To adjust the consistency, add more wax for a firmer salve or more oil for a softer one.

When stored properly in a cool location, salves generally last from one to three years.

Chapter 16
Healing

The Moon Goddess Speaks

Like the river, my compassion is ever flowing. I eternally listen for the cries of the world, and I come to soothe all pain with my gentle, unconditional love.

When you are suffering, I offer my tears as a sacred salve. Lean into my loving arms whenever you ache, and I will bring softness, healing, and harmony to your tender heart.

Born of the lotus, I will envelop you with its healing essence, gently cleansing you of all that hurts. I am your refuge when life is sharp and hard. I am your sanctuary of serenity and restoration. I am mercy herself.

I am Quan Yin.

Journal Inquiries for This Gateway

What healing do I seek from the Moon during this lunation? Where would I like to be in my healing one lunar year from today? When do I feel most joyful and free?

Affirmations for This Gateway

I am ready to heal. I accept the healing power of the Moon into my body, mind, heart, and spirit. I recognize when I am healed enough.

Healing is a journey, and it is rarely linear. We spiral around and back again, endlessly returning to ourselves.

In order to heal, we must create space, a sacrosanct container devoted to *being here now*, within the holiness of the present moment. Each moment is connected to all of the other moments of our lives, both in our past and in our future, and each is another opportunity to reinforce our connection to the fullness of our own being, to discover, to learn, to grow, and to heal.

The Moon reminds us that wherever we are, and whatever we are experiencing, there is a blessing to be found there, that each moment of our lives can be a blessing.

We can partner with the Moon in her guise as healer, utilizing her powers to rejuvenate, renew, and facilitate healing for ourselves and others, creating space for self-love, self-trust, and self-care in all realms: body, mind, heart, spirit.

The call to healing—the desire to heal something specific—only arises when we are ready to do the work. When we are not ready to heal something, it will not be present in our consciousness. It is best, therefore, not to push or force anything. When our psyche is ready and the situation is right, the healing naturally begins.

It is also important to be aware that our healing is never complete. There will always be something else we hope to heal in ourselves, and there will almost always be another layer of something that we thought we had already healed rising up into our consciousness.

Freed from the bounds of the Earth and yet still composed of her cells, beaming powerful energies down to us throughout all of her phases, the Moon can be a fierce ally for us in our individual healing processes and a collaborator in healing the world.

She can help us to leave unhealthy, dangerous, and toxic situations; she can help us to illuminate our own hidden depths; and she can bring us the courage needed for profound self-reflection, self-compassion, and self-understanding. The Moon amplifies our own inner voices, helping us to better hear our own inner wisdom, reminding us that all we seek is already within.

The Medicine of the Moon

Ancient mythology from cultures the world over teach that the planets were all once alive—including the luminaries, our Sun and Moon—and that each of these planets carries an individual vibrational medicine that is transmitted to Earth.

In the context of energy healing, the word *medicine* means the energy, power, vibration, or frequency that is inherent within an object, event, location, or happening. Two purposes of medicine are healing and curing.

As briefly discussed in chapter 6, every planet has a specialty, a particular type of energy that can be used to both power and amplify magic and ritual.

Because the Moon is already intimately intertwined with emotions—and because she is forever present in our lives in one form or another—she is an optimal collaborator in mending the emotional body and increasing emotional health.

Our most difficult and uncomfortable emotions are often the ones that hold the most essential lessons and deepest truths, and lunar energies can be of particular assistance in aiding us to feel them fully, in releasing grudges and unmet needs, and in mitigating past traumas (especially regarding her particular provinces of mothering, hearth, and home).

In medical astrology, the Moon is said to rule the stomach and upper digestive tract, all bodily fluids and mucus membranes, the uterus, and the breasts and chest. Working with her to increase health through nutrition, movement, and hydration is indicated.

Since the Moon is phasal, she can help with mood regulation. She also rules all habits, both beneficial and not. Unite with her to loosen entrenched patterns, notably those that no longer serve your highest good.

Because she is continually in flux through both sign and phase, the medicine of the Moon evolves more rapidly than that of any other celestial body. If her phase or sign isn't conducive to the work at hand, it will be soon.

Lunar medicine is dark and quiet, involving rest, replenishment, and dreaming. It is invisible and intuitive, and often quite irrational. The elixir of Lunar is cool, calming, and soothing—instrumental in settling energies that are too high, too hot, or too frenetic.

Moon medicine is one of tender awakening, revelation, and inner illumination. It is liminal: of the thresholds and of the crossroads, of everything and of nothing, of all that is secret and shadowy. Surrender and yielding are mandatory. We can steer, but we cannot direct.

As the foil, solar medicine is visible and rational; hot, bright and uplifting; and opportune for shifting energies that are too slow, too cold, or too sluggish. It is goal oriented, concerned with action, events, and productivity.

Both solar and lunar medicine are necessary for life and for living. The restful, tranquil light of the Moon is just as necessary as the invigorating blaze of our Sun Star.

Lunar medicine is the domain of the Shapeshifter, the one who cannot be contained. There is risk inherent in her remedies, and they tend to work in mysterious ways, ways that can't always be reliably replicated or consciously understood.

Healing Through the Lunar Phases and Frequencies

Each Moon phase contains specific energies that can be used to facilitate healing. Just as in lunar spellwork and ritual, waxing and waning are the two most broad and perhaps most important components. After that, each phase can be used to further hone the type of healing sought.

The Lunar Phases

Here are some keys for crafting your healing work during each phase.

- *New Moon:* begin healthy habits; start an exercise program; increase self-love
- *Waxing Crescent Moon:* rededicate to mental, spiritual, emotional, and/or physical fitness; focus on nurturing self and others
- *Waxing Half Moon:* strengthen connections with self and others; address communication issues; return relationships to full health
- *Waxing Gibbous Moon:* activate and alchemize all aspects of health and healing; solidify foundations
- *Full Moon:* offer gratitude and add energies to the healing that is already in progress; saturate your work with radiance and power
- *Waning Gibbous Moon:* revise healing affirmations; set healthy boundaries; integrate loving self-reflection
- *Waning Half Moon:* focus upon self-love, self-compassion, and self-care; forgive self and others; begin releasing poor habits
- *Waning Crescent Moon:* conclude unhealthy or unsupportive relationships; banish or shed what isn't working; rest, restore, and renew yourself

The Lunar Frequencies

You can also pair your healing work with the astrological signs as the Moon passes through them. Here are some of the beneficent qualities that you can channel toward healing:

- *Aries:* bold, enthusiastic, exuberant, optimistic, passionate, quick
- *Taurus:* appreciative, grounded, sensual, stable, steadfast, sturdy
- *Gemini:* communicative, humorous, flexible, quick-witted, social, versatile
- *Cancer:* empathic, expressive, feeling, intuitive, nurturing, protective
- *Leo:* charismatic, creative, entertaining, fun-loving, generous, joyful
- *Virgo:* analytical, dedicated, logical, particular, practical, service oriented
- *Libra:* balanced, caring, charming, connected, helpful, refined
- *Scorpio:* astute, deep, discerning, intense, resilient, transformational
- *Sagittarius:* adventurous, cheerful, curious, gregarious, intellectual, upbeat
- *Capricorn:* ambitious, committed, devoted, disciplined, industrious, structured
- *Aquarius:* egalitarian, imaginative, independent, observant, principled, visionary
- *Pisces:* compassionate, creative, emotional, feeling, flowing, sensitive

The Moon and Nervous System Regulation

Often considered the link to the soul, the nervous system can be likened to the body's headquarters. It is composed of the brain, spinal cord, and nerves, which send electrical messages from the brain to every other part of the body. This complex system regulates every aspect of our lives both physical and emotional: from muscle movement to heartbeat, from breathing to remembering, from feelings to digestion, and beyond.[51]

The Nervous System in Brief

The nervous system has two parts, the central nervous system (CNS) and the peripheral nervous system (PNS). The peripheral nervous system is then further categorized into the somatic nervous system, which is responsible for body movements, and the automatic nervous system, which handles all the involuntary body processes.

It is the automatic nervous system that we will focus on here, principally the sympathetic and the parasympathetic components. The sympathetic nervous system stimulates and energizes our bodies and is responsible for our fawn, fight, flight, and freeze reactions. The parasympathetic branch is concerned with relaxation, which needs to be activated in order for us to rest, restore, and heal.

In this modern world, most people live in a state of nearly constant stress, with overactivated adrenal glands and bodies drenched in cortisol, suffering from primal sensations of continual danger, exhausted yet unable to sleep through the night, contending with high blood sugar, and experiencing digestive problems. As a collective, contemporary humans have difficulty pausing, relaxing, and just *being*. We license stress and guilt to drive our everyday lives and then wonder why we are chronically fatigued, drained, disconnected, and unhappy.

This seems to happen for two reasons: (1) in a patriarchy-kyriarchy, our value is perceived as rooted in our productivity and (2) many of us are walking with deep-seated trauma either from our own childhood experiences and/or from the epigenetic trauma that has been passed down to us through our DNA.

When we are not experiencing an emergency, our bodies should be living in a parasympathetic state of relaxation and regeneration with regular heart rates, slow breath, easy digestion, and balanced hormones. It is impossible to fully heal if we are not in this state.[52]

We can train ourselves to dwell here, though—to prioritize rest, to release stress, and to learn healthy ways in which to move through our seemingly automated fawn-fight-flight-freeze responses. That is where the Moon comes in.

51. "Nervous System."
52. "Health or Disease, Directly Dependent on the Vagus Nerve."

Regulating the Nervous System

Nourishing your nervous system—including recognizing your stress responses and identifying your traumas—leads to a better appreciation of your own capacity and needs, enhancing your trust in your own Earth body, your own vulnerable and authentic truth.

When you feel safe and regulated enough to fully incarnate in your physical body, this accelerates your abilities to heal, to create magic, and to express the greatest possible version of yourself. Learning to slow down, to track intuitive messages and notice your bodily sensations, increases your ability to access your own powers, vision, and wisdom.

Making small changes, one at a time, is easier for the nervous system to process than making one big, sudden transformation. A marvelous first step is to discover how your body responds to those things that activate you and then to develop gentle, compassionate practices to soothe yourself, alleviate stress, and reduce trauma.

What are *your* body's go-to responses to pressure, discomfort, shock, and stress? When you are activated, what do you do?

- Do you fawn? Do you try to appease someone who is upset or angry? Do you find yourself acting submissive, or agreeing verbally even if you don't agree internally? Do you people-please or try to gain favor?
- Do you fight? Are you known for having a hot temper, for flying off the handle, for going from zero to sixty in one moment? Are you defensive or aggressive? Are you a perfectionist? Do you try to control situations? Do you bully or harry others to do your bidding?
- Do you flee? Do you run away from tense situations or perceived danger? Do you try to avoid people who are upset or acting out? Do you create physical or emotional distance?
- Do you freeze? Do you check out or dissociate? Do you lose your words or even your ability to think clearly? Do you feel stuck in place, paralyzed, unable to move? Are you unable to take action against a perceived threat?

Once you understand how your nervous system generally acts and reacts, you can create the resources you most need to relieve stress, soothe and calm yourself, and increase pleasure, activating the parasympathetic part of your nervous system.[53]

Lunar Techniques for Nervous System Regulation

As Moon Witches, we continually strive toward the most awakened, empowered, and embodied expression of our authentic selves that is possible. It is our mutual intention to remain open and

53. Long, "How The Parasympathetic Nervous System Can Lower Stress."

receptive to the lunar energies that are flowing into our lives whilst at the same time holding a firm and solid container for ourselves, coupled with a fastidious awareness of what we are allowing into our physical and etheric vessels and into our realms.

It is vital to develop practices that help us to manage our own energies, as well as detailed cognizance of the energies that belong to others—the energies of other people, the thoughtform energies of the collective unconscious, as well as the cosmic energies that are constantly streaming down onto the Earth and into our bodies and our lives.

Moon-based energy practices can help with this, training us to contain and then direct our own energies and our own receptivity in the healthiest of ways, supporting us in sitting upon the thrones of our own lives, knowing what we are truly responsible for and have authority over, and what we do not.

Here are some strategies to synchronize your nervous system with the lunar vibrations, which, in turn, will help you to heal yourself and hold space for the healing of others. Use these ideas as jumping-off points for refining your ability to hold your own container and conduct your own energies.

The Fundamental Exercise

This simple four-step practice is meant to be done throughout the day, whenever you find yourself feeling ungrounded, reactionary, or overwhelmed. It is helpful for bringing all parts of yourself together, salving jagged energies, discharging stress, and returning you to center.

Stop and deliberately observe your surroundings. Notice the sensations happening in your body. Notice the Earth beneath you and the energies of the Moon above.

Place one hand on your heart and one hand on your stomach and slowly breathe in calming lunar energies. Visualize the rays of the Moon entering your body with each inhalation and all unwanted energies leaving your body with each exhalation.

The Nourishing Practice

This exercise is intended for daily use, to help empty the body of stress and to fill it with the nourishing powers of the Moon. Laying loving hands upon your own physical vessel helps to both release and regulate your energies, fostering sensations of safety, security, and belonging.

Begin with gentle breath, connecting with yourself and then with the Moon.

With great awareness, slowly touch your body, part by part, with loving yet firm palms. As you make contact with each part of yourself, focus on drawing the energy of Luna into that place. See-sense-feel this energy—perhaps as a color, a sound, a scent, a texture, a taste, or something else.

Pay particular attention to anywhere that needs some extra love: your heart, your stomach, your eyes, your forehead, your neck, and so on. Stay with this practice for as long as it feels pleasant, and then release your channel to the Moon with gratitude and move softly back into your day or evening.

The Evening Reset

This final nervous system–focused practice is designed for nightly use, immediately before sleeping.

Get yourself comfortable in your bed, placing your hands lightly upon your heart or stomach. Breathe in through your third eye and then out through your legs, allowing energies to exit through your feet.

Breathe in through your crown and then out through your legs, allowing energies to exit through your feet. Breathe in through your Moon Center and then out through your legs, allowing energies to exit through your feet.

Now, imagine yourself floating under the Moon, upon the surface of a warm sea. Smell and taste the salt in the air. Feel the soothing energies of the sea and of the Moon in the phase and sign she is currently traversing.

Feel the energies of the Moon entering your body through your third eye, crown, and bindu chakras, and then feel these energies gathering in your hands.

Surrender to the ebb and flow of the salty sea and the powers of the Moon above. Place your hands wherever you most need the energies of peace, calm, and healing.

Breathe here—lengthy, slow inhalations and exhalations—for as long as it takes to clear your body of unwanted energies and emotions, at least three cycles of breath. Thank the sea and the Moon and drift off to sleep.

The Body

In this section, I will share a series of somatic tools and techniques for you to explore as you enact your healing work with the Moon. Once you've played with them a few times, adapt them to your needs and make them your own.

Bodyscanning with Moonlight

Bodyscanning is a meditative practice that can help you to slow down and connect with what is going on in your physical, mental, emotional, and spiritual bodies. It is a beautiful way to take a present-moment inventory, resetting and regulating the nervous system.

This method uses the light of the Moon to illuminate what is happening for you in any given moment; it increases your self-awareness and reorients you within yourself. Regular lunar bodyscans can help you to become more present and embodied, grounded into who you are and what you are feeling.

The Process

Step 1: Begin by making your body comfortable, sitting or lying down, even standing if desired or necessary.

Step 2: Close your eyes, slow your breath, and connect with the Earth and Moon. Feel into the lunar phase and transit that is happening in the sky. Open your channel to the Moon and draw down her energies.

Step 3: Beginning with your crown, breathe lunar energy into your body. With loving curiosity, focus upon your crown, noticing any sensations that are present there for you today.

Step 4: Slowly and deliberately, breathe lunar energy down through and into each part of your body now, pausing to simply observe the sensations present for you in each location before moving on: From your crown, move to all parts of your head, to your throat, to your shoulders, to your heart, to your arms and hands and fingers, to all of the organs contained inside your torso, to your solar plexus, to your sacral chakra, to your legs, your feet, your toes. Witness and acknowledge whatever is present for you in each part of your body.

Step 5: When you reach the soles of your feet, stop and draw additional peaceful lunar energy down into any place that is tight or painful or uncomfortable. Breathe these soothing rays into any place that asks for it.

Step 6: Breathe lunar energy all the way through your body—from your crown to the soles of your feet—sending it down into the Earth.

Step 7: When you are complete, stop the current of energy and give gratitude to the Moon. Open your eyes and return your attention to your surroundings, awakening to whatever is happening there, giving your body some soft rubs or taps and a tight hug before moving on with your day or evening. Blessed be!

Lunar Breathwork

We can calm anxiety and increase relaxation through lunar breathwork. Anyone can do breathwork, and even though it is a fascinating discipline, it is not necessary to master a separate system in order to engage with it. In fact, humans have probably been using breathwork for healing and well-being for thousands of years.

Try starting out with this practice for only one minute. When you feel accomplished here, build up to three minutes, then five, then ten, and then fifteen, with a goal of regularly reaching twenty or more minutes for your lunar breathwork sessions.

If you wish, you can write an affirmation of support to use during breathwork, or just engage with it in this way.

The Process

Step 1: Begin by connecting with your breath, then the Earth and Moon through your roots and branches. When you are grounded and centered, visualize your crown chakra gently opening to receive lunar energies.

Step 2: Breathe in for a count of three, concentrating upon taking in the healing light and frequencies of the Moon. Hold for a count of three. Exhale for a final count of three, releasing anything you want to be rid of.

Step 3: Notice what part or parts of your body you are storing unwanted feelings or old patterns in, and breathe the Moon's light into these places, ushering out the unwanted feelings or patterns with every exhalation. Allow the Moon's vibrations to heal these parts of you, restoring them to full health and beauty.

Step 4: When you are complete, take in one more long full inhalation, see-sense-feeling the energies of the Moon filling you up, circulating through every part of your body through your blood, and then seal this healing lunar energy into your body by envisioning your crown chakra closing almost completely to hold it in. Take a few more relaxed breaths before opening your crown chakra to the aperture you prefer for going about your everyday life.

8-8-8 Breathing

This exercise aligns your body with the cycle of the eight major lunar phases, helping to eradicate unwanted energies from the lungs and the body as a whole.

Working with lunar breathwork can also be incredibly satisfying to do with your partner or close friends and especially within a coven of Moon Witches or even an open circle, if you are feeling brave!

The Process

Step 1: Inhale: Breathe in slowly and evenly for a count of eight, envisioning the Moon moving through her eight major phases as you do so: New, Waxing Crescent, Waxing Half, Waxing Gibbous, Full, Waning Gibbous, Waning Half, Waning Crescent.

Step 2: Pause: Pause and hold your breath for a slow count of eight.

Step 3: Exhale: Breathe out slowly and evenly for a count of eight, envisioning the Moon moving through her eight major phases as you do so: New, Waxing Crescent, Waxing Half, Waxing Gibbous, Full, Waning Gibbous, Waning Half, Waning Crescent.

Moving with the Moon for Health and Healing

A swift and enjoyable way to connect with the Moon for healing is through movement. This can be done in concert with music or not, depending upon your personal preferences. You can do this practice standing or sitting, even lying down.

Feel into the phase and sign of the Moon, then feel into how your body is resonating with these vibrations. What feels stuck inside of you; what trapped emotions or experiences need freeing?

Begin by slowly moving in a way that flows with what the Moon is doing in the sky and how she is interacting with the zodiacal frequency she is transiting.

Is she in an air sign? A fire sign? A water sign? An earth sign? Express the energies of the Moon through your human vessel, using the lunar vibrations of the energies of this element to shift yourself into better health, into releasing that which must go.

You may find yourself stretching your arms, rotating your torso, exploring yoga poses, jumping, skipping, even leaping or dancing. The most important thing is to do what feels good to your body.

Moonrest

In times of mild weather, you can sleep outdoors in the fresh air. Yes, without a tent! Build a cozy, welcoming nest for yourself, an altar for your magnificent human body. Lie down in the nest, recognizing that *you* are the sacred offering. Feel how nourishing it is to be a holy offering to the Moon, to offer your body up to the Moon in exchange for her healing rays.

The Process

Step 1: Settle yourself, recalling your wholeness and holiness. If you have need of specific healing, speak it aloud to the Moon Mother.

Step 2: Ground yourself securely into the Earth Mother below, then send your etheric tendrils up, up, up, caressing the Moon with love and appreciation. Draw her energies down, down, down into your body. Fill yourself up with her curative rays.

Step 3: Breathe her peace into your body. Pray to her, meditate with her, and ask her for a healing dream. Soak in her vibrations, as deeply as you can. Harmonize your frequency with hers.

Step 4: Observe how vast the Cosmos is and how small you are. Let your troubles slip away into the infinity of the Multiverse. Send and receive love; send love to the Moon and receive her unconditional love into your body. Make a healing wish for yourself.

Step 5: Allow yourself to drift off to sleep, holding the intention for health and healing and rest and renewal in her image.

Step 6: When you wake up, note whatever dreams or dream fragments you remember in your Moon Journal or Dream Diary. Remember to check back on your dream or dream fragments later to see if there is any information she delivered for your health and healing.

Lunar Toning

This is a simple activity to connect with the healing powers of your own voice. If this modality speaks to you, begin with five minutes of practice and work up to fifteen-to-thirty-minute weekly sessions. Five minutes gives you time to immerse yourself in the sound, stepping away from self-judgment and into lunar flow and cosmic perception.

The Process

Step 1: Before beginning, be aware of the sign and phase of the Moon.

Step 2: Sit or stand in a position that is comfortable for you and facilitates the full expansion of your chest. Ground and center yourself and invite the Moon to join you in your practice.

Step 3: Begin to gently play around with your voice, exploring notes that feel natural and right for you today and also feel somehow connected to the lunar sign and/or phase. These notes should create no pain or strain, and the sound produced can be anywhere within your vocal range, high or low. Begin with soft sounds and add volume as your voice heats up.

Step 4: Try extending your sound outward as far as you can, envisioning it going all the way up to the Moon. Your inhalations should be controlled, deep, and full through each cycling of breath to power the sound for as long as possible.

Step 5: Start experimenting with other sounds—especially vowels—or even words that are satisfying and fun to you, helping you to connect with whatever the Moon is doing in the sky. If you don't feel like articulating discernible notes, try humming or buzzing like a hive of bees.

My favorite word to tone for this practice is *Luna*—it helps me to connect my personal frequency with hers. I like to draw out the vowel sounds; they create a resonance that accentuates my feelings of belonging to the Moon.

Step 6: Notice any sensations happening in your body and any emotions arising in your heart.

Step 7: Extend your love to the Moon upon the sound you are creating. Feel her love entering into your body with each inhalation.

Step 8: When you are complete, allow your sound to gently succumb to sacred silence. Return your breath to your normal pacing and give your body some gentle attention before moving into your next activity or about your day or evening.

Lunar Affirmations

Affirmations can be created to support healing through every phase and/or sign of the Moon. Affirmations, sometimes called intentions, only work when they truly match both our desires and our emotions—and if they feel good to us.

These supportive phrases are best written and spoken in the positive, naming what you do want instead of what you do not. Present-tense affirmations starting with *I am* a splendid place to start.

Moonwater for Affirmation Support

If you are working with a specific affirmation for your healing and growth, you can infuse a moonwater to match the vibrations and support your intentions. Consider first your affirmation and then the lunar sign and/or phase that will be most helpful to you. Choose the date you want to work with and write it on your calendar.

Look up on an app or a website to see when moonrise will take place that day or night.

To Gather

- A glass jar or bottle with a lid
- Water. Water from your tap is fine, or you can use a sacred water that you have on hand or gather specifically for this magic.

- One or more crystals, herbs, and/or plants that support your intention
- Alcohol (to preserve your water)
- Labels or paper and tape, paint pens, or other such implements

The Process

Step 1: Write your affirmation—or a symbol or sigil that represents it—upon the glass of your jar or bottle (or write it on a label or piece of paper and affix that to the exterior).

Step 2: Directly before moonrise, fill your container with water and bring it outside (if this is not possible for you, you can place it somewhere in your home instead). Surround your jar with the supportive crystals, herbs, and/or plants that you chose.

Step 3: Ask for the Moon's witness and help. Open your jar or bottle and speak your affirmation aloud into the water three times (or more). Add the alcohol preservative before closing the jar.

Step 4: Leave your jar out under the Moon for thirteen hours.

Use this water to bless yourself as you continue to work with your affirmation, anchoring your intent into your physical, mental, and emotional reality.

Moon Moodboards

This is a creative exploration to clarify your feelings, to communicate your own inner emotions and visions to your outer, rational, worldly Self. I primarily work this practice within the waxing half of a lunation, to support my emotional healing. You could choose a waning phase, though, if you would like to do releasing work, and then later burn, bury, or sink the moonboard.

Moonboard Healing Practice

You don't have to share your moonboard with anyone, so do not edit yourself or worry about what others may think, say, or do. This is about *you* and your healing.

To Gather

- A white, silver, gray, or black candle, depending on the Moon phase you have chosen to work with

- A lighter or matches
- A large piece of paper (such as posterboard, cardboard, or a broken-down shipping box)
- Interesting magazines or other sources of images (e.g., printouts from the internet or books, old greeting cards, drawings you made)
- Scissors
- A glue stick

Optional

- Markers in various colors
- Glitter, sequins, beads, dried flower petals or herbal allies, or other decorative items

The Process

Step 1: Light your candle in the name of the Moon or Moon Goddess and ask her to be with you, to witness your work, to guide your hands and your heart.

You can cast a formal circle to better contain the energies of your working—or not; it's completely up to you. Do ground, center, and open the channel before you begin, though. Connect with breath, roots, and branches, with Self, Earth, and Moon.

Step 2: Page through the images and set aside those that match your mood, your energies, your emotions. Don't overthink this; in fact, don't think at all. This is not an intellectual exercise but an emotional one. Let your heart and your gut take the wheel.

You may look for people who seem to share your feelings, or you may choose pictures of symbols, objects, or items that match your emotions, or perhaps you may pick images that share a color or colors that match your energies. Or perhaps you may go for a combination of all of these things or something else entirely. Whatever appeals to you!

Step 3: Cut your chosen images to better fit your board if necessary, then glue them on. After everything is attached, you can use markers to add words, affirmations, symbols, and additional drawings, and/or attach the other items you've selected.

Step 4: Once your moonboard is complete, sit with it, taking it all in. Permit whatever sparks for you to rise into your consciousness. Note these things in your Moon Journal for later reference.

Step 5: Make a wish for yourself and your life. Bless and charge your moonboard—and yourself!—with the vibrations (and rays, if they are visible) of the Moon. Then, depending on the type of board you made, either display it or dispose of it.

Healing with Water

Aquatherapy and other forms of healing with water can help to relax and rest your physical vessel in connection with the revitalizing rays of the Moon and her natural rapport with the power of water.

Ritual Bath

I often use a simple bath to help calm myself before performing a rite. Here are some ideas for more elaborate ritual baths to promote healing.

Heart-Healing Moonbath Ritual

This ritual can help to regulate emotions and heal heartache; it is ideally done directly before bedtime. This is a ritual bath, so treat it as holy; you could burn incense, light candles, meditate. Allow yourself to be both cleansed and healed.

It is advisable to leave the components of this bath on your skin overnight before showering in the morning. This enables the regenerative qualities of your moonwork to soak into your body and your subconscious while you sleep, bringing greater restfulness, rejuvenation, and healing.

To Gather

- 2 cups of powdered milk
- 1 cup of Epsom salt
- ½ cup of baking soda
- One rose upon the stem. If there are thorns, remove them before your bath.
- 9 drops of rose otto e.o. plus 9 drops of rose geranium e.o., diluted in ⅛ cup of carrier oil
- 1 batch of moonwater of your choice (see chapter 10)
- A pitcher, bowl, or other large container
- A mixing spoon

The Rite

Step 1: One by one, add each of the ingredients to your bowl or pitcher, combining them as you intone this chant:

By Moon, by rose,
By water and salt,
Beneath the rays of Luna,
I heal my heart.

Step 2: As you fill your tub with water, pour the potion from your vessel into your bath as you would a libation for the Goddess.

Step 3: Swirl the bathwater around to distribute all of the ingredients, and then submerge yourself in the healing waters.

Step 4: Stay here as long as it is satisfying, and then head promptly to bed.

Night Jasmine Moonbath Ritual

For an acute situation, I like the Heart-Healing Moonbath Ritual above. For routine emotional maintenance, this next bath is in my regular rotation. I especially appreciate the gentle power, scent, and vibration of jasmine, one of my particular plant friends.

To Gather

- Jasmine bath salt (recipe follows ritual)
- A moon magic candle (white, gray, silver, or black, depending upon the phase you are working with). If you are called, dress the candle for your purpose.
- A lighter or matches
- Jasmine essential oil diluted in a carrier oil in a small, unbreakable vessel

Optional

- Other candles
- Incense of your choosing
- Soft and relaxing music

The Rite

Step 1: Fill your tub and add your prepared bath salt. Swirl your waters around so everything mingles and becomes one. Ground, center, and open the channel using breath, roots, and branches.

Step 2: Turn off your bathroom lights and light your candle. Hold it up to the Moon (whether you can see her or not) and ask for her blessings. If you'd like, use a sky app to discover exactly where she is situated in relationship to your location. Set the lit candle down in a safe place where you can see it.

Step 3: Carefully submerge in the tub. Whilst here, breathe the Moon's light (or dark!) into your body, feeling into the sign and phase she is residing in.

Step 4: Ask the Lunar Lady to cleanse, clear, and bless you, body, mind, heart, and spirit. When you are ready, take up your small vessel of oil and anoint your body, stopping at each chakra and checking in with how you feel there before anointing yourself. I like to begin at my crown and move downward. Remember your bindu chakra and the palms of your hands and bottoms of your feet!

If there is any place where you need extra support, cleanse, clear, and bless that place (or those places) as well.

Step 5: Relax in your bath for as long as you'd like, then mindfully move back into regular life.

Jasmine Bath Salt Recipe

The following yields enough for one moonbath. If you are creating this product for future use, store it in a glass jar. Additionally, you may increase the proportions to make enough for more than one bath. Simply combine the following ingredients:

- 1 cup Epsom salt
- ½ cup jasmine flowers (*Jasminum officinale*)
- 13 drops of jasmine e.o. diluted in about ⅛ cup of carrier oil

Note: If you have access to fresh jasmine during her long blooming season, gather her blossoms and prepare this recipe for immediate use. If you aim to store this salt for a future bath, use dried flowers.

Lunar Healing Water

Lunar healing water is used for blessing the self and others when the healing and loving energies of the Moon are needed.

Lunar Healing Water

Since this project involves collecting salt water from a natural source (e.g., the ocean), you will most likely need to plan your pilgrimage in advance. Choose a sign and/or phase of the Moon that reflects the energies you want to store.

To Gather

- A biodegradable, animal-safe offering
- A container to collect water in
- A sterilized glass jar or bottle with lid
- Grain alcohol or vodka
- Labels or paper and tape, paint pens, or other such implements

Optional

- Essential oil from one of your personal plant friends, or e.o. that corresponds to that particular lunar phase or sign

The Process

Step 1: Commune with the body of water you have chosen to visit, and connect with the sign and phase the Moon is in.

Step 2: Make your offering, and ask the water permission to gather some of it to use in your healing work.

Step 3: If you receive an affirmative answer, collect water from the ocean, sea, or saltwater lake, expressing your gratitude and respect.

Step 4: Bring your water home and pour it into a sterilized glass jar or bottle. To preserve the water, add 25 percent of grain alcohol or vodka. If you wish you may also add several drops of an essential oil from one of your personal plant friends or that corresponds to that particular lunar phase or sign.

Step 5: Label your jar with the name of the water gathered, the preservative, and any other additions. Don't forget the date and the lunar sign and phase.

Healing with the Shadow Self and the Inner Critic

Self-love is one of the foundational pieces of developing a rich life, one where we unequivocally know our worth, own our sovereignty, and are compassionate with ourselves no matter what.

This is *soul work,* and although it can be difficult and sometimes tricky, it is the good and necessary work that ushers profound movement, innovation, and transformation into our lives, the precursors of self-acceptance, fulfilment, and power-within.

A Self-Love Healing Ritual

This ritual moonspell can facilitate rapid and powerful change. Be gentle with yourself afterward: Rest, eat healthy foods, and be very slow and kind as the energies settle. It may take time for the fullness of your working to land.

Ideally, this self-love rite is performed outdoors. However, it is not always warm enough—or safe enough!—to do this. Ensure you are in a protected space whenever you do magic, ritual, or spellwork.

For this ritual, you need a Full Moon night when you can see Luna in the sky.

To Gather

- A mirror
- A wet erase marker. Note that these are different than dry erase markers, which only wipe off of specific surfaces. Wet erase markers can be easily washed from glass, metal, mirror, and other such surfaces.
- An ID card with your picture on it. You can use your driver's license, passport, or school or work card; ideally, you will choose a card that you carry with you daily.
- Fresh flowers. Use your favorite if they are available.

- An altar. This can simply be the ground—the Earth herself—should you wish, or it can be more involved. Set up your altar so the light of the Moon shines down upon it unimpeded.

The Rite

Step 1: Settle your body comfortably. Ground, center, and open the channel.

Step 2: Place your mirror on your altar in such a way that you can see both your reflection and the reflection of the Full Moon. This may take some finagling; stay calm. It *can* be done!

Step 3: Using the wet erase marker, write the following affirmation on your mirror: "I am worthy of self-love."

Step 4: Surround your mirror with the flowers you have chosen.

Step 5: Hold your picture ID in your hands. Look into the mirror and see the Moon. Now read the affirmation aloud at least thirteen times. Look at the Moon in your mirror and then gaze into your own eyes.

Step 6: Feel the energies of self-love and compassion rising up within you. Fake it until you make it if you have to! Remember that we are all One, that *all* is One, and that you are both a reflection and a manifestation of divinity.

Step 7: Feel the Moon shining her loving, healing beams upon you from above and reflecting those healing, loving beams up from the mirror into your eyes. Feel yourself completely surrounded by her loving, healing vibrations—above you, below you, around you, and within you.

Step 8: Speak your affirmation again thirteen times.

Step 9: Send the energies of self-love and compassion and the loving, healing vibrations of the Moon through your body and then out of your heart and out of your hands into your ID card. Feel your connection with All That Is. Feel your divinity *and* your humanity. Feel your completeness and your complexity, your light and your shadow, your wholeness and your holiness.

Step 10: Speak your affirmation again thirteen times.

Step 11: Offer gratitude to the Moon both within your mirror and above you.

Step 12: Release your sacred space, grounding and centering yourself before moving back into ordinary reality. It is done, done, done!

If possible, leave your altar set up overnight or at least until the Moon sets. Offer the flowers to Luna in some special fashion once the energies you have set into motion have finished their work.

Conclusion

As I write this, our Lunar Lady is in the sign of Taurus, growing toward her fullness, her glow increasing, her powers sweeping, benevolent, and kind. As I stood under the Moon tonight, I thought of you. Was her sparkle keeping you awake, too? Could you feel the star-steeped air humming with potential and possibility? Were you feeling the same sense of kinship?

I imagined all the Lunar Witches around the world standing together in the Ethers, hand in hand, our hearts joined in joyous cohesion as we sung her praises.

As Lunar Witches, we are not only connected to the Moon; we are connected to one another. In a world that seems increasingly sharp and jagged, here is a similarity all humans share: We are all subject to the queenly benevolence of Luna, the cosmic tides of our lives pulled and pushed by her traveling, our existence timed to hers.

We all deserve lives that are rich, regenerative, and filled with well-being, community, and camaraderie. The dance of the Moon across the sky can offer us a unified focus, supporting us in wading further into the flow of life itself.

Perhaps it sounds too simple, and yet I cannot help but think that this link we all share with the Moon could be a starting place. Perhaps we could learn to listen to one another through listening to her, centering our commonalties instead of leaning into our differences, coming together as One beneath her brilliant luminosity.

Whether or not this big dream is attainable, I hope that you have learned how impactful it can be to align yourself with the powers of the Moon, her transformations a guide toward integrating your inner realm with your outer realm, to inhabiting the confluence of Above and Below and Within and Without, allied with both Earth and Cosmos.

Lunar Witchcraft is a lifelong practice built upon lived experience. Keep practicing, keep centering your relationship with the Moon, keep trusting in spirit and in yourself, keep surrendering to her beauty.

As each lunar phase marks another passageway, may you accept her loving offer of integration and connection with the most-ancient—and modern—parts of your being. May you accept these opportunities for healing, wholeness, and holiness as you progress through her never-ending cycles, growing your love, wisdom, resilience, perception, and power-within.

The Moon never reflects the same sunlight twice. Every reflection, every moment, is unique, just as you are. As you walk the Path of Lunar Witchcraft, you carry your moon magic and your moon medicine—your special gifts—along with you. Continue following the path and own it as yours.

Partnership with the Moon is one of the greatest blessings of my life, and I credit her soft, gentle, and compassionate gifts of bright illumination and dark stillness with gifting me the courage to step deeper and deeper into who I truly am and who I am meant to be. I hope that you have found this connection and belonging, too.

I will meet you under her silvery beams.

Acknowledgments

With the deepest of appreciation and gratitude, I thank all who have traveled with me to this place. I especially thank Debra, the gracious torchbearer who illuminated the way; Jason for generously sharing guidance with compassion, understanding, and humor; and Gus, for his unwavering patience, constant support, and steadfast love.

To the excellent, wise, and dedicated people of Llewellyn, thank you. You took my limited vision and expanded it into something far larger than I could have ever seen on my own.

This book would not exist without each of you. Thank you for your support and your love. Thank you for believing in me.

To all whose hands helped to bring this book to life, I bow in gratitude.

Recommended Reading

Affirmations

The Creative Visualization Workbook by Shakti Gawain

Daily Rituals: Positive Affirmations to Attract Love, Happiness and Peace by Phoebe Garnsworthy

Quantum Affirmations: The New Energy Science of Conscious Manifestation by Monte Farber

Astral Travel

Astral Projection for Psychic Empowerment: Practical Applications of the Out-of-Body Experience by Carl Llewellyn Weschcke and Joe H. Slate

The Astral Projection Guidebook: Mastering the Art of Astral Travel by Erin Pavlina

Astrology

Astrology: A Cosmic Science by Isabel M. Hickey

Essential Astrology: Everything You Need to Know to Interpret Your Natal Chart by Amy Herring

The Inner Sky: The Dynamic New Astrology for Everyone by Steven Forrest

Candle Magic

The Art of Hoodoo Candle Magic in Rootwork, Conjure, and Spiritual Church Services by Catherine Yronwode

Candle Magic: A Witch's Guide to Spells and Rituals by Lucya Starza

The Lighting of Candles by Christopher Penczak

Chakras

Chakra Healing: A Beginner's Guide to Self-Healing Techniques that Balance the Chakras by Margarita Alcantara

Llewellyn's Complete Book of Chakras: Your Definitive Source of Energy Center Knowledge for Health, Happiness, and Spiritual Evolution by Cyndi Dale

Wheels of Life: A User's Guide to the Chakra System by Anodea Judith

Crystals

Crystal Magic: Divination, Healing, and Spellcraft with Gems and Minerals by Rev. Dr. Jon Saint Germain

Crystal Magic for the Modern Witch by Devin Hunter

Crystals for Witches: Rituals, Spells, and Practices for Stone Spirit Magic by Eliza Mabelle

Stones of the Goddess: 104 Crystals for the Divine Feminine by Nicholas Pearson

Dreaming

The Art of Lucid Dreaming: Over 60 Powerful Practices to Help You Wake Up in Your Dreams by Clare R. Johnson

The Awakened Dreamer: How to Remember & Interpret Your Dreams by Kala Ambrose

A Field Guide to Lucid Dreaming: Mastering the Art of Oneironautics by Dylan Tuccillo, Jared Zeizel, and Thomas Peisel

A Witch's Book of Dreams: Understanding the Power of Dreams & Symbols by Karri Allrich

The Elements

Four Elements of the Wise: Working with the Magickal Powers of Earth, Air, Water, Fire by Ivo Dominguez Jr.

The Missing Element: Inspiring Compassion for the Human Condition by Debra Silverman

The Way of Four: Create Elemental Balance in Your Life by Deborah Lipp

Essential and Magickal Oils

Llewellyn's Complete Formulary of Magical Oils: Over 1,200 Recipes, Potions & Tinctures for Everyday Use by Celeste Rayne Heldstab

Mixing Essential Oils for Magic: Aromatic Alchemy for Personal Blends by Sandra Kynes

The Sacred Art of Anointing by Allison Stillman

Sacred Oils: Working with 20 Precious Oils to Heal Spirit and Soul by Felicity Warner

Flower and Gem Essences

Bach Flower Therapy: Theory and Practice by Mechthild Scheffer

Flower Essence Repertory: A Comprehensive Guide to North American and English Flower Essences for Emotional and Spiritual Well-Being by Patricia Kaminski and Richard Katz

Flower Essences and Vibrational Healing by Gurudas

Gem Water: How to Prepare and Use More than 130 Crystal Waters for Therapeutic Treatments by Michael Gienger and Joachim Goebel

Goddess Asteroids

Asteroid Goddesses: The Mythology, Psychology, and Astrology of the Re-Emerging Feminine by Demetra George and Douglas Bloch

Green Witchery

Cunningham's Encyclopedia of Magical Herbs by Scott Cunningham

Garden Witch's Herbal: Green Magick, Herbalism & Spirituality by Ellen Dugan

Herbal Rituals by Judith Berger

Hoodoo Herb and Root Magic: A Materia Magica of African-American Conjure by Catherine Yronwode

Natural Magic: Potions and Powers from the Magical Garden by John Michael Greer

Healing

Inside-Out Healing: Transforming Your Life Through the Power of Presence by Richard Moss

Magick of Reiki: Focused Energy for Healing, Ritual, & Spiritual Development by Christopher Penczak

You Can Heal Your Life by Louise Hay

Journeying

Shamanic Breathwork: Journeying Beyond the Limits of the Self by Linda Star Wolf

Shamanic Journeying: A Beginner's Guide by Sandra Ingerman

Medicinal Herbalism

Herbal Healing for Women: Simple Home Remedies for Women of All Ages by Rosemary Gladstar

A Modern Herbal (Volume 1 and 2): The Medicinal, Culinary, Cosmetic and Economic Properties, Cultivation and Folk-Lore of Herbs, Grasses, Fungi, Shrubs & Trees with Their Modern Scientific Uses by Margaret Grieve

The New Holistic Herbal by David Hoffmann

Moon Magic

In the Shadow of 13 Moons: Embracing Lunar Energy for Self-Healing and Transformation by Kimberly Sherman-Cook

Mysteries of the Dark Moon: The Healing Power of the Dark Goddess by Demetra George

Sisters of the Dark Moon: 13 Rituals of the Dark Goddess by Gail Wood

Pendulums

Pendulum Magic for Beginners: Power to Achieve All Goals by Richard Webster

Protection Magic

The Witch's Shield: Protection Magic and Psychic Self-Defense by Christopher Penczak

Shadow Work

Meeting the Shadow: The Hidden Power of the Dark Side of Human Nature edited by Jeremiah Abrams and Connie Zweig

The Secret of the Shadow: The Power of Owning Your Whole Story by Debbie Ford

Shadow Work: A Spiritual Path to Healing and Integration by Michelle Wadleigh

Spellwork

The Big Book of Practical Spells: Everyday Magic That Works by Judika Illes

The Casting of Spells by Christopher Penczak

Tarot Spells by Renée Janina

Tarot

Around the Tarot in 78 Days: A Personal Journey Through the Cards by Marcus Katz and Tali Goodwin

Psychic Tarot: Using Your Natural Psychic Abilities to Read the Cards by Nancy Antenucci with Melanie Howard

Tarot for Your Self: A Workbook for the Inward Journey by Mary K. Greer

Trancework

Trance-Portation: Learning to Navigate the Inner World by Diana L. Paxson

The Trance Workbook: Understanding & Using the Power of Altered States by Kay Hoffman

Water Magic

The Hidden Messages in Water by Emoto Masaru

The Way of the Water Priestess: Entering the World of Water Magic by Annwyn Avalon

Bibliography

Aceves, Ana V. "What are the Phases of the Moon?" *Sky & Telescope*, July 6, 2016. https://skyandtelescope.org/astronomy-resources/what-are-the-phases-of-the-moon/.

Begum, Tammana. "The 1883 Krakatau Eruption: A Year of Blue Moons." Natural History Museum. Accessed December 21, 2024. https://www.nhm.ac.uk/discover/the-1883-krakatau-eruption-a-year-of-blue-moons.html.

Bethune, Meredith. "The Medicinal Roots of Modern Liqueurs." Tales of the Cocktail Foundation. March 22, 2017. https://talesofthecocktail.org/medicinal-roots-modern-liqueurs/.

"Bindu Chakra." Yoga in Daily Life. Accessed November 2, 2024. https://www.yogaindailylife.org/system/en/chakras/bindu-chakra.

Cameron, Julia. *The Right to Write: An Invitation and Initiation into the Writing Life*. TarcherPerigee, 1999.

Coha, Renee. "Scents in the Summer Garden." Chicago Botanic Garden. August 2, 2023. https://www.chicagobotanic.org/blog/learning/scents_summer_garden.

"Cultural Objects Names AuthorityÒ Iconography Display." Getty Research Institute. Accessed January 6, 2024. https://www.getty.edu/cona/CONAIconographyRecord.aspx?iconid=901000069.

Cunningham, Scott. *The Complete Book of Incense, Oils & Brews*. Llewellyn Publications, 1989.

Davis, Josh. "The Moon." Natural History Museum. Accessed November 2, 2024. https://www.nhm.ac.uk/discover/factfile-the-moon.html.

"DHL Moonbox: Astrobotic Technology." Astrobotic. Accessed December 20, 2024. https://www.astrobotic.com/lunar-delivery/send-to-the-moon/.

Dobrijevic, Daisy. "What Are Lunar Eclipses and How Do They Occur?" With contributions by Robert Roy Britt. Space.com. March 14, 2025. https://www.space.com/15689-lunar-eclipses.html.

"Eclipses and the Moon's Orbit." NASA. Updated January 12, 2012. https://eclipse.gsfc.nasa.gov/SEhelp/moonorbit.html.

"11 Essential Oils: Their Benefits and How to Use Them." Cleveland Clinic. December 14, 2021. https://health.clevelandclinic.org/essential-oils-101-do-they-work-how-do-you-use-them.

Espenak, F. "Length of the Synodic Month: 2001 to 2100." AstroPixels. Updated January 7, 2022. https://astropixels.com/ephemeris/moon/synodicmonth2001.html.

Gadon, Elinor W. *The Once and Future Goddess: A Sweeping Visual Chronicle of the Sacred Female and Her Reemergence in the Cultural Mythology of Our Time*. HarperOne, 1989.

Gawain, Shakti. *Creative Visualization: Use the Power of Your Imagination to Create What You Want in Your Life*. New World Library, 2010.

Hart, John C. "Modeling Transformations." Accessed November 2, 2024. https://courses.grainger.illinois.edu/cs418/fa2017/slides/everything-ch7.pdf.

"Hawaiian Moon Phases and Traditional Natural Resource Management." Western Pacific Regional Fishery Management Council. Accessed January 3, 2025. https://www.wpcouncil.org/wp-content/uploads/2019/05/Indigenous_Display-1.pdf.

"Health or Disease, Directly Dependent on the Vagus Nerve." Imunomedica. December 30, 2021. https://www.imuno-medica.ro/news/Health-or-disease-directly-dependent-on-the-vagus-nerve-23.

Helmenstine, Anne Marie. "Sidereal Month Versus Lunar Month (Synodic)." ThoughtCo. Updated February 1, 2020. https://www.thoughtco.com/sidereal-lunar-month-4135226.

Hiscock, Philip. "Where Does the Phrase 'Once in a Blue Moon' Come From?" *Sky & Telescope*, August 24, 2012. https://skyandtelescope.org/observing/once-in-a-blue-moon/.

"Is The 'Blue' in 'Blue Moon' a Reference to Betrayal?" StackExchange: English Language & Usage. Accessed January 4, 2025. https://english.stackexchange.com/questions/437111/is-the-blue-in-blue-moon-a-reference-to-betrayal.

Ives, Martyn, dir. "If We Had No Moon." Discovery Channel, 1999.

Katz, Marcus, and Tali Goodwin. *Secrets of the Waite-Smith Tarot: The True Story of the World's Most Popular Tarot*. Llewellyn Publications, 2015.

Kronfeld-Schor, Noga, Davide Dominoni, Horacio de la Iglesia, Oren Levy, Erik D. Herzog, Tamar Dayan, and Charlotte Helfrich-Forster. "Chronobiology by Moonlight." *Proceedings of the Royal Society B: Biological Sciences* 280, no. 1765 (2013). https://doi.org/10.1098/rspb.2012.3088.

Laios, Konstantinos, M. M. Moschos, Evangelia Koukaki, E. Vasilopoulos, Marianna Karamanou, M.-I. Kontaxaki, and G. Androutsos. "Dreams in Ancient Greek Medicine." *Psychiatriki* 27, no. 3 (2016): 215–21. https://doi.org/10.22365/jpsych.2016.273.215.

Lee, Nellie Ming. "Grape & Grain | Steeped in History: A Cordial, Liqueur or Schnapps Is a Tonic Whatever You Call It." *South China Morning Post*, updated October 6, 2016. https://www.scmp.com/lifestyle/food-drink/article/2024975/steeped-history-cordial-liqueur-or-schnapps-tonic-whatever-you.

Lin, Che-Hung, Shunichi Takahashi, Aziz J. Mulla, and Yoko Nozawa. "Moonrise Timing Is Key for Synchronized Spawning in Coral *Dipsastraea Speciosa*." *Proceedings of the National Academy of Sciences* 118, no. 34 (2021). https://doi.org/10.1073/pnas.2101985118.

Long, Chelsea. "How the Parasympathetic Nervous System Can Lower Stress." Hospital for Special Surgery. August 30, 2021. https://www.hss.edu/article_parasympathetic-nervous-system.asp.

Luke, David. "Psychoactive Substances and Paranormal Phenomena: A Comprehensive Review." *International Journal of Transpersonal Studies* 31, no. 1 (2012): 97–156. http://dx.doi.org/10.24972/ijts.2012.31.1.97.

"Lunar Geology." Bowling Green State University Department of Physics & Astronomy. Accessed November 2, 2024. https://physics.bgsu.edu/~layden/Eclipse24/Activities/Act_AldayT_LunarGeology.pdf.

"Lunar Sidereal and Synodic Periods." Durham University Department of Physics. Accessed November 2, 2024. https://astro.dur.ac.uk/~ams/users/lunar_sid_syn.html.

McDonough, Molly. "The Connections Between Smell, Memory, and Health." *Harvard Medicine Magazine*, April 1, 2024. https://magazine.hms.harvard.edu/articles/connections-between-smell-memory-and-health.

"Moon Composition." NASA. Updated February 10, 2025. https://science.nasa.gov/moon/composition/.

"Moon Formation." NASA. Updated February 14, 2025. https://science.nasa.gov/moon/formation/.

"Moonlight May Affect Sleep Cycles." Harvard Health Publishing. May 1, 2021. https://www.health.harvard.edu/staying-healthy/moonlight-may-affect-sleep-cycles.

"Moon Phase and Libration 2024." NASA. December 22, 2023. https://moon.nasa.gov/resources/519/moon-phase-and-libration-2024/.

"The Moon's Phase and the Sun-Earth-Moon Geometry." University of Sheffield School of Mathematical and Physical Sciences. Accessed November 2, 2024. https://www.hep.shef.ac.uk/cartwright/astro1/MoonPhases.pdf.

Morgan, Ffiona. *Goddess Spirituality Book: Rituals, Holydays and Moon Magic*. Daughters of the Moon, 1995.

Morrison, Dorothy. *Everyday Moon Magic: Spells & Rituals for Abundant Living*. Llewellyn Publications, 2003.

Mountainwater, Shekhinah. *Ariadne's Thread: A Workbook of Goddess Magic*. Celestial Arts, 1991.

Murray, Margaret Alice. *The Witch-Cult in Western Europe; A Study in Anthropology*. Clarendon Press, 1921.

"Nervous System." Cleveland Clinic. November 16, 2023. https://my.clevelandclinic.org/health/body/21202-nervous-system.

Novak, Sara. "The Science Behind Your Chakras: What Are Chakras and How Many Are There?" *Discover*, updated October 23, 2024. https://www.discovermagazine.com/health/the-science-behind-your-chakras.

Perry, Christopher. "The Jungian Shadow." The Society of Analytical Psychology. August 12, 2015. https://www.thesap.org.uk/articles-on-jungian-psychology-2/about-analysis-and-therapy/the-shadow/.

Petrovska, Biljana Bauer. "Historical Review of Medicinal Plants Usage," *Pharmacognosy Reviews* 6, no. 11 (2012): 1–5. https://doi.org/10.4103/0973-7847.95849.

"Pineal Gland." Cleveland Clinic. June 22, 2022. https://my.clevelandclinic.org/health/body/23334-pineal-gland.

Prema, Chappa Krishna, and Tarun Joshi. "Dream Interpretation: Ancient Cultures and Scientific Research." *The International Journal of Indian Psychology* 12, no. 2 (2024). https://doi.org/10.25215/1202.36.

Shelley, Percy Bysshe. "Alastor; or, the Spirit of Solitude." The Poetry Foundation. Accessed January 3, 2025. https://www.poetryfoundation.org/poems/45113/alastor-or-the-spirit-of-solitude.

"Solar and Lunar Eclipses." National Weather Service. Accessed November 2, 2024. https://www.weather.gov/fsd/suneclipse.

"Solar and Lunar Eclipses That Are Coming Up, and How They Influence Us." We'Moon. Accessed December 12, 2024. https://wemoon.ws/blogs/journey-into-astrology/solar-and-lunar-eclipses-that-are-coming-up-and-how-they-influence-us.

SpaceRef. "A 'Blue Moon' Heralds the Harvest." SpaceNews. August 29, 2012. https://spacenews.com/a-blue-moon-heralds-the-harvest/.

Stanley, Sarah. "Lunar Gravity Measurements Hint at a Partially Molten Mantle Layer." Phys.Org. September 30, 2024. https://phys.org/news/2024-09-lunar-gravity-hint-partially-molten.html.

"Supermoons." NASA. Updated February 14, 2025. https://science.nasa.gov/moon/supermoons/.

"Supermoons & Micromoons." Star Walk. June 30, 2023. https://starwalk.space/en/infographics/supermoons-and-micromoons.

Talbert, Tricia. "Why Can You See the Moon During the Day? We Asked a NASA Scientist: Episode 19." NASA. January 5, 2022. https://www.nasa.gov/solar-system/why-can-you-see-the-moon-during-the-day-we-asked-a-nasa-scientist-episode-19/.

Tarlach, Gemma. "Our Oldest Ancestor: It's in the Bag." *Discover*, updated November 19, 2019. https://www.discovermagazine.com/planet-earth/our-oldest-ancestor-its-in-the-bag.

Tavernier, Lyle. "When Do Lunar Eclipses Happen?" NASA: Jet Propulsion Laboratory. Updated October 25, 2024. https://www.jpl.nasa.gov/edu/teach/activity/when-do-lunar-eclipses-happen.

"Tidal Locking." NASA. Updated December 10, 2024. https://science.nasa.gov/moon/tidal-locking/.

"Tides." NASA. Updated January 27, 2025. https://science.nasa.gov/moon/tides/.

"Top Moon Questions." NASA. Updated February 25, 2025. https://science.nasa.gov/moon/top-moon-questions/.

"Void of Course Moon Dates and Times." We'Moon. Accessed November 2, 2024. https://wemoon.ws/blogs/journey-into-astrology/moon-void-of-course-data.

Walker, John. "Inconstant Moon: The Moon at Perigee and Apogee." May 1997. https://www.fourmilab.ch/earthview/moon_ap_per.html.

Warnock, Christopher. "Planetary Hours and Days: Rulership of the Days and Hours in Traditional Astrology." Renaissance Astrology. Accessed November 2, 2024. https://www.renaissanceastrology.com/planetaryhoursarticle.html.

Water Science School. "How Much Water Is There on Earth?" U.S. Geological Survey. November 13, 2019. https://www.usgs.gov/special-topics/water-science-school/science/how-much-water-there-earth.

Water Science School. "The Water in You: Water and the Human Body." U.S. Geological Survey. May 22, 2019. https://www.usgs.gov/special-topics/water-science-school/science/water-you-water-and-human-body.

"Weather on the Moon." NASA. Updated February 10, 2025. https://science.nasa.gov/moon/weather-on-the-moon/.

"What Are the Three Types of Solar Eclipses?" Exploratorium. Accessed January 3, 2025. https://www.exploratorium.edu/eclipse/three-kinds-solar-eclipses.

Whitt, Kelly Kizer. "Black Moon Coming on December 30–31," EarthSky. December 29, 2024. https://earthsky.org/moon-phases/black-moon-december-30-31-2024/.

Wolchover, Natalie. "If It Isn't Blue, How Come It's Called a 'Blue Moon?'" NBC News. August 28, 2012. https://www.nbcnews.com/id/wbna48814398.

Yarborough, Kaitlyn. "What Is Cherry Bounce? Learn about North Carolina's Oldest Drink." *Southern Living,* updated July 11, 2024. https://www.southernliving.com/what-is-cherry-bounce-7559431.

"ZODIAC – Ancient Astral Science in Transformation." Freie Universität Berlin. Accessed November 2, 2024. https://www.geschkult.fu-berlin.de/en/e/zodiac/index.html.

To Write to the Author

If you wish to contact the author or would like more information about this book, please write to the author in care of Llewellyn Worldwide Ltd. and we will forward your request. Both the author and the publisher appreciate hearing from you and learning of your enjoyment of this book and how it has helped you. Llewellyn Worldwide Ltd. cannot guarantee that every letter written to the author can be answered, but all will be forwarded. Please write to:

Jesamyn Angelica
c/o Llewellyn Worldwide
2143 Wooddale Drive
Woodbury, MN 55125-2989

Please enclose a self-addressed stamped envelope for reply, or $1.00 to cover costs. If outside the U.S.A., enclose an international postal reply coupon.

Many of Llewellyn's authors have websites with additional information and resources. For more information, please visit our website at https://www.llewellyn.com.